The Grandest Trek

Unforgettable People, Stories, and Lessons for Life
from Hiking the Length of the Grand Canyon

Tom Myers

Puma Press
Flagstaff, Arizona

Copyright ©2025 Thomas Myers
Puma Press, Flagstaff, Arizona

Produced in the United States of America. All rights reserved. No part
of this book may be reproduced or transmitted in any form or by any
means, electronic or mechanical, including photocopying, recording,
or by an information storage or retrieval system— except by a reviewer
who may quote brief passages in a review to be printed in a magazine
or newspaper—without permission in writing from the publisher. For
information, please contact Puma Press, 336 Horny Toad Road, Flagstaff,
AZ 86003 USA.

Although the author and publisher have made every effort to ensure
the accuracy and completeness of information contained in this book,
we assume no responsibility for errors, inaccuracies, omissions, or any
other inconsistency herein. Any slights of people, places, companies, or
organizations are unintentional.

FIRST EDITION / FIRST PRINTING
ISBN: 978-0-9847858-6-8 (Hardcover)
ISBN: 978-0-9847858-5-8 (Paperback)
Library of Congress Catalog Number: 2024926257

Front cover photograph: Gary Ladd. Hikers in the Muav Gorge, near
    150 Mile Canyon, September 1989. From closest to farthest: Lee Steck,
    George Steck, Dick Long, and Brooke Long.

Back cover photo: T. McCullough. Closest to farthest: Weston Myers and
    Connor Phillips hiking in the river near Dry Canyon, River Mile 265.

Editor: Susan Tasaki

Book design and production: Mary Williams Design

Book jacket and cover design: Bronze Black Design and Mary Williams Design

All Rights Reserved

All proceeds from the sale of this book will be donated to the Grand Canyon Conservancy in memory of Robert Eschka Benson, one of the Grand Canyon's greatest hikers.

His life ended far too soon,
but may his legacy live on.

Praise for The Grandest Trek

The Grandest Trek is a gripping adventure story. By traversing one of the world's most unforgiving landscapes together, Tom Myers and his teenage son Weston forged a bond as deep as the Grand Canyon itself. But their unique hike through the natural wonder is not the only page-turning tale in this book. In addition to chronicling the ups and downs of his own expedition, Myers masterfully weaves in stories of other noteworthy Grand Canyon end-to-end hikers. The Grandest Trek is as much about Grand Canyon history as it is a multifaceted journey through parenting. Ultimately, Myers proves that often the best way to overcome life's challenges is to surround yourself with natural beauty and simply keep putting one foot in front of the other.

— Annette McGivney
Author of Pure Land: A True Story of Three Lives, Three Cultures, and the Search for Heaven on Earth

It's almost impossible to go anywhere or read anything about Grand Canyon without following a trail cut by Tom Myers. Having such an extensive medical knowledge of the Grand Canyon is impressive on its own, but Tom also possesses a deep and historic understanding of the place. And its all in one brain. There is nobody else like him. He is Mr. Grand Canyon. He's the physician who's spent decades practicing medicine on the South Rim while simultaneously co-writing not one but two seminal texts: Death in Grand Canyon, the most authoritative primer on fatalities at the crown jewel of America's national park system, and Grand Obsession, the definitive biography of Harvey Butchart, godfather of below-rim hiking. Now comes The Grandest Trek, Myers' crowning achievement as one of the Canyon's finest voices and advocates.

— Kevin Fedarko
Author of The Emerald Mile and A Walk in the Park

Contents

Sometimes it's on the path most rocky that
you will find your footing most true.

Honest Pillow Talk

Never underestimate the power of the pillow. For backpacking, a good camping pillow is worth every penny. If you buy a nice comfy pillow, you'll never regret it. Without one, what you will regret is sleeping in misery, your cheek embedded on a rigid seam of wadded-up clothes or a lumpy zipper. Trust me, I've been there. Miserable sleep begets a miserable day. Invest in your sleep and you will reap dividends; fail to invest and suffer the consequences.

Here's another helpful tip for a good night's sleep: "An honest man's pillow is his peace of mind."

With that aphorism, I must admit that I didn't set out to hike the length of the Grand Canyon in order to join the surprisingly short list of length-of-the-Canyon hikers. But it ended up that way. In fact, in the mid-1980s when I first thought of attempting it, no such list existed. I didn't know if anyone had managed to scramble all of the 600 or so taxing miles from the beginning of Grand Canyon at Lees Ferry to its end at the Grand Wash Cliffs. And I honestly hoped no one had.

Eventually, I learned that I wasn't the only one to have had this big idea; roughly a half-dozen others had done it while staying well below the radar. That discovery didn't change a thing. Moreover, when I learned that the newly emerging list included a fine little coterie of dedicated Canyon hikers—an eclectic mix of kindred spirits, like-minded brothers and sisters who love Grand Canyon about as much as anyone can—my determination to be included in that group became even stronger. I'd be lying if I said otherwise.

Further truth be told, because of its demands and dangers, hiking the Grand Canyon, especially off-trail, is not for everybody. The Canyon can be as brutal as it is beautiful, as indifferent as it is inspiring, and as deadly as it is dramatic. After hiking several thousand miles over four decades, working as a physician on the Canyon's South Rim for more than three of those decades, and coauthoring *Over the Edge: Death in Grand Canyon* (a chronicle of below-the-rim fatalities), I am well acquainted with the Canyon's hazards, and their consequences. These hazards have claimed the lives of far too many well-intentioned but often poorly prepared hikers.

Despite the book's success, it would do my heart good if there were no new names or tragedies to add in future editions of *Over the Edge*.

Importantly, while *The Grandest Trek* is an assemblage of stories about people and their experiences—including my own with my son, Weston—hiking the Grand Canyon from end-to-end, it is *not* a how-to guide. I hope such a book is never written; there are too many downsides, including the Canyon's inherent dangers leading to more deaths, potential crowding, trail scars, and loss of the sense of mystery and discovery that comes with route-finding on your own.

Yet I also realize that some with minimal (or no) Canyon backpacking experience may be stirred by these stories to challenge themselves on foot below the rim. Having been in those proverbial hiking boots, I completely understand. But with all sincerity, I say to anyone who decides to heed the Canyon's siren song, use maximum caution. Potentially negative consequences come with the territory. I've personally suffered my share of trials and tribulations below the rim, including bashed body parts, heat exhaustion, and terrifying moments. I also take no pride in admitting that I've had some very close calls in the Canyon, generally as a result of my own lapses in judgement. Frankly, I'm lucky to be here to write this.

If nothing else, know this: It's seriously dangerous to hike or backpack remotely or deep into the Grand Canyon. Never do it on a whim. Do your homework—read about where you're going—and come prepared. Avoid the hottest times of the day and the year. Bring appropriate food and gear. Carry adequate water and know how to find more before you run out. Resist scrambling or climbing beyond your skill level or preparedness. And before going off-trail, get worn-out and dusty on the maintained ones first. Also, hone your ability to read a Canyon map. Then make sure to always bring at least one that doesn't require a battery.

Above all, appreciate that the Grand Canyon can be merciless. It's a bone-dry, jagged, and vertical world, as well as a really rocky place. Any backpacking there is going to be hard. *So bring a nice pillow.*

INTRODUCTION

Dancing Lessons

Here is an occasion for trumpets,
For the beating of great drums,
And, if for dancing, a dance in which one leaps into the air.
There is nothing like the Canyon Country in all the world.

Roderick Peattie
The Inverted Mountains (1948)

I can't dance, but I don't let that stop me. Arms flailing, feet shuffling, head bobbing, body spinning, totally without rhythm, I let loose when the opportunity arises. My wife, Becky, both laughs and cringes when I do this. Though she reminds me that dance isn't one of my skills, she knows I am far better now than I once was. She also knows her laughter inspires me to dance even more.

Why? I'd rather have her and others laugh at me while I try to dance—and laugh with them and at myself—than not laugh at all. I learned that lesson a long time ago, albeit rather painfully, from the Grand Canyon.

Like Roderick Peattie's giddiness for Canyon Country (which I share), my early Canyon "dancing" lessons came with an even broader spectrum of emotions. There were times when my breath was snatched away, my heart skipped beats, and tears streamed down my face ... emotions typically found in a love story. Beyond the hiking tales presented here—some hazardous, some humorous, some educational—this book is, in fact, a love story.

First, it's about love of the land, in this case, the Grand Canyon. Second, love of exploring the region on foot and off-trail. And third, sharing the first two with someone you love.

Further, for many, backpacking in a place like the Grand Canyon is a search for self-worth as much as for adventure and natural scenic beauty, a hunt for personal dignity and an antidote for insecurity. Consequently, and for reasons that will become apparent, much of the book morphed into memoir.

Equally highlighted are others who have walked the Canyon's entirety, several whom have fallen into folklore. Intentionally, my emphasis is not so much on the *how* and *when* of their journeys, but the *who* and the *why*. Their captivating accounts are interwoven between my personal ones. In doing so, I came to realize how fortunate I was to have known, even hiked with, many of those featured. In particular, it is with misty eyes and a sentimental smile that I share memories of Canyon hiking legends and friends Harvey Butchart, Kenton Grua, and George Steck, all of whom have long since passed away.

As love stories often do, this book includes thrills as well as laughter and delight, some moments worthy of dancing and leaping. There are also times of anger, fear, intense sorrow, and heartbreak. Taken together, it's a heady mix of lessons for life learned on one of the most spectacular dance floors on earth.

And while the Grand Canyon clearly rewards efforts made to learn the steps and rhythms Mother Nature serves up here, it is just as clear that it is a place where bad decisions or bad luck can end the dance forever. *Yet the steps are worth it.* Though some have suffered, grieved, or even lost themselves in this dance, far more—including me—have rejoiced in being found.

for Weston

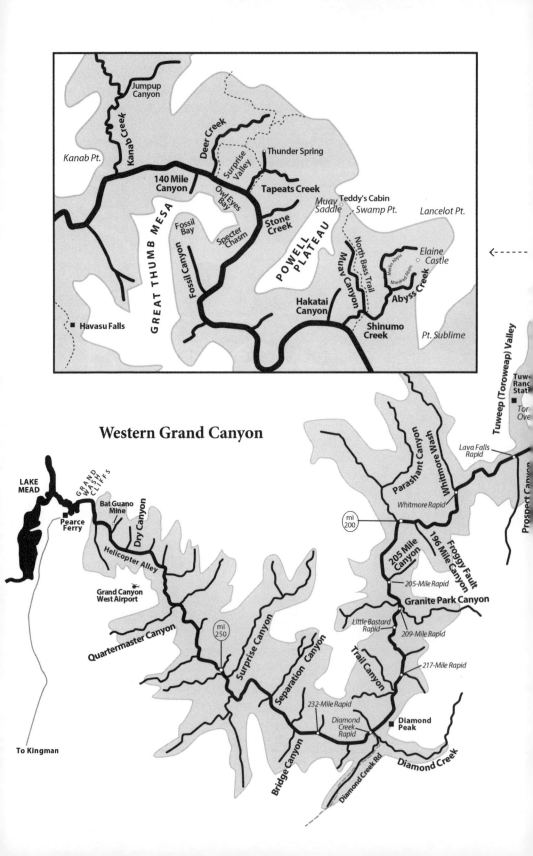

Western Grand Canyon

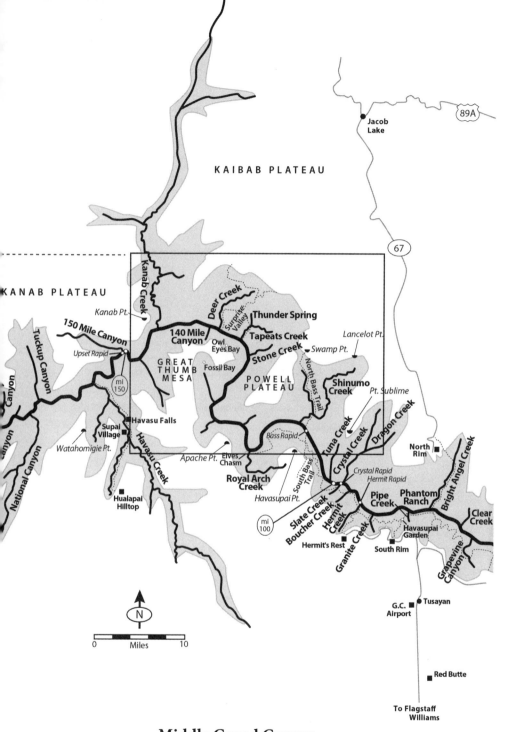

Middle Grand Canyon

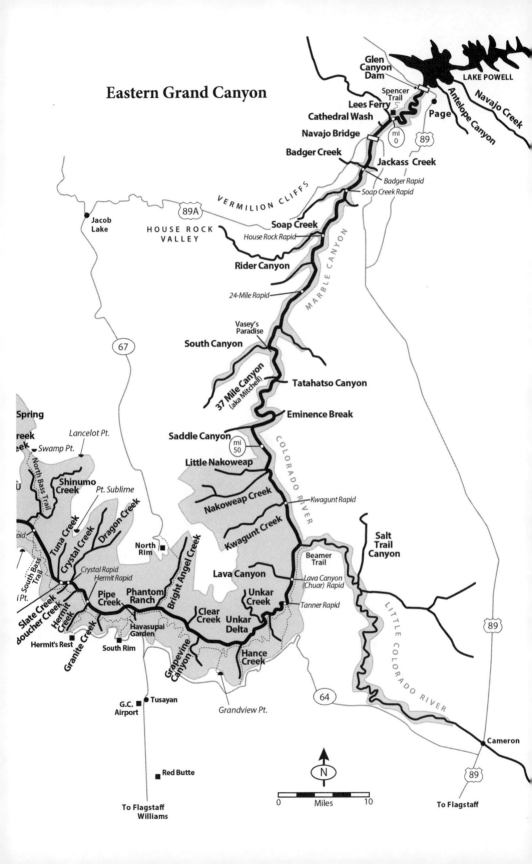

Eastern Grand Canyon

Glen Canyon Dam
LAKE POWELL
Navajo Creek
Spencer Trail
Lees Ferry
Cathedral Wash
Page
Antelope Canyon
Navajo Bridge
mi 0
89
Badger Creek
Jackass Creek
Badger Rapid
Soap Creek Rapid
VERMILION CLIFFS
89A
Jacob Lake
HOUSE ROCK VALLEY
Soap Creek
House Rock Rapid
Rider Canyon
MARBLE CANYON
24-Mile Rapid
67
Vasey's Paradise
South Canyon
37 Mile Canyon (aka Mitchell)
Tatahatso Canyon
Eminence Break
Saddle Canyon
COLORADO RIVER
mi 50
Little Nakoweap
Spring
Lancelot Pt.
reek
eek
Swamp Pt.
North Bass Trail
Shinumo Creek
Pt. Sublime
Nakoweap Creek
Kwagunt Rapid
Salt Trail Canyon
Tuna Creek
Crystal Creek
Dragon Creek
North Rim
Kwagunt Creek
Beamer Trail
pid
South Bass Trail
Crystal Rapid
Hermit Rapid
Pipe Creek
Phantom Ranch
Bright Angel Creek
Lava Canyon
Lava Canyon (Chuar) Rapid
89
i Pt.
Slate Creek
Boucher Creek
Hermit Creek
Granite Creek
Havasupai Garden
Clear Creek
Unkar Creek
Unkar Delta
Tanner Rapid
Hermit's Rest
South Rim
Grapevine Canyon
Hance Creek
LITTLE COLORADO RIVER
G.C. Airport
Tusayan
Grandview Pt.
64
Cameron
Red Butte
89
To Flagstaff Williams
N
0 Miles 10
To Flagstaff

CHAPTER ONE

Cliffhanging

CATHEDRAL WASH TO SOAP CREEK (THE FIRST LEG)

"It's a dangerous business, Frodo, going out of your door," he used to say. "You step into the Road, and if you don't keep your feet, there is no knowing where you might be swept off to."

Frodo, quoting Bilbo Baggins
J. R. R. Tolkien,
The Fellowship of the Ring (1954)

October 2008

"Hey, Wes?"

"Yeah, Dad?"

"Ummm, if you feel yourself falling, make sure you jump out as far as you can..."

Clinging to the cliff face like a spider, Wes craned his neck to look down over his shoulder at me, thirty feet below. He seemed befuddled by my advice. Then it hit me: *Jeez. Did I really just say that?*

For a moment Wes remained frozen, then scanned the terrain beneath him. No doubt he was contemplating the pros and cons of my guidance. Meanwhile, I contemplated my contribution to his current cliff-hanging predicament. How does anyone get into a situation like this? And why? And are the risks worth it?

Looking back, the day had started well enough. Only a few hours earlier, my friend Peggy Kolar, a National Park Service ranger at Lees Ferry, had dropped us off at the head of the Cathedral Wash drainage. Less than a minute after Wes and I had shouldered our packs, we stood at the apex of this tributary canyon, part of the Marble Canyon section at the beginning of Grand Canyon. We had already explored the fascinating Cathedral Wash gash—a jagged erosional wound in the rough hide through the region's Kaibab and Toroweap limestone—twice before, the first time when he was five years old. This time, rather than return the way we came, we'd continue downstream and camp for the night. On day two we'd hike along the river to Soap Creek Canyon at River Mile 11. From there we'd go up Soap, back to the rim and my truck, which Peggy had helped me shuttle there.

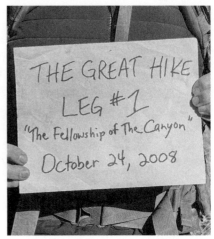

Our trip banner. *Suzi Martin*

We both regarded this trip as the first part of a truly epic journey. Wes was convinced it would be similar in scope to Frodo's and Sam's daunting walk through the land of Mordor to Mount Doom in *The Fellowship of the Ring*. My adolescent son loved this J. R. R. Tolkien book (and the other two in the trilogy), as well as the movies adapted from them. So did I. In the spirit of this fantasy, we now carried a small banner: "THE GREAT HIKE. Leg #1. The Fellowship of the Canyon. October 24, 2008." Prudently, we left out the "Doom" part.

"Dad, can I be Frodo? You can be Sam," thirteen-year-old Wes suggested.

"Are you calling me fat?" I teased. Sam was Frodo's overweight, somewhat bumbling but loveable Hobbit sidekick, and I knew I had a "dad bod." Wes just smiled.

Cathedral Wash runs in an easterly direction for about one-and-a-half miles, from the Lees Ferry Road to the Colorado River. It's three miles downstream from Lees Ferry, which is designated River Mile 0 for its position along the Colorado and which also marks the geographic and bureaucratic beginning of the Grand Canyon. I told Wes we'd knock off the three miles between Lees Ferry and Cathedral as a separate leg on another day.

Named in conjunction with the small butte (the "cathedral") that towers over it, like the majority of Grand Canyon's tributary canyons, the wash is bone dry until an occasional rain or snowstorm fills it. Considered a slot canyon, it is far deeper than it is wide, and drops at a relatively gentle 160 feet per mile. By comparison, the popular South Kaibab Trail, chiseled through the cliffs nearly ninety miles downstream near Grand Canyon Village, drops 700 feet per mile. Also, unlike the very distinct and well-maintained South Kaibab Trail, Cathedral Wash provides no such hiker assist. Here, you follow where others have gone, usually the path of least resistance, by scuff marks in the dirt. Cairns, small stacks of rocks here and there, also signal the way.

Cathedral Wash varies in width from twenty to eighty feet as it dissects the 270-million-year-old, cream-to-brown-colored limestone. One spot requires stooping under a low-hanging ledge. At times, tawny honeycombed sections can be seen. Bulging and constricting, this drainage bends and twists like a giant vein on its way to the river. Punctuated with minor exposures, such as small cliffs, it is straightforward route-finding. While a bit of a gamble, like any Canyon hiking, overall it's a fairly easy introduction to off-trail traversing.

Cathedral Wash. *Mike Buchheit*

Within less than thirty minutes, we stopped at the top of a small downclimb. Feeling the skin beneath my pack already getting sweaty and sticky, I readjusted my waist and shoulder straps, giving my skin a few seconds of a breather. Then I cinched both down to minimize any sideways shifting of the pack that might knock me off balance, or worse, off a cliff. Wes followed suit with his own. At about thirty pounds, my pack was a little heavier than his because I carried a few extras, including the tent.

About half an hour after departing Lees Ferry Road, while leading us through the narrows, I began to hear a faint, low-rushing rumble, carried up-canyon to us on the crisp October breeze. Compelled by a personal ritual, I asked Wes to stop, hold his breath, and listen, as though trying to hear a heartbeat with a stethoscope.

He did this, then turned and grinned at me. I smiled back. Yep. The muted murmur we heard informed us that the Colorado River, the greatest surgeon on the planet, was still busy down there. Six million years without a day off, it continues to incise and sculpt the Grand Canyon into the most gorgeous gorge on earth.

As we approached the mouth of Cathedral Wash, the river's low-pitched roar grew louder. The cliffs now soared 250 feet overhead. Sunlight poured in. Catching sight of the famous Colorado invigorated us. For Grand Canyon hikers who frequently spend hours descending its depths to reach the Colorado, the river coming into view is like the feverishly anticipated entrance of a rock star at a music concert. It's a guaranteed thrill every time.

Minutes after arriving at the river's edge, we turned right, headed south, and started boulder-dodging downstream. The going immediately got rough as we worked around willow thickets, threaded through tangles of tamarisk trees, and clambered over boulders and small ledges. Every now and then, a cool, moist breeze wafted off the river. At one point, I stopped, closed my eyes, and inhaled deeply, gratifyingly.

After so many years, I was officially—*and finally*—starting my quest to trek the Canyon's entire length. More meaningfully, my son was stepping right along with me.

As we walked, a monkey on my back seemed to loosen its grip. The pestering little primate had taken up residence there a decade before Wes was born and had been intermittently nagging me to walk the Canyon from end to end ever since.

Unfortunately, as the monkey's grip loosened, my stomach tightened. This dichotomy was directly related to an unavoidable cliff now coming into view. This cliff would be our first real test, likely one of hundreds of similar tests we would need to negotiate to pull off our ultimate goal. Indeed, when engaging in remote Canyon hiking, all goals—daily, weekly, even yearly—are distilled to the exigencies of the moment. And each one can literally make or break you. Although I knew some exposed climbing could get us beyond this cliff, the bigger question was the wisdom of being here at all.

CHAPTER TWO

The Ringing Bells

CATHEDRAL WASH TO SOAP CREEK (CONTINUED)

So. Tell me. What do you think? Which is better? To take action and perhaps
make a fatal mistake—or to take no action and die slowly anyway?

Ahdaf Soueif,
The Map of Love (1999)

It should go without saying (unfortunately, it doesn't), but *any* remote, off-trail hiking deep into the Grand Canyon ought to be considered daunting and dangerous. That said, why would anyone embrace such a formidable and risky goal as hiking the Canyon's length? While deeper, more personal motives vary, on the surface, most seek something similar, albeit in differing proportions: spectacular scenery and solitude, outdoor adventure, and the personal challenge of accomplishing something done by very few others. All but one of these "reasons" are subjective; the last one, "accomplishing something done by very few others," plainly is not; it's a well-defined and tangible goal. Is it ego-driven? Certainly, ego is involved, but speaking for myself and from what I have learned about others who have walked the length, I don't think it's the primary driver. Ultimately, I leave that for the reader to decide.

Beyond the big stuff, there are also minor, spur-of-the-moment triggers. For Wes, the reason for this hike and this cliffhanging moment was simple. It was the result of some calculated brainwashing I'd laid upon my boy in the form of a "fun weekend hike with a cool little climb," and the bribe of a cheeseburger at Vermillion Cliffs restaurant when we finished.

For me, on the other hand, this moment manifested a long-standing big idea. Really big. *Too big?* When I first thought of walking the Grand Canyon from end to end, I had no idea what it might entail, nor did I know if anyone had ever managed to scramble the entirety, all 600 or so taxing miles. Not that it mattered. What I really wanted then was to see hard-to-reach, hidden areas of unique Canyon beauty. I also wanted to challenge myself physically and emotionally in the biggest way I could think of, and to do it in my favorite landscape, with a buddy. *All of it. The whole shebang. The grandest trek in the grandest place.*

At the time, I was incredibly determined, my simple mindset fueled by twenty-two-year-old energy and naivete. But then, suddenly, life happened: a career as a medical doctor, marriage, kids, bills. Big, fantastic, and—let's face it—chancy ideas abruptly yielded to the demands of a more responsible reality. Solitary or "selfish" pursuits such as hiking the length of the Grand Canyon became a trivial tin can, one I kept kicking down the road.

Leapfrog ahead a quarter-century. Middle age had infused my previous physical confidence with physical concern. Gray hair (or worse yet, no hair) was replacing what used to be dark brown. Feeling Father Time's increasingly heavy breath on my aging neck, I had a sense of urgency to resurrect my long-delayed goal, and chose to spring it on the youngest of my three kids, my unsuspecting son, shortly after Weston officially became a teenager.

"Hey, Wes. Wanna hike the length of the Grand Canyon with me?"

He couldn't have registered every physical implication I loaded into that simple question. (As it turned out, neither could I.) But the gist of what I was really saying was this: *Please come do this with your Pops! I'm getting old fast! It's now or never! Plus, what an amazing chance for some father-son bonding! It'll be really fun. Here's how it'll work: You'll give up all your weekends and vacations for what seems like the rest of your life to hang out with me. You'll use all this free time to be physically assaulted and emotionally abused by the Grand Canyon. You'll convince yourself that you love it and it'll be worth it, because at the end you'll emerge as a stronger, better person. Whaddaya say?*

Wes and me, New Years Day on the Bright Angel Trail, 1999. *Becky Myers*

His nonchalant "Sure" reflected a more qualified decision than one might guess. I had been hiking him into the Canyon since he was an infant. At thirteen, Weston had already taken part in at least a half-dozen Canyon backpacking trips with me, as well as multiple day hikes and two river trips. Plus, he spent his first four years living on the South Rim. He seemed ready.

In preparation for this hike, I consulted *Grand Canyon Loop Hikes*, a book by renowned Canyon hiker George Steck. In this book, George discusses the cliff-hanging spot Weston and I now faced.

> The river route from Lees Ferry to Soap Creek is straightforward except for a short bypass required just upstream from Navajo Bridge. This bypass goes up a ramp and then down a 30-foot cliff—steep, but lots of handholds and footholds.

"Look," I told my wife, Becky, before we left, "the cliff has lots of handholds and footholds; George says so right here." I pointed to the all-important line in Steck's book. Understandably, despite my efforts to put her mind at ease, she was still nervous about Wes going on this hike. For one thing, no one nearly as young had ever walked the Canyon's length. Kenton Grua, the youngest person of the known few who preceded us, was a Canyon river guide. At twenty-five, twice Weston's age when he completed the journey in 1976, Kenton traversed the bulk of the Canyon in a thirty-six-day continuous hike.

In contrast, because of my work and Weston's school obligations, our endeavor would stretch out over several years. During school breaks and work vacations, we would make loop hikes into and out of the Canyon, achieving a linear gain downstream with each trek—like forging links in a chain. While we weren't in it to break any record(s), knowing Wes could become the youngest-ever to walk the Canyon's length (if he finished before he turned twenty-five) appealed to both of us.

As a young teenager, Wes enjoyed baseball, video games, *Lord of the Rings*, and *Harry Potter*. He was a good student, had friends, and avoided troublemakers in his peer group. Yet his mother and I sensed his boyhood innocence slipping into adolescent aloofness. At times, he seemed to brood and disconnect. This alarmed us both.

Luckily, hiking was a healthy outdoor activity he still enjoyed, especially in the Canyon. He seemed to appreciate the natural beauty, the challenge, and the sense of accomplishment involved in completing a hike. And when we hiked, we talked. Technology (computers, cell phones, video games) was intentionally missing in action. We were a captive audience of two with no distractions other than the terrain. Getting his buy-in to my dream trek would mean a multiyear commitment to staying connected with me. In turn, we believed, that connection would extend to the rest of the family.

Becky's concern about us risking our necks was moderated by knowing how much I longed for that kind of positive relationship with my son, something my siblings and I had never experienced in any form with our own father.

But both of us also knew that Canyon hiking, especially off-trail, came with significant physical demands and risks.

Despite the fact that my prime was now in my rearview mirror, my health and fitness levels were good. Wes, whose prime was still years away, also had good health and plenty of vigor. During a recent growth spurt, he had outgrown most of his clothes and transformed from slightly chubby to relatively lean, seemingly overnight. At five feet, seven inches and 120 pounds, he had also skipped the clumsy, gangly stage many adolescents endure. He also had outgrown his childhood asthma. Yet, as a physician, I knew all too well that fate could slam shut this window of good health—for either of us—at any time.

We needed to jump through the window now, while we both could.

Becky understood all this. Even so, her understanding did nothing to diminish the hazardous real-world risks of off-trail hiking in one of the harshest topographies on earth. By circumstance more than choice, she knew these risks far better than many people who claim to know the Grand Canyon. After all, she had been there during the creation and exhausting research needed for *Over the Edge* (coauthored with Michael Ghiglieri). As research for the book developed, I read her one horror story after another. She learned more than most would ever want to know about who/what/when/where/how/why people have died in the Canyon. To tell the truth, the facts my coauthor and I dug up proved that things below the rim were worse than either of us had initially imagined.

Tragedies occur down there. Most are the result of poor judgment (dehydration and heat stroke from hiking without enough water during extremely hot weather; falls from risky, unprotected climbing on treacherous terrain; swimming in the river without a lifejacket; or similar foolhardiness), while other misfortunes come about simply through bad luck or freak accidents (rock falls, flash floods, lightning strikes). On the other hand, horror stories aside, we also knew the vast majority of Canyon adventures have happy endings.

That's where George Steck came in.

While the idea of hiking the length of the Grand Canyon had been collecting cobwebs in my mental closet for more than two decades, George had finished his own Canyon end-to-end mega-hike in 1982, three years before I happened upon the notion. That year, George and his small entourage succeeded in weaving in and out of one side canyon after another, finding routes through dangerously exposed areas. They accomplished a feat that has been rarely repeated: the first nonstop, full-length, below-the-rim Canyon thru-hike—more than 600 miles in eighty days.

Years ago, a friend referred to George as "the godfather of lengthwise hiking in Grand Canyon." I totally agreed with the term. In fact, it was under George's tutelage and encouragement that my own ambition to walk the length blossomed, me becoming a grateful godson, proud to follow in his footsteps.

"George Steck did it right," I reassured Becky, "We're going to do it like George, not all at once, but in pieces."

Like me, Becky had been well acquainted with George. We both knew that over forty years, he had hiked thousands of miles in the Grand Canyon. During none of his amazing trekking accomplishments had he been an over-the-top thrill-seeker. Nor had he been one to understate the hiking risks of routes described in his *Grand Canyon Loop Hikes* books. More importantly, his own hikes never ended badly. No one died on his trips, nor were helicopter rescues needed for anyone hiking with him. Becky considered all this.

While she still appropriately assigned George partial blame for my troubling inspiration to walk the length, she had also respected and admired him. He and his wife, Helen, had been our friends, and Becky knew George was a carefully calculating survivor of decades of Canyon hiking. Similarly, since George was a theoretical mathematician, his calculation of "lots" of footholds and handholds for the cliff I would be placing our son on was likely to be accurate.

"Okay, fine," Becky relented. I heaved a sigh of relief and silently thanked George, but I did not delude myself that her "fine" meant what Webster said it did.

While I was relieved to have her borderline blessing, I found myself constantly second-guessing my plans. What if Becky's apprehensions proved correct? What if Wes fell and died or suffered a crippling injury? It would devastate all of us. What if I fell and ditto? More of the same. For either of us to tragically qualify for entry into the book I cowrote would also be mortifying for the surviving family members. To avoid such scenarios, countless times I considered quitting all Grand Canyon adventuring.

Even during our walk today, the alarm bell of worst-case-scenarios intermittently rang in my head. Within the clanging I heard, "Don't do this. It's too risky. Go back. Watch the video instead."

Yet just as loud was another bell, one that signaled an even gloomier message: regret. Regret for turning around, opting for the "safe" alternative. I imagined hearing its mournful sound well into the twilight of my life, long after my hiking days had passed, Wes had moved on, and this opportunity had slipped away. As the cliff came into view, that bell rang loudest.

⌒〜⌒

Just upstream of Navajo Bridge, Wes and I came to a halt. The sandbank we had been traversing abruptly ended at the jagged cliff that I had been dreading, one that dropped directly into the river. The climb required to bypass this cliff, "George's obstacle," was obvious.

I looked at Wes. "What do you think?" I asked.

"I can do this, Dad," he asserted with the profound confidence of his years.

Chunks of bedrock protruded from the cliff, like broken treads of an ancient staircase clinging to the outer wall of a crumbling castle. After leading up to the height of a three-story building, these "steps" then descended more vertically to a vegetation-choked riverbank about twenty feet downstream from where we now stood. The river was flowing too high for any attempt at wading below the cliff, and short of swimming the river, this convoluted cliff bypass was the only way to reach that downstream riverbank. Once there, we could then continue walking the shoreline.

Fortunately, the cliff offered excellent knobby handholds and footholds. I scrambled up, ascending the rock holds like a ladder. Moving horizontally, I then downclimbed the sketchy vertical descent. The final move required shoving and yanking myself and my backpack through the branches of a tamarisk tree inconveniently rooted in the bank at the bottom of the downclimb.

Wes watched me, then followed while I watched him. *Stay focused, Wes. Check, then double-check, each foot and handhold for stability. Stop and turn around if you have to. When it comes to the Canyon, never overestimate your ability and never underestimate the terrain. Never let your guard down. And never, ever be cavalier.*

Again, I knew the risks here were very real. Things could easily get dicey. What I didn't know yet was just how life-or-death dicey—and truly terrifying—it would get for Wes and me.

At the highest point of the traverse, Wes paused directly above the frigid Colorado River, which has claimed more than 100 lives in the Grand Canyon alone. That's when I made the jump comment. He looked down at the roiling flow, then at me.

"Really? Jump?" Weston asked, surprised by my suggestion that he launch himself off the cliff and into thin air.

"Yeah, and if you jump, make sure you clear those boulders near the shore and land in that deeper water," I instructed as I pointed to a spot in the river several feet from the bank.

"Okay," he replied.

Wes turned back to the cliff face and began adjusting his hands and feet, prepping for his next move. I held my breath before realizing I needed to tell him something else that might prove important.

"Oh, Wes?"

"Yeah, Dad?" He twisted to look at me once more.

"If you do end up in the river, make sure you undo your pack first, *then* swim to shore."

CHAPTER THREE

The Grand Deception

CATHEDRAL WASH TO SOAP CREEK (CONTINUED)

Some things you miss because they are so tiny you overlook them. But some things you don't see because they're so huge.

–Robert Pirsig
Zen and the Art of Motorcycle Maintenance (1974)

The eye cannot see what the mind does not know.

–Proverb

October 2008 (continued)

After traversing the first problem cliff below Cathedral Wash, Wes and I parked ourselves to eat lunch amidst boulders on an angle-of-repose slope in the shadow of Navajo Bridge. The midday sun had pushed the temperature to near 90°F. No breeze.

Both the shade's coolness and the knowledge that we'd surmounted the trek's first big hurdle felt great. Scattered on the talus around us were rusting metal pieces: bolts, angle iron, rebar, old soda cans. We also spotted weather-beaten chunks of wood, mostly relics from the bridge builders. The silvery green Colorado River flowed lazily 100 feet below. Muted thunder echoed off the sheer walls as vehicles crossed the bridge above.

When completed in 1929, Navajo Bridge—with its twin steel spandrel arches—not only became the highest bridge of its type in the world, it immediately relegated Lees Ferry to a "ferry" in name only. During a final crossing the year before the bridge's completion, the ferryboat capsized in the season's exceptionally high water and all three men aboard drowned. This tragedy sealed the ferry's fate.

Besides offering a safe crossing, this first of two Navajo Bridges reduced the time and distance to reach the opposing rim—a pre-ferry, 400-mile, day-long endeavor—to a mere 830 feet and less than twenty seconds. In 1995, the year Wes was born, the Arizona Department of Transportation (ADOT) completed a second Navajo Bridge, a wider replica of the first. (The original structure remains in place for foot traffic.)

The bridges seemed to soar overhead, around 470 feet above the river.[1] Matchbox-size cars and trucks moved on the new bridge, while Lilliputian people roamed across the old one. They looked way the hell up there, which they were. This perspective made the Canyon walls seem even higher, reflecting their true height.

Navajo Bridges. *Pete McBride*

Without something familiar for scale, it's difficult to grasp the Canyon's immense size when looking up from below or down from above. Either view can be illusory. Consider what happened to the first Europeans to peer into the Canyon. In 1540, a contingent of Coronado's conquistadors seeking the Seven Cities of Gold (or *Cibola*) gazed over the edge and concluded that the Canyon was less than half as deep as it actually is. Further, they saw the mighty Colorado as an unpretentious little creek, assuming it was about as wide as a man is tall; in reality, on average, the Colorado in the Grand Canyon is wider than an eight-lane freeway.

Then, confident they could reach the bottom within hours, the conquistadors began a scramble into the depths below, only to be stymied and likely terrified by the terrain's ruggedness and exposure. Thoroughly exhausted and humbled after taking three days to make it only about one-third of the way down, they wisely turned around.

---

1 For comparison, the New River Gorge Bridge in West Virginia, is 876 feet high.

Five hundred years later, their experience at both underestimating the Canyon's size and the physical effort needed to negotiate it is reenacted daily. Why? One word: Deception.

The deception may seem academic, and, to those only seeing it from the rims, the river, or an airplane or helicopter, it is. But it can quickly shift to potentially fatal when a person contemplating a hike scans the Canyon's interior from the rim view and is convinced the features are far closer than they appear, and far easier to reach. Maps of the Grand Canyon can also be misleading in terms of providing a true sense of the challenges.

Staring at a heavily inked contour line representing a 200-foot free fall is far less informative than peering off the sheer lip of the real thing or looking up from below for a navigable break. The same thing can be said about the chaotic shoreline of the Colorado River, which, despite its smooth appearance on paper (or in pixels), is *not* a viable option for an end-to-end stroll. Even the best Canyon maps lack essential detail. Thus, perhaps more than any other landscape, the Grand Canyon exemplifies the saying, "The devil is in the details."

For those who have never hiked off-trail in the Canyon, these details are nearly impossible to comprehend. Start by imagining an infuriatingly unstable, crumbly topography, where walking is only possible on seemingly endless steep slopes of rock and loose dirt. Sometimes, the only route is situated precariously and immediately above a terrifying drop, where a single misstep could result in a fatal fall.

Beyond the fear factor and unstable footing, add in the dead weight of a bulging backpack and envision

My daughters, Brittany and Alex, "hiking" along the river in Marble Canyon, 2014. *Tom Myers* lugging it and your top-heavy self up, then down, and through boulder-choked chutes and layered cliffs. Routes that sometimes demand thousands of feet of elevation change in a single day are energy-sapping. Under this strain, torsos teeter. Legs buckle. Falls occur. Blood flows.

Making travel even more challenging, some of the best routes are clogged by thorny, seemingly hostile plants. Jumping cholla cactus (*Cylindropuntia fulgida*) for example, has detachable segments covered with inch-long, barbed spines, the equivalent of miniature harpoons, as well as tinier, hairlike spines called glochids. They give the cactus a fuzzy, even cuddly, appearance that inspires its oxymoronic nickname: "Teddy Bear" cholla. No matter how innocuous the contact, the cholla's spines easily attach to the fur or flesh of any passerby (for seed distribution), where they stick with painful and worse-than-Velcro tenacity.

Catclaw acacia (*Senegalia greggii*) is even worse. The stinging pain generated by brushing against its barbed, tentacle-like branches makes the plant seem like a desert version of a Portuguese man o' war. The razor-sharp, hooked spines latch on for the seemingly sole purpose of shredding skin and torturing trespassers.

There's a reason desert vegetation is so surly: It evolved to protect the precious moisture locked in its respective tissues. This reality highlights another quintessence of this unforgiving place: lack of water. The broken and convoluted lunar landscape (in the late 1960s the Apollo astronauts trained briefly in the Grand Canyon, but the environment proved a bit too severe for them) is virtually devoid of the most important molecule, aside from oxygen, needed to sustain life: water.

Day after day, the Canyon bakes under a relentless sun. In fact, 99.7 percent of the Grand Canyon's 1,902 square miles is desiccated. Yet from the rims, the inner Canyon's drought-resistant vegetation, especially on the Tonto Plateau 3,000 feet below, can look misleadingly lush and green, like a sparse but grassy lawn, perfect for a midday picnic with the kids, teeing off, or a nap—all part of what I call the Grand Deception.

◦~◦

As we gazed at the bridge, Wes and I reminisced about the time we used it for a bragging joke. Years earlier, I had persuaded four-year-old Wes and his seven- and nine-year-old sisters, Alexandra and Brittany, to walk back and forth repeatedly with me to "set a world record" for the most rim-to-rim (R2R) crossings of the Grand Canyon in a single day. (Most people accomplish an R2R using the South and North Kaibab Trail system and are lucky to stagger the twenty-one-miles once in a single day.) We finished eight back-and-forths on the Navajo Bridge before my kids became too bored to be coaxed any further. Those eight "rim-to-rim" crossings took us about an hour. A whimsical "world record" that as far as I know still stands.

Now, nine years later, it had taken Wes and me about the same time to walk the mile-and-a-half from the mouth of Cathedral Wash to below the twin bridges. It was harder and took much longer than my initial estimate, another reminder that traversing the Canyon is not only deceptive but can also be grueling and monotonous. To hike the entire length, we obviously needed to factor in plenty of time.

Once again, George Steck came to mind. He walked for eighty straight days to complete his 1982 thru-hike. Where possible, he walked along the Colorado River. For 279 miles within the boundaries of Grand Canyon National Park, the Colorado twists and bends like a sidewinder; in many areas, cliffs make the river's shorelines unwalkable. Consequently, it's often necessary to traverse ledges high above and far away (sometimes miles) from the river or from any other water source. This topographic reality piles on the walking miles.

The Grand Canyon is a dendritic-shaped labyrinth of more than six hundred side canyons. Starting high on the rims as small ravines, they form into channels that grow and spread like cracks in a windshield or airways in the lungs, each plunging into ever-larger and deeper tributaries before consolidating into major side canyons. Hikers must negotiate each of these side drainages by either transecting them directly (in often-risky descents and ascents), or by less dicey (but more time-consuming and laborious) walking around their many-fingered upper branches. As an example of the latter, it takes five miles of walking around a massive side canyon called Grapevine on the inner Canyon's Tonto Trail to net just a single downstream mile.

George, who estimated that making one river mile of linear distance downstream required an average of 2.2 miles of walking, tallied a grand total of about 600 miles on his eighty-day hike. (He also added another hundred miles or so of tough treks done in advance to stash the eleven caches of food needed for resupply along the way.)

Using George's experience as a yardstick, if a backpacker hiked for eight hours per day at one mile per hour (as Wes and I just did), he or she would net eight miles per day. Using simple math, 600 miles would require about 75 hiking days, or nearly one-fourth of a year. Serious trail runners and backcountry hikers may scoff at this tortoise-like pace.

Why so slow? It comes down to one other major factor beyond the torturous topography: there is no single end-to-end trail in the Canyon.

Trails are key to getting around quickly and safely in nearly any wilderness, but especially in the Grand Canyon. In fact, finding a trodden path in the remote

Canyon backcountry is often a physical and emotional godsend, even if the "path" is nothing more than isolated tracks made by the hardened hooves of mule deer (*Odocoileus*) and desert bighorn sheep (*Oivs canadensis*) and marked by their droppings. For one thing, it provides certainty that the route "goes." For another, it's very likely the proverbial path of least resistance; animals, like humans, prefer to take the easiest route from point A to point B.

Yet, for more than 95 percent of the route George Steck and his crew trekked during their thru-hike, there was (and is still) no trail. There are a number of reasons for this. A lengthwise trail would be impractical, unbelievably expensive, and prone to frequent failure. Collapsing cliffs, rockslides, and flash-flood erosion would make any such trail a challenge to maintain, even with unlimited funds. While a thru-hike in the Grand Canyon would still be incredibly difficult and dangerous if such a trail existed, the existence of one would change everything. *Everything.*

To illustrate this point, consider that the Grand Canyon has yet to see a total of 100 full-length hikers. Yet, of about three million annual hikers, nearly a thousand complete a full traverse of the famous, 2,200-mile-long Appalachian Trail (AT) each year.[2] The fastest traverse was done in a blazing forty-six days, for an average of nearly fifty miles a day. Another example is the Pacific Crest Trail (PCT) that runs from Mexico through California, Oregon, and Washington to Canada. It's 2,653 miles long and has around a million total hikers annually, 800 to 1,200 of whom are attempting a thru-hike. As a third example, each year, the 800-mile Arizona Trail (AZT)—from Arizona's border with Mexico north to its border with Utah—has about three million people hiking portions of the trail and about a hundred thru-hikers.[3] Also important to note, these numbers do not include individuals who completed their trail's length as section hikers.

In short, if the AT, PCT, and AZT trail systems were roads and their hikers were vehicles, they would be the equivalent of sports cars zipping along busy autobahns. In contrast, hiking off-trail in the Grand Canyon equates to four-wheel drive rock crawling in granny gear, all done in the god-forsaken boonies, no less.

Another difference is that all three of these major trail systems are described in depth in guidebooks and on the internet. Further, while they traverse mostly wild lands, each also has portions that wander through towns and/or follow roads. These waypoints into civilization offer places to resupply, shuttles, medical assistance, water, motels, restaurant meals, warm showers, and—perhaps most importantly—predictable bailouts and reliable safety nets.

These cushy support systems, plus guide services, have helped push total

2 Appalachian Trail Conservancy FAQs, 2023 https://tinyurl.com/3af8enaj
3 Arizona Trail Finisher Report https://aztrail.org/the-trail/trail-finishers/

thru-hiker numbers for each trail into the thousands. The sheer volume adds yet another potential security system via mutual assistance, especially in situations where aid or rescue is needed.

Meanwhile, a thru-hiker in the depths of the Grand Canyon has but one touchpoint with civilization: Phantom Ranch at River Mile 88. It offers commercial lodging, restaurant meals, food and water resupply, and a nearby National Park Service (NPS) ranger station for medical and other support. Aside from that, there is nothing, except the occasional passing river trip, and that's assuming you can safely reach the river. This reality has contributed to keeping the total number of Canyon thru-hikers surprisingly low. At the same time, and again by comparison, the number of deaths among Grand Canyon hikers is relatively high. In fact, the Grand Canyon has roughly triple the number of hiker deaths than all three of those other trails combined.[4] This despite having a comparatively minuscule number of hikers.

Fortunately, in 2008 when Wes and I started, there had been no fatalities among those attempting to hike the Canyon's length. If there had been, Becky would have probably nixed our whole length-hike idea. Then again, at that time, only fifteen people had hiked the entire length of the Canyon. How did I know this obscure statistic? Using connections within the small but relatively close-knit community of off-trail Canyon hikers, I tracked down each one, and I told Wes what I had learned.

Like most kids, Wes aspired to be famous, to do something amazing. His dream was baseball. He often wondered out loud to me about playing at a big-time college or going pro. I knew that he knew that it was a long shot. But after he realized how few had hiked the length of the Canyon, he became equally inspired by this possibility to stand out from the crowd.

"Wow! It'd be really cool to get on that list, Dad," he said. "It would be even better to become the youngest to do it."

"Yeah, it would be cool, for sure, Wes. But we need to keep this in perspective. If it doesn't happen, that's okay, because it's more about you and me spending time together. Getting you into a record book that no one really cares about is not our priority. Plus, I never want you to think your achievements are what define you, or what I value about you. I would much rather have you be a good person who never walked the length than a jerk who did. Is that okay with you?" I smiled at him.

"Yep," he grinned back.

---

4 As of 2025, approximately 270 hikers have died in Grand Canyon (*Over the Edge: Death in Grand Canyon*) versus fewer than about 75 on the AT, PCT, and AZT combined (various sources).

After lunch, Wes and I began poking through the accumulated junk below the bridge. Wes found an old coffee pot and took an imaginary drink. Then, a little dehydrated from exertion and our time in the sun, we both took real gulps from our water bottles. I knew our dehydration could have been far worse. We had intentionally chosen the fall season for our hike to avoid the worst of the Canyon heat. Still, stepping out from the coolness within the bridge's shadow and back into the sun came as a shock.

Sunlight comes with a "solar load," a phrase that describes heat absorbed by objects (including people) via ultraviolet radiation. When you're cold, it's great, but when you're already overheated from exertion, it's awful. In the case of the latter, "load" seems like the perfect word. Excessive heat engulfs the body which soaks up the radiation like a sponge. And just as a sponge feels heavy when soaked with water, the body can feel weighty when saturated by sun. The hotter the temperature, the heavier the load. The harder to move. The harder to breathe. Without question, heat poses the greatest danger to Canyon hikers and is the deadliest element of the Grand Deception. Just like being intoxicated by alcohol, bad things—from impaired judgement and physical dysfunction—happen when one is under its influence. Heat becomes the ultimate predator. Unseen and silent, it creeps up then slowly devours the unwary who venture into its path.

And this predation starts on the rim.

Descending into this inverted mountain range from the much cooler rim country is seductive. Like an earthbound version of a black hole, the combination of lower temperatures and gravity sucks people in. Early on, cool air and fresh legs can make a descent seem deceptively comfortable and surprisingly easy, even during summer. One simply needs to pick a foot up and lean forward. Then repeat. Gravity and momentum do the rest. By comparison, continually lugging a heavy load against the force that keeps us "grounded"—like mountain climbers—weeds out the majority of potential summiters from the onset. Further, temperatures tend to drop as you ascend. On the other hand, with a descent into the Grand Canyon, it only gets hotter the deeper you go. As you near the bottom, the full temperature differential often comes as a tremendous shock. Summer temperatures between rim and river sometimes fluctuate by up to 60°F or more.

For example, in June, it's not uncommon to leave the rim during a relatively cold, 50°F sunrise and encounter broiling heat—more than 115°F in the bottom of the Canyon—by midafternoon. In fact, the Grand Canyon is one of the few places on the planet where such an extreme variation in air temperature may be encountered while traveling only a few miles on foot. For far too many Grand Canyon hikers, this deception has been fatal, resulting in horrible deaths.

Despite the relatively mild October heat, Wes and I downshifted our already-slow pace. As we walked, we talked about those on the tiny but unofficial list who had walked the length. I told Wes a few stories about George Steck, my favorite person to make the earliest cut. A decent, hard-working family man, George, who had died five years earlier, really loved the Canyon, I said, then expounded on how I came to learn that he loved a good practical joke almost as much.

George Steck circa 1977. *Steck family archives*

CHAPTER FOUR

Dear John ... Sort of

MEETING GEORGE STECK

*If I have ever made any valuable discoveries, it has been due more
to patient attention than to any other talent.*

Sir Isaac Newton (1642–1727)

April 1996

His question caught me off guard, so before I answered, I paused to study his face during this, my meeting with famous Grand Canyon hiker George Steck. He had just driven from Albuquerque to the South Rim to pick up a hiking permit, then detoured to the Grand Canyon Clinic where I worked as a doctor to meet with me. The man was a living legend and I was flattered, but cautious, since I'd sometimes been blindsided by out-of-the-blue medical requests from people I knew only casually. I had only met George briefly once before.

"Could you do me a favor?" he had asked.

George was a tough read, even for someone who did it for a living; his serious expression revealed little. His face, with its terracotta-on-beige skin tone and deep, craggy wrinkles, reminded me of Grand Canyon geology: intimidating and difficult to decipher.

What sort of favor did he need? Was he sick? He didn't look it. Still, I imagined his request would be something medical; perhaps he wanted me to look at a rash, discuss an ailment, or write prescriptions for his personal medical kit, like antibiotics or pain pills. But since he'd gone out of his way to drop by, I felt obligated to help him if I could.

I knew he hadn't come to see me for hiking advice. By the mid-1990s when this visit took place, George had already rambled several thousand remote miles during his thirty years of Canyon exploration. When it came to complex, off-trail route-finding in the Grand Canyon and sharing this knowledge and experience, he was an undisputed expert. Indeed, if there had been an advanced degree in off-trail Grand Canyon hiking, George Steck would've had one. Further, in my eyes, he had only one peer: the enigmatic former Northern Arizona University (NAU) mathematics professor Harvey Butchart. Harvey, a generation older than George, had racked up 12,000—mostly difficult—off-trail miles during

Harvey Butchart. *Bill Belknap*

a Canyon hiking odyssey that lasted forty-two-years, from 1945 to 1987. George, I had to admit, hiked in his footsteps. (We all do, actually.) Still, I knew he was formidable in his own right. Harvey, nearing ninety at the time of my meeting with George, hadn't laced up his hiking boots in more than a decade.

George was still notching Canyon miles, but now in his early seventies, he, too, was well into the twilight time of his own amazing Canyon hiking career. He knew he would never match Harvey's record, but that had never been his objective. His experiences in the Canyon were intentionally far different. Little did I guess, but that was what I would eventually come to appreciate the most about George Steck. It wasn't the miles; it was the man.

His visit was both humbling and intimidating for someone with my limited experience. Despite my nearly fifteen years of Canyon hiking, mostly on trails, I was the equivalent of a naive undergraduate meeting with a collegiate dean.

George was also an actual scientist. With a master's degree in physics and a PhD in probability and statistics, for twenty-five years, he had worked at Sandia Laboratories in New Mexico for the Department of Defense in developing nuclear arsenals. He was meticulous in his profession, a trait that carried over into his Grand Canyon hiking.

He had written the backcountry guidebooks *Grand Canyon Loop Hikes I* (1989) and *II* (1993), which were later combined into one volume. Both are collections of incredibly detailed and methodically documented off-trail hikes that can be conveniently done as loops beginning and ending at the hiker's vehicle, thus avoiding difficult or time-consuming shuttles. At the time George wrote these, his "loop" concept was original and clever. It was also a prime difference between his books and conventional hiking guidebooks, including those written by Harvey Butchart.

Like Harvey, George had a photographic memory and paid uncanny attention to detail. His descriptions included estimated hiking times, water sources, interesting natural or potentially dangerous features, and best places for camping. Scattered among the descriptions are charming vignettes, such as stories about foiling mice that raid food supplies and schemes to wheedle beer from river runners.

While I found George's loop hikes appealing, what most impressed me was that he was one of a tiny handful of people to walk the entire length of the Canyon. Only two others—Kenton Grua and Bill Ott—preceded him. George was either third or seventh, depending on how he's sequenced in the group of people who accompanied him during his "Ordeal by Rubble" hike in 1982. (Because he organized and led the entourage, I give him the bronze for lengthwise hikers.) During that 1982 blitz, he also became one of the first three people to complete a non-stop Canyon thru-hike. For that, he garners a gold. In any event, it was George's meticulous planning and leadership that made these accomplishments possible—even fun. He was a walking encyclopedia of arcane, hard-won Canyon hiking knowledge, and luckily for those who followed, he shared his secrets to success in his books.

I had purchased George's *Grand Canyon Loop Hikes I* a few years before we met and remembered being pleasantly surprised. Not only did the book contain priceless information about off-trail Canyon hiking, it was also key to our meeting. In the book, he encouraged readers to correspond with him, going so far as to provide his personal mailing address. Finding this humility appealing, I wrote him. I let him know how much I enjoyed and was impressed by his books. I also mentioned that I lived and worked as a doctor at Grand Canyon Village and invited him to drop by if he ever needed some assistance or a place to crash prior to a Canyon hike. Although I was sincere in my offer, I mostly just wanted to meet this unique man. Honestly, I never thought he'd take me up on my invitation, but a year later, here he was. And he felt comfortable enough to ask me for a favor.

George—with a small pot belly on an otherwise lean, six-foot, two-inch frame and wearing a long-sleeved shirt, khaki pants, and Hush Puppy-type shoes— seemed relaxed. Add his thinning white hair and glasses, and he appeared far more doctor-like than I did. In fact, his look suggested a soft, outdoor-shunning professional rather than a tough and seasoned hiker.

George squinted at me through his bifocals, taking in my no-doubt rude stare. His eyes, slightly sunken and watery, reminded me of rain-filled potholes. Then suddenly, they seemed to twinkle.

"Don't worry," he offered seconds later, smiling. "It's nothing bad."

I let my guard down and smiled back.

"Sure, George," I finally replied. "What sort of favor do you need?"

"I'd like you to write a letter for me on your stationery. It's a practical joke on John Southrey, a friend of mine."

A practical-joke letter? This was a refreshing surprise, and a far cry from advice on a bunion or a bellyache or a prescription for amoxicillin or codeine. From George's books, I knew he had an unusual sense of humor. And a mischievous streak.

In *Loop Hikes*, for example, he describes a joke played on an NPS superintendent (Bill Dunmire of Carlsbad Caverns) over what he called "CLFs," or "Cheery Little Fire" coupons. Like most people making an overnight hike during a cold winter, George relished a campfire after dark. But he also knew campfires were outlawed in the backcountry by the NPS unless you built them in a fire pan, a piece of equipment typically too bulky and heavy for a backpacker to tote. Moreover, the park service also required that ashes and other fire-related debris be packed out.

To vent about the absurdity of needing a fire pan to avoid freezing to death, George wrote in his book that he told the superintendent (Dunmire) about the CLF coupons he'd bought. Further, he added, the coupons were being sold in the Backcountry Reservations Office at Grand Canyon. They came in books of five, he proclaimed, each one allowing the bearer to legally have a "cheery little fire" when needed.

George also explained that, to prevent hoarding or scalping, the coupons were dated and nontransferable. Even so, CLFs were priced very reasonably at only $5 per book. Dunmire shook his head, appalled. George described him as becoming increasingly indignant about a product that scorned NPS backcountry rules, and then chastised George for buying them. When George finally spilled the beans about making the whole thing up, Dunmire not only remained unmollified, his agitation endured long after the two parted. That, in my mind, was the hallmark of one mighty fine joke.

So, I was intensely curious about what George had in mind with this mysterious official letter he wished me to write. And, I have to admit, I felt a thrill at the prospect of being part of a potentially great "George Steck practical joke." Basically, I was willing to play along. Maybe too willing.

"John Southrey? Hmmm… I don't know him, but that's okay," I acknowledged. "So, is it a 'Dear John' letter?" Wink, wink.

"Well, sort of," George smirked.

"Uh, okay, George. So, who is John and what is it you want me to say in this letter?"

"John's from Texas. He's a young guy, like you. He's a real good hiker and climber. I've done a couple of Canyon hikes with him. He really loves this place and backpacking the remote areas. He pretty much shuns the trails because of all the people. Unfortunately, he recently broke a bone in his hand in a climbing accident. It's actually a pretty minor injury, but I want you to say he is "skeletally disadvantaged" because of his injury and will no longer be allowed to hike the Canyon, except for the maintained trails. He'll be banned from anything in the backcountry. That's the part he's really gonna hate," George chuckled. "I'll actually write the letter," he went on, "but I want it on your stationary to have it appear as though *you* wrote it."

"Okay, gotcha. '*Skeletally disadvantaged?*' Really? That's hilarious, George. It has an annoying but believable bureaucratic ring to it," I laughed. "Don't you think your friend will be angry?"

"Oh, yeah! He'll definitely be angry. That's the goal," George acknowledged, the grin on his face growing wider. He was clearly delighted with his own deviousness.

"What if he's so pissed off that he wants to retaliate or get a lawyer or something?"

"Oh, don't worry about that. I'm pretty sure he won't blow a gasket," he said, brushing off my concern. "John's a good guy, and he'll eventually get a laugh out of it when I break it to him that it was all part of a joke. I'll just give him a little time to stew about it, because I'm sure he'll call me."

"Well, alrighty then." I handed him some of my clinic letterhead stationery. "Here you go, George. Make me proud and make me sound smart."

"One more thing," George asked. "How do you sign your name?"

"Messy. I'm a doctor, remember? Just promise me again you won't put anything really inappropriate in it that might come back to haunt me. I need this job. I have a wife and three kids."

"Right. Don't worry," he reassured me. "It'll be fine."

Famous last words, George. Knowing George's science background, I thought of Isaac Newton's third law, one I frequently remind myself of, especially in

33

medicine where it couldn't ring truer. Newton, the legendary physicist who has a butte in the Grand Canyon named after him, wrote: "For every action, there is an equal and opposite reaction." Before parting, I thought George needed a reminder, in the vernacular.

"Okay, George, but remember, sometimes paybacks are a bitch."

"Yeah, well, I suppose," he chuckled, "but it's worth it."

Several weeks later, George sent me a handwritten note and a draft of the letter. Little did either of us know that George's payback would eventually come. And it would be a doozy, proving Sir Isaac right yet again.

But that payback was two years away. In the meantime, George and I became friends. On multiple occasions, I asked him about walking the length. Some of those talks included a discussion about an unusual Grand Canyon river guide, a revered boatman who had been part of the fastest river trip in the Canyon's history. We agreed on one thing in particular: ironically, the boatman left his biggest mark in the Canyon while on foot.

Thomas
M
Myers
MD

Grand Canyon
Samaritan Medical
Center
PO Box 489
Grand Canyon
National Park AZ
86023
520.638.2651

1 August 1996

Mr. John Southrey
8443 Fern Bluff Avenue
Round Rock, TX 78681-3542

Dear Mr. Southrey,

Pursuant to recent severe budgetary constraints imposed upon us, it has been necessary to curtail Search and Rescue missions here at Grand Canyon. In an effort to reduce the need for such services in the future, the Backcountry Management Plan (BMP) has been revised to eliminate use of the backcountry by those who are skeletally disadvantaged.

In this regard, routine processing of permit changes by this office indicates John Azar has requested a change to a permit citing as justification the fact that you have suffered a climbing fall with subsequent bone fractures. Since you now fall within the scope of the definition of "skeletally disadvantaged," I regret to inform you that you can no longer be permitted to hike in the Grand Canyon backcountry. This prohibition is for a period of ten years after which you may apply to this office for relief from this regulation.

Be assured, however, that you will be welcome on any of our many maintained trails.

Hoping for your cooperation in this matter, I am
Sincerely yours,

Tom Myers

Dr. Thomas M. Myers MD
Grand Canyon Samaritan Medical Center
Grand Canyon, AZ 86023

Samaritan Health
System
Phoenix AZ

**Grand Canyon
Samaritan Medical
Center**
Grand Canyon
National Park AZ

Bullfrog Clinic
Glen Canyon
National Recreation
Area AZ

Corporate Offices
Phoenix AZ

Kenton Grua circa 1972. *Rudi Petschek*

CHAPTER FIVE

In Kaibab Moccasins

THE STORY OF KENTON GRUA

There is a road, no simple highway/between the dawn and the dark of night,
And if you go no one may follow/That path is for your steps alone.

– Robert Hunter
The Grateful Dead, "Ripple"/American Beauty (1970)

You ask why I do this? I think the answer must be that each life is a search for self-
understanding and in the course of this searching, each soul is led down a certain
path by a very high spiritual longing. I am but following my own path home.

Kenton Grua
Journal Entry, September 30, 1973

September 1973

Sitting on a boulder, Kenton Grua painfully plucked out the broken cactus spines embedded in his foot. Unfortunately, as cactus spines routinely do, several had broken off at surface level, making them unpluckable and potential infection sites. As he tended to his foot, he contemplated the journey ahead. Only thirty-six miles downstream from Lees Ferry, he was still several hundred miles from his very ambitious—and unique—goal.

Deciding to tough it out and continue, Kenton hobbled downward through a rare break in the Redwall cliffs to the Colorado River, where he camped for the night. For the next two days, he limped along, making slow progress while hoping his foot might miraculously recover. Seven river miles farther, he reached Eminence Break, a geologic fault slashing in from the east side that opened a route leading 3,800 vertical feet from river to rim.

He stopped to reassess his foot. The cactus-spine punctures were now red and swollen, and they hurt. There was no denying it; infection had set in. Resigning himself to the inevitable, he propped up his foot and waited.

No matter which direction Kenton looked, the views were stunning. Dominating the scene were massive, nearly 600-foot-thick Redwall Limestone cliffs. In this section of the Canyon, which geologists call the Redwall Gorge, the river sometimes flows wall-to-wall, leaving no shoreline for walking. It took up to perhaps a million years for the mighty Colorado to fully breach this incredibly erosion-resistant formation; its bedrock put up a stubborn fight before its lowest inch succumbed to the river. Today, within this section of Grand Canyon, the Redwall seems to cradle its fluid conqueror. In sharp contrast to the easy passage it grants the river, Redwall Limestone is far less accommodating to hikers. Its gigantic ramparts pose a nearly impenetrable barrier to any creature without wings.

No one disputes that cliffs are the biggest obstacle to foot travel in the Grand Canyon. Many of the other hindrances, such as cacti, can be annoying but are relatively trivial. In fact, stepping on a cactus or brushing against one is almost inescapable when hiking off-trail. Typically, cacti present less of a problem if you're wearing hiking boots or sturdy shoes. In the fall of 1973, twenty-three-year-old Kenton Grua wore neither. By choice, he was wearing moccasins, shucking conventional footwear much as he had shed his previous life four years earlier.

He first encountered the stony ledges of the Canyon in 1969 when he was nineteen and hired by Hatch River Expeditions to guide trips down the Colorado. When he started, his feet were pale and soft; he'd worn cowboy boots for most of his life up to that point, a reflection of his conservative upbringing in northern Utah. Now, nearly forty river trips and hundreds of hiking miles later, his feet—usually in flip-flops, or bare—were tan and tough, far different than they had been originally.

Very deliberately, so was he.

Four years earlier, Beatles' fans cried when *Abbey Road,* touted as their final album, was released. A quarter-million furious activists crammed the Mall in Washington, D.C., and shouted protests against the Vietnam War. In contrast, around 400,000 rock-music lovers happily screamed and danced with abandon to songs from Jimi Hendrix, The Who, Janis Joplin, Creedence Clearwater Revival, and many more in the field of a New York dairy farm near a town called Woodstock. Most noteworthy from the final year of that tumultuous decade, however, is what many still consider one of the supreme feats in the history of humanity: Apollo astronauts Neil Armstrong and Buzz Aldrin took "one small step for man, one giant leap for mankind" on the moon.

Meanwhile, thousands of miles away in the bottom of the Grand Canyon, new river guide Kenton Grua spent much of 1969 lauding his own personal hero, Major John Wesley Powell, a man he considered equal to any rock star or courageous moonwalker. One hundred years earlier, Powell had completed the first Grand Canyon traverse by boat, and Kenton (along with a handful of other river-running Powell "groupies") proudly celebrated the historic centennial. While the Powell story captured his imagination, the Colorado River and the stupendous landscape it carved seized Kenton's entire being. It would hold him captive the rest of his life.

Another hallmark of the time was the anti-establishment hippie culture: carefree, non-materialist living; free love; drugs; antiwar sentiments; long hair; tie-dyed clothes; nudity; headbands; and peace signs. "Hippie" flourished in the river-running community, and Kenton readily adopted both.

In 1962, Kenton Grua's father moved his trucking business from Salt Lake City to Vernal, Utah. Located in the eastern part of the state, Vernal had fewer than 8,000 residents. The railroad system bypassed the medium-sized town, which made trucking critical to the community's survival. For Kenton's dad and their commonplace Mormon family, which included Kenton's mother and his two brothers, it was a good financial move. For the twelve-year-old middle child, however, it would prove far more consequential.

Vernal differed from most traditional Utah communities in one unique way: river running. The Green River, one of the West's largest rivers and the Colorado River's biggest tributary, streamed only twenty minutes from town. Within a few blocks of the Gruas' new home stood the headquarters of Hatch River Expeditions, nucleus of the local river-running faction. Not surprising, within months of arriving in town, the Grua family took a river trip with Hatch.

By chance, legendary Hatch boatman Shorty Burton led their introductory trip down the Yampa River. Nearly six-foot tall, "Shorty" and the other guides rowed twenty-two-foot rafts made from surplus military bridge pontoons lashed together. Burton, thirty-nine years old and a seasoned, respected guide, proved to be the perfect mentor for the middle Grua boy. He let Kenton do some rowing, then taught him how to cook biscuits in a Dutch oven.

Shorty and the other free-spirited, outdoorsy Hatch boatmen fascinated Kenton, but it was the river itself, with its thrilling rapids and sublime flatwater, and the haunting beauty of the sculpted Yampa Canyon that really beguiled him. In fact, this Hatch trip affected the entire family. Soon after, Kenton's father bought his own boat, a military surplus ten-man raft. He rigged it with oar

Vernal High School yearbook, 1968.

locks and a frame and began taking his three sons on annual summer river trips down the Yampa. Within a few years, the river seemed to flow in his family's blood, especially that of his second son.

Even so, after graduating from high school, Kenton moved back to the Salt Lake City area and enrolled in the University of Utah's mechanical engineering program. Yet he found his mind continually drifting home, and to the river. During the 1968 Christmas break, the eighteen-year-old moved back to Vernal. Throughout his stay, one idea kept dominating his thoughts; with that thought in mind, he hopped into the family car and drove to the Hatch warehouse. There, he spoke with company owner Ted Hatch, telling him that he wanted a job. Knowing and respecting the Grua family, Ted offered him a position there and then.

Still, he chose to test Kenton's commitment by assigning him the mundane duties of fixing equipment and patching boats, chores every prospective guide had to master on-shore before working as a guide on-river. Kenton didn't mind. While the work didn't pay much, he didn't need much. Besides, the warehouse had a laid-back, inviting vibe, and he knew the position would familiarize him with the boats and equipment, preparing him to eventually achieve his goal: to run his own boat.

As summer approached and Kenton became increasingly comfortable with the work, he made a few Yampa trips as an assistant. A quick learner and diligent worker whose five-foot, six-inch, lean, 130-pound frame was agile and strong, he was eventually scheduled for a Grand Canyon trip with Ted Hatch himself as trip leader. Three trips later, Kenton began piloting his own thirty-three-foot Hatch motor rig through Grand Canyon rapids, including the formidable Lava Falls (rated a 10 on the Grand Canyon rapid scale of 1-10 in difficulty).

In addition to shucking his cowboy boots, Kenton wore cut-off jeans and stopped cutting his prematurely thinning hair. Shaving, too, became a thing of the past. Before long, he sprouted an unruly, thin-topped mop on his scalp and a beehive beard off his chin. Combined with his short stature and perpetually bare feet, it gave him a rather unflattering resemblance to one of Tolkien's Hobbits. Having given up Mormonism for hippie-ism, he gravitated toward music by the Grateful Dead and John Prine; their tunes were his new hymns. He also dumped the idea of becoming a mechanical engineer. Instead, the college dropout "fell into" nature, sleeping outdoors and embracing vegetarianism.

He also started smoking marijuana and using peyote. (He remained a staunch vegetarian for life, but reefers and peyote buttons came and went.) But his real addiction was the Canyon itself. As drugs were to Hendrix, the Grand Canyon was to Kenton. From his first "hit" in 1969, he was a lifelong, hopeless Canyon addict. He wanted, then needed, this place.

By 1973, between several dozen Grand Canyon river trips, Kenton had racked up a few hundred Canyon miles on foot, albeit mostly on side hikes from the river, wearing flipflops or high-top tennis shoes and carrying a daypack. The majority of these hikes also involved leading commercial passengers on well-tramped trails. Soon—maybe too soon into this four-year, fast-tracked apprenticeship in the subtleties of traversing the Canyon off-trail—Kenton's level of confidence convinced him he was ready for the complex trekking and route-finding that a really long, really hard backpack trip would take to complete: a never-been-done-before, hike-the-entire-length-of-the-Grand-Canyon jaunt. Burning in his mind since the start of his Canyon odyssey, it was a trip he believed he needed to do.

In preparation, during a fall 1972 river trip, Kenton cached food along his intended hiking route near strategic waypoints. Romanticized notions about American Indians led to his decision to tackle this monumental trip while wearing moccasins. His intention was to "connect" with the Canyon's ancient peoples, who had trod its depths in simple footwear. "You ask why I wear moccasins?" he once queried in his journal. "Because it's the next best thing to going barefoot."

Unfortunately, no matter how well-shod, feet will eventually lose clashes with rocks or cactus spines. In moccasins rather than hiking boots, they lose even quicker. Kenton learned this the hard, needle-sharp way. Surprisingly, he hadn't stinted on his throwback footwear; his thick-soled, high-topped "Kaibab Moccasins" were top of the line, made in Tucson and modeled after northern Arizona's Navajo-style moccasin. (*Kaibab* is actually a Paiute word, meaning "mountain lying down," or "Grand Canyon.")

Despite the Kaibab's whopping (in 1972) $60 price tag, within two days, they sported silver-dollar-sized holes, and their soles had been chewed up by the Canyon's carnivorous rock. Making matters worse, Kenton's parsimony kept him from swapping them out for the extra pair in his pack until it was too late; he was saving that pair for downstream. (He also had a third pair cached in western Grand Canyon.) By the time he made the switch on the third day of his hike, the damage was done.

While sitting by the Colorado and nursing his protesting foot, Kenton gazed upward at the steep route threading the Eminence Break Fault. Trying to coax his sore feet into hobbling the near-vertical, almost three-mile route was futile. Even if he did, he'd end up in a true middle-of-nowhere section of rim country in Navajoland, a sparsely populated and desiccated landscape where neither help nor water would be easily found. The dangers of a relatively waterless world were fresh in his mind. Only days earlier upstream, after having grossly underestimated his water needs, he had become seriously dehydrated while traversing the Supai cliffs high and away from the river. Acknowledging those realities he wrote, "I resolve to end it here. I have no choice. I have a way out and I take it. I am lucky. I've walked 42 miles in faulty moccasins, a very foolish thing to do. One foot is badly infected, both feet sorely bruised. I am beaten. I was beaten before I began. But I've learned important lessons."

As he sat on a beach waiting for a passing river trip he knew would be coming by so he could hitch a ride out, Kenton considered the surrounding view. The Colorado River, flanked by a chaos of boulder fields, cactus-choked talus, and indomitable cliffs, slithered out of sight. That view beckoned him, dared him, even.

By the end of 1973, a total of one dozen people had walked on the moon. Also by the end of that year, a thirty-seventh and thirty-eighth person would officially make it to "the ceiling of the world," the summit of Mount Everest. But becoming the first person to hike the entirety of the greatest canyon on earth— obviously not the moon but arguably the canyoneering equivalent of summiting Everest—was still up for grabs. Kenton Grua knew this and was motivated by the possibility. In many ways, his failed trek actually strengthened his resolve, for it answered his most haunting worry. He now knew his courage, wits, and physical fitness were a match for the Grand Canyon's forbidding terrain. In his journal, he noted: "I can see little point in continuing farther for the purposes of becoming the first person to walk through the Canyon or to prove it is possible since I already know that it is."

Deeply introspective, he added:

> Sitting by the river ... has allowed me a lot of time to ponder what I am doing and I am now of the conclusion that merely to be the first (and probably the only...) person to walk through the entire Grand Canyon is in itself a very poor reason to be hiking here. I love and respect the Canyon a great deal and have learned many of life's practical lessons from it. Perhaps this is a lesson of life for me.

Kenton Grua contemplating in his dory. *Rudi Petschek*

If he felt being first "in itself a very poor reason" for hiking the Canyon's length, Kenton Grua would admit to me and others that he actually had a very good reason, a personal one, for doing so. Indeed, for him it became more about correcting something done wrong than fulfilling what felt right. His quest to walk the length would turn into a battle of principle, one he was determined to win, cactus spines or not.

For now, this battle would have to wait. He'd become a field casualty of a hostile cactus. But like a good soldier, he'd be back. Though his infected foot ached, for him, this place was worth the pain.

A Grand Canyon Expeditions river trip eventually floated up to his beach. Guiding it were two of his buddies, O'Connor ("O.C.") Dale and George Billingsley. With mixed emotions, Kenton waved them over and hopped on board.

Kenton Grua, Diane Boyer, Becky, me and Wes. December 30, 1995. *Tom Myers*

CHAPTER SIX

Hiking With an Elf

THE STORY OF KENTON GRUA (CONTINUED)

Should auld acquaintance be forgot/And never brought to mind?
Should auld acquaintance be forgot/And auld lang syne?

Robert Burns
Auld Lang Syne (1788)

The days seem to pass so quickly in this life. I turn around and another canyon
experience is over.... I guess I love the canyon about as much as anything.

Kenton Grua, Letter, ca. 1971

December 1995

"Alrighty, Big-Guy-Fill-'Em-Pants, you got any surprises in there for mommy?"
Becky said aloud while sniffing Weston's diaper.

"Big-Guy-Fill-'Em-Pants? *What? You call him that!?*" Kenton Grua asked
with a chuckle.

"Oh, yeah. You'll find out why soon enough, trust me," Becky grinned.

It was December 30, 1995, and five of us were about to head down to
Phantom Ranch. Kenton and his wife, Diane, accompanied my wife, our infant
son, and me. We were tickled the hike was actually happening; just a week
earlier, we hadn't been so sure it would. Grand Canyon National Park was closed
because President Bill Clinton and the Democratic House minority were at a
budget impasse with Newt Gingrich-led Republicans. The federal government,
including the National Park Service, had "shut down." No visitors were allowed
in the national parks.

"Are we still going?" Kenton had asked.

"Oh, yeah!" I crowed.

"How's that?" he pointed out. "Phantom Ranch is closed."

I was hoping he'd ask that. I flashed him an eye wink and a cheesy grin. "It pays to have friends in low places," I said.

By low places, I meant in the bottom of the Canyon. And by friends, I meant my favorite bottom dwellers: the Phantom Ranch employees that worked down there, aka "the ranchers." The park was indeed closed, but I had spoken to Warren Tracy, the ranch manager, and he said we were still good to go. *How?*

Warren pointed out that we were already living in the park. Thus, we didn't need to be "allowed in." So, come on down, he told me. He also informed me that while he wouldn't be there, most of his employees, the other ranchers, would. In response to the rare opportunity of having Phantom all to themselves, the ranchers planned to throw a big party and dance in the canteen on New Year's Eve—an event they vowed would be epic and unlike any before. We were welcome to join them.

"Nope. No landmines in there," Becky announced, smiling as she finished the whiff test. Stuffed into a baby backpack hanging on my back, Weston cooed while flailing his feet and arms. We interpreted this as all systems go.

Starting over a dozen years earlier in 1982, hiking into the Canyon on New Year's had been a tradition for me, an annual source of inspiration. For ringing in the New Year, no more amazing place on the planet existed, and for very personal reasons, which I share later in the book, I decided to keep my "Canyon New Year's hike tradition" going.

This tradition garnered Becky's blessing, and as a young family, we had already hauled Brittany and Alexandra, Weston's older sisters, into the Canyon several times for this holiday. This time, they stayed with their aunt and cousins on the rim as we took their eight-month-old brother on his "official" first hike.

Kenton had spent much of 1995 in the Canyon as a boatman for the US Geological Survey's research-related river trips, and Diane was a research librarian at Northern Arizona University's Cline Library. I was both surprised and flattered when they took me up on my invitation to join us, especially when it came to Kenton. I'd thought this would be a relatively mundane and unappealing way to spend New Year's for a man who had spent most of the last quarter-century adventuring in the Canyon's depths. But then, I didn't know Kenton that well, and didn't yet appreciate the extent of his Canyon passion.

Fortunately, the winter had been fairly dry, so the trail had (thankfully) no ice to negotiate as we started down. Even better, it lacked tourists. With no other hikers to dodge, we made good time, chatting and getting to know one another better.

I had met Kenton three years earlier, in 1992, on a National Park Service river trip led by Grand Canyon's resource management specialist Kim Crumbo. Crumbo, a former Navy Seal and Vietnam vet, had written *A River Runner's Guide to the History of Grand Canyon,* which had a foreword by legendary environmentalist and author Edward Abbey. I was eager to spend time with Crumbo, who was fascinating in his own right, but became even more excited about the trip when he told me he'd hired Kenton as one of his boatmen.

By this time, within Canyon circles, Kenton was widely known and held in high regard for several reasons, the biggest being his storied 1983 "speed run": the Canyon's fastest oar-powered river run, made by a three-man crew he'd organized and led.[5] Less than a decade later, the tale had already escalated into folklore. While I hoped to speak to him about the speed run, most of my curiosity eddied around his lesser-known 1976 end-to-end walk through Grand Canyon.

Crumbo and I had hiked in to meet the trip at the boat beach near the foot of the South Kaibab Trail. I gawked when Crumbo introduced me to the man nicknamed "the Factor."

"Wow! It's really great to meet you," I said as I shook Kenton's hand. "I definitely want to hear about the speed run, but I really want to talk about your walking the length of the Canyon, if you're up for it."

"Sure, we can talk about those things, but what about you? I understand you're a doctor on the South Rim. Have you done much hiking or boating down here?"

In that moment, the small man with the big reputation suddenly loomed large and intimidating. His unique nickname didn't help. Rumor had it that Kenton acquired "the Factor" sobriquet because he was a difference maker, "factoring into" just about everything related to the river and Grand Canyon boating. Intelligent and opinionated, he also had a reputation for occasionally slowing down trips because of sometimes annoying, spur-of-the-moment ideas—for example, searching for an archeology site or rock art—and was disinclined to budge if challenged. Trip leaders knew that with Kenton along, they almost always had to "factor in" more time and flexibility.

"Yeah, but nothing like you," I sheepishly admitted to him. "I've been hiking

---

5 They accomplished the feat using Kenton's dory, the *Emerald Mile,* in a blazing time of thirty-six hours and forty-two minutes during high-water releases from Glen Canyon Dam. For more on this accomplishment, read *Speed* (published in *There's This River: Grand Canyon Boatman Stories,* edited by Christa Sadler) by Lew Steiger, or National Outdoor Book Award winning *The Emerald Mile* by Kevin Fedarko.

down here since the early '80s, but mostly just on trails; I've only been on a couple of river trips. One was with Crumbo last year and another with Glen Canyon Environmental Studies to do beach surveys. I try to get down here every chance I get, but time is tight."

Kenton shrugged. "You know what, Tom? We can't all be down here. We all have roles in this place. We need someone like you on the rim to take care of us if something happens. Thanks for being up there. Anyway, it sounds like you love the Grand Canyon. For me, I just like meeting other Grand Canyon lovers, and it's great to meet you."

That line stuck with me.

I suppose that, at one level, I was putting it to the test when I invited him to join our New Year's hike. Would he venture into the Canyon without getting paid or meeting a river trip? Would he go in with not only an uncool non-guide but the non-guide's wife and baby, no less? Over my years as a Grand Canyon hiker, I'd learned that, aside from day hikes from the river, many river guides never hiked or backpacked the place, and thus, couldn't relate. Frankly, if it weren't for the river or getting a paycheck, a large percentage of river guides wouldn't be in the Grand Canyon at all. Yet here we were.

"Want me to carry Weston?" Diane asked as we neared The Tipoff, four miles in and two miles from Phantom.

"Oh, Diane, you don't have to do that!" Becky protested.

"No, really, I'm fine carrying him, unless of course, you don't want me to."

"Heck, no!" I blurted. "Carry all you want!"

After Kenton helped switch the baby backpack to Diane, we walked single file, me at the rear and Kenton just ahead. I couldn't help but notice how steady and effortless his stride seemed. Hands stuffed in his pockets, feet in tennis shoes, he made his way down the trail with a minimum of effort.

How did he walk the length? Quick. Steady. Sure-footed. That seemed obvious. Far less apparent was the *why*. I'll never forget the when and how I got the answer.

On that 1992 river trip, I had intentionally hopped on Kenton's raft as Crumbo's flotilla headed downstream into the chilly November air. After ten to fifteen minutes of small talk, I decided to ask the oarsman the question foremost on my mind.

"So, why'd you do it, Kenton? What made you want to walk the length?"

Kenton, wearing sunglasses, looked at me briefly, but kept rowing, apparently contemplating.

Despite the cool conditions, Kenton wore only a cotton tee-shirt and shorts, unlike most of the rest of us (including me), who were clad in raincoats and rain pants. I also couldn't help but notice how his stature allowed him to easily row

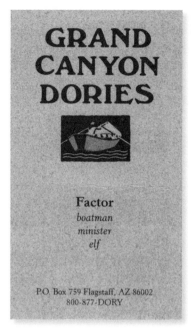

GRAND
CANYON
DORIES

Factor
boatman
minister
elf

P.O. Box 759 Flagstaff, AZ 86002
800-877-DORY

standing up. His hands—each of which had a stranglehold on an oar handle—were also memorable; in sharp contrast to my soft white ones, his looked tough, brown, leathery. Wiry forearm muscles declared themselves with every stroke, and like his arms, his legs were lean and sinewy.

He occasionally removed his cap to wipe his brow, revealing a horseshoe-shaped band of thin brown hair desperately clinging to the perimeter of his head. His scalp glistened white, indicating that the hat rarely came off. He also had small feet, which had inspired years' worth of teasing about being elf-like. Reflecting the playful, self-effacing side of his personality, Kenton eventually embraced the elf characterization. He even put "elf" on his personal business card.

Kenton rowed effortlessly, the blades soundlessly slicing the water. More than twenty years earlier, he had jumped ship, so to speak, moving from piloting motor rigs to rowing boats. He got on board with Grand Canyon Expeditions in 1971, piloting large, motorized rafts, then transitioned to Grand Canyon Dories in 1973, rowing the wooden boats that were part of environmentalist Martin Litton's elegant fleet. In running dories Kenton found his true niche, becoming highly respected by peers and passengers alike.

However, willful as he was, Kenton once defied his boss, factoring heavily in something that would prove vital to the health of the Canyon's river corridor: hauling human waste out of the Canyon by boat. In 1977, NPS river ranger and future Grand Canyon superintendent Steve Martin and environmental scientist Steve Carothers presented the idea at the first-ever NPS Boatman Training Seminar.

"People can poop in army surplus rocket boxes," they rationalized, and the human waste could then be hauled out rather than buried in the beaches. This would eliminate unsightly and disgusting sandbar surprises and mitigate a very real health hazard. A year earlier, at an outfitter's meeting with NPS officials, Litton had bristled at the concept, declaring, "There is no way in hell I'll have my passengers shit in a can."

Steve Martin recalled how Kenton immediately jumped on the "mobile crapper" concept for the health of river runners and the Canyon's beaches. "Let's be proactive," he announced, and vowed to convince Litton (which he did). If Dories could do it, so could the other outfitters, as well as the do-it-yourself (also called independent or private) boaters. Kenton set an example that many embraced. Ultimately, everyone had to comply.

"Have you ever read *The Man Who Walked Through Time?*" Kenton finally asked me in response to my question.

"Yup."

He paused at the oars, then locked eyes with me.

"That's why."

∽∼⌒∾

In his 2014 book, *Walking Man*, Robert Wehrman refers to *The Man Who Walked Through Time* by Colin Fletcher, officially released on January 15, 1968.

> The book's release was not without its detractors; among them was Harvey Butchart and more particularly, his disciples. The debate over who was the first man to walk the length of Grand Canyon National Park heated up…. The argument over who really was the first person to walk the length of the park flared into a full-blown feud, with people lining up to give solid support to their man.

One year after the book's publication, newly anointed Canyonphile Kenton Grua got his hands on a copy.

Unlike Kenton, Colin Fletcher was not a Canyon obsessive. In fact, in 1962, when the forty-year-old native of Wales came up with his idea for walking the length of the Grand Canyon and writing a book about it, he had never even visited it, let alone hiked it. Therein lies at least one seed of the future discontent with the book, especially among those who were serious Canyon hikers.

While he had no Grand Canyon experience whatsoever, Fletcher had an impressive resume when it came to wilderness walking. For example, over a period of six months in 1958, he walked the length of California, pre-Pacific Coast Trail, from Mexico to Oregon. He chronicled the journey in *The Thousand-Mile Summer* (1964).

Fletcher would later admit that his revelation to walk the complete length of Grand Canyon—and to write a book about it—came as he sat on the rim and looked out over the Grand Canyon for the very first time. Eventually, he whittled down his goal from walking the entirety to only the length of the Canyon within its then-national park boundaries, what he later called "the Canyon's major and most magnificent part."

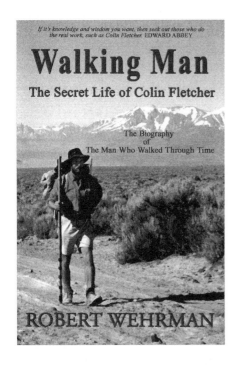

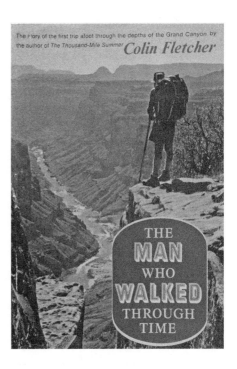

Following the initial brainstorm, his mind likely raced with more ideas to hook readers. *Would he be the first? How splendid that would be! What else? Ah, yes! Do it nonstop and stay below the rim for the entirety! And a kicker? Do it alone!*

While confident in his abilities as a solo hiker, one familiar with the dangers of the desert from his traverse in southern California, Fletcher acknowledged that he knew little about the Grand Canyon's specific challenges. What he *did* know for certain, however, was that if he wanted to live to tell the tale and sell books, he would need to draft an intended route, a blueprint for success and a game plan for survival. This meant acquiring data about hiking the inner Canyon from any source he could find while keeping his ultimate goal a secret, lest someone beat him to the punch.

He gave himself a one-year crash course in remote Canyon hiking by leaning on the collective knowledge of those who had already earned sweat equity in foot exploration of the place. Unbeknownst to Fletcher, the mother lode of this knowledge resided in one man. Call it dumb luck or providence, but this man practically fell into Fletcher's lap.

By happenstance, Fletcher lived near Otis "Dock" Marston, a Canyon river-runner and obsessive-compulsive collector of all the river-running history he could get his hands, ears, and eyes on. Marston understood the best information on remote hiking in the Grand Canyon resided with a solitary individual in Flagstaff, Arizona. In his book, Fletcher acknowledged this discovery: "So I set about tracking down the experts on foot travel. In the end I discovered that they totaled one: a math professor at Arizona State College[6] in Flagstaff."

By 1962, math professor Dr. Harvey Butchart had set himself apart as the Grand Canyon's foremost hiker, bar none. He had covered more miles in the Canyon than anyone else in its recorded history. Since 1945, he had logged more than 500 days below the rim and about 6,000 total miles. By the time the transplanted Welshman waltzed into the Canyon scene, Harvey had been adding to his own record for years.

Determined, Fletcher tracked him down. After several letters, they scheduled a meeting at Harvey's Flagstaff home. It's likely Fletcher hesitated before rapping on the door, as he hadn't divulged the full intent of his plan, lest someone scoop him, including Harvey. Earlier, on December 7, 1962, he had written to Harvey, saying, "For various reasons, I'm anxious to keep my project quiet at the moment, so I hope you'll forgive me for not going into details." By this March 1963 meeting, he had yet to come clean.

After likely awkward, ice-breaking formalities with the somewhat reserved Harvey and his equally reserved wife, Roma, Fletcher got around to his reason for the meeting—and his true intent: He wanted to hike the length of Grand Canyon National Park in one fell swoop.

Harvey knew that Fletcher had a lot of experience walking in the deserts of California. Still, his goal seemed far-fetched. Not only had Fletcher never hiked the Grand Canyon, but he also appeared to be out of condition and overweight. As Harvey later wrote, Fletcher sported "a bay window in front." But rather than laugh, the polite math professor patiently began to explain what such an endeavor would entail.

Harvey, who had a genius-level IQ and a photographic memory, rattled off names of places and features that might be challenging, which likely befuddled Fletcher. For clarity and to better illustrate where Fletcher might go, Harvey retrieved his most prized Canyon possession: his map, the product of seventeen years of Canyon hiking. Fletcher likely held his breath as Harvey unfurled the map, the equivalent of a sacred scroll for his purposes. Any subconscious breath-holding was probably disrupted by a sudden gasp when Fletcher laid eyes on the hundreds of squiggly red lines representing Harvey's routes. A masterpiece in maneuvering, the lines painted a picture of possibility for Fletcher that would have exceeded his wildest dreams.

It also quickly became obvious that despite nearly seventeen years of

---

6 In 1966, it officially gained university status and was renamed Northern Arizona University.

obsessive hiking in the place, even the great Harvey Butchart hadn't "officially" completed what Fletcher was gunning for. Of the 250 or so miles that made up the length within park boundaries, Harvey pointed out a very small section— perhaps five miles—below the tip of a feature called Great Thumb Mesa that he hadn't done. The fact that Harvey hadn't walked it yet meant that no one, at least in modern times, had.

As plotted out, the meandering lines connecting his hikes showed that Harvey had completed about 98 percent of the route. This map, plus the meticulous notes Harvey kept in his hiking logs, could be the key to Fletcher's success. Before leaving, Fletcher knew this, without a doubt, to be true.

It's easy to argue that the ethical and honorable thing for Fletcher to have done at that point would have been to invite Harvey to join him on his hike and allow him to finish what he had started and worked so diligently toward for nearly two decades. However, doing so would ruin Fletcher's plan to reap the singular glory as the first to hike the park's length, acquiring not only fame, but also spurring book sales. Instead, with apparently no guilty twinges, Fletcher boldly asked to copy his map. This put Harvey on the spot.

Fletcher had driven in from California. Obviously educated, he oozed with Welsh charm. For Harvey, the virtues of generosity and humility were deeply ingrained in his character, a result of his devoutly Christian upbringing. *How could he say no?* In the end, he couldn't. So, he smiled and nodded yes, asking for nothing in return. Before parting, Harvey made a friendly, one-nickel bet that Fletcher wouldn't make it, and they shook hands.

A thrilled Fletcher enjoyed that handshake. With it and Harvey's no-strings-attached assistance, the "walking-the-length-of-Grand-Canyon first" title was also now firmly within his grasp.

Much to Kenton Grua's disdain, Fletcher would never let go.

Colin Fletcher, self-portrait June 1966, below Havasu Canyon.
The Huntington Library, San Marino, California

CHAPTER SEVEN

Flap Crap and the Factor

THE STORY OF KENTON GRUA (CONTINUED)

Listen you bastards, I've got something to tell you!
Colin Fletcher
"Fletcherisms," in *Walking Man* (2016)

There was this little note that somebody'd written, some hiker, and left in Tapeats Cave. I don't remember the gist of it, but it was like, you know, "Got here. It was an incredible hike down from the rim. Blah, blah, blah. Almost died. Blah, blah, blah. Blah, blah, blah." And then signed "Colon Flexor." [laughter] And that kind of cracked me up.

Kenton Grua
Interview with Lew Steiger, 1997

April 1963

Clouds and melancholy hung heavy as Colin Fletcher neared the stretch below Great Thumb Mesa. It had been snowing for days. With each step, his boots squished an inch or two into the muddy soil, leaving distinct impressions. Then he stopped dead, eyes widening in disbelief. Ahead of him, across the snow and mud, dark and definite and impossible, stretched a line of human footprints.

He stooped to inspect them…

For Harvey Butchart, whose work and family obligations restricted much of his hiking to weekends, completing the final piece in a Grand Canyon National Park boundary-to-boundary hike had never been a high priority. Too time-consuming. Too straightforward. Relative run-and-gun discoveries of rim-to-river routes had far greater practicality and appeal. Still, after almost twenty years, all that remained for Harvey to complete the length of the park within its boundaries were the five desolate miles below the tip of Great Thumb. Part of it remaining for Harvey hinged on yet another reason.

For generations, people of the nearby Havasupai tribe believed this stretch below Great Thumb Mesa—with its three incredibly steep, large bays (amphitheaters) and lack of water—was impassable, and potentially deadly. Harvey, who hiked alone fifty percent of the time, knew this. From previous hikes in the area, he had also been able to confirm these hazards by direct observation, gazing down from above and horizontally from either end.

"They're steep, those amphitheaters," Harvey had told Fletcher when they met. "Very steep. But I'd guess they're both passable. Still, you can never really tell with these things until you give them a try. And as for the middle one—I guess we'll just have to wait and see."

⌇⌇⌇

Amidst flurrying snow on a wet day in April 1963, the "Walking Man" discovered irrefutable evidence that confirmed what he had learned only days earlier. The "wait and see" was over:

> I stood up, smiling. When I walked on through the snowstorm, following the dark imprints into the gloom, I found my tiredness had gone. It was good to know, beyond any real shadow of doubt, that I was following, with a most artistic symbolism, the footsteps of the man who had blazed my trail and who had, a week before, fulfilled a seventeen-year ambition.

Indeed, two days before Fletcher started hiking, Harvey set out to fill in that five-mile gap below Tahuta and Great Thumb Points. Again, this segment equated to the last stitch he needed to connect his hiking seam through the park's length. Beyond this, he had sincere concerns about the water situation for Fletcher and wanted to check it out. In one overnight trip, he completed both goals.

The timing could not have been better. Recent wet weather in the region had filled potholes along his route on the Esplanade level and recharged the spring near the head of 140 Mile Canyon. After filling the gap, he returned to the rim via a route around the tip of Great Thumb at Fossil Bay.

Next, Harvey arranged to get a written note to Fletcher at Supai Village letting him know that the nebulous section was no longer a mystery. Not only were the treacherous bays passable, he informed Fletcher that abundant pothole water also existed. Harvey offered the reports as charitable reasons for his gap-filling hike just days before Fletcher set out, which was true. Yet just as true, despite Harvey never articulating it, was his need to establish what was rightfully his before the Welshman essentially stole it.

Harvey's actions caught Fletcher off guard. He, like most people, had failed to recognize Harvey's extremely competitive nature. Why? Because the subdued, cerebral, even insecure persona Harvey displayed on his thin, five-foot, seven inch frame belied the fierce competitor he actually was. To "wait and see," as Harvey told Fletcher, was not an option the math professor intended to exercise.

After inspecting the tracks he discovered during the snowstorm, Fletcher reported he smiled. At some point, however, his smile likely inverted to a frown. While he understood it was far more appropriate for Harvey to hold the distinction of being first, he felt conflicted. Something he had been both literally and figuratively banking on would never be. Henceforth and forever, he would only be second.

Yet, when the first edition of *The Man Who Walked Through Time* came out in 1967, the dust jacket proudly—and falsely—proclaimed otherwise: "The story of the **first** trip afoot through the depths of Grand Canyon." [emphasis added] An erroneous boast on the dust jacket's front flap was worse:

> The Grand Canyon had been run by boat, **but no one had ever attempted the journey by foot, and the experts said it could not be done**. The remarkable classic of nature writing by **the first man ever to have walked the entire length of the Grand Canyon**. [emphasis added]

Again, Fletcher hadn't hiked the "entire" length of the Grand Canyon; nor was he "first." Ironically, in the text, Fletcher refuted these declarations. He even spotlighted the discrepancy. Several times, he gave Harvey the credit he deserved for being first, heaping praise on the math professor's legacy and unconditional generosity.

So why the falsehoods on the cover?

"There are a few possible answers," explains Robert Wehrman in *Walking Man*. "Copy on book slipcovers isn't written by the author; it is created by publishers' marketing departments and is referred to in literary circles as 'flap crap.'

"Had Harvey wanted the text on the cover changed, Fletcher would have insisted that Knopf [the publisher] make the correction in later editions. But Harvey did not ask, and the claim on the cover still stands." Wehrman credits this argument to Carl D. Brandt, Fletcher's literary agent and friend. Brandt, like Wehrman, also concluded, "It's just flap crap."

Chalking up the false advertising to "flap crap" is one thing, but pushing the flap-crap failing on Harvey seems unfounded, no matter how you look at it. Brandt suggested that Harvey deserved blame for not speaking up. Brandt's assertion that it could have been changed for later editions at Harvey's request also seems to brush off the huge slap-in-the-face it was to Harvey from the get-go. Yes, that could have equated to "damage control," but irreparable damage was done by allowing the dupe to be printed even once.

And the duping wasn't limited to the cover. A photo caption within the text:

> "Conclusion of the journey: At the last camp, a satisfied look back—
> for success had meant far more than becoming **the first man to walk the
> length of Grand Canyon National Park**." [emphasis added]

Using the same jargon as Fletcher's publisher, this false caption might be better known as a "craption."

In the end, whether the hoodwinking originated from Colin Fletcher or his editor or publisher is irrelevant. As the author, Fletcher allowed a falsehood in his favor to be printed to sell his book. And people bought it. In droves. They still do. Hence, more than a half-century later, the book remains in print, the best-selling Grand Canyon book of all time. It is considered a classic.

Yet Kenton Grua came away less than impressed. Instead, after he got to know Harvey, the "flap crap" riled him. In 1992, we talked about it as he rowed. We recalled sharing similar bewilderment—a "What-the-hell?" moment—after reading the passage about Fletcher finding Harvey's footprints, then flipping to the cover which declared Fletcher had been first.

"Yeah, that really pissed me off," Kenton summarized.

In 1997, more than twenty years after Kenton's seminal trek, Lew Steiger interviewed him for the Grand Canyon River Runners Oral History Project. Kenton reflected in more detail about reading Fletcher's book. He essentially reiterated what he had told me in the boat five years earlier:

> It was pretty interesting, but as anyone who knew the Canyon could see right away, [Fletcher] didn't really walk through the whole Grand Canyon, or hike or whatever, through the whole Grand Canyon, by any means. He only went about 100 miles out of about 300 river miles—not quite. So, slightly more than one-third of it was all he did and claimed to have walked through the Canyon. And I didn't like his attitude much— that came through in his writing of the book, that he was pretty proud of

himself, and he really—not even subtly—put down Dr. Harvey Butchart, who was one of my heroes in terms of Canyon hiking.

Kenton felt Fletcher used Harvey, plain and simple. He profited, big-time, from the priceless aid Harvey had so generously provided, only to disrespect his benefactor in the end—or, worse in Kenton's mind, stab Harvey in the back. Kenton also believed Fletcher did it to "massage his ego." Further, he disliked Fletcher's writing style, with its metaphysical undertones. For example: "[T]he sense of the union had become explicit, intimate, totally involving. It embraced everything. Not only man and beaver and mouse, lizard and rattlesnake and toad, sandfly and slug." Kenton called the writing a "turn-off."

Perhaps equally galling to serious Grand Canyon hikers like Kenton was seeing a one-hike-wonder like Fletcher garner so much attention in their most revered landscape. Fletcher made the limelight without paying his dues. The stunt seemed almost sacrilegious. It left Kenton with such a bad taste for Fletcher and his book that he came to this conclusion about hiking the true length of the Grand Canyon: "Somebody else needs to do it, just to do it, and do it right, do it light, and do the whole thing, and start at the top and go with the river, end up at the bottom."

Clearly, Fletcher's misconduct was a major inspiration for Kenton's hike. Yet, another factor may have spurred him into action three years after his first attempt.

In 1975, one year before Kenton started his epic first full-traverse hike, the Grand Canyon ballooned in size. At least on paper. The National Park Enlargement Act doubled the area of the park to include the entirety of the Grand Canyon proper. The following were added: Marble Canyon National Monument, comprising the beginning of the Grand Canyon at Lees Ferry, River Mile 0, to the Little Colorado River Gorge at River Mile 61.5; Grand Canyon National Monument, from Havasu Canyon at River Mile

Kenton and Harvey, Old Timers river trip at Lees Ferry, September 1994. *Richard Jackson*

59

157 to Diamond Creek at River Mile 226; the Lake Mead National Recreational Area (NRA) section from Diamond Creek to Grand Wash Cliffs, the end of the Grand Canyon, at River Mile 277; plus portions of Kaibab National Forest and Glen Canyon NRA.

Thus, on January 3, 1975, with a stroke of President Gerald Ford's pen, the true geographic boundaries of the national park claiming the greatest canyon in the world were politically defined.

Within that wake, in January 1976, Kenton wrote: "I find myself in Flagstaff, seriously, at times, considering trying it again." The back pain and sciatica that had caused him to abort a second attempt two years earlier were gone. Healthy but hesitant, he unenthusiastically put in a cache at the South Bass Trail. That done, he wrote "Still, I decide not to do it." He needed more inspiration. But what? Better yet, *who*?

> Then comes Bart Henderson. A lot of energy.... Really turned on about the idea. He wants to do a book together, picture essay. We come together on it. His energy brings mine back up.

A freelance river guide, Henderson, like Kenton, had grown up and gone to school in Vernal. A year behind Kenton in high school, he'd considered the upperclassman a friend. Also Kenton-like, he had been exposed to the river early,

Bart Henderson. *Courtesy Bart Henderson*

hearing boatman stories from Hatch river guides (several guides had worked for Henderson's dad, a local contractor, as assistant carpenters during the off-season), then became a Canyon boatman himself. By this juncture, his experiences made him just about as Canyon-savvy as Kenton.

Both had transitioned from the conservative, stereotypical Utah male to shirtless, barefoot, hippie river guides. Both had dropped out of college. And both had similar upbringings and life interests that connected them on multiple levels, including sharing marijuana pipes or peyote. They were able to discuss virtually any topic, from politics and war or science and money to Canyon geology and river guiding, love, sex, drugs, and family. They also discussed Kenton's resolve to walk the length, something Henderson admired.

By early February 1976, spurred into action by Henderson, Kenton began

Kenton's Scout parked at Watahomigie Point, start of hike into Havasu Canyon to leave a food cache, February 1976. *Ellen Tibbetts*

planning in earnest, preparing for a start date later that month. "Kenton quickly developed a sense of urgency about it," Henderson recalls. "Not just because it was something historic but also because he needed to finish before the onset of the river-guiding season and hot weather set in."

As he had in 1973, he planned to do the hike all on one side: south, or River Left. Along with Henderson; Kenton's then-girlfriend Ellen Tibbetts (whom he lived with in Flagstaff); and Skip Jones, another friend, he cached supplies in six round, five-gallon honey cans, spacing them out in what he thought would be about two-week intervals. Then, on February 27, the four of them—Kenton, Ellen, Jones, and Henderson—left Flagstaff, heading for the top of Jackass Canyon, eight miles downstream from Lees Ferry.

For this trek Kenton decided to use a new, relatively small North Face rucksack with an internal frame. Another adjustment included swapping out moccasins for JC Penney work boots with heavy-duty crepe soles. He credited this sturdy upgrade in footwear to Harvey, who swore by the brand. First, they laced up high

Kenton with Ellen Tibbetts. *Bart Henderson*

above the foot and provided lots of ankle support, and second, they kept out debris. In Kenton's words, they were "plain old high-topped, lace-'em-all-the-way-up work boots."

Unquestionably, however, the biggest changeup from '73 included a hiking companion; he invited his energetic buddy, twenty-four-year-old Henderson, to join him. Before starting, Kenton took one look at Henderson's old boots and knew they didn't have a prayer of going the distance. So they detoured to Page to pick up a pair of steel-toed boots for Henderson as well.

Companionably hiking downstream, the two young men made good time, quickly establishing a rhythm: Get up shortly after sunrise, hike for several miles. Stop for lunch. Maybe smoke a little weed. Walk the rest of the afternoon. Set up camp before early evening. Relax, share meals like soup mix with noodles, almonds, pecans, cashews, cheese, and bread crumbles. Discuss the setting, the day, maybe smoke a little more weed. Go to bed. Get up the next morning and do it all again.

Kenton also made time to write daily about their experiences. Determined to capture the essence of the journey, he sometimes made notations on the relative fly—writing during rest breaks:

Wednesday, March 3rd, day 5

What a fantastically special day this is…. Near the mouth of tata [Tatahatso Canyon] find a perch levitating us out over the gorge. We break for a smoke. Return to walking and peering. Some incredible vistas from every pier. Changing light, clouds, light snow, a magical scenario, a stage for spirits. Bart's going crazy with his Nikon, wearing out the shutter. We think we must have died and gone to heaven. This day will be with us forever.

At Eminence Break, River Mile 43, where Kenton had previously aborted his hike in the 1973 attempt, they met Skip Jones, who'd hiked in to spend a celebratory night with them.

After the overnighter, Jones hiked out and Henderson and Kenton headed downstream. Nearing the Little Colorado River, they encountered a Museum of Northern Arizona river trip. The river runners offered the hikers a ride and invited them to share their camp that night. Tempted by the food and fixings of a river trip, Henderson accepted, but Kenton declined. He said he needed to be true to himself and his goal: staying completely on River Left.

Henderson met him the next day at the Little Colorado after being dropped off by the river runners, and from there the two hiked to the Tanner Trail at River Mile 65. It would be their last night together; shortly after sunup the next morning, Henderson hiked out. "I told Kenton I would be rooting for him and felt honored to have been part of his grand plan."

Alone, Kenton wasted no time. He blazed downstream along the Escalante Route and Tonto Trails. Planning to meet Ellen at Hermit Creek, River Mile 95, added to his incentive. Still, being alone gave him pause. "Finally feeling what it's like to be alone in the Canyon—the greatest challenge—being Alone [sic] with myself."

By early afternoon on Friday, March 12, 1976, day 14 of the hike, that aloneness ended abruptly when an excited Kenton rendezvoused with Ellen at Hermit Creek Campground:

> Happy time. Happy day. We roll on down to Boucher Creek for the night. Bathe, have hot cocoa, then Ellen brings out the kicker. Enchiladas, ready-made—pop into the pan and heat—eat soo good. [sic] Just what I needed. Warm love, my good-hearted woman.

A native of Madison, Wisconsin, twenty-four-year-old Ellen Tibbetts grew up with a love of both drawing and horses. Combining this with a love of the outdoors and a fascination with the American West, after graduating from high school, she came to Northern Arizona University, where she majored in art. Weekends and holidays were frequently spent hiking with friends and exploring nearby areas. She quickly fell in love with the Grand Canyon and joined the university's hiking club. She even went on Canyon hikes with Harvey Butchart, the club's longtime sponsor.

Summit of Pollux Temple, 1970. From left, Jim Sears, Ellen Tibbetts, Al Doty, Harvey Butchart, and Bob Packard. *Al Doty*

Ellen met Kenton in the fall of 1973 on a honeymoon river trip for George and Sue Billingsley on the San Juan River. As fellow river guides with Grand Canyon Expeditions, the couple knew Kenton, and were friends with Ellen from the hiking club. Ellen and Kenton ultimately shared a nine-year romance. For her, in addition to Kenton's personality and charm, much of the spark to the relationship came from the landscape they loved to explore together. "Grand Canyon's the most romantic place in the world," Ellen would later say. "It's easy to fall in love there."

Well-fed, comfy, and snuggling with his sweetheart, Kenton had no problem drifting off that evening. That bliss ended abruptly a few hours later when a deer mouse (*Peromyscus maniculatus*) invaded their camp. Although the moonlighting marauder escaped Kenton's wrath, he captured his reaction to the little booger (something nearly every seasoned Canyon backpacker or longtime river runner can relate to) on paper:

> Beautiful night—calm, clear until about 2 AM when the most fuckin' outrageous mouse in the Grand Canyon came around and wouldn't give up. I'd throw rocks time and again and he would be right back, chewing on the packs. By 4, I finally give up trying to get any more sleep. He has really brought out the killer instinct in me. Wish I had a trap, he'd be a dead one and I'd be happy. I believe in live and let live but this little shithead just can't be put off.

Despite the mouse, the next morning Kenton journaled:

> "I had a real good night's sleep. The stars glisten like 10,000 jewels. In the background the soft music of running water. Ellen breathing quietly at my side, I'm a happy man."

Unfortunately for Kenton, Ellen's uplifting companionship would be short-lived. Like Bart Henderson, she couldn't commit to hiking the entire distance, but at least he could enjoy her company as far as Havasu Canyon. She also brought far more experience than Henderson when it came to off-trail hiking in the Grand Canyon, having done more miles on foot below the rim than nearly all of her female peers, as well as most men, including Kenton. Of Ellen, who'd also guided Kenton in placing two of the caches, he wrote:

> "I'm learning a lot about hiking from Ellen. She's a real hiker. I'm a riverman. There's a real difference between day hikes from the river and actual packing in the Canyon. An entirely different reality.... I'm glad for

what I know, for what I've learned, mostly from Ellen, makes the canyon a lot more enjoyable."

Her "Tibbett's Stew," as Kenton called it, a mixture of potatoes, nuts, cheese, and Zwieback breadcrumbs, added to his pleasure. Once, while preparing the stew in the dark, they accidentally dumped a stash of peyote[6] buttons instead of the breadcrumbs into the mix. Laughing at themselves and the mistake, they made sure neither went to waste.

Appreciating Ellen's expertise and cooking skills, uplifting demeanor, and their relationship, Kenton had zero qualms about inviting her to join him on what would be the most dangerous and challenging segment of his entire walk: the spectacular Muav Gorge.

Beginning below Kanab Creek at about River Mile 145.5, the Muav Gorge extends for more than thirty miles. Laid down like lasagna layers, its stacks of limestone formations—specifically, Muav, Temple Butte, and Redwall—are thicker than in any other Canyon reach. Dominated here by the gray Muav, this industrial-looking corridor is formidable; in places, only a quarter-mile separates the 1,200-foot-high clifftops on one side of the river from those on the other. Besides their mesmerizing atmosphere, something else within these soaring cliffs appealed to Kenton.

Kenton drying out fresh peyote during his length hike, March 1976.
Ellen Tibbetts

On multiple river trips beginning in his early Hatch days, he had spotted desert bighorn sheep in this area, steadily maneuvering along a sketchy Muav ledge averaging 100 to 150 feet above the river. This ledge, despite tremendous exposure in places—including several gaps that the bighorn had to jump—offered a consistently passable route for the agile sheep. Confident in his own and his

---

6 Peyote (aka mescal) buttons contains the hallucinogenic drug mescaline. The "buttons" are dried caps of the peyote cactus (*Lophophora williamsii*) which grows wild in Texas and Mexico. Buttons can be crushed and smoked but are generally chewed or ground for addition into liquid drink then ingested. Historically, peyote was used by the Aztecs and Native Americans in religious ceremonies. Recreational sale or use outside of Native American religious ceremonies is illegal in most states.

girlfriend's sure-footedness, he decided that if the bighorn could do it, so could he and Ellen. They'd just mimic where the bighorn (in Kenton's words, "truly the lord and masters of the Canyon") went and what they did.

Far easier said than done, it turned out. Sometimes the going became terrifying, as Kenton later explained in his interview with Steiger:

> So, it's one of those things you either—on that ledge you could move really fast, if you did the bighorn trail, and just did those jumps. And even not doing the jumps, just walking along, you're right on the edge, and it's kind of "ball-bearing-y" and loose, but there's a little faint trail there that the bighorns use…. It was a pretty scary, pretty hairball ledge to do…. There were a couple of jumps [where I just went], "Unh-uh! No way."

The two made it through to Havasu Canyon unscathed and euphoric. "The energy of being the first people to traverse that bighorn route, probably since the Anasazi, was absolutely thrilling," Ellen recalls. "And for me, being able to do that Muav section, the best part of his hike, with Kenton was incredible." Kenton was totally in sync with her on this. In camp he wrote, "This has been an incredible day. A thrill a minute, much better than I had thought it would be. We feel exhilarated, exhausted."

After ten days together, Ellen hiked the eighteen miles out the Havasupai Trail. Meanwhile, Kenton began picking his way through the cliffs downstream. About one-eighth of a mile down from the mouth of Havasu, he retrieved one of his caches. The densely packed five-gallon can contained about ten days' worth of supplies, essentials like candles, penlight batteries, maps, notebooks, matches, and clean socks. The fifteen pounds of provisions also included salt, cayenne pepper, granola, dried milk, hot chocolate, coffee, wheat berry bread, Rye-Krisp, sesame/PB/honey spread, mixed nuts, raisins, assorted dried soups, spinach [dried], and noodles. Then, to satisfy an apparent sweet tooth, M&Ms, Cadbury chocolate bars, and carob fudge.

Resupplied, recharged, and once again on his own, Kenton pushed himself to walk all day and camp when it got dark; he covered fifteen to twenty miles most days, sometimes even close to thirty. On March 28 (day 30), he reached the mouth of Diamond Creek at River Mile 226, where he and Ellen had placed another cache. From a sloping cliff, he saw a few Hualapai men milling around the road near the delta area 200 feet below.

Other than the road to Lees Ferry, Diamond Creek provides the only other access to the river by vehicle. Its road is entirely on the Hualapai Reservation and its use comes with a toll to non-Hualapai. So does any hiking on Hualapai land. While obtaining clearance to use the road is relatively easy, for several reasons (discussed in Chapter 30) the Hualapai are disinclined to approve hiking permits in their backcountry. To avoid the hassle (not the nominal fee), Kenton had decided to take his chances and go permit-less across the Hualapai land. To catch trespassers, the Hualapai stationed tribal rangers at the mouth of Diamond Creek, and if caught, the trespassers would have to pay a hefty fine.

Knowing this and despite a slight drizzle, Kenton stayed intentionally out of sight and waited for the men to leave. When the coast was clear, he hiked down and began scouting around for a dry camping spot. He eventually found what he was looking for. He pulled out his journal and, per protocol, commenced writing. "So here I lie, trying to cook dinner from underneath a stupid picnic table."

⌒〜⌒

Downstream from Diamond Creek, the walking remained fairly easy and straightforward, allowing him to intermittently follow burro trails and do some sidehilling along the Hurricane Fault. After a week, though, he encountered yet more horrible bushwhacking, as bad or worse than anything upstream.

> "Sometimes I think I'm in Hell, but then I think even Hell couldn't be this bad. It wears me to the bone. Tears at my hide. Claws at my eyes. Every rock is loose and I'm down as much as up … truly miserable last 3 miles. Wouldn't want to do it again in a million moons."

Later that same day, while camped at River Mile 272, his mood did a 180. As he noted in his journal, "The river flowing beside, a perfect shower spot to wash away the traces of a hard day. Crimson monkey flower adds a dash of red. Columbines high up in glorious yellow. Frog singing in a chorus of everlasting love. The wisdom of falling water. My mind soars, my spirit is lifted. I'm camping my last night in heaven, if heaven could be this fine."

On Saturday, April 3, 1976 (day 36)—more than 400 miles by his estimate from his starting point at Jackass and nearly two weeks earlier than the April 15 date he had been shooting for—Kenton awoke to sunlight illuminating his finish line. "[T]oday I pass out the Grand Wash Cliffs and on to the ferry. Surely has been a fine experience. I rise early at 4:00 o'clock, sit and gaze out at the Grand Wash Cliffs in the distance. In ways I'm glad it's over, in ways I wish it weren't, but then it really never ends, only begins again."

Shortly before ten a.m., he passed by the Grand Wash Cliffs "to stand in the sunshine on the other side of the Canyon."

The hike now history, he sat and contemplated how best to capture the moment's significance on paper. His answer? "Think this over. Smoke the canyon hash pipe." Then, within the collective high, he found the words he was searching for:

What are my feelings here at this spot just footsteps from the Canyon? Joy, sadness, completion, disbelief. Can it really be that I have just done what I dreamed of but in reality never thought I would or could do? I look up from my notes. At the openness, the space outside the Canyon. Yes, I'm here. I've walked through the Grand Canyon stem to stern, done what I set out to do. The weight is off my mind. I feel most of all freedom to go on with life. I've finished something I'd left part done, something I had to do for some reason.

⌒〜〜⌒

As an aside, that "reason," he emphatically told me and others, including Bart Henderson and Lew Steiger, was Colin Fletcher. Yet in more than 400 pages of journal notes penned during his hike, he never referenced the book *The Man Who Walked Through Time* and mentioned Colin Fletcher only once. That single mention didn't show up until his final week of hiking and had required a bit of a prompt.

Near River Mile 213, he encountered a commercial river trip, Cross Tours. After describing his novel endeavor to the passengers, Kenton wrote, "I'm asked, 'sort of like Colin Fletcher, huh?'" Apparently not offended by the comparison, nor by several curious passengers ("dudes," per Kenton) taking snapshots of him, he gave them a three-word response. "Yep, sort of."

With more shades of Fletcher, Kenton took his writing very seriously. "Writing is like taking pictures," he jotted. "the scope is limited, making use of but one sense." He also wrote, "This is a tricky business—playing with pen + ink + words—trying to catch thoughts and stick them between paper, press them as one would a flower."

Unlike his hiking hero Harvey's just-the-facts-ma'am style, Kenton's prose— like Fletcher's— frequently described his emotions in the moment. For example, he talked about feeling fear many times, especially in the Muav Gorge while following bighorn trailing sometimes "300-400 feet, vertical to the river below." To negotiate this headspace, he convinced himself he needed to do one thing:

Think like a bighorn … they move as shadows. Always just out of minds' grasp. Fascinating animals. Pioneers of the kingdom. Wizards, sorcerers, magicians, strange and wonderful creatures. Almost a transcendental experience to see one.… Bighorns have no thought of fear … I swallow mine. It tastes worse than peyote. I move fast, sure and determined. Now

One of Kenton's three journals kept during the 1976 length hike.

and then my fear creeps back … then swallow it again and again. I feel, at times, no fear…. Fear kills. I can see it perfectly. Perhaps someday I will have no fear—hence no death—only being.

Metaphysical references were common, and he often used a reverent tone describing the landscape, sometimes personifying the scenery: "The Mormon tea plant besides me sighs" or "The canyon walls hug me close … I love you too, Grand Canyon, you who have cared and loved me so."

Kenton also didn't skimp on words when it came to philosophizing. His writing waxed heavy with nostalgia and is loaded with take-home lessons:

Life is always moving along the edge. One wrong step and it's over. Eventually we all have to face the slipping away into eternity, to move through life without fear brings one through that last step, that pain or longing. One just experiences the falling, the eternity. An observer watching the final act in the play—the beginning of a new play. And as my body walks, my spirit flies. Having no casing of arms and legs to keep it earthbound, it soars past the cliffs, then beyond, circling, circling in the mists of the heavens…

After stowing his precious journal, he started walking again. Within minutes, he came upon two men and their wives fishing off their boat. The "sweet old folks," brothers Eric and Jack, and spouses Mildred and Bertha—retired snowbirds wintering in Meadview—not only offered Kenton coffee and a peanut butter sandwich, but also dished up a boat ride so he could bypass hiking the last two miles to Pearce Ferry. Without hesitation, he accepted everything.

Just before noon, less than an hour after the foursome had dropped him off, Ellen arrived. A welcoming party of one, she rolled up in his old International Scout, a vehicle his parents had given him. Kenton wrote, "Gosh, how good it is to see her at last. It puts the finishing touch on a memorable experience."

Of that meeting and the completion of his journey, there is no photographic record. There were no balloons or bells or whistles. Per Ellen: "It seemed like just another day." Indeed, the only out-of-the-ordinary commotion came when Kenton introduced Ellen to the generous couples who gave him the ride, followed by both of them assisting a boatman acquaintance with derigging his raft. Once completed, they loaded Kenton's pack into the Scout, hopped in, and drove off.

In Kingman, Kenton bought a new shirt and some gloves, then they ate Mexican food, "lots of it," at La Casita on the east side of town. After lunch, they drove to Peach Springs, then down Diamond Creek Road to the river to pick up his food cache can and camp for the night.

Unlike the stealth he displayed when he'd accessed the cache two weeks earlier, this time he sought out a Hualapai tribe representative—Monroe Beecher, a man who frequently hung out in the area. He knew he owed the Hualapai tribe for his time on their land and driving on their road. His confession to Monroe about the twelve days he'd hiked there sans permit impressed Monroe to the point that he only charged him half the normal daily rate: one dollar a day ($0.50 per day to hike, $0.50 to camp). In total, Kenton paid the Hualapai $17. "I'm glad I told them about it," he wrote. "Spent a lot of useless energy worrying about how'd they react since I'm telling them after the fact… It made me feel much better to have paid them honest." He added, "I feel real, real good, at ease, complete."

Conscience clear and feeling as fulfilled as he ever had in his life, he and Ellen camped that night on the sandbank at the mouth of Diamond Creek. Beneath a starlit sky, deep within Grand Canyon, next to his gal and his beloved river, he driftied off to sleep.

Upon returning home, it was business as usual. Indeed, his endeavor received no press. No book, no glossy magazine account, not even a local newspaper article documented it. But Kenton felt content. Mission accomplished. Fletcher would never be able to claim to be the first to hike the length of the Grand Canyon, whether defined by either its geographic or bureaucratic boundaries.

Two decades later as he reflected on his achievement, Kenton told Steiger, "I really don't know why I had it as a goal, other than because of the way I'd felt about Colin Fletcher doing it…. I didn't want him to be able to claim to be the first man to have walked through the Grand Canyon. I didn't care who did, per se, but I thought that he was a poor choice of a human to have that distinction."

That's how it would remain for Kenton. He never pulled punches when he discussed Fletcher. But, to Fletcher's credit, he came back to do far more Grand Canyon hiking. There's a good chance a jaded Kenton Grua might have felt differently had he been aware of Fletcher's other serious Canyon hikes. For example, in the spring of '66, Fletcher returned to the Grand Canyon for another long solo journey. This time, he went from Havasu Canyon to Diamond Creek, River Mile 226. In 1971, he walked from Diamond Creek, to Bridge Canyon, River Mile 235. Then in 1977, he returned a third time to hike from Bridge Canyon to the Grand Wash Cliffs, River Mile 277.

All of these, several hundred more miles, were done without accolades or having another book in the works. They were likely done because Fletcher, like so many, probably fell in love with the landscape. In fact, by 1977, a year after Kenton Grua finished the length, Fletcher had racked up the second-most lengthwise miles hiking below the rim. Only a river guide who joked about being an elf had done more.

Yet they both acknowledged and bowed their heads to the millennia-long legacy of humans who had walked below the rims. When it came to appreciating foot travel within the Canyon by its ancient human inhabitants, Harvey Butchart perhaps said it best: "We might all be cautious in claiming to be the first, because native people have been in the Canyon for at least 4,000 years and seem to have been everywhere."

Like Harvey, Kenton developed a unique appreciation for the Indigenous people who'd gone before. Indeed, he felt he owed much of his length-hike success to those who walked the same earth long before him, people and animals alike. "Routes all worked out, thanks to the Anasazi and the Bighorn." In his Steiger interview, he added this vignette about the Canyon's prehistoric people:

> All the way, the things that struck me, you could see evidence of Anasazi[7] … a historic trail that we know of that had never been used by a white man. And mescal pits. So it was definitely done by the Anasazi. I don't know if anybody ever just kinda walked the whole distance, or hiked the whole distance, per se. They moved through there, did everything

---

7 The label "Anasazi," a Navajo word for "ancient enemy" or "non-Navajo ancient ones," was applied to the Ancestral Puebloan people by early Anglo-American archeologists; it is no longer used.

that I did, in terms of hiking. And that was kind of a neat feeling, to be in their footsteps.

Kenton on a Redwall cliff in Marble Canyon. *Bart Henderson*

Evidence of humans within the Grand Canyon dates back thousands of years and appears in countless locations. Beginning with Paleo-Indian hunters (10,000 BCE) and continuing with Desert Culture (2000 BCE) and Ancestral Puebloans (1250 BCE to 800 CE), long walks below the rims were likely common on both sides of the river. Often, these were made by hunters following game trails.

While it seems highly possible that over the millennia, a collective line of foot travel by the region's Indigenous people would connect one end of the Canyon to the other, no conclusive evidence of this exists. Also, given the need for strategically cached food and water (an extremely difficult undertaking even by today's standards), and that the various tribes were not always friendly with one another, and that such a time-consuming and difficult walk would serve no real purpose to a hunter gatherer, it seems unlikely that any single individual had walked end-to-end before Kenton Grua.

If anyone did, they would probably agree with Kenton: Among other things, success hinges on healthy, happy feet.

CHAPTER EIGHT

Grand Addiction

CATHEDRAL WASH TO SOAP CREEK, (CONTINUED)

*The Canyon becomes a mind-altering drug, the canyoneer an addict. He
wonders if ordinary people can understand what he's experienced; he becomes
"born again," sharing a bond only with others of the same persuasion. It becomes
"his" or "her" Canyon. Only the initiated can truly understand the power of this
fanatic possessiveness.*

Bill Beer
We Swam the Grand Canyon (1988)

You can get the monkey off your back, but the circus never leaves town.

Anne Lamott
Grace (Eventually) (2007)

October 2008 (continued)

Once Wes and I had maneuvered past the cliff near Navajo Bridge, I thought
we'd be home free for our first leg, certainly panic-free. That cliff had been the
crux. After we'd eaten lunch in the shade of the bridge, the going, once again,
became very tedious, consisting of seemingly endless boulder dodging and peg-
legging on sloping talus. All under direct sun. Naturally, we began to drag, our
pace slowing to maybe one mile per hour. I had consumed most of my water.
At River Mile 5.5, we descended a break to the river; I needed to refill. Shortly
thereafter, a soft hissing sound erupted from close by. *Very close.*

Pffssttt! For a split second, it didn't register. Pffssttt! *What the hell is that?!* It
seemed even louder. Pffssttt! Suddenly the source of this sound became obvious.

"No! NO! NO! Oh, crap!" I yelled, mostly to myself but loud enough to be heard by Wes on the cliff above.

Pffssttt! Pffssttt! As the terrible caterwaul continued, I imagined a stroke, a ruptured aneurysm spurting blood inside the brain. *My brain.* Specifically, I thought of a "wet stroke" (bleeding), as opposed to a "dry stroke" (no bleeding), in which a clot blocks a blood vessel and obstructs flow. Both are bad. After all, a stroke is a stroke. Each can result in a potentially disabling or lethal injury from damage to the surrounding tissue. While I felt nothing, I still knew a crippling event could be happening. Every second mattered. A wave of panic began to rise in me like heat from a bonfire…

Eight years had passed since the millennium. I had resisted getting a cell phone, likening the technology to a tenacious tether. While training to be a doctor, I had no choice about carrying a pager—an electronic leash—everywhere I went, including the bathroom. Sure, I knew cell phones were different; unlike a pager, which only flashed a phone number or location, they offered two-way communication.

Finally, after Becky gave me her old flip phone and convinced me of its benefits, I caved, admitting it might come in handy; I also liked the camera feature. Besides, it gave her a sense of security, though I told her I'd be shocked if we'd have any cell service where we were going in the Canyon. So, prudently, I stuffed the device into my backpack's aptly named "brain pouch."

This pouch rests on top of the main body cavity of a pack, like the head atop a human torso. Sitting high, it's typically protected. No weight or pressure from other items above crush it; it's far above the water if wading's required; and when the pack is set down or accidentally dropped, the impact is usually on the bottom or sides, not the top. The brain of the pack, like the human head, typically protects important stuff. For example, backpackers often place their most valuable items in there: flashlight, camera, eyeglasses, medications, lighter, map, toilet paper, and so forth. On this trip, in addition to the phone, I also added another unusual but important item, one I valued more than the phone: a can of Tecate beer.

After scrambling down the eighty-foot slope to the river's edge to refill my water jug, I had swung my pack off my shoulder and flopped it on the rocks. The flop seemed innocent enough, certainly not careless, but the pack's brain hit against a chunk of Kaibab Limestone and a pointy little spicule.

Then the hissing began.

Frantic, I lunged for my pack. I knew my beer was dying, bleeding out. I had two goals. First: guzzle the remainder of the beer so its death would not be completely in vain. Second: rescue the damn phone. Faster than I had ever done before, I yanked open the zipper only to get immediately sprayed by a small geyser shooting from the Tecate can.

"No!" I bellowed.

While I've never had an addiction issue with alcohol, I do enjoy a beer now and then. I also loathe anything going to waste. So, I grabbed the wildly spraying can, popped the top, tilted the can vertically, then chugged what remained. That done, I sighed as beer dribbled off my nose and chin.

"What a bummer!" I moaned to Wes before belching.

Still grumbling about the unfairness of it all, I looked inside the brain pouch.

"Oh, crap!" I shouted as I snatched my phone from a puddle of beer.

Once again, I thought that speed was of the essence. I flipped the phone open, gave it a few vigorous shakes and quick drying swipes with my tee-shirt, followed by a few sharp puffs of air. (Like a version of the three-second rule, I suppose, where one quickly "cleans" food dropped on the floor before eating it.) Then, despite my gut telling me otherwise, I pushed the phone's power button.

The screen flashed on, just like normal, the date and time superimposed on a scenic backdrop. *Cool!* This encouraging sign of life lasted about a microsecond before the screen disintegrated into a kaleidoscope of purples, reds, blues, and oranges.

"Awww, crap!" I knew the bruised appearance signaled a mortal injury. Electronics clearly fried, I shut it off and threw it back into my pack. "What a double bummer! I feel bad about the phone and your mom will be mad, but I really wanted that beer in camp!"

"Jeez, Dad," Wes chuckled. "It was only a beer."

"False! It is *only* a beer if we are at home," I countered, holding up my pointer finger to, well, make a point. "But down here, a beer is no ordinary beer, son! It becomes nectar of the gods!" Still grinning, Wes then rolled his eyes.

A half-hour later, Wes and I found a good spot to camp at Six Mile Draw, a short side canyon coming from the right. We parked our tent on a small, sandy, flat bank situated between short willow and tamarisk trees on the downstream end of the draw's debris fan that river runners frequently use. A cool upstream breeze wafted through our camp as we ate freeze-dried Mountain House Mexican rice and talked about the day. I asked Wes about the climb.

"It was fun, Dad. I don't think the cliff was all that scary, and the hiking wasn't all that hard."

His response boded well for future hikes, I thought, and today's hike had been a good initial test run for us. Relaxing, Wes took off his boots and started rubbing his feet.

"Shoot! I think I'm getting a blister," he moaned.

I took a look. Yep. He had a small one on his big toe.

I started to cut a moleskin pad for it.

"Do you think we can have an Airsoft war when we get back?" he asked while watching me place the moleskin on his foot. "Airsoft" involves shooting little plastic pellets from plastic replicas of military guns. I looked at him.

From his silly grin and my past experience, I instantly knew his plan. He always gave me the cheaper of his two guns, the one that required being within twenty feet of your target to hit it.

"Yeah, sure," I smiled.

"Do you think I'd be good at a food challenge?" he queried next, referencing *Man v. Food,* our favorite television show. In it, the show's host, Adam Richman, traveled the country, sampling cuisine famous to a city or region. Then he took on a "food challenge" that involved downing a huge (or hot and spicy) meal within a time limit. I looked at Wes, shook my head, my smile widening. I loved how his thirteen-year-old brain could change direction on a dime.

"Yeah, I think you could hold your own."

He nodded in approval.

"I bet you'd be really good," he told me.

I laughed.

"Are you calling me fat?"

"No. You just like to eat a lot."

He grinned broadly as he started to climb into his sleeping bag.

"Umm, Dad?"

"Yeah?" I saw him looking at me, his expression now sheepish, hopeful.

"Do you think I could ever be good enough to play baseball in college?" In a game the year before, Wes struck out seventeen of eighteen batters.

"You know, Wes, there's always a chance."

"What about the pros?" he asked, even more pensive.

"You'll never know unless you try. It could happen with a lot of hard work and luck. Luck in genetics." I held up my hand, fingers crossed. "Time will tell."

"Right." He flashed a small smile, yawned, then closed his eyes. "Goodnight, Dad."

I lay down too but couldn't sleep. I looked out the open tent door at the bright moonlight reflecting off the cliffs and the river. The lazy upstream breeze with its typical October chill had cooled even more. I snuggled my sleeping bag to my chin. Our choice for camp had been perfect.

The Colorado glided by. Like always for me, I found its soft murmur as soothing to my mind as my inflated sleeping pad was to my body. Shadows from the surrounding cliffs loomed spectacularly, epic in scale.

God, I love this place. For the humbling perspective. For the tear-jerking beauty. For the bust-your-ass challenges. For the head-clearing inspiration and natural highs.

Then, in spite of myself, I thought of my "brain bleed" earlier in the day. With it came another recurrent thought. For years, hiking the Canyon has reminded me of *The Fantastic Voyage*. In this 1966 film, a submarine crew reduced to microscopic size is injected into the bloodstream of an injured scientist to repair damage to his brain.

Similarly, hikers in Grand Canyon are like tiny blood cells moving through a dendritic vascular system of side canyons, ancient, hardened arteries of seemingly infinite proportions—each different in size, shape, texture, depth, and uniqueness. My favorites are the deepest and narrowest. Within these varicosed, dark canyons, what's around the next twist is anyone's guess. *Can we even pass by this constriction? Will there be a cliff or big chokestone? Will other organisms appear ahead? A deer? A bobcat? A bighorn? Or will we stumble upon a to-be-coveted watery desert oasis, a real-world Shangri-La?* That "unknown-around-the-next-bend" sensation is one of the thrilling essences of Canyon hiking that keeps me coming back—a fantastic voyage each and every time.

I've also learned to crave the feeling of being "microscopic in size," not just physically, but in the perspective of time, and thus, my life. While I've never been able to fully wrap my mind around the immense geologic age of the Canyon, then and there I had a revelation, a comparison I *could* relate to. At the time, I was nearing fifty years old and knew that my heart had beat about 1.8 billion times. This number is roughly equal to the age of Elves Chasm gneiss, the Canyon's oldest rock. If the Canyon's geologic age were a fifty-year-old human's and my life were represented by its heartbeats, in that moment my entire existence equaled a single, solitary beat. *Only one.*

As I watched the Colorado, I also couldn't help but think of my friend Kenton Grua. Like so many, he too, thought of the river as blood and something alive. Camped at Tanner Beach during his lengthwise hike, contemplating and listening to the river, he journaled:

Total 78 RM 68

Sunday March 7, 1976 Day 9

The river the aorta the lifeblood the creator and in the end the destroyer of the canyon...

A smooth, sleek, living thing with long flowing hair. The river talks on, keeping me spellbound, lost in a beautifully woven tale—having no beginning, no end, only an everlasting musical murmur... The river laughs and gurgles, a cricket chirps. My mind is quiet and alive, just listening. No thought- a peaceful feeling. Just here + now.

I easily imagined Kenton ferociously rowing his dory through here in 1983, his own heart pounding, blood surging through his body in a marathon effort to set the record for the fastest rowing trip. He passed this spot before moonrise.

My next thought went to Kenton's tragic and unexpected death in August 2002, the result of a spontaneous aortic dissection while mountain biking. As blood tore through the lining of this artery—the body's largest—the layers separated, which almost instantly obstructed all blood flow. Unconscious within seconds, he crashed his bike and died soon thereafter. He was only fifty-two.

One of the last places I had spent any significant time with Kenton was here in Marble Canyon several months before his death; Wes had also been with us. We were attending the Spring 2002 Grand Canyon River Guides Training Seminar (GTS). At the time, the twice-divorced Kenton had recently re-married. His new wife Michelle came with three small children. He appeared the happiest he'd been since I'd known him. During get togethers, it became obvious he embraced his new marriage and fatherhood with commitment and vigor. It seemed unfair that he'd never had the chance to hike with his two sons and daughter down here.

Sleep still eluding me, I then imagined Kenton hiking in his Kaibab moccasins atop the shadowy cliffs across the river. He had tromped through here during daylight, of course, but in my mind's eye, I could see his short legs churning fast, buzzing a hole in the sole in one of his moccasins, ultimately leading to the cactus-spine puncture and infection. Between the thought of Kenton's injury and Weston's blister, I recalled yet another image involving them both.

During our hike out the South Kaibab Trail after we celebrated New Year's at Phantom Ranch in 1995, the weather turned windy and bitterly cold. Eight-month-old Wes, on my back in his baby backpack, lost one of his booties as we neared the freezing rim. Kenton found it stuck in the backpack's frame, grabbed it, then took Weston's tiny, cold foot in his hands. "Let's warm that baby up," he declared as he started massaging and exhaling his warm breath on it. Once he'd done that, he slipped the booty back on. "You have to take care of these feet, Weston; you're gonna need them so you can hike this place." I had considered Kenton a kind and inspiring friend, but that gesture made me love the man.

I also loved how deeply he loved this place, something we shared. For seekers of beauty, solitude, and adventure within canyon country, there is none greater. The Grand Canyon with its Colorado River is the earth's gloryhole, the geologic jackpot and lithic nirvana.

Can I ever get enough?

During more than thirty-five years of practicing medicine, I've learned that addictions, in some shape or form, are ubiquitous. I've been hooked on the

Canyon since my first "hit" at age ten, staring into its depths for the first time. Been hooked ever since.

Fortunately, I've put a lot of my obsession into good use: working as a doctor on the rim; assisting the NPS with emergency medical services; researching and teaching about Canyon history as well as desert wilderness medicine, and co-writing a book on how to avoid dying in the Canyon—like preventative medicine with doctoring.

I should have seen my now-hopeless Grand Canyon addiction coming. Besides my own adventuring, I had spent significant time in the Canyon with one of the greatest Canyon obsessives of all time, Kenton Grua. During those times together, we reveled in the same euphoric high.

Risking obsession within our family, I deliberately (abetted by Becky) began hiking our girls into the Canyon as toddlers and, in Weston's case, as an infant. A well-intentioned, thoughtful enabler, I wanted our kids to love the Canyon as much as I did so that we could share it.

During the first stage of the mega-hike with Wes, we found the ancient vasculature of Cathedral Wash lacking water, petroglyphs, or the historic artifacts that sometimes make a Canyon hike more beguiling. Yet its convoluted beauty still held us in suspense. Weston, despite prior hikes here, seemed hot to trot, hustling downcanyon as lead.

Indeed, for several weeks prior to me popping the "wanna-hike-the-length-with-me" question, he had been asking, almost begging, for another Canyon hike, as though he were going through a sort of Canyon-hiking withdrawal. "Dad, this is awesome! It feels really good to be back in here again," Wes had chanted almost immediately into the hike as we scurried down Cathedral.

I turned my gaze from the moonlight and looked at him. He slept soundly, content after getting his Canyon fix. At thirteen, he was well on his way to what Kenton and I and others shared, and I felt at ease with this.

I took my pulse, another ritual. It was normal. I had rehydrated. Had I taken it a few hours earlier, it would have likely been a little fast, a sign of dehydration. As I felt the pulsations under my fingertips, I imagined each beat as a blip on a heart monitor. *What if one blip equaled one lifetime?* To capture 1.8 billion blips (again, the age of the Canyon's oldest rock, in years) on a rhythm strip, at least 32,000 miles of paper would be needed, more than enough to wrap the entire earth.

I am a single blip.

My daughter, Brittany, hiking along the top of the Redwall near River Mile 25. *Tom Myers*

CHAPTER NINE

Read, Run, and Type 2 Fun

CATHEDRAL WASH TO SOAP CREEK, (CONTINUED)

One day, in retrospect, the years of struggle will
strike you as the most beautiful.

Sigmund Freud (1856–1939)

October 2008 (continued)

Morning broke with a wake-up call from a Canyon wren (*Catherpes mexicanus*). Slightly bigger than a hummingbird and cute as can be, they are cinnamon in color, have long curved bills, and little pot bellies. They dart and flit about with seemingly carefree enthusiasm. The males also have a beautiful mating call. Its repeating, high-pitched fluting cascades in delightful decrescendos, each lasting about five seconds. Along with my strong cup of coffee and the Canyon's sunrise panorama, that little bird's rhapsodic reveille was morning glory.

We were on the move by seven and soon were following mule deer trails, little footpaths that wound through the geological chaos. These paths made the hike so much easier; we followed a good one for nearly a mile. I told him if we were lucky, there would be more such trailing to come, especially adding in the bighorn sheep downstream.

"Dad, deer and bighorn are like the Grand Canyon's natural CCC!" Weston blurted, delighted by the relatively easy walking. By CCC, he meant the Civilian Conservation Corps, part of President Franklin D. Roosevelt's New Deal plan to get young men back to work during the Great Depression of the 1930s. Wes knew that CCC crews built several amazing trails in the Grand Canyon, including the North Kaibab and the River Trail blasted into the cliff walls near Phantom Ranch.

Following the tramped routes of these intrepid ungulates would be a recurring theme for us over the next seven-plus years. However, in off-trail hiking in the Canyon, easy walking is rare and never lasts.

Near River Mile 8, we dropped into Badger Creek Canyon. This drainage is perennially dry, despite the "creek" name on maps (such misnomers contribute to the Grand Deception). Immediately downstream we encountered a huge, rocky landslide. The Kaibab and Toroweap ramparts directly above looked like they'd been dynamited, sending an avalanche of broken limestone, gypsum, and shale crashing down. Over the eons, water, wind, and sun had varnished the slide, giving it the appearance of a massive rusting junkyard of blocky steel. The quarter-mile-wide pile extended from the base of the Toroweap cliffs to the river, as though unloaded over the edge from a giant dump truck on the rim. Much like river runners facing a rough rapid, we scouted for a route through the rocky maelstrom. None existed.

Read and run.

Unfortunately, similar to a leaf in a rocky stream, our plunge turned into a stop-and-go stutter. In some places, we had to climb up ten feet or more, move horizontally about the same, then climb back down yet another fifteen feet.

Hikers' reality on the top of the Redwall with oblivious boaters below. *Rich Rudow*

Basically, three dozen feet of cattywampus stitching to net a ten-foot hem of downstream progress.

If boulder dodging on the thirty- to sixty-degree slope wasn't bad enough, many of the rocks we had to navigate proved precariously unstable. And the hazardous ones weren't always obvious. At times the rocks' shape, their angle on the slope, or the crumbly soil underneath projected the danger clearly. We avoided those. At other times, the rocks—like cleverly hidden landmines—offered a perfect invitation (more Grand Deception) for a weighted foot: flat surface, level, and sandwiched between other rocks. Yet far too many are prone to giving way, sending the unlucky hiker crashing down. And, from experience at the Grand Canyon Clinic, I knew that the heavier the pack, the harder the fall and the worse the injury. Thus, our bulky packs made the effort that much tougher.

As an assist, at times we also had to resort to grabbing and pushing off rocks. At best, the abrasive rock felt like sandpaper against the skin and at worst, like a cheese-grater. I kicked myself for forgetting to bring gloves.

A hundred yards beyond Badger Creek Rapid and downstream of the rockslide, we stopped to watch a river trip float past. By this time, the temperature had jumped into the mid-80s. Panting, sweat dripping in our eyes and soaking our backs, we stared with fascination and envy as the four rafts moved lazily past us. One reclining rafter sipped a canned beverage. *Probably a cold beer, lucky bum.* He looked at us, yawned, then turned to chat with the guy at the oars who, too, looked relaxed, his oar handles tucked under his knees and reclining against a duffle pile. The boat, drifting in the swift current, whisked them past our torturous boulder field in a tiny fraction of the time it had taken us to navigate it.

The contrasts between our two modes of Canyon travel were striking. For boaters, running the eight miles from Lees Ferry to Badger Rapid is relatively effortless. It's mostly flat water with current. Absent upstream winds, you could probably be asleep at the oars until Badger. For backpackers like us, wind or not, covering that same distance is guaranteed to be mentally and physically exhausting. Every step has to be calculated. Every step takes effort. And every step counts. Complicating matters for the hiker, there is a constant balancing act of throwing glances at the scenery versus those to the feet. Beauty beckons, but gawking around and not at the ground risks a stumble. One such misstep could break an ankle, rip the skin, or crack a skull.

"That's Type-1 Fun, Dad," Wes informed me as the boaters drifted past. Previously, he'd explained a theory that claims whatever you're doing can be rated on a "Fun Scale." Type-1 Fun means it's fun when you do it and fun looking back on having done it. Type-2 Fun is not that much fun when you're doing it but is fun looking back on. Type-3 Fun is awful when you're doing it and still terrible when you remember it.

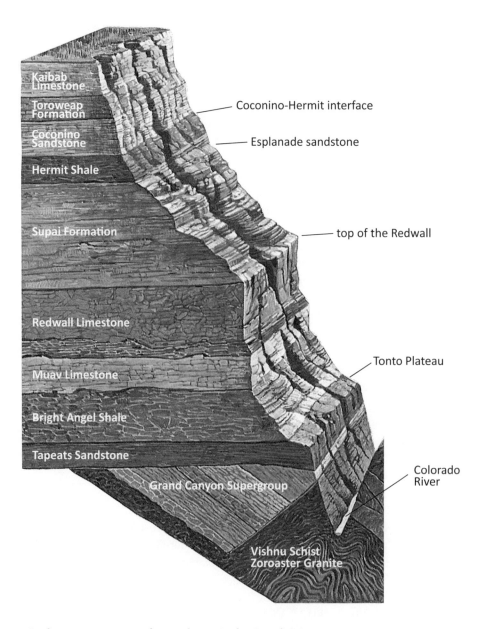

Geologic cross-section of major layers in the Grand Canyon.
(Of note: there are twenty-seven total rock units with formal names.)

Most lengthwise or horizontal traversing is usually done along the top of sedimentary formations with consistent ledges and benches, such as the Esplanade Sandstone, the Redwall Limestone, and the Tonto Plateau. Rim-to-River trails typically switchback through the layers, following fault lines.

"Oh, yeah?" I replied. "What's this, then?"

"It's definitely not Type-1. It's probably Type-2, but we'll see. We're not done yet."

His words were prophetic. The sloping talus ahead became steeper and steeper. We veered to the top of the maroon-colored Hermit Formation, which begins to appear around River Mile 5. Comprised of mudstones and siltstones, "the Hermit" was laid down about 265-million years ago by a system of meandering rivers and streams when the region was thought to be "semi-arid." Our chosen pathway had us marching along the top of this formation where it came into contact with the bottom of the layer above it, the Canyon's Coconino Sandstone. This interface, a hard-packed crust often covered by loose rock (broken chunks of the more resistant Coconino Sandstone and Kaibab Limestone fallen down from above) is marked by sharply eroded, wave-patterned gullies. In Marble Canyon the Hermit tops out at about 300 feet thick, but in the western end of Grand Canyon, it triples in thickness to almost a thousand feet. We tried to negotiate it horizontally, then by zigzagging while angling our boot edges into the slope. It reminded me of a frozen black diamond ski run, its sheer surface covered with ice kernels.

"This is awful, Dad," Wes complained. "It's like the rock changed. What is it?"

Mirroring Wes's Fun Scale, I thought it was time for another metaphor, one which has evolved over the years. The initial version went something like this:

"It's called the Hermit Shale, and for backpacking, it can really suck. Shales are ancient mud and clay—layered, crumbly crap, super-steep and super-flaky. Reminds me of people I know. In fact, most of these rock formations seem to have human-like personality traits and moods. Some can be fun to be around and some can make you miserable."

<hr/>

Quick confession. I have no formal training in geology. And while I find a lot of it fascinating, it's not my bailiwick. Or to put it another way, when it comes down to the nitty-gritty of rocks—where geologists frequently nerd out—I tend to zone out. (Instead, I channel most of my nerdiness into Grand Canyon wilderness medicine minutia and historical hiking trivia.) Still, a basic understanding of the nuances of the Canyon's rock layers can be helpful in figuring out what to expect when navigating through or across them.

Sandstones (like the Esplanade and Tapeats) are usually friendly. Because of their sandstsone composition, they literally (relatively speaking) have a softer side; their edges are less sharp and their gullies less sheer. Plus, sandstone surfaces are grainy, thus grippy, and offer great traction. And because they're sedimentary, they're layered and ledgy. Walking on them can not only be possible but fun. (Until it's not. And that's usually because the route pinches out, gets too exposed, or has been obliterated by rockfall.)

Limestones (e.g. the Redwall and Muav), on the other hand, are relatively antisocial. Calcium carbonate makes them very dense and much harder. In turn, they are hard on hikers. Far more erosion-resistant, their edges are sharper—sometimes razor-sharp—and more jagged. Their surfaces are also often slick, and they retain more verticality and sheerness. Unless faulted, their bypasses usually require ropes and climbing gear to navigate. To whit, of his twelve thousand miles in over four decades of exploring, Harvey Butchart found only 116 ropeless routes through the Redwall (a.k.a., the Dreadwall or Shredwall) Limestone. On the flip side, limestones generally offer stability and, similar to sandstones, can be excellent to walk on. Plus, they've eroded into some of the most spectacular slots and grottos, not only in the Grand Canyon, but in the entire world.

Shales (such as the Hermit and Bright Angel), as mentioned, are flaky. Their eczema-like surface often peels, or simply breaks off. But they have a beneficial tradeoff—their slopes are less sheer, and their surfaces are often soft enough to allow backpackers to dig the edge of their feet in when sidehilling.

Metamorphic and igneous rock found deep in the Canyon (e.g. the Vishnu Schist and Zoroaster Granite) are extremely dense and frequently sheer. Visually fascinating, they can be a frustrating hodgepodge for someone on foot. They are wildly unpredictable and almost schizophrenic when it comes to geologic patterns. Because they frequently lack ledges, horizontal traversing can be maddening, very dangerous, or impossible.

A few final thoughts regarding the Canyon's geologic dispositions: Learn to read the rock. Be deferential to their moods and avoid pushing your luck where the stratum seems to be in a particularly bad one. Appreciate that each formation's relationship to hikers is and always will be, well, rocky. And never forget the one trait they share: stony indifference. Lethal exposure and instability give all of them the potential to become seemingly unrepentant killers. *All of them.*

❧

We eventually descended one of the steep gullies down to river level, thankfully without mishap. Then we worked our way over to a heaven-sent flat, sandy bank running along the river near what river runners call Ten Mile Rock, a giant vertical slice of the Toroweap Formation poking out of the Colorado. We passed it and arrived at Soap Creek Canyon in time for lunch and to watch another group of boats run the rapid formed by the drainage. After resting, we hiked the four miles up Soap Creek, topping out around four in the afternoon.

"We did it!" Wes hooted at the top, fists in the air. "Our first leg! That's so cool!"

I mimicked his jubilation. Another part of the Grand Addiction is the nearly indescribable emotional and physical relief you luxuriate in after exiting the Canyon's depths, hoofing it out under your own power. Somehow you defied the unrelenting, weighty pull of gravity, as well as defeatism, and escaped the abyss. Like reaching the Colorado River after a full day of hiking, arriving back on top after yet more toil evokes equal ecstasy—a nearly instantaneous feel-good buzz worth the hours of emotional and physical toil. It's incredibly addicting.

A couple of hours later, we were in the Vermilion Cliffs restaurant eating the cheeseburger and fries I'd promised. One of us savored a cold beer.

"So, what would you give it, Wes?" I asked. "What kind of fun was it?"

"Most definitely Type-2," he declared, waving a French fry at me and smiling. "Yeah, Type-2."

It had been a good test, I told him. We'd have a learning curve as we worked toward our goal of hiking the whole thing. This had been our Marble Canyon Hiking 101 entry-level class. *And we passed.*

"Think you'll want to keep doing this until we go the whole way?" I asked.

"Yep. I do."

"Cool."

"By the way, how much did we do of the length, Dad?" he cheerfully (and naively) inquired.

I quickly did the math in my head: one-and-a-half miles down Cathedral Wash, eight miles to Soap Creek, four miles out: so, thirteen-and-a-half miles, plus probably another 50 percent for the up and downs, ins and outs. A grand total of nearly twenty miles. Next, I compared this number versus our likely total mileage.

"I think we're just under 2 percent," I responded, bursting both our bubbles.

"Dang," Wes groaned.

Knowing he needed a relatable pick-me-up, I thought of our banner and Frodo and Sam's daunting walk through the land of Mordor to Mount Doom in *The Fellowship of the Ring.* "Yeah, well, remember what your Hobbit buddy Samwise Gamgee said? 'It's the job that's never started as takes longest to finish.' At least we've started. That's huge."

During the car ride home, Weston fell asleep, his head cushioned against the window. I couldn't help but notice that while he'd grown bigger, he still had a baby face. It looked relaxed, content. Like so many parents, I wanted to freeze-frame the moment, keep him from heading further into adolescence, then adulthood. Protect him from life's disappointments, and always keep him as my little boy, a human version of a puppy dog who never tires of hanging out with

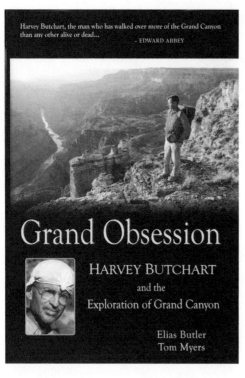

Harvey Butchart, the man who has walked over more of the Grand Canyon than any other alive or dead...
— EDWARD ABBEY

Grand Obsession

HARVEY BUTCHART
and the
Exploration of Grand Canyon

Elias Butler
Tom Myers

his pops. And hiking with me. *How do I do that? Has any father before me done it, and done it right?* While I didn't have an immediate answer for a role model to use, I did have one for who *not* to use.

Jim Butchart, son of the hiking legend, once confided to Elias Butler and me, "My dad wasn't a great father, but he didn't work at it, either." Elias and I had come to know both Jim and his older sister Anne, as well as their mother Roma, while researching our 2007 Harvey Butchart biography *Grand Obsession: Harvey Butchart and the Exploration of Grand Canyon.*[8] *Backpacker Magazine* accurately labeled Harvey Butchart as "the undisputed king of extreme and obsessive Grand Canyon hiking." To claim this crown, he had spent over 1000 days, the equivalent of three-and-a-half years away from his family, down in the Canyon. Then, when home and not fulfilling the obligations of full-time professorship, he spent hundreds of hours recording his exploits in encyclopedic form, his logbooks totaling more than 1,200 single-spaced, typewritten pages. But as Harvey's hiking legacy grew, his family ties withered. A canyon-like chasm eventually split their lives.

Regarding his dad, Jim added, "Unless you were math, chess, or a Grand Canyon junkie, you couldn't talk to him. He was completely focused and overwhelmed by his own pursuits.... There were some bitter feelings growing up. On an analytical level, he excelled. On an emotional level, my dad often failed. Geniuses are quirky. They often exclude all else for compulsion. My dad was without question a Grand Canyon genius, but there's a price for quirkiness."

That price? In Harvey's case: family estrangement. When it came to his dad, Jim went from feeling bitter to mostly indifferent, like his sister. Meanwhile, Roma became—and remained—resentful. Not believing in divorce, she endured

---

8 *Grand Obsession: Harvey Butchart and the Exploration of Grand Canyon* won the 2008 National Outdoor Book Award for history/biography. "Of all the Grand Canyon books out there, this one stands alone as a classic work showcasing man and nature at their best." Lynn Arave, book review, *Desert Morning News*, 2007.

Harvey's obsession until his advancing age and physical decline finally did what she and the kids couldn't. Although Harvey didn't hike the Grand Canyon during the last two decades of his life, unfortunately, irreparable damage had already been done to the marriage and family dynamic. Jim and Anne stayed aloof, while Harvey and Roma mostly just co-existed. Sadly and sardonically, Roma referred to herself as a "hiking widow."

Knowing that I didn't want to make Becky a hiking widow (either literally or figuratively) or my kids hiking orphans, I immediately scratched Harvey off my list of dad role models. At one level, George Steck seemed like a good fit, but his boys had been older—teenagers—when their hiking the Canyon together took off. I wanted a father who'd been younger, ideally closer to my age, and similarly with a younger son. *But again, who?* I eventually found my guy, a man named Ron Mitchell. Not only were his hiking achievements humbling, the level to which he included his boy left me speechless.

Ron and Randy Mitchell at House Rock Rapid, 1973. *Dale Graham*

CHAPTER TEN

Bruno and Roscoe

The Story of Ron and Randy Mitchell

People, let me tell you 'bout my best friend
He's a warm-hearted person who'll love me to the end
People let me tell you 'bout my best friend
He's a one-boy, cuddly toy
My up, my down, my pride and joy

Harry Nilsson
"Best Friend"/The Courtship of Eddie's Father (Television Series, 1969–1972)

April 1974

The upcoming Easter weekend presented eight-year-old Randy Mitchell with two options. He could stay home; sleep in; then, after waking, enjoy the thrill of searching for candy while still in his pajamas and satisfying his sweet tooth after finding it.

Or, he could huff and puff and sweat for hours hiking to the bottom of Grand Canyon with his dad. Go to bed feeling sore and tired, then wake up to being missed by the Easter Bunny and, with the sun beating down, repeating the grueling hike in reverse.

When thirty-six-year-old Ron Mitchell heard son Randy opt for the hiking trip, he wasn't surprised. He knew his son enjoyed their Canyon outings almost as much as he did. Ron also knew something Randy didn't: the Easter Bunny would, in fact, show up. He'd make sure of that. Rewarding Randy was rewarding himself, and he would do whatever it took to keep his pride and joy hiking with him.

Over the previous four years, Ron had continually invented, then re-invented, ways to keep his son happy and entertained on their Canyon trips. At the same time, he had another personal goal: becoming the first person to walk the entire length of Marble Canyon below the rim. To fulfill that and have Randy tagging along? Proverbial icing on the cake.

For his age, Randy already stood out as one of the most accomplished hikers the Canyon—or even the state of Arizona—had ever seen. Besides more than a half-dozen Canyon hiking trips, including several to the bottom, he had hiked to the top of the 12,637-foot San Francisco Peaks, backpacked in the Superstition Mountains near his Phoenix home, and hiked trails in Sedona and Oak Creek Canyon. Even more shocking, he had gone willingly and happily on these trips.

In reality, it had proven to be astonishingly easy for Ron to get Randy to tag along. Randy always seemed to be game for adventuring outdoors. He loved plants and animals and camping. Building fires and forts and setting up a tent were exciting escapades for him, entertainment he and his dad created. Randy's mother, Holly, not only approved, but also supported and encouraged the endeavors, despite the strenuous nature and inherent dangers some of the hiking posed. Ron assured Holly he would be careful, and she trusted him. She also knew her son needed an outlet for his boundless energy.

Seemingly unfazed by the terrain, Randy channeled that energy into scrambling efficiently through the landscape. His deft maneuvering triggered a memory for Ron.

"Randy, you remind me of my favorite old truck, Roscoe. The way you get up and down these trails and through these cliffs—it's like a tough old truck!"

"I'm Roscoe! I'm a truck! Varoom!" he would say to his dad. "You're a truck, too, Daddy! What's your name?"

"I'm Bruno," Ron would laugh, playing along, "Bruno" was another of his former trucks. "Yeah, you and I are just a couple of tough ol' trucks!"

Also truck-like, Randy hauled much of his own gear: sleeping bag, clothes, and food. More important to Randy, however, were two hitchhikers he always made room for in his backpack: a rubber deer and a rubber snake. The two buddies had to come. Ron also brought something he considered just as important: a bulky 8mm movie camera. He had it aimed and clicking away on Easter Sunday morning when Randy woke up and rubbed his eyes.

"Guess who showed up?" Ron asked while he filmed.

Randy, remembering what day it was, scurried around, scanning under ledges and behind boulders. Within a few minutes, he had an assortment of Easter candy and wore a huge grin. For father and son, it was a very sweet moment during what had otherwise been a somewhat bittersweet hike.

Another father-son pair, Dale Graham (a friend from Phoenix) and his 14-year-old son, Kimmel, had hiked in with the Mitchells, and the four immediately found the going both rough and exhausting, especially for the eight-year-old.

Ron adjusted his pace and itinerary to accommodate his son, but they were only making a half-mile per hour when a steeply sloped and boulder-choked reach along the river slowed them to a relative crawl. Finally, far short of their goal, they camped above the river in the Supai sandstone ledges at River Mile 15.5.

In the morning, knowing their goal of reaching Vasey's Paradise at River Mile 34 within

Randy and Ron in Marble Canyon. *Ron Mitchell archives*

two days was impossible, Ron decided they should turn around. After Randy ate a hefty portion of his Easter candy for breakfast, they packed up and headed back upstream. Soon, they were spotted by a commercial pontoon motorized raft. Shocked to see backpackers, especially a little kid, the boatmen motored over to chat.

After Ron explained his now-abandoned goal, the lead boatman kindly offered an option to salvage the trip: a ride downstream. Ron, Randy, Dale, and Kimmel hopped aboard, and later that day, shared camp with the boaters. While sitting on the beach that evening, Randy looked up, then pointed at the cliff overhead. "Daddy, isn't that what you call a fault up there?" Ron looked overhead, then his mouth dropped open.

Sure enough, the steep, boulder-filled chute that split the cliffs was a fault. To Ron, it also looked like a route that might help a hiker negotiate much of the 1,500 feet to the rim. (Indeed, two months later, in June 1974, Ron and Frank Charron, a thirty-four-year-old NAU geology student, as well as Randy, descended the route near River Mile 19, which Ron whimsically named "Randy's Fault.")

The next day, the boatmen motored the foursome a short distance to another river-to-rim route near Vasey's Paradise. Despite tremendous exposure in places, young Randy managed to scramble to the rim unscathed. How his boy never complained—not even once—or cried, nor seemed terrified, left Ron astonished.

Ron also felt surprised by how far his own Canyon hiking had advanced since his first hike with his brother down the Bright Angel Trail in 1966. After growing up as a flatlander in Illinois, at age nineteen Ron had moved to New Mexico in 1957. A year later, he moved to Phoenix. There, he took a job at Motorola as a machinist, following in the footsteps of his father, who had similar work at General Motors back in Illinois.

In May 1967, Ron's dad accompanied him on Ron's second Canyon hike and first lengthwise section. The two descended the Hermit Trail, traversed the Tonto Trail to Indian Garden (now Havasupai Gardens), then returned to the rim via Bright Angel Trail, about twenty-five miles total. The hike proved pivotal in Ron's life, one that triggered his interest in extended, lengthwise hikes below the rim. When Fletcher's book, *The Man Who Walked Through Time*, came out a year later, Ron lapped it up. Like Kenton Grua, but more enamored with than annoyed by Fletcher, Ron felt inspired. He set a personal goal to do what only Fletcher and Harvey Butchart were known to have done: walk the length of Grand Canyon National Park from end to end.

Newspaper article about Ron and Randy Mitchell in *The Arizona Republic*, May 1976. *Ron Mitchell archives*

Ron began planning for his trek in 1969. He knew his biggest challenge would be finding time. He and Holly had a young family; daughter Cindy was born in 1959 and son Randy in 1965. To provide for them, Ron needed full-time work. Could he combine his hiking goals with his professional career and personal life? Yes, he concluded; he would just have to be creative and efficient with his time off.

From reading Fletcher's book and following the same route, Ron knew the hardest, most dangerous part of completing the length of Grand Canyon National Park would be walking the 100 remote and mostly waterless miles around the massive Great Thumb peninsula, which juts twenty miles into the Canyon from the south. To mitigate the risks, he would need to be smart and devise a fail-safe plan.

In May 1969, Ron, Randy, and Holly made an inaugural reconnaissance trip to check out the Thumb and scout for water. Five hours after leaving Phoenix, including two hours on dirt roads, they arrived at one of the most remote spots in the lower forty-eight states: Great Thumb Point.

They set up camp on the rim and the next day, while Holly and Randy hung out around camp, Ron hiked into the Canyon to Great Thumb Spring, 1,000 feet below and marked by an impossible-to-miss cluster of leafy green cottonwood trees among barren, rocky terrain.

Fortunately, when Ron arrived at the rare water source, he found it trickling. The water, cool and clear, ran for about 100 feet, then disappeared into gravel. Fortuitously, the spring was also located near the halfway point around Great Thumb. Ron instantly recognized it as a perfect place for a food stash and layover day.

In early 1970, Ron made two more trips to Great Thumb. The first included hiking with five-year-old Randy ten miles to Supai Village from Hualapai Hilltop, then scrambling several miles up to the Esplanade level. There, Ron and Randy carefully buried a cache before they returned to their car. Randy did so well that Ron took him on another stash-burying trip, this time on a route off Great Thumb between a point called Hamidrik and another called Gatagama. Dropping to the Esplanade below, they buried two cans of Pepsi, two gallons of water, and extra food and film.

The following year, Ron and Dale Graham took fourteen days to walk around the Thumb. The stashes were intact and vital for the trip. After completing the Great Thumb section, Ron returned with six-year-old Randy, as well as Dale Graham and his son, Kimmel, for a thirty-mile, four-day leg, forging another

'IT'S HARD NOT TO PANIC, AIN'T IT?'

searing heat and a dwindling water supply made it doubtful if he would be the first to walk through Marble Canyon or the object of Search and Rescue

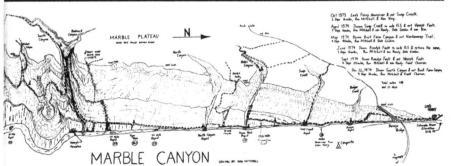

Marble Canyon can't be taken for granite. It took Ron Mitchell eleven attempts over a period of fifteen months to walk the 52 miles along the river.

Hand drawn map by Ron Mitchell, published in the *Arizona Republic*.
Ron Mitchell archives

link in his lengthwise chain by starting off at nearby Apache Point and coming out South Bass Trail. Two years and four more hikes later, in September 1973—after fifteen separate legs and all the tedious back-and-forth driving from Phoenix—Ron became the third person (unofficially) known to have walked the entire length of the park, all on the south side.

While Randy had been a huge help as well as a source of inspiration, Ron also credited Harvey Butchart, whom he had contacted at the beginning of his quest. They wrote each other multiple times and met at Harvey's Flagstaff home. As he had done with Fletcher, Harvey shared his maps, hiking logs, advice, and encouragement.

On a personal level, Ron also felt a connection to Harvey. Both were husbands and fathers. Both held a full-time job while doing the bulk of their hiking. And both approached the Canyon with the same run-and-gun style: burn runs mainly over weekends. Harvey, however, held an advantage: living in Flagstaff (2.5 hours closer to the Canyon) and having summers off. Meanwhile Ron remained tethered to Motorola and Phoenix year-round.

Still, finishing the park's length inspired Ron to do more. Believing the Marble Canyon section of Grand Canyon, which lay outside the park boundary, hadn't been done, he consulted Harvey on whether he or anyone else had ever completed it. This had to be a déjà vu moment for the math professor.

As with Colin Fletcher's inquiry, Harvey knew that no one—at least, in modern times—had walked the length of this part of the Canyon. Similar, too, Harvey only needed a single section to complete it himself. He told Ron so. Any déjà vu with Fletcher's request likely ended with Ron's response: "Why don't you come with me, Harvey? You can finish what you started. You earned it."

Harvey's reply left Ron feeling humbled but excited.

"I've had plenty of firsts. You can have this one." Nearing seventy, with dozens of hiking firsts and thousands of miles behind him, Harvey knew he could never be dethroned as Grand Canyon's hiking king. Another first wouldn't change that.

As a downside and as mentioned earlier, this legacy had come at a high cost: estrangement from his family. As also previously noted, Ron Mitchell took a far different approach to accommodate his boy. Perhaps it was inevitable then, that Ron would push both his luck and his son a little too far.

In late April 1974, Randy accompanied his dad and Frank Charron (another friend of Ron's) on a hike to bury a cache Ron would use in Marble Canyon. It would require hiking fourteen miles, down and out the Nankoweap Trail, burying the cache halfway down. Referred to by the NPS as the Grand Canyon's "MOST difficult trail," Nankoweap—with its 6,000-foot elevation change, steepness, length, and significant exposures—is considered a serious challenge to even experienced hikers.

For their April hike, the weather proved unseasonably hot, the inner Canyon temperature hovering around 90°F. At about five miles in, Randy started throwing up and became too weak and dizzy to stand. Ron found a small patch of shade and tucked Randy into it, then began pouring water over him to cool his body down. Then, while Randy rested, Ron buried the water and food. Being out of the sun seemed to help Randy, but his nausea persisted. Knowing they needed to return to the rim, Frank took Randy's pack; Ron, still carrying his own pack, hefted his forty-pound son onto his shoulders and toted him the seven miles back out.

When they reached the rim, Ron gently settled Randy into the front seat of his truck. Fortunately, by this time, Randy's skin had cooled and his vomiting had stopped. Ron shuddered to think what the consequences might have been had he kept pushing Randy earlier. Driving off, he sighed in deep relief as Randy fell asleep.

A month later, the buried water proved just as lifesaving for Ron and Dale Graham as water for cooling his body had been for Randy. When Ron and Graham reached the water cache spot on the afternoon of day four of their hike, the air sizzled over 100°F. They had been rationing water for more than twenty-four hours and had not eaten anything substantial for thirty-six. Desperate, Ron began digging at the cache site with his bare hands until he unearthed the water jug. "I picked that dude up and gave it a big hug and a kiss."

Eight months later, on December 22, 1974, Ron and Frank Charron reached Buck Farm Canyon, stitching in the last section Ron needed to accomplish his goal of becoming the first person known to traverse the length of Marble Canyon. It had taken six separate hikes for a total of 138 miles and 21 days. Ron threw his hat and hiking pole in the air in celebration.

Ron Mitchell's Grand Canyon hiking legacy remains special. He became the third person to hike the Canyon's bureaucratic length and the first to hike through Marble Canyon; completing both also gave him the longest continual hiking line in the Canyon: from Lees Ferry to Havasu Canyon. That record would stand for two years until a certain dory boatman came along. Perhaps most unique about Ron Mitchell's Canyon hiking legacy? Including his young son.

Marble Canyon, ironically, turned out to be the last Grand Canyon hiking Ron and Randy did together. By the mid-1970s, despite having been promoted, getting an award and a raise at Motorola for developing X-ray camera technology for imaging silicon wafers, Ron had grown tired of the big city, his job, the corporate world, and the desert. He wanted to live and work in the outdoors, preferably near water.

Fortuitous for his future employment, Ron had worked a few Canyon trips as a swamper, then as a guide, for Sanderson River Expeditions. It gave him some river-running experience. Although his dad poo-pooed it, with Holly's approval, Ron quit Motorola in April 1976 and moved the family to Idaho, where he'd been offered a manager's job at Frontier Expeditions, a company that led boating trips down the Salmon River.

Randy continued to hike with his dad, primarily in the Bitterroot Mountains. They also went to other places, including Escalante Canyon in Utah. Ron kept the fun but relatively low-paying Idaho job for three years, then returned to work as a machinist, mostly in Missoula, Montana. At seventeen, Randy graduated from high school, then joined the US Air Force and moved away. He eventually earned a private pilot's license and settled in Vancouver, Washington.

After twenty-five years of marriage, Ron lost Holly to cancer. He remarried, but after fifteen years, his second wife also succumbed to cancer. In retirement, he married a third time; he and Patti live in northern Utah.

I first heard of Ron Mitchell in the early 1990s from accomplished Canyon hiker and Butchart protege, Jim Ohlman. Jim told me he'd met Ron in the mid-1970s and had seen some of Ron's film footage, which included a snippet of the legend hiking below the rim. Ohlman also gave me copies of two newspaper articles written about Ron and his Canyon exploits.

After learning all of this, I knew Ron Mitchell was a man I wanted to meet. Using tips and contacts from Ohlman, I began to search for him in earnest. Those pre-Internet searches mostly involved phone calls and letter-writing. After nearly a year, all my leads exhausted, I gave up.

Later, around 2010, after I started hiking the length with Wes, my interest in tracking down those who preceded us became more intense. Highest in priority was Ron Mitchell. So, I resurrected my goal. Unfortunately, time had made the scent a dozen years older and the trail a dozen years colder. During this second effort, an acquaintance told me he had met Ron Mitchell and his wife at the North Rim a couple of years earlier. He said he had a short conversation with Mitchell, who appeared to be in poor health. He suspected Ron had cancer. He also speculated that in the years hence, Ron may have died, something I didn't want to believe.

Despite this possibility, I continued my pursuit. With the help of another friend, Tom Martin, and the expanded search powers of the Internet, much to my surprise, I eventually tracked Ron down in 2018. Perhaps it's fitting that we finally connected the old-fashioned way, via handwritten letters. Fortunately, it turned out that Ron didn't have cancer and he lived south of Salt Lake City. I found him cheerful, quick to laugh, and easy to relate to. He told me about his Canyon adventures, about hiking with Randy, and about his movies.

For history's sake, after gleaning Ron's story, I encouraged him to have digitized copies made of his 8mm movie archive, and strongly suggested that he narrate his films. He painstakingly did both, even adding background music. Ron's films condensed five years of hiking into four hours. The end result, which he sent me copies of, didn't disappoint.

When I watched the footage for the first time, a few things stood out. First, Ron did in fact have film of Harvey Butchart hiking below the rim in the Grand Canyon (to date, the only such film known). In a twenty-second excerpt, Harvey waves at the camera, then is seen carrying a daypack and wearing a bandana on his head as he walks along the Supai rim of Buck Farm Canyon. As a faithful Butchart follower for decades, I was beyond thrilled to finally see the fabled footage. I felt like a born-again Christian watching a video of Jesus Christ walking on water.

Second, the movies provided an enthralling time capsule of a bygone era of Grand Canyon hiking: external-frame backpacks, heavy hiking boots, denim jeans, canned food, metal canteens, and open fires on the ground.

Third, and perhaps most surprising, was the footage that included Randy. Scenes include him nonchalantly scrambling up boulders and free-climbing cliffs. Next he is gathering Easter candy in one of the most unlikely spots on earth, a Supai sandstone ledge. Then he's happily chasing a butterfly, playing on a sand dune, or splashing in the river or a pothole. Other frames show

Harvey Butchart and Ron Mitchell circa 1974, Marble Canyon Lodge. *Ron Mitchell archives*

an innocent-looking, wide-eyed Randy with a plastic deer poking out of his backpack. Ron knew these were some of fatherhood's special and fleeting moments, ones he would cherish, and clearly tried to capture as many as he could.

Some scenes filmed by others, including Dale Graham or Holly, show "Bruno" and "Roscoe" together: Ron playfully tugging a rope tied around Randy's waist and father and son hugging, or hiking holding hands or sharing a fire. Occasionally, the footage turns a little herky-jerky, with Ron the subject and Randy holding the camera. In Randy's footage, Ron is the proud papa, young, handsome, full of life. With big smiles, Ron clearly shares his son's joy. The final scenes seem to whiz by. Then, before you know it, it's over.

May all your potholes be full.

Ron Mitchell

The complimentary close of a letter to Harvey Butchart, 1974.

CHAPTER ELEVEN

The Pot-Bellied Old Fart

The Story of George Steck

There are strange things done in the midnight sun
By the men who moil for gold;
The Arctic Trails have their secret tales
That would make your blood run cold;
The Northern Lights have seen queer sights
But the queerest they ever did see
Was that night on the marge of Lake Lebarge
I cremated Sam McGee.

Robert W. Service
The Cremation of Sam McGee (1907)

December 2000

George Steck leaned in toward those seated around him. Then his eyes narrowed.

"I cremated Sam McGee," he rasped slowly, sinisterly.

My wife, kids, and I were mesmerized as he recited the famous poem.

George, who had invited us to visit him at his New Mexico home, loved to entertain guests with the poem, and he didn't miss a beat in this performance. Sixty years earlier, as a teenager, he had memorized Robert Service's nearly 1,000-word, fifteen-stanza poem for a Sierra Club youth camp. I remember feeling pretty smug when I memorized the Gettysburg Address at about the same age. At a whopping 272 words, it amounted to less than a third of the length of "Cremation."

Earlier that evening, George, along with his wife Helen and their daughter Ricia, had taken us out to eat at Furr's Cafeteria, a few miles from their

Albuquerque home. Eating dinner at Furr's had become a ritual for the Stecks. After we ate, as we crossed the parking lot, George ran ahead and swatted "Elmo," their Volkswagen van.

"Touched it first!" he announced with a big grin.

Like the recitation of Service's epic poem, he reserved this playful ritual for family and friends. During the drive to the restaurant, we were surprised when George leaned his head out the driver's side window and barked like a dog at a pedestrian. The man went from startled to irritated, and we went from bewildered to entertained. Even Helen, who had no doubt witnessed the behavior dozens of times, chuckled.

Helen's good mood belied her fragile health. Fifteen years earlier, she had received an accidental overdose of a prescription medication. The mistake sent her kidneys into slow failure and left her homebound. Prior to that, she and George had often hauled their brood of three—Michael, Stanley, and Ricia— into the Grand Canyon.

Now, Helen could barely navigate her home's hallways, let alone hit a trail. Mostly bedridden, she made short meanders around the house, to doctor's appointments, or to Furr's. A devoted husband for nearly a half a century, George was her primary caregiver. We saw him reflexively assist her in and out of Elmo and her chair at the dinner table during our evening out.

Tucked into an Albuquerque subdivision called the New Area, George and Helen had the home designed and built in 1961, when the area was, literally, new; forty years later, their neighborhood showed its age. Most of the single-story houses appeared to be higher-end tract homes, well-kept but dated. Nearly all had xeriscaped yards, well-suited for Albuquerque's high-desert environment. As a result, we were unprepared for what we saw when we entered the Steck home on that first visit.

George and Helen greeted us as we stepped into a large foyer with a vaulted ceiling and skylights. A sprawling deciduous tree reached high toward the skylights, and large leafy plants edged the space. Damp and musty, the interior came as a sharp contrast to the dry New Mexico air outside. Several small birds flitted about in this mini rainforest. Like Becky and I, our three kids stared in amazement.

A small painting hung on the wall. I instantly recognized the image as the Deer Creek Narrows, one of the Grand Canyon's slot canyons. I nosed close. A whimsical wooden sign posted as part of the picture declared: "George Steck Retirement Home." Adair Peterson, a mutual friend, had painted it.

Next, the living room. A couch, two lounge chairs, and a coffee table dominated one side, a baby grand piano the other. Both Helen and George played, but George had a reputation as being fairly accomplished on the ivories, with a repertoire of two dozen classic numbers, from Brahms to Beethoven. (Of note, he is not related to the George Steck of piano manufacturing fame.) Helen led us to an adjacent hallway and the guest bedroom, where she told us we'd be sleeping. At the end of the hallway was the couple's master bedroom and the place of Helen's confinement.

A multitude of pictures, nearly floor to ceiling, covered the walls of the long corridor between the two rooms. The pictures were a time capsule of the Stecks' lives: George and Helen as young parents, with their young kids. School pictures. Graduations. Shots from family adventures in the Grand Canyon. Photos and cards from extended family and friends. Becky and I were shocked when we spotted two Christmas cards we'd sent pinned to their board of memories.

After taking our luggage to the guest room, we returned to the living room, where we found George sitting in his recliner, smiling and relaxed. Helen took Becky and the kids into the kitchen for snacks and drinks while I sat and chatted with the man of the house.

"So, George, do you *really* have a banner asking river runners for beer?" I asked, having heard about it from another mutual friend.

He smiled. "Come with me."

We veered through the living room, the kitchen, and into the small room that served as George's study. Stacks of boxes and framed pictures cluttered the floor. I tried not to kick anything as I shuffled in. A stunning painting of the Sierra Nevada dominated one wall. On another hung a gorgeous, three-by-four-foot framed photograph of Lake Powell. More outdoor paintings, photographs, and other art pieces co-opted the walls' free space.

The largest wall—eight feet high by about twelve feet long—was covered from floor to ceiling with books. Over several visits, I remember scanning the titles, which included an intriguing spectrum: from *War and Peace* to *Abraham Lincoln* to *Pinocchio*. To my surprise, only about two feet of one shelf contained Grand Canyon books.

After dodging the floor obstacles like I had done, George sat down at a desk, the top of which was buried in papers, pens and pencils, magazines, and stacks of yet more books. He opened a desk drawer and pulled out what appeared to be a small blanket. He unfolded it. It boldly read: LAST CHANCE TO DISPOSE OF EXTRA BEER BEFORE ENTERING RAPIDS.

"Gary made that for me," he proclaimed with a big grin, referring to Gary Ladd, a well-known Arizona photographer based in Page. He also told me that Ladd had taken the framed Lake Powell shot, as well as the photo on the cover of *Loop Hikes II*, and wrote the foreword.

Ladd and George met during a Sierra Club hike in the late 1980s, and the photographer began hiking with him in the Grand Canyon shortly thereafter. In

George Steck and Craig Childs in Marble Canyon.
Gary Ladd

doing so, Ladd joined a group casually referred to as Steck's Army. The "army" went with George on backpacking adventures. Ladd recalled that on hikes, George was an "endless source of surprises, and typically planned and executed everything." That included giving his troops their marching orders.

Yet, by no means was George a hiking dictator. Steck's Army had a shared fondness for their good-natured brigadier, and the feeling was mutual. Consider the following passage from *Loop Hikes*. In it, George describes how he, Ladd, and a young recruit named Kyle Harwood playfully teased each other.

> During one of the rests Kyle and I were trading insults, as we often did, and tossing pebbles at each other, and Gary said, in a sad voice, "You know, there's one thing about this trip that I wish were different."
> "What's that?" we chorused.
> "I wish I knew Kyle well enough to insult him, too." My name for Kyle was Buckfoot Nibbin Prancin Paws, a perfectly good name that was even vaguely complimentary, and in return he called me PBOF.
> Later, Gary asked, "George, do you know what PBOF stands for?" I struggled for a while and finally said, "No, but if it were GBOF, it would be "Great Balls of Fire." Kyle couldn't think of anything either so we gave up. "Pot-Bellied Old Fart," was Gary's answer. After that I was known as PBOF.

Born in Berkeley on January 11, 1925, George Steck entered the world as part of a brilliant, multigenerational California family. His father, Leo Varner Steck, had a PhD in chemical engineering; his mother, Eleanor Catherine Allen, despite having no formal college education (common for women of that era) was reportedly even smarter. Leo and Eleanor welcomed a second son, George's younger brother Allen, in 1926. Four years later, the couple divorced, splitting

104

Allen and George Steck with their father, Leo, circa 1930.
Steck family archives

George begins his backpacking career in California.
Steck family archives

up both their assets and their children. Eleanor, who believed five-year old George didn't need his mother as much as younger Allen, took primary custody of the four-year old and moved the two of them north across San Francisco Bay to Sausalito. Meanwhile, George stayed with his dad in Oakland.

Unfortunately, Leo's work with Shell Oil Company required extended periods of travel, sometimes for months on end. Because Eleanor felt she had her hands full with Allen, Leo placed George in an orphanage for the better part of two years.

For the remainder of their childhood, the Steck brothers saw each other only once or twice a month. Visits typically required Allen to take a ferry across the bay to meet at his dad's home. Eleanor admitted to Leo that she often felt overwhelmed by having both boys at the same time, and didn't enjoy it.

Later in life, the boys learned that their mother had never been fond of children, including her own. Despite that, she remarried and had a third child, the boys' half-sister, Lillian, born in 1940. (Eleanor later divorced a second time and moved to Carmel, California. In 1960, at age sixty-one and depressed, she committed suicide.)

Leo Steck also remarried. He met Frances Johnson, a schoolteacher from Boston, on a business trip. As Frances embraced step-motherhood, Leo became a devoted father. Both parents stressed the value of education, emphasizing reading, especially the classics. Likewise, music ranked high in priority, as did the outdoors. In turn, George learned the piano and Allen percussion. And Leo, an avid outdoorsman and fly fisherman, frequently hauled his sons on outdoor weekend adventures, including into the nearby Sierra Nevada and Yosemite National Park. While their dad fished, the boys wandered. Once they hit adolescence, they often ventured out on one- to two-day hiking excursions of their own. During one such trek in 1942, the teenage Steck brothers unofficially made the first ascent of Yosemite's Mount Maclure using the 12,900-foot mountain's northwest ridge line, George leading the way.

At seventeen he joined the Sierra Club. George's maternal grandfather had been acquainted with John Muir, the most famous of the club's 182 charter members. George represented the third generation of Steck Sierra Clubbers, a proud family legacy. The Steck family also took pride in Grandfather Powell's possible connection to one of the Canyon's most famous explorers, John Wesley Powell. Both families had lived within twenty miles of one another in England. (George's middle name was Powell.)

For George, the Sierra Club fulfilled two needs: to be outdoors and to socialize. Shy intellectuals from a broken family, he and his brother had relatively poor interpersonal skills. Both could come across as cold and aloof. To change that for himself, George became a Sierra Club camp counselor. He built a telescope to share with campers, then memorized *The Cremation of Sam McGee* to amuse the camp's grade-school attendees. Reciting the narrative poem forced him out of his cerebral comfort zone and into socializing.

After graduating from Piedmont High School in 1943, rather than enroll in college, George chose to explore the backwoods of Washington and Oregon for several months on horseback with a buddy. Inspired, he briefly considered life as a horse rancher, but with World War II ongoing, nineteen-year-old George joined the US Navy as an apprentice seaman. He worked on radars and used his first paycheck to finance his lifetime membership in the Sierra Club.

George didn't see combat in World War II, which he chalked up to luck, his young age, and the imminent end of the war. During his Navy stint, however, he achieved the rank of lieutenant, which helped him talk his way onto another ship—the USS *George*—where Allen (who had also joined the Navy) served as a seaman.

Honorably discharged in 1946, George enrolled in the University of California, Berkeley, and studied physics. After earning a bachelor of science degree, he decided to go to graduate school at the California State Institute of Technology (Cal Tech). Much to his annoyance, before he could pursue a master's, he discovered he needed to take a required undergraduate math class. After signing up, he discovered that he'd already missed several days of lecture, and a test loomed. He needed notes.

During the next day's class, George, who knew no one, stood up and looked around at his fellow classmates, all younger than himself. "Could I borrow someone's lecture notes?" he asked. No one responded. Dejected, he sat down. After the class dismissed, a pretty brunette approached George.

"They're not very good, but you can use mine," she told him.

The dark-haired twenty-one-year-old was Helen Smolenski, a math major from a Polish farming family in Massachusetts. "I hope you do well," she said as she handed him the notes. Red-faced but grinning, George gladly accepted. The notes helped, as did an aptitude for math and a genius-level IQ; he got an A and Helen got a B.

Within Steck family folklore, she reportedly saw him slumped against a hallway wall later that semester. Dressed in a raggedy tee-shirt, shorts, and sneakers, he looked gangly and lost. Once again feeling sorry for him, Helen invited George to join her and some of her girlfriends for coffee. They were unimpressed. It didn't matter. She was. And the feeling proved mutual.

A few months later, on August 26, 1950, they married. Two years after that, George received his master's degree in physics. He then taught the subject for a year at the University of California, Davis, agricultural college before returning to Berkeley for more graduate school. Though he briefly considered a PhD in philosophy, he switched his degree to what he enjoyed most: probability and statistics. Those who work in this field (the realm of geniuses) create mathematical models to predict outcomes of random events through collection, analysis, interpretation, and display of numerical data. While in the thick of his PhD work, George and Helen also started a family. Sons Michael and Stanley were born in 1952 and 1955. In 1956, George completed his PhD; his thesis focused on theoretical statistics.

Meanwhile, a decade had passed since the August 1945 dropping of atomic bombs on the Japanese cities of Nagasaki and Hiroshima, weapons that vaporized 100,000 people in less than a second. The world had witnessed the devastating power of splitting uranium and plutonium atoms and by the late 1950s, American and Soviet political leaders remained convinced that permanent world peace hinged on splitting even more. This evolved into what became known as the Cold War, one that required both countries to maintain a constantly looming threat of nuclear annihilation, or "mutually assured destruction" (the MAD doctrine).

In the early 1940s, development of the atomic bomb, a "weapon of mass destruction" (WMD), became something Albert Einstein had urged President Franklin Roosevelt to pursue before Adolph Hitler and his Nazi scientists did. With a clear sense of urgency to achieve this goal, Roosevelt and the United States Army chose New Mexico's remote high desert for its clandestine work. They also selected physicist Dr. Robert Oppenheimer to organize and lead the research. Code named the "Manhattan Project," the federal Atomic Energy Commission, overseen by the US Department of Energy, funded a national laboratory to research and develop a bigger and better nuclear arsenal in Los

Alamos. In 1945, Los Alamos created an arm for the ordnance design, testing, and assembly portion. In spite of (or because of) the grim nature of the work, they chose to give the lab a tasteful title. "Sandia" means watermelon in Spanish.

To stay ahead of the USSR in the nuclear arms race—WMD for MAD—Sandia needed a supply of smart physicists, chemists, and mathematicians. Basically, it needed people like George Steck. Shortly after graduation, Sandia recruited George, and in 1957, he and his family left California for Albuquerque, New Mexico's most populous city. Helen, pregnant with child number three, gave birth to daughter Ricia shortly after their arrival.

That same year, feeling the need to come up for air after years of academia, work, and domestic duties, George signed up for a several-day Grand Canyon river trip chartered by the Sierra Club. This trip, taken with Helen's blessing, would be his first to the famed national park. It turned out to be a unique introduction, one that sadly coincided with the end of an era.

Pioneering commercial river runner Georgie White, the "Woman of the River," guided the trip. With the completion of Glen Canyon Dam still seven years in the future, the Colorado River flowed freely through Grand Canyon. An extremely wet 1956–1957 winter resulted in a runoff that pushed the river to a whopping flow of 124,000 cubic feet per second (cfs), one of the highest of the century, more than a dozen times higher than typical present-day flows.

For those on the trip, seeing the Colorado overflowing its banks and so loaded with silt that it could almost be called gravy would've been similar to seeing the last of America's sprawling buffalo herds before sport killing, railroads, and market demand for buffalo products nearly made the buffalo go extinct. Glen Canyon Dam, which came online in 1963, did essentially the same thing to the wild Colorado. Aware of the river's eventual fate, George took a small video camera to document the experience. Then, reluctantly, he left the trip at Phantom Ranch and made his way up to the rim—his first Grand Canyon hike.

George fell in love with the Canyon and the river. Feeling "sucked in by capillary action," he vowed to return.

In 1958, he made good on that promise when he took another Sierra Club river trip on the Colorado, again with Georgie at the helm. This time, they explored the also-doomed Glen Canyon immediately upstream of the Grand, where the Colorado flowed through sensuous slickrock. Glen Canyon's beauty and the river enthralled him. After the trip, George bought a "marine assault raft" for $65 and a 7.5 horse-power motor for $150; for the next five years, he led his own two-week river trip each summer through Glen Canyon.

In 1963, the completion of the dam and the filling of Lake Powell drowned not only much of Glen Canyon, but also much of the allure that river-running on the Colorado held for George Steck. Luckily, his Canyon destiny didn't require moving water, only moving feet.

⌒⌒⌒

"There's something else here you might like to see," George told me. He pulled out another banner, a red one about two feet by three feet. "Down the Gorge with Uncle George," stenciled in white, emblazoned across the top. Below were the names Dale, Greg, Lee, Paul, Sara, and Stan. "The kids made that for me," he smiled.

Before I could comment, he added, "There's something else that goes with the banner." He rummaged in the desk for a few more seconds. "Here it is." He handed me "Down the Gorge with Uncle George: A Commemorative Calendar for 1979." A photo of George with the banner sticking out of his backpack adorned the cover.

I looked at him. He had a big smile.

"Tell me about that trip, Uncle George."

George hiking with the "Down The Gorge With Uncle George" banner, 1977.
Steck family archives

CHAPTER TWELVE

Down the Gorge With Uncle George

THE STORY OF GEORGE STECK (CONTINUED)

*In the 1977 trip, it was me and six kids, just newly graduated from high school.
I called them the galumphers. They just galumphed along and in no time at all,
they'd be way out in front. So, I had to develop the theory of leading from the rear.*

George Steck
Interview with Mike Quinn, 1997

1976

George waltzed into the office of friend and Sandia co-worker Don Mattox without knocking. On one wall, Mattox had a map of the Grand Canyon. George veered over and squinted at the zigzagging lines representing the Canyon hikes Mattox had completed. While not near the density of Harvey's, Mattox's map had quite an assortment of inked-in, spiderwebbing contours. Like pictures of children and grandchildren, Mattox took pride in those lines. So did George; having organized and led the hikes, most of the "lineage" was his.

A military veteran and North Carolina native, Mattox moved to New Mexico in 1961 after being hired for Sandia's Material Science Metallurgy Group as a materials science engineer. He and George met at a New Mexico Mountain Club event in 1962 and immediately hit it off. A year later, at Mattox's urging, George went backpacking in the Grand Canyon with him and eight others from the local New Mexico branch of the Sierra Club. They descended the Tanner Trail, traversed the Beamer Trail, ascended the Little Colorado River (aka, Little C) gorge, then topped out on the Hopi Salt Trail. For both men, the thirty-five-mile hike proved exceptionally difficult—grueling but rewarding. Seven years younger, Mattox's maturity, easygoing nature, and sturdiness impressed

George, and the feeling was mutual. The twosome pledged to come back, and they did, many times.

George eventually took the lead in planning their Grand Canyon hikes, each more difficult and remote than the one before. Mattox never shied away. The Canyon helped forge a once-in-a-lifetime friendship, Mattox becoming the first and foremost member of Steck's Army.

When *Grand Canyon Loop Hikes* came out in 1989, George let his steadfast infantryman know how much he appreciated his contribution to making the book a reality. In the copy he gave Mattox, he inscribed: "For Don Mattox, without whom there would be no book because there would be no hiking Grand Canyon. You took me on my first Grand Canyon hike and nearly killed me."

∽∼⌒∘

Eyes fixed on Mattox's map, George mused, "Maybe I'll do a hike from Lees Ferry to Lava Falls."

"Well, if you do, you're going to have to beat me."

Mattox's tongue-in-cheek comment didn't come as a surprise to George. Similarly, George's immediate planning for the hike, done with the same focus and attention to detail as his research, came as no surprise to Mattox. George estimated that the hike would be about 400 miles and consume at least a month. He offered Mattox a chance to join, but the latter declined, saying he didn't have time to do the whole thing. Mattox could, however, commit to starting with George and going about a quarter of the distance.

With his usual sidekick mostly out of the picture and not wanting to go it alone, George drafted others to join him. First, he tried to enlist his sons, Michael and Stanley. Both boys had cut their backpacking teeth hiking in the Grand Canyon. Mike, then twenty-five, capable and athletic, lived in Colorado. He told his dad he couldn't make the entire trip because he'd committed to play in a Denver soccer club tournament, but, like Mattox, he could link up for at least part of it. George's s twenty-two-year-old son Stan, however, was game for the whole thing.

For George, having Stan along came with a unique bonus. Though he had a degree in mechanical engineering, Stan worked as a river ranger for Grand Canyon National Park. Like Kenton Grua, he had spurned a mainstream engineering job for one that paid him to be in the outdoors and on the river. Also like Kenton, he'd already seen much of George's proposed route from his boat and could speak to the challenges of the different reaches along the way. Furthermore, being a river ranger might come in handy if they needed help from the NPS.

George next talked his brother Allen's kids, Sara and Lee, into coming. Like their cousins, Sara and Lee had begun their Grand Canyon hiking careers as preadolescents, tagging along on family trips with George and Helen.

When Helen was still physically able and her three kids capable teenagers, she and George took them on Canyon trips tailored to their hiking levels and interests. These included strenuous but not overly difficult hikes down trails to scenic places with water, such as Thunder River and Deer Creek. Also invited along for group camaraderie and family atmosphere were Allen, Sara, and Lee; Mattox, with his wife and daughter; and Albuquerque friends, the Petersons and the Kleybockers and their kids. Typically two weeks in duration, these outings became a summer highlight for the Steck family and friends, a tradition that lasted about five years until the mid-1970s.

In 1977, Sara, then twenty-two, lived in California and worked for Mountain Travel—a company cofounded by her father, specializing in international wilderness adventure trips—as an agent and guide. Her older brother, twenty-four-year-old Lee, attended Stanford. Both had grown up in Berkeley, their parents a liberal contrast to their more conservative Aunt Helen and Uncle George, whom they saw only once or twice a year. Lee recalled the typical greeting from Uncle George when they met.

"You know, Lee, you're my favorite nephew," George would say.

"I'm your only nephew," Lee would remind him.

"Well, that doesn't change a thing. You're still my favorite."

By summer 1977, as a member of the Sandia Hiking Club, George had organized and led multiple trips with local Albuquerque high school kids. Several boys in the club gravitated to George's adventuring spirit and playful personality, and George enjoyed their company as well; he offered three of them—Greg Edgington, Dale Finn, and Paul Doolittle, all recent high school graduates—an invitation to join the Lees Ferry-to-Lava Falls expedition. Like Sara, Lee, and Stan, they eagerly committed to the entire trip.

Shinumo Creek. *Steck family archives*

With his fledgling Grand Canyon hiking army now assembled, George planned their Canyon assault for the fall of that year. He spent weeks plotting the exact course on his map, including route details and intended camp sites as well as calculating food needs and water resupply points. During the sweltering heat of late August and early September, George, Stan, Dale, Greg, and Lee spent about ten days hiking in and out of the Canyon caching food and water at strategic points below the rim. Each cache contained a note specifying who it belonged to, when the owners would use it, and a plea to not raid it. As a send-off and to honor their leader, George's recruits surprised him with the "Down the Gorge with Uncle George" banner they'd made.

On September 16, 1977, they arrived at Lees Ferry after being dropped off by Helen in the Stecks' Elmo van. At the campground, they encountered Lees Ferry ranger Tom Workman. He approached the group.

"I thought I better check in with you guys," Workman announced. "So, where are you going?" he continued, directing his attention to the elder statesman and apparent leader, fifty-two-year-old George, whose "Down the Gorge with Uncle George" banner proudly jutted out of his pack.

"We're hiking to Lees Ferry!" George boldly—but mistakenly—declared.

"Really?" Workman replied with raised eyebrows and a smirk. "All the way to Lees Ferry?" They laughed off the faux pas. Workman wished them well, and they headed downstream. George later wrote in the calendar:

> To start off finally on THE TRIP after a final look back at Helen and Elmo and the end of the pavement was an anticlimax—a sort of this is the way the world ends, not with a bang but a whisper kind of feeling. Where are the speeches and the brass band?
>
> THE TRIP ... so long in the planning ... yet always is my delicious late evening ruminations about if we succeed. But now that we are actually under way, the reality of only partial success for whichever of a million possible reasons, is briefly faced, acknowledged, and then firmly tromped into the mud and forgotten. It is a wonderful day and ... we have miles to go before we sleep. U.G.

Other than ringtails invading their camp and stealing food on the second night, they were off to a good start, getting their hiking legs and developing a marching rhythm. Unfortunately, shortly after breakfast on day three, Paul Doolittle misstepped and badly twisted his ankle. Gritting his teeth, he sucked it up and limped along. In his honor, the little platoon's nickname for the trip, which had been "March or Die," jokingly became "March *and* Die."

In a change of luck later that same day, Stan found a six-pack of Miller lite beer at

24 Mile Rapid, which they renamed "Six-Pack Rapid." They hipped and hoorayed at the find, thanking and toasting their unknown benefactor. During the celebration, Stan tripped and broke his walking stick. While righting himself, he fell again, putting his hand in a cactus. They all laughed, savoring the merriment and the beer.

Six-Pack Rapid aka 24-Mile Rapid.
Steck family archives

Alcohol on one of George's hikes epitomized the biggest change for Stan, Lee, and Sara. Indeed, they never saw it on their family trips in the early '70s. Except once. Sara was in her late teens when she brought a beer on a trip, causing George and Helen to "freak out." Until then, they reserved alcohol for special occasions, limiting themselves to a single glass of wine. Lee was shocked when, on his arrival at George and Helen's house at the start of the caching trip, Aunt Helen welcomed him with open arms and an exuberant, "Hi, Lee! So good to see you! Want a margarita?"

Where the Redwall Limestone emerges near River Mile 23, the group had to veer up and away from the river to hike atop the formation that rises eighty feet per linear mile. Each hiker now carried multiple quarts of water, the added weight making progress downstream slow and tedious. At River Mile 36.7, they crossed a side drainage George called "Mitchell Canyon," honoring Ron Mitchell, who had pioneered the route three years earlier. George, who had read about Mitchell's accomplishment in a newspaper article, had discussed this section with the group. In the calendar, Lee noted his impression of the area:

> Today sho' ain't what Mitchell said it would be. He said it would probably be the hardest day. Doesn't seem to me to be any harder hiking than yesterday. Wasn't easy, mind you, but it wasn't super killer hard. Back at camp, we even had time to kick up our heels and that is something. Washed clothes, washed ourselves and generally relaxed next to the overhang at House Rock. It's funny but it seems like we've been here longer than three days.

Day six came with a welcome reprieve. They laid over at Nankoweap Creek at River Mile 53 and waited for Don Mattox, Hugh Peterson (another hiking buddy), and Mike Steck. The three planned to rendezvous with the group by descending a route to the mouth of Nankoweap Creek. While Hugh would hike out from

Nankoweap after spending the night, Mattox and Mike planned to spend another week trekking with the hikers to Phantom. Mattox, who could always be counted on for a laugh, provided another dividend: He packed in George's favorite cake—apricot, from La Chantilly Bakery in Albuquerque; it arrived in fine shape. The three hikers also brought half a case of beer for a mini celebration.

During the festive moment, Mattox offered up a trade. "Who will carry two gallons of water to Vishnu for a full round squeeze-tube of peanut butter?" he asked. Later, in the calendar, he joked about his wampum bribes to get the younger ones to ease his burden: "Who wants a raisin? Uga Uga Boo, Uga Boo Boo Uga.... Don M."

Unfortunately, before reaching Phantom Ranch, the lighthearted mood soured. Frustrated by the kids hiking faster than he could, George became cranky and began to grumble, even talked about abandoning the hike. He couldn't do his job of "leading" from the rear when the kids were way out in front and out of sight.

Helen met them at Phantom. As always, seeing her lifted George's spirits, as did her advice. In soothing tones, Helen suggested a compromise to unite the team again: George, lighten up on the leash! Kids, rein it in! Her cheerfully delivered solution, heeded by all, began to heal the rift. Getting silly drunk and laughing for hours in the Phantom Ranch canteen also helped. In the morning, Mike, Don, and Paul (still nursing his sore ankle) hiked out with Helen.

Spirits lifted, the six remaining members of the team—George, Stan, Lee, Sara, Greg, and Dale—plodded downstream. At one point, in a side canyon filled with pothole water, the route narrowed. Skirting a large pool without falling in became an entertaining challenge. Greg Edgington, who had been given multiple nicknames, including "the thin Edge," "mud man," and "the wilderness junkie," was the first to try inching around the pool. Lee described the comical outcome:

> As he traversed, three feet off the water, he slipped in, and as he did so, he rotated around and hit the other wall in a perfect layout. It was fantastic! He's down! He's up! Oh no! As he went further, he slipped again and caught himself again! Hysteria set in!

On day thirty, they arrived at Deer Creek (River Mile 138), a true Eden if there ever was, and worthy of the toils of the trail for its slickrock pools, patios, and waterfalls, all lushly shaded by cottonwood trees. There, they played and lounged most of the day. Not uncommon for George's hikes, "easy days" had no agenda other than to have fun. They took turns enjoying dips in a jacuzzi-like tub formed by the creek rushing through the Tapeats Sandstone. A huge swimming hole had also formed at the base of the nearly 100-foot Deer Creek Falls. Stripping naked, Stan climbed to a ledge twenty-five feet above and jumped into the ten-foot-deep pool at the falls' base, emerging shocked but exhilarated. Hours later, they hiked to Fishtail Canyon and set up camp. There, they played in the sand like little kids, running, rolling, sliding, spinning.

By this time, late October, mornings broke colder as they headed into the final leg from Kanab Creek to Lava Falls. After leaving the river, they ascended Kanab Creek, then climbed up through the Canyon cliffs. High in the drainage, they discovered autumn had descended. An elated Lee made note:

> That morning was <u>fantastic</u>!!! It was fall and all the maples were turning. Deep reds, oranges, purples and gold. As we hiked along we would spot a patch of changing color and unconsciously head for it. We stuck our heads in the midst of the Reds and walked in and joyfully tramped around. We stuck leaves in our ears and our headbands. I felt ecstatic! Wondrous! It was truly magical.

Sara also journaled:

> Woke up, got out of bed, threw a comb across my head…. Another pretty, peaceful dawn. The light of the sun starts out diffused and slowly brightens. I walked alone this morning …

The trip's final mornings often began with George waking those trying to sleep in by cheerfully joking, "Last call for seconds on pancakes!" They knew George had no pancake mix.

With only days remaining and tension long behind them, the hikers became more sentimental, reflecting on the approaching end of their special journey. On their last night, Dale Finn entertained the group with renditions of John Prine songs; he couldn't sing, but he put sincere heart and humor into it by intentionally botching some of the lyrics. Lying around in their sleeping bags, they shared silly limericks before they called it a night.

Stan wrote with mixed emotions about the trip's finale.

> I was depressed by the trip's ending. The whole last five days were nothing more than a "long goodbye" and I don't like long goodbyes. But then something happened … some kayakers came by … and suddenly I was excited about talking with "outsiders."… And I was excited about seeing people I thought about. The trip has been a monumental part of my life … now it is a monumental memory.

To preserve this "monumental memory," George came up with the calendar concept. His "army," on board again, contributed journal entries for each month, while George designed a unique pattern to display the days. For example, February featured a photo of Lee Steck, spiderlike, climbing a cliff. To accompany the shot, George drew a spider web representing the days of the month. Beside the photo is a caption that George loved, confirmation of the success he hoped for all of his trips. Simple, yet eloquent, the caption sums up what Grand Canyon backpacking means to so many.

> The hiking is a bitch but when we rest it is so beautiful. The Colorado is green and crystal cold … the deep blue sky highlights the reddish gold cliffs. I could watch and listen forever.
> —"Spider Man" Lee

When I handed the calendar back to George, he began flipping through it, something he had probably done a hundred times before. I'll never forget the pleasure and sentimentality that radiated from his pothole-watery, seventy-five-year-old eyes.

Later, I browsed the calendar myself. For November, George had artistically laid out the days of the week as pie slices. One caption stood out: "There is a young fellow named Finn/Who keeps most marvelously thin/He uses a fork for his soup/And loves to go poop/And leaves all his food on his chin. U.G."

One word, almost guaranteed to make any kid (big or little) both giggle and cringe, caught my attention and transported me back to my own, first lengthwise section hike, and a hallelujah moment I've never forgotten.

Stan, Sara, Lee, Greg Edgington, George and Dale Finn, 1977. *Steck family archives*

CHAPTER THIRTEEN

Go Go Boots

FLASHBACK: HERMIT TO BRIGHT ANGEL

Even today, the canyon has not been synthesized in our history, art or literature; its only enduring place on paper is an endless succession of color postcards and slick photographs.

Bruce Babbitt
Grand Canyon: An Anthology (1978)

When you see someone putting on his Big Boots, you can be pretty sure that an Adventure is going to happen.

Winnie the Pooh
A.A. Milne, *Winnie-The-Pooh* (1926)

April 1985

"Top Cats! Ed Pinckney Powers Villanova Past Georgetown." This headline dominated the cover of the April 1985 *Sports Illustrated* I held in my hands. As a huge basketball fan, I immediately read the story of how underdog Villanova beat the heavily favored Georgetown in a shocker for college basketball's championship. Then, thumbing through the issue, I came across another article that I found more intriguing: "Grandeur and Torment."

Written by Kenny Moore, the piece chronicled a midwinter, forty-two-mile, cross-country skiing journey from Jacob Lake in the Kaibab National Forest to the North Rim of the Grand Canyon, then hiking across the Canyon rim-to-rim via the North and South Kaibab Trails. Moore had completed this outing with Bruce Babbitt. Moore launched the story with "Traversing the Grand Canyon

Grandeur and Torment, *Sports Illustrated*, April 1985.

in midwinter is no picnic, the author found, especially with a go-go governor as guide."

I remember considering that line. *"Our 'go-go governor,' huh? I wonder if he hikes in go-go boots."*

At the time, Arizona residents knew Babbitt was a man on the move, both outdoors and in politics, but even for him this was unique. A member of a pioneering northern Arizona family and a wilderness advocate, he had a special affinity for the Grand Canyon, having done his master's research in geology near the two Kaibab Trails. He also compiled *Grand Canyon Anthology*. Elected governor of Arizona in 1978, Babbitt served until 1987. He eventually became secretary of the interior under President Bill Clinton, and later, made his own run for the Democratic presidential nomination. I had met Babbitt once, briefly. As an eighth grader, I went with a handful of others from East Flagstaff Junior High School to the state capital as a reward for academics. We met Governor Raul Castro and the state's then-attorney general, Bruce Babbitt.

Anyway, I digress. The *Sports Illustrated* belonged to the Travelodge Motel on old Route 66 in Flagstaff, where I worked graveyard shifts as a clerk. I took it from our lobby into the office.

"Pretty cool story here you should read, Mark. Governor Brew-ski Babbitt is in *Sports Illustrated*." I handed him the magazine opened to the article, which he began to scan.

Mark Crane and I alternated night shifts at the motel. A pre-med student like me, Mark also ran on NAU's cross-country team. In training, he ran up to 120 miles per week. At six feet, two inches, he weighed 145 pounds. I used to call him Ichabod Crane, after the skinny protagonist who's hit in the head with a pumpkin in Washington Irving's *Legend of Sleepy Hollow*. In contrast, I happened to be what I'd call "fit-fat." I had good cardiovascular fitness, toned muscles, even six-pack abs. The only problem? All were concealed under a layer of pudge. Despite our physical discrepancies, I had done a few runs with Mark, as well as several hiking trips, including the Grand Canyon.

Our first hike together there had taken place two years earlier, in the summer of 1983, shortly after I purchased *A Guide to Hiking the Inner Canyon*, written by a man named Scott Thybony and published by Grand Canyon Natural History Association. I read the description for Hermit Trail, 8.5 miles from rim to river, to Mark: "Trail conditions: Secondary trail. Occasional washouts may require some route-finding ability."

"This is a perfect trail for us," I told him.

With "some route-finding ability" required and having only two previous rim-to-river hikes under my belt, it constituted a step-up in difficulty for me, and would be a fine first hike for him. I thought we could hike into Hermit Creek on our first day. Then, to make it a greater challenge, the next day we would go from Hermit Canyon fifteen miles across the Tonto Trail to Havasupai Garden

Arizona Governor Bruce Babbitt near Phantom, February, 1985.

(formerly known as Indian Garden until 2022), then hike out 4.5 miles to the rim via the Bright Angel Trail.

Despite the heat, the timing seemed perfect for another reason: the Colorado River was raging through Grand Canyon. Because of the exceptionally wet 1982-83 winter and huge runoffs into an already full-to-capacity Lake Powell, dam operators couldn't release enough water fast enough to keep the dam from self-destructing. It was all over the news. "Who knows?" I quipped to Mark. "With the high water, this big rapid called Hermit might be a giant tsunami! We need to see it!"

That summer, I had a job as a pizza delivery boy for Flagstaff's Alpine Pizza. To further entice him, I promised I'd bring his favorite pizza. With that, he was all in.

We started at sunrise as planned and made

good time in the cool morning air. Hours later, the heat hovered near 110°F as we neared the river. Engulfed in the suffocatingly hot air felt like total submersion in a waterless hot tub, the heat filling every crease and cranny. Even my eyeballs felt hot and sticky. Between blinks, squiggly heat waves filled my vision like the visual aura of a migraine headache. It came as no surprise when I felt my own head starting to pound. *Jeez! How can anything live in this god-awful heat?*

But things do.

And some of those things buzzed with life as we neared Hermit Creek: cicadas, big, flying insects hidden in the foliage. Cousins to the cricket, they too are dedicated noisemakers. A cicada's intense, high-speed buzzing can be startling and is often confused for a pissed off rattlesnake. (The clatter is the male's mating call, created by wing movement, the volume and speed of which are directly proportional to the heat. *A male in heat?*)

At the confluence of Hermit Creek and the Colorado, we plunked our overheating manly bodies onto a sandbank and commenced cooling down with splashes of river water. The cold Colorado flowed a pea-soupy green, but the creek ran nearly crystal clear which was good, as next on our agenda was rehydrating. In our charge down the Canyon, we had polished off all the water we carried. Fixated on it and on food, we filled our empty water bottles directly from the creek, then dug several baggies of oily pizza out of our packs. We washed down gooey, congealed wads with the unfiltered creek water. Blissfully ignorant (and lazy), neither of us had thought to bring a filter or disinfectant tablets.

Fortunately, but not surprising according to what I learned decades later, neither of us got sick. Research on the Canyon's waterways carried out over several years in the late 1990s revealed that free-flowing streams are "relatively pristine" and typically free of infectious microorganisms like bacteria and parasites, especially when they're running clear. If the water is turbid or dirty, however, all bets are off. Why are the Canyon's waters so pure? The rock layers above, especially the massive Redwall, act as giant filters. So does Glen Canyon Dam. Another big reason streams like Hermit Creek are safe to drink from is that there aren't enough hooved animals or beavers or people pooping directly in or near the water to foul it.

Anyway, I was about to change that.

"That rapid doesn't seem as big as I thought it would," Mark griped as we stared from the beach.

"Yeah, but those trees underwater are pretty cool. Let's check them out!" I suggested, pointing to the tamarisks swaying in the current twenty feet from shore. We both jumped into the cold water (which was slightly warmer than usual because of the higher releases) and swam over to the partially submerged, six to ten-foot-tall trees that would normally be high and dry. After a few minutes, Mark waded back to shore. I continued to paddle around. Then Mother Nature called.

"Hey, Mark, do you have any TP?"

"Nope. Sorry."

"Oh, crap! I gotta go bad, like now."

"Just go in the river."

"What?! Really?"

"Why not? Shit flows downstream," he added with a laugh.

I stood there for several more seconds, trying to decide how to proceed. Shivering, arms folded across my chest, I felt my stomach cramp and my legs start to go numb. Uh-oh, waited too long. Clueless about the dynamics of river currents, I decided to take Mark's advice. After all, shit does flow downstream. *Right?*

I relaxed and let things happen, then spun around. An oversized tootsie roll immediately bobbed to the surface. Unbelievably, it headed in my direction. *Upstream.*

"Oh, crap! Here comes my crap!" I shrieked.

"Run!" Mark hollered back.

Run? Of course! It seemed logical: get away by running upstream. Neither of us knew that eddy currents circulate upstream in opposition to the main current. Unfortunately, I had just launched my turd torpedo into one of those eddies.

Every other second or so, I glanced back. Despite my attempted upstream sprint in what felt like waist-deep, freezing molasses, the little brown scupper closed in on me. The river had justifiably marked me as a target of my own torpedo, payback for pooping in it. I watched with fear and fascination as it picked up speed in a faster current and made a final "dead wake" toward me.

"Dive! Dive!" I yelled. I dove in, then popped up closer to the bank. Clearing my eyes, I saw the poop several feet to my left, still riding the eddy. The dodge worked. Before it could change course and chase me farther, I ran for shore.

"Incoming!" I yelled at Mark, flopping onto the sand nearby.

He turned to me with a serious look. "You know what, Tom?"

Panting and dripping wet, I turned and looked at him.

"That was some pretty funny shit," he dead-panned.

For a while, we watched the turd circle around in the eddy. It eventually joined a small pile of driftwood, blending in, bobbing and weaving within the morass. It's embarrassing to admit all these years later, but I found it mesmerizing. It also became an eddy lesson for life, one I never forgot: What goes around comes around, so be careful where you crap.

That night, we camped up-canyon along Hermit Creek. The relentless heat and intermittent wind gusts kept me from sleeping. Plus, I felt nearly every chunk of rock underneath me through my deteriorating egg-crate foam pad. My single sheet felt like a quilt. The only thing that made my wadded-up backpack a slightly better pillow than my ratty cutoffs was the smell. In the dim starlight, I thought I saw my cowboy hat about to be blown into oblivion. When I lunged for it, I smashed my face against what turned out to be a sombrero-shaped boulder.

No surprise, in the morning, my cheek felt and probably looked like a botched facelift, the result of sleeping on backpack seams. The air temperature turned piping hot even before full sun. For breakfast, we dined on more pizza and Doritos. As we got ready to leave, we both downed plenty of water, using our bellies as canteens. Then we filled up our real ones.

"I'm not sure I'll have enough water," Mark remarked about his two-quart canteen, an old, military-style metal model.

"Don't worry. I got plenty," I boasted as I slapped the one-gallon plastic milk jug I had just filled. It resounded with the dullness of a ripe watermelon.

As we marched out into the already furnace-hot air, the cicada cackling swelled louder and louder. The temperature once again topped out at well over 100°F by the time we reached Havasupai Garden that afternoon. Parched and our water long gone, we bellied up to the spigot like two drunks in desperate need and downed about a half-gallon each before trudging out.

⌇⌇⌇

I snatched the *Sports Illustrated* back from Mark.

"We should do something epic like that!" I declared.

"Like what? Ski, then hike rim-to-rim?"

"No, even better, Mark! We should hike the Canyon from end to end!"

"You mean, like hike the whole thing?"

"Yeah, walk the whole darn thing, from end to end. It'd be fun, don't you think? I bet we could do it! The Tonto wasn't that hard!" I proclaimed, naively referencing our one-and-only lengthwise dodder from the "turd trip" two years earlier. I assumed the Tonto Trail probably went the whole way.[9] "I wonder if anyone has ever done it. What do you think?"

"I have no idea," he answered, looking dubious.

"Ahhh, who cares if anyone else has done it," I challenged, getting more excited. "It could be really cool! Seriously, what do you think? Wanna hike the length of the Grand Canyon with me?" I pressed again.

"Yeah, sure," he shrugged. I could guess what he was thinking: *Why not? It's only the length of the entire Grand Canyon, after all. And I got nuthin' else to do...*

---

9 The Inner Canyon Tonto Trail System is 122 miles (if one includes connections to the Beamer and Escalante Trails) in length but only nets 53 downstream river miles.

My duct-taped copy of Scott
Thybony's book.

The spark to hike the length fizzled about as fast as it had ignited once we both embarked on our all-consuming careers in medicine. Years of intense education and training gobbled up the rest of our twenties. I moved to Tucson for medical school and he moved to California for the same. Mark eventually became an oral surgeon, while I became a general practice doctor. I never left Arizona, nor did the dream of trekking the length of the Canyon ever leave me; I just moved it to the back burner.

For consolation, I vowed to explore all fifteen trails detailed in Thybony's hiking guide, the one we used for our Hermit hike. I kept that vow. Once I'd done that, my simmering idea to walk the length began heating up again; Landing my first "real doctor" job at Grand Canyon Clinic at the South Rim and meeting serious Canyon hikers—like Harvey Butchart, Kenton Grua, and George Steck—acted as a blow torch, as did Scott Thybony's book.

Unbeknownst to me, Scott had his own remarkable story of being the first to hike the length of Grand Canyon within its national park boundaries on the north side. An incredibly accomplished Canyon explorer but an extremely private man, Scott completed this little-known endeavor with his only brother, John. Ironically, neither book nor epic hike would have happened if not for something regrettable and deadly that took place two decades earlier and a world away. That something involved John.

John Thybony, circa 1966. *Courtesy Scott Thybony*

CHAPTER FOURTEEN

The Warrant Officer

THE STORY OF JOHN AND SCOTT THYBONY

*The bastards have never been bombed like they're going to be
bombed this time.*
President Richard Nixon (on his Vietnam War strategy)
April 4, 1972

We can bomb the world into pieces but we can't bomb it into peace.
Michael Franti
"Bomb the World" (2003)

Early 1980s

For John Thybony, flying a "mission" over the Grand Canyon was about as different from flying missions in Vietnam as were the two terrains. The views flashing past his helicopter's windshield included a kaleidoscope of colors in jagged cliffs within a mostly barren landscape.

More significant was what *wasn't* whizzing past: smoke, rice paddies, jungle, and—above all—tracer bullets or rockets. Plus, thrill-seeking tourists were picking up the tab for his flights, not Uncle Sam.

In Vietnam, John's passengers were often damaged, desperate, and terrified young men who wanted only a quick getaway with their lives and limbs intact. Some were battle casualties, infantry grunts he'd dropped off hours or days earlier, now wounded, dying, or dead. For them it wasn't about the ride; it was about the escape.

Also, unlike those in Vietnam, Grand Canyon missions almost never involved tricky flying or a complex goal. Outside of the rare but more challenging

127

flight into the Canyon for the NPS, they were mostly modest endeavors, even mundane, other than dealing with the winds or weather. Fly out of Tusayan with a chopper-load of tourists, drop a little below the rim, buzz the standard route with its routine right turns, point out some of the geologic features (buttes, side canyons, the Colorado River, etc.), tell a story or two of local interest, throw in a few jokes, then return, ideally, to a decent tip. In fact, for John Thybony the only thing the two types of "missions" had in common was the goal: bring everybody back alive, including himself. He'd take the Grand Canyon any day for the beauty, peace, and a steady paycheck.

Several times on his Canyon flights, John noted redtail hawks. When caught in updrafts the hawks would circle serenely. This sharply contrasted to Vietnam, where John once observed a comrade's helicopter in a death spiral before it crashed to the ground, exploding into a ball of fire. Yes, the Grand Canyon was a vastly different world.

In Vietnam, John had been a warrant officer, a helicopter pilot with the 119th Assault Helicopter Company. His job? Fly into combat zones, deposit soldiers and extract casualties. He also hauled ammunition and supplies; ferried VIPs; and, on occasion, made beer runs. His helicopter, Bell Model 205A-1/ UH-1H (a "Huey"), had two-bladed main and tail rotors and ran on a large Lycoming 1,400-horsepower turboshaft engine. Its passenger compartment could transport up to thirteen people—a souped-up, flying minibus. Hueys were built in greater numbers than any other helicopter model.

During a mission on December 12, 1967, twenty-one-year-old Thybony's helicopter was tailing another helicopter near Kon Tum, the capital of the Kon Tum Province in South Vietnam. A Special Forces Unit had gotten overwhelmed and needed immediate extraction. As the choppers approached, the lead ship sustained serious damage from Vietnamese artillery; the pilot radioed that he was going down. Despite intense enemy fire, John broke off his chopper's approach and steered for the stricken aircraft. After landing nearby and loading the lead helicopter's personnel into his aircraft, he took off again. Although his copter took several hits from a barrage of ground gunfire, the crews of both ships made it out alive.

After medevacking the wounded to a staging area, John and his crew flew back to the combat zone to provide cover for a gunship trying to recover the weapons system of another downed ship. Six months later, in recognition of his efforts, John received the prestigious Air Medal of Heroism, the Eighth Oak Leaf Cluster. It would be just one of more than two dozen medals for young John Thybony.

While the Grand Canyon was a far cry from Vietnam, it was also a far cry from John's home state of Virginia. He turned twenty in 1966, the year he spoke to a US Army recruiter in his hometown of Falls Church. He told the recruiter that he hoped to learn to fly and, for that reason, wanted to enlist rather than risk being drafted into the infantry. The recruiter assured him his wish would likely be granted. Waiting for confirmation, he got cold feet and, hoping for a last-minute student deferment, applied to a small local college. The army got to him first; an acceptance letter from the college three days after he signed his commitment forms couldn't make him renege. His father, an army colonel, administered the oath of allegiance at his swearing in. Young Thybony remained faithful to this oath for the rest of his life.

As a boy, John Thybony aspired to be a magician, developing his own magic act and creating business cards for "Jonathan the Magician." As he grew into his teens, however, this faded, and he became something of a wild child who increasingly butted heads with his somewhat overbearing father. At sixteen, frustrated and moody, grades tanking, John dropped out of high school and moved out of the family home. He took unpaid jobs with the local fire department and ambulance service in exchange for room and board. Within a year, he was driving the ambulance, handling drunks, car-wreck traumas, heart attacks, and gunshot wounds. He even helped deliver two babies. But eventually, he'd had enough and moved back home.

One month into his enlistment, he reported for entrance into the army's accelerated helicopter pilot training program. On August 1, 1967, after nine months, he received his wings and warrant officer status. The timing coincided with some of the heaviest fighting and worst combat missions of the war. Almost immediately, John found himself in the thick of it. For example, on October 25, 1967, his unit received word that a ground patrol in a dire situation needed immediate assistance if any were to be rescued. John volunteered for the mission even though "the evacuation area was infested with known enemy positions." He flew into the site under fire, then lifted out with a chopper-load of casualties. After dropping them off, he returned two more times, both under fire. He would be credited for saving fifteen men that day and earning his second Air Medal for Heroism, the Sixth Oak Leaf Cluster.

Yet his and other servicemen's efforts made little dent in the larger war. US intelligence drastically underestimated the resilience of the North Vietnamese, whose collective resolve seemed unwavering. They would rather see their country blown to smithereens than have their internal politics dictated by the US and its anticommunist allies.

Privately, President Lyndon B. Johnson vowed there was no way in hell he'd be the first US president to lose a war. Later, Nixon followed suit. In the end, the bombing of Vietnam more than tripled that of World War II (partly because the war lasted almost five times longer). Ultimately, the nineteen-year-long military catastrophe cost billions of US dollars and claimed the lives of more than 58,000 Americans and 3.5 million Vietnamese. While this astronomical expense—both in dollars and in the lives of young, naïve soldiers—would ultimately reveal itself, at the time it was still being falsely sold to recruits and to the American people as a noble and necessary crusade.

Still in the thick of it but with the war's futility becoming ever more apparent, John started to lose faith. During one mission, he transported more dead in body bags (many of whom he had flown in alive days before) than the total official death toll listed for that day in the *Stars and Stripes* (an official military publication). He knew the American government was lying to its citizens.

After his Vietnam tour ended in 1969, the US Army sent him to a base in Georgia to serve as an instrument flight instructor for his final year of duty. Increasingly disenchanted, he couldn't wait for his walking papers. Yet when they arrived, re-entry into private life proved anticlimactic. No hero's welcome. No warm embraces. No parades. No pats on the back. Not even a simple "thank you."

Instead, like many other returning Vietnam vets, he discovered that much of the American public resented him, considering him complicit in an immoral war. To a degree, he understood that perception and their frustration. His own disenchantment grew into an intolerable disgust. Eventually, he became active in the group Vietnam Veterans Against the War. In April 1971, he took part in the famous "March on Washington," aka the "Battle for the Mall."

Anticipating violence despite the assurance it would be a peaceful demonstration, the federal government readied troops in the basements of several nearby federal buildings and erected a fence on the mall to prevent advancement on the Capitol itself. It proved unnecessary. Ironically, the protestors' most devastating blow came not through violence but through silence and a singular gesture.

On the final day, one by one, veterans threw their heroism awards—medals and ribbons—over the fence. John tossed in a handful of his own. One veteran reportedly threw away nine Purple Hearts. This sent a strong message, as strong as they could deliver about this horribly misguided war. Yet the "Resistance War Against America" continued for another four years, and John was intensely relieved that he no longer had to fly into the fray.

In 2018, Jack Heslin, John's platoon commander in the 119th, wrote *Thunder: Stories from the First Tour*, detailing the missions he had flown, many with Thybony. For decades after the war, Heslin, who took his oath of secrecy as seriously as John did, wouldn't speak in detail about what he had witnessed. Then, at his wife's behest, he finally wrote the book in which he recalled the chaos of those missions.

It's impossible to describe the absolute pandemonium of exploding bombs and gunfire and everything going on around you—the screeching engine, the roar, the headset alive with chatter. You're on this edge all the time of maintaining control. The only way to do that, no matter how terrified you felt, was to stay totally focused on what you were doing.

More than a decade later, while flying in the Grand Canyon, John's focus remained similarly sharp, just as it had in Vietnam. While he constantly reminded himself how fortunate he was not to be flying into gunfire, he also reminded himself how lucky he was to still be flying at all. More than 5,000 of the 7,000 Hueys flown in Vietnam, as well as nearly 2,000 of their pilots, didn't make it home. Now, the serene terrain below him, and its superheated drafts, uplifted his helicopter and his spirits like a massive, healing breath of fresh air, free of death and mayhem and horrific memories.

Also unlike Vietnam, which he saw almost exclusively from the air, by the early 1980s, John Thybony had a unique earth-bound connection to the Grand Canyon. Memories of hiking trips weren't as visceral as combat, but they were just as real. One stood out.

Over nearly two weeks in the fall of 1972, John and his younger brother, Scott, completed an epic hike, the first traverse of the entire north side of Grand Canyon National Park on foot below the rim. Neither brother made a point to broadcast the accomplishment. To this day, even within the relatively close-knit circle of serious Canyon hikers, it's gone mostly unnoticed.

Buzzing over the Tuna Creek area, John could easily spot where he and Scott had backpacked after getting caught by a flash flood. As the weather turned foul,

Scott Thybony, 1972. *John Thybony*

they had veered around Dragon Creek. Then, pummeled by a tremendous rainstorm, they took refuge under a tight overhang—a space with barely room for two and only a few inches between head and ceiling—as the flood raged by.

After it receded, they crossed, then hiked farther west and camped under another overhang in an area called Tuna Creek, ten river miles downstream of Bright Angel Creek and Phantom Ranch. Soggy, shivering, and still

131

3000 feet below the rim as the sun set, they gathered sticks and built a fire within the overhang's confines to dry out and warm up. Within minutes, Scott recognized the outcropping as an archaeological site and had misgivings about sleeping there, let alone having a fire. Yet they were at risk of hypothermia, so hunkering down was their wisest option. Soon, they shared dinner and conversation within the fire's comforting warmth.

As they got ready to leave the next morning, they began to clean up all evidence of their presence. Scott used his cup to remove the ashes and dump them into Tuna Creek. He then swept the site clean. Before he could throw out the excess wood they had gathered, John began stacking it in the back of the overhang.

Scott quietly watched. He knew that time and time again, John had risked everything to aid distressed comrades, a need that had been burned into his psyche. When he finished, the young veteran turned and looked at his younger brother.

Of John Thybony, a friend once mentioned, "What I remember most about him were his blue eyes. They were uncompromising, just so clear. He would look straight at you, unflinching."

"Someone might need this someday," he told Scott.

CHAPTER FIFTEEN

Porcupine Quills

THE STORY OF JOHN AND SCOTT THYBONY (CONTINUED)

In the end, all we are left with are the big questions and the small kindnesses.
The rest falls away.

Scott Thybony
Burntwater (1997)

1966

While in Vietnam, John Thybony received a letter from his younger brother.
In it, Scott casually mentioned possibly dropping out of college to join the US
Army's Special Forces and live with one of the mountain tribes in Vietnam. He
felt it would allow him to fight the war and "do a little anthropology on the side."

Introspective, Scott sharply contrasted with his brother in terms of personality.
Among other things, he was far less inclined to clash with their father.

It usually took weeks for John to answer a letter. This reply came sooner than
usual.

"It's not what you think," he wrote. Again, sworn to secrecy and staying true
to his vow, he didn't go into detail in the letter, but added, "As a personal favor
to me, stay in school."

So, instead of enlisting, after graduating from J. E. B. Stuart High School in
Falls Church, Scott ventured west in 1966 to attend the University of Arizona
in Tucson. His keen interest in human history prompted him to major in
anthropology; soon, venturing out into Arizona's Sonoran Desert became his
favorite activity. Scott had only been at U of A for a semester when, in December
1966, John asked him in a letter to move closer to home in case he died in

Vietnam. Reluctantly, Scott transferred to George Mason College, a branch of the University of Virginia. The move turned out to be a good thing; at George Mason, he met Sandy, who would later become his wife. Though the war saturated the news, they heard very little from John.

Having become enamored with the Southwest and bored living in the East, Scott returned to Tucson in 1967 for the fall semester. He also resumed his extracurricular explorations. Friends eventually invited him along on a trip to Havasupai Falls within the Grand Canyon. Impressed, Scott went back to the Canyon a few months later, bringing his girlfriend Sandy; they hiked down the Bright Angel Trail to Havasupai Garden. The spectacular landscape seemed to summon him, and over the next four years he returned multiple times.

Then, in 1971, Scott heard from a friend about a unique opportunity he couldn't ignore. An elderly Navajo man living on the tribe's reservation near Red Lake in northern Arizona had become too feeble to tend his sheep. He and his wife, neither of whom spoke much English, needed help herding the animals. The friend explained that the couple was so desperate for assistance that they'd accept help from a *bilagáana* (a Caucasian). Compensation consisted of room (a hogan) and board (which occasionally included the treat of traditional fry bread and mutton stew prepared by the man's wife). Intrigued by what he could learn from the experience, Scott drove up and "interviewed" for the job. Despite the language barrier, Scott's soft-spoken demeanor sold him to the couple. Knowing John had reentry wanderlust, Scott asked the couple if he could invite his brother to come up and help as well. After an affirmative yes, for two months the brothers fulfilled their sheep-herding responsibilities.

When they returned to the world of the *bilagáana*, John, still seeking escape from traditional American culture but wanting to further his education, went to Mexico to study for a semester. While there, he even joined a dangerous demonstration against the Vietnam war in Mexico City. Meanwhile, the Grand Canyon remained in the forefront of his little brother's mind. Indeed, Scott drove to the South Rim and began camping in the forest off Rowe Well Road. From this base camp, he began reconnoitering the Grand Canyon on solo hikes. For two weeks, he hiked every day, first exploring trails, then probing routes off the rim.

One day, Scott ventured into Tusayan just outside the park for supplies and saw that a backpacking shop had just opened. He introduced himself and learned that the owner, Norm Johnson, lived in Flagstaff. He also found out Johnson wanted to set up a trail-guiding service.

Upon hearing this, Scott met with Johnson in Flagstaff to ask about a guiding job, although he did confess, "I've only been hiking the Canyon for two weeks."

"Well, it's more than me," Johnson retorted. "You start in two months."

Needing something in the interim, plus more Canyon hiking experience, Scott phoned Phantom Ranch and inquired about temporary work.

"You're in luck," the manager announced. "Someone just quit. Apply at Human Resources on the rim." After hanging up, Scott immediately went to the Fred Harvey Company HR office in Grand Canyon Village, and they hired him on the spot.

For the next two months as the weather heated up, he worked ten days on and four days off at the ranch as a "houseman," assisting when called upon in housekeeping, maintenance, and dishwashing. On the first of his four days off, he'd hike up to the rim, check his mail and run errands. Days two through four, he hiked back into the Canyon, exploring routes to increase his knowledge and expertise for his imminent guiding job.

In June, Johnson's new hiking business took off. Scott led hikes in and out of the Canyon, mostly to Phantom Ranch on the Bright Angel Trail. He loved the role, even though the trail hiking quickly became routine.

Things changed after Johnson set up an agreement with Gaylord Staveley, owner of a river company, Canyoneers, to include a river portion with the Grand Canyon adventure, as well as the idyllic Havasu Canyon, famous for blue-green water and towering waterfalls. Customers would be guided down into the Canyon on the Bright Angel Trail, hop on the Canyoneers motor rig when they reached the river at Pipe Creek, then head downstream nearly seventy river miles to Havasu Canyon. From there they would hike nine miles up the Havasupai Trail to Supai Village, stay in the lodge, then hoof it another eight miles the following day to an awaiting shuttle ride at Hualapai Hilltop. Johnson's hiking guide would get a free river trip in exchange for assisting on the boat. Scott enthusiastically signed on for the last such trip of the 1972 season.

While on the river, he jumped right in as part of the Canyoneers crew. He found the river fascinating and a boatman's adventurous and relatively carefree lifestyle appealing. Working hard, he impressed the other guides. Rave reviews about Scott eventually reached Joan Staveley, Gaylord's wife and company co-manager. Equally impressed, she offered him a job as part of her river crew for the next season.

Around the same time, in October 1972, after his first trip on the river, Scott concocted his plan to walk the length of Grand Canyon National Park below the North Rim. The idea originated while chatting with a Bright Angel Lodge bartender about the book *The Man Who Walked Through Time*. They knew Fletcher had walked the length of the park on the south side, but had anybody done it on the north side yet? It seemed unlikely.

"Why don't you do it?" the bartender suggested.

Scott thought for a moment before replying. "Okay. I think I will."

He immediately began his homework. The first assignment? Contact *Grand Canyon Treks* author Harvey Butchart. No surprise, Harvey had nearly completed the routes along the park's northern boundaries, from Nankoweap to Tapeats Creek, in sections. And as he had done with Fletcher and Mitchell, Harvey graciously shared his expertise and maps, asking nothing in return.

Scott laid out his route with an intent to stay mostly along the top of the Redwall Limestone but would occasionally require climbing below. Harvey thought Scott's proposed route, although shorter than what he would have chosen, might be riskier for lack of water, and possibly more difficult. Yet to Scott, despite this and the twelve major side canyons that would need to be crossed, it made sense. It also made a beautiful, sweeping arc on the map.

With the potential route laid out, he painstakingly planned meals down to the ounce. He decided not to take a stove, making meal preparation faster and his pack lighter. Nor would he take a tent. Within these self-imposed parameters, he also concluded that going solo would be best.

Then John called.

"Can I come?" he asked. Scott had taken his brother on a hike in the Canyon two years earlier. It had been a short one, and Scott remembered it well:

> In the spring of 1970 John drove west in his red MG-B as soon as he got out of the army. He had already started letting his hair and beard grow. Darrell Howard, a friend who had flown with him in Vietnam, came along. On the spur of the moment, the three of us hiked down the Bright Angel Trail with whatever gear we could fit in my pack. It was John's first trip into the Grand Canyon.
>
> About an hour into the hike, John and Darrell started complaining. We had just begun, and when I called them on it, they blamed the army. They had learned to start complaining long before they needed a break, since the sergeants always waited an hour before paying any attention.
>
> We continued down the trail, and John began telling me of a mission he had flown where a helicopter got shot down on a hidden North Vietnamese bunker. All hell broke loose. His aircraft landed to pick up the other pilots and flew out under heavy fire. Darrell gave him a hard look and John broke off the story, having never been released from his oath of secrecy. As we descended below the rim, the war continued half a world away.

John Thybony had been out of the army for a year, and his first year back had been a bit unsettling. Around Christmas, Scott and John's younger sister, sixteen-year-old Meredith, ran away from home. Together, the brothers began tracking her down. After a two-week search, they found her alive but emotionally struggling in New York City. They eventually coaxed her into coming home.

Looking to escape family stress and Virginia, and wanting a fresh start, John bought that red MG sports car and eventually headed west to Tucson to join Scott, now in his senior year in college.

In 1976, John left Arizona for Idaho, hoping to find work with the US Forest Service as a seasonal smokejumper. Though he had little interest anymore in helicopters, he still found flying fascinating, as well as the concept of jumping out of aircraft into rugged territory where helicopters couldn't land and vehicles couldn't navigate.

Three hundred people showed up for eight spots. John drove up in his old, beat-up truck. Hiring boss Bobby Montoya saw the long-haired, bearded driver and leaned toward a nearby colleague, "Well, here come the Clampetts," he snidely mused, referencing *The Beverly Hillbillies*, a popular television show. As John strolled up, Montoya started singing the show's theme song.

But in the end, Montoya found John Thybony surprisingly well-spoken and confident; his appearance didn't matter. From his application, which Montoya had received before John arrived in Boise, Montoya knew he had tremendous experience with helicopters. He'd already chosen John as one of the eight hires, sight unseen.

Fighting fires as a smokejumper is potentially hazardous, to say the least. For example, in 1949 in the Mann-Gulch fire in Montana, thirteen smokejumpers (all but one World War II veterans) were overtaken by the fire after jumping into it. Former smokejumper Bill Mader, in his essay from the 1970s, "The Run for the Top," writes about the connection between veterans and smokejumpers:

John Thybony, circa 1980.
Scott Thybony

It was my take that they transitioned to smoke jumping because they liked the free-wheeling lifestyle and adventure, and a life with a touch of risk. They were also not without blunt humor and I think needed the sense every day that they didn't know where they were going.

John held the firefighting job for three summers, making dozens of jumps around the West, from Alaska to Nevada and New Mexico. In the off-season, he returned to the Grand Canyon to work as a hiking guide. He also made friends with a Grand Canyon local, a Swiss native named Eric Gueissaz (pronounced "GAY-suh"). An outdoorsman and El Tovar chef, Gueissaz had recently purchased the South Rim's historic Highland Mary Ranch. Built in 1899, the rustic property resides five miles south of the rim, down Rowe Well Road. Gueissaz let John live in a small guesthouse on the property.

John had never been intimidated by challenging or risky endeavors. In fact, too often, he welcomed them. He once snuck himself and Scott into a bar when they were fifteen and thirteen, respectively. Another time, in April 1965, the Eagle Scout brothers were recruited to assist in a harrowing diving expedition to save four men trapped in a flooded cave in Arkansas; John had been calm, level-headed, and focused. Scott followed suit.

John Thybony tweezing cactus spines from Eric Gueissaz. *Scott Thybony*

At twenty-four, John had a lean, athletic build, carrying 160-pounds on his five-foot, eleven-inch frame and by this time, had nearly as much Canyon hiking experience as his brother. Like Scott, he had worked as a hiking guide for Johnson the previous summer. Scott knew John would make a good companion on his mega-hike.

They started out on October 10; Scott estimated that it would take three weeks, half the time it took Fletcher to walk the south side. Within two days, John proved his worth by finding a critical route in a cliff that Scott, who had been leading, had given up on. For the next week, machine-like, they moved steadily, surprising even themselves with their speed. They reached Phantom Ranch days ahead of schedule.

Walking into the canteen, Scott nonchalantly approached his old boss, Mel, to say hello. The Phantom Ranch manager's eyes widened when Scott explained their undertaking. "Ah-ha! So that's why you came to work down here!" Mel exclaimed. "I was wondering why a college boy would be washing dishes down here. You were planning this trip all along!"

John during the north side hike, 1972. *Scott Thybony*

He then tossed them a couple of towels and told the brothers to hit the showers. Once there, John peeled off a sweaty, ripe-smelling sock. "So, if you throw your sock against a wall and it sticks," he instructed Scott, "it's time for a change." He chucked the grimy wad at the wall. They laughed when it easily stuck.

A week later, after enduring torrential rains and nearly freezing, they arrived at the western boundary of Grand Canyon National Park at Tapeats Creek, exiting to the rim near the Thunder River trailhead.

The brothers then parted ways. Scott went back to Flagstaff, eventually leaving his guiding gig with Canyoneers and taking a job as an NPS river ranger. He and Sandy married, and they had a son. Meanwhile, John headed to Idaho.

In the summer of 1978, while hanging out at a bar in Boise on his day off, thirty-two-year-old John met twenty-year-old Mindy Hume. A western New York state native, Hume had hitchhiked across the country with a female friend. Mindy and John chatted. The good-looking veteran, sporting long hair and a wrist bracelet given to him in Vietnam, impressed her. His piercing blue eyes also caught her attention. Mindy found John's gaze and manner of posing questions rather intimidating. She also found his appearance and his demeanor alluring. And vice versa. They went their separate ways that day but vowed to stay in touch.

That same summer, while fighting a fire in Idaho, John and his crew were running low on food. After radioing in, they hiked to a landing zone and waited for the resupply. Squeezing his eyes shut, John clutched his hat firmly on his head and squatted on the ground as the chopper hovered overhead. While caught in a tornado of dirt, gravel, sticks, leaves, and other debris kicked up by the rotor wash, he had an epiphany. *This is nuts,* he chided himself. *I'm a pilot. Why am I down here eating this shit? I should be up there.*

He returned to Arizona permanently in 1979, intent on three things: First, he would fly again; he went to Phoenix to update and recertify his pilot's hours. Second, he would return to the Grand Canyon to take a pilot's job; Helitech Helicopters hired him without question. Third and most important, he would propose to, then marry, Mindy; on June 21, he completed his trifecta when he slipped a ring on Mindy's finger at the Grand Canyon Village courthouse, a local judge presiding. Scott and Sandy served as witnesses.

Within three months, however, second thoughts crept in about flying scenic helicopters for a living. It turned out to be what he thought it might: poorly paid and relatively boring. He quit the job to cut and sell Christmas trees. But things changed when Mindy got pregnant.

Needing a better and more stable income, John resumed flying helicopters, this time in Utah and Grand Junction, Colorado, for Shell Oil. About the same time, Mindy delivered their first child, a daughter they named Prairie. When they decided to settle down, they chose to be near the place they loved most and where they had close friends: the Grand Canyon. They rented the little house from Gueissaz once again, and John took a pay cut to go back to flying scenic helicopters. Orion, their son, was born in 1982. Life became idyllic for John Thybony: raising a family in the woods near the rim of the Grand Canyon, gardening, cutting firewood, and flying.

On the morning of June 18, 1986, three days before his seventh wedding anniversary, John woke up to the whimpering of the family's dog, Ladue. They had named him after a river in Alaska where John had worked a fire. Unfortunately, their pooch had gotten quilled in the face from contact with a porcupine. The husky-mix yelped as John, one by one, yanked out the quills.

Knowing he'd be gone before the kids got up, John left a note on the kitchen counter with the quills. Mindy smiled when she read the note. He told her what happened to Ladue and asked her to show the quills to the kids, as they'd likely find them and the story fascinating.

The day came with the characteristically clear, hot, and sunny conditions common in mid-June at the Canyon. Accordingly, Mindy had planned to do laundry, then hang it to dry.

Around nine that morning, pilots Bruce Grubb and Jim Ingraham lifted off the Tusayan Airport runway in a mid-sized scenic airplane, a de Havilland Twin Otter Vista Liner operated by Grand Canyon Airlines. With several years of experience flying the Canyon, Grubb and Ingraham prepared for another routine flight. Filled to capacity, their one-hour flight had eighteen passengers, mostly international tourists: eleven Dutch citizens, four Americans, two Swiss, and one South African. At nearly the same time, John Thybony and his four passengers, three Germans and one American, lifted off a Tusayan Airport helipad for the first tour of the day, a forty-minute flight in the Bell Jet Ranger. He headed in the same direction as the Twin Otter.

About one in the afternoon, as Mindy did laundry in Grand Canyon Village with the kids, Eric Gueissaz appeared. A small entourage of John's closest friends trailed behind. Heads initially bowed, their shell-shocked, tearful eyes eventually met hers.

"I knew in that instant," Mindy recalled, "John was gone."

Fifteen minutes into the flight, John's Jet Ranger and the Twin Otter had closed in on the same area over Tuna Creek. They collided when the airplane's exposed landing gear contacted the helicopter's rotor blades. The main rotor mast tore away, the rotor blades ripping into the Vistaliner's tail section as it went. Mortally wounded, both aircraft plummeted to the ground. Exploding in flames as fuel ignited, the burning aircraft produced massive smoke clouds that could be seen from the South Rim. Several eyewitnesses made the NPS aware of the crash, triggering an immediate helicopter search and rescue reconnaissance flight.

Charlie Peterson, one of the NPS rangers on board, reported what they came upon on the Tonto Plateau, near River Mile 99: "I saw two aircraft totally involved in flames, about 30 to 40 feet high." The site burned for hours, the heat so intense that melting aluminum ran in rivulets from the wreckage. All twenty-five people aboard both aircraft died. It remains the second-deadliest air disaster in Grand Canyon history. (The worst had happened thirty years earlier, nearly to the day, on June 30, 1956, when two planes collided midair over the Canyon and 128 people perished.)

The news reached Scott in Virginia. Only two days prior, he and John had attended their grandmother's funeral. During their stay, Scott talked John into visiting the Vietnam Veterans Memorial in Washington, D.C. John had been reluctant—he knew he would see the names of comrades. He'd also said he hoped he didn't see his own name there.

Well aware of his mortality, he once showed Scott what he called "the last bullet." Because captured American pilots were often tortured and executed, "I saved the last bullet for myself," he told Scott, "in case I was ever shot down. I wasn't going to let them capture me." Then he added, "The bullet reminds me to keep things in perspective."

Only once did John convey to Scott the emotional toll the war had taken on him. He told Scott that during his first leave home, driving alone, he suddenly started crying. "It came out of nowhere," John recalled to Scott. "I don't know why. Then it stopped." He also admitted to his brother that he didn't regret his part in the war. What he regretted was the loss of so many lives.

He viewed the Vietnam Memorial with anger and sadness as he read the names. Following the funeral, John caught a red-eye flight back to Arizona; he had to work the next day.

Stunned and deeply saddened by the news of the crash, family and friends across the country saw headlines in the weeks that followed reflect speculation as to why the aircraft had collided. Fingers were pointed at both pilots, yet the actual cause of the crash remained a mystery.

Two months after the accident, during a mid-August heat wave, Scott set out on foot for the crash site. When asked why, he couldn't say specifically. Maybe he was looking for answers. Maybe for closure. Swells of superheated air billowed up from the Canyon depths as he bushwhacked off the rim at Point Sublime, aiming for Sagittarius Ridge, 1,500 feet below. He arrived by evening and set up camp for what would be a fitful night's sleep. In the morning, he decided to go light and fast to the crash site. Carrying little food and a single water bottle, he set out. After tedious downclimbing, he eventually made the bone-dry, sizzling-hot Tonto Plateau. The temperature hovered near 110°F. He passed a single pothole shimmering with what looked like about two gallons of oily water, the only water in the otherwise dry bed of Tuna Creek.

Still carrying a quart of water, which he believed would be adequate, Scott looked at the pothole but didn't top off. Instead, he decided he would fill up from it on his return.

As he struggled to find the crash site, he ran out of water. He had also forgotten to bring a hat. Despite sensing his body becoming dehydrated, he continued to push on. Singularly focused, he eventually found what he hoped for.

The largest pieces of debris had been removed. Wracked with emotion, Scott built a small stone cairn, the hot rocks burning his hands. He offered up a prayer for his brother and the others who died. Then, turning to leave, he suddenly found himself disoriented. He walked up a hill, then down, then through one ravine after another. Desperate to find that elusive pothole water, he unintentionally came across something that would prove to be almost as important.

On a ridge above him, away from the main crash site, lay another manmade object. Scarred from the impact of metal on metal, he could still identify it as one of the helicopter's rotor blades. It had been missed by the search parties. Scott left it in place but marked the location on his map.

Still exposed to the unrelenting sun, he needed that pothole water, badly.

Although confident he could find it, he knew that in his current state, he couldn't reach it. Going much longer without water under the direct sun meant certain death from heat stroke. A sense of urgency crept in. For his wife and toddler, he had to get out of the sun. *Now.*

Auspiciously, he found a ledge, crawled under it, then tucked himself into the deepest, coolest part of the recess. He began to hallucinate. An American Indian elder, grim and unsmiling, appeared; he stared at Scott, then spoke, advising him to wait until the sun went down. Then the effigy disappeared.

Five hours passed. Finally, the sun set behind Sagittarius Ridge and Scott crawled out. Still feeling dehydrated and weary, at least his body had cooled off. Thinking and seeing more clearly, he retraced his steps. Within an hour, he reached the tiny water pocket he had passed on the way in and slowly drank. Exhausted and chilled as darkness set in, he scanned for a bivouac.

The area seemed familiar. An overhang came into view. He walked over for a closer look, then remembered. Fourteen years earlier, soggy and freezing, he and John had camped there. Now, Scott moved under the stony outcrop and lay down. Lacking a sleeping bag, he scooped shallow indentations for his hip and shoulder and curled up. As the night grew colder, his thoughts shifted to keeping warm.

Then he remembered something else.

At the back of the overhang, lay a small pile of firewood. It was just as John had left it, undisturbed after all those years. Scott grabbed several pieces and lit a fire. Staring into the flames, he felt the fire's warmth surround him. *Someone might need this someday.*

Eventually, Scott led an air crash investigator and a lawyer to the site to retrieve the rotor blade. Using it, federal investigators were better able to reconstruct the cause of the collision. A critical piece of evidence, it helped investigators come to the conclusion that each aircraft had likely been in the other's blind spot. And that John Thybony had not been at fault.

Within a year after this crash, the Federal Aviation Administration (FAA, founded after the 1956 airline collision over the Canyon) began recommending that all turbine commercial passenger aircraft have Traffic Collision Avoidance Systems (TCAS) installed. It also developed rules and regulations to standardize air tour routes and minimum flying altitudes within Grand Canyon.

Mindy and her children; Scott, Sandy, and their son; and other family and friends came to the South Rim's Havasupai Point in September for a memorial service. Prairie and Orion walked to the edge with flowers and dropped them into the Canyon. For Scott, no tears came. He had already done his grieving. He opened the urn containing John's ashes and spilled them out, then tossed the ceramic pot into the Canyon as well.

Several weeks later, family and friends held a second memorial at Havasupai Point. During it, a redtail hawk appeared. Scott recalled John commenting that he sometimes flew with hawks, their eyes meeting. Scott watched the hawk. Caught in an updraft, it circled serenely for several seconds, then disappeared.

CHAPTER SIXTEEN

Dirty Little Secrets (Part One)

SOAP CREEK TO RIDER CANYON

Exploration, like seduction, puts a premium on the virgin.
Wallace Stegner
Beyond the Hundredth Meridian (1953)

February 2009

"Look, I'd like to tell you more, but we're trying to keep this kinda secret."

Wes and I glanced at each other, puzzled.

"Oh, okay," I replied in hushed surprise, taking the hint.

As Wes and I approached the Soap Creek trailhead, clouds swirled and wind gusted. To reach the river before dark, we needed to hustle. But then we spotted a group sitting in camp chairs, hanging out, chatting. The backpacks scattered nearby suggested they were hikers. Despite the urgency, I told Wes I wanted to say hi, so we walked over.

Several in the group glanced our way as we drew near, then without a wave or smile, just as quickly turned back to resume talking amongst themselves. Perhaps they thought we wanted to bum something off them. Then, a middle-aged man I guessed to be near my age, stood and approached us. He walked several feet away from the circle, standing outside it as if to keep us from breaking an invisible barrier.

"Hey, how's it going?" I inquired, trying to strike up a conversation.

"Fine. Doing pretty good," he answered. He seemed tired.

"Uh, good. So, what are you guys up to? Are you going down Soap Creek?" I asked.

"Well, actually …." He stopped. He studied us briefly. "We're going down Badger," he finally offered.

"Really?" I responded, truly surprised. "I tried that years ago. You get cliffed out by the river," I reported.

"We're going to rappel to the bottom."

"Whoa! Awesome! How are you getting back out?"

He paused, eyeing us both again.

"So, we're actually a canyoneering group from Phoenix. Several of us are going down Badger, and we have other friends going down Jackass Canyon at the same time." (Jackass Canyon is directly opposite Badger.) "We're packrafting across, above the rapid," he continued. "Then we're exchanging keys, picking up each other's cars and driving back to Phoenix."

"Wow!" I had heard of people "canyoneering" in Grand Canyon, a relatively new thing that involved rappelling through narrow or "slot" canyons. Combining it with packrafting added a novel twist. "That sounds really fun." I looked at Wes, who nodded in agreement. "How long have you been doing this?" I asked the man.

"Well, we've been doing it for, er … a while."

"Cool. What else have you done?"

He hesitated.

"Look, I have a buddy here writing up these routes, and right now, we really don't want too many people knowing about it."

The rest of the group, still sitting and unengaged with us, seemed to confirm his words. They were clearly avoiding eye and verbal contact.

"Okay, I get it," I replied, enthusiasm deflated.

The man sensed this. He seemed conflicted.

"Hang on a second," he said. Going back to his pack, he rummaged inside, then began writing something on a piece of paper. Seconds later, he returned, paper in hand. "Look, I wish I could tell you more, but here's my phone number. Call me if you want to talk about it."

I took the paper and looked at the group still ignoring us, aloof in the name of secrecy or from lack of interest in what they probably assumed was our relatively boring hike. Perhaps both.

He handed me the paper. For a moment, I imagined a rock star with his band confronted by groupies—in this case, Wes and me. The guy handing me the phone number ran interference. *Here's an autographed picture, dude. Now go away…*

"All right. Thanks," I said flatly when I took the paper. "Have a nice hike."

"You, too," he responded, even though he had no clue about what we were doing. Wes and I walked away and he went back to his chair.

"So, what are you going to do, Dad?" Wes finally asked me when we were out of earshot. "Are you going to call him?"

"Here, I'll show you what I'm gonna do, Wes." We stopped. I took the paper with the phone number and crumpled it in my hand.

"You know, Wes, this is a big place. Bigger than any of us. It's fun to share it with people who are like-minded. I've been coming here a long, long time and I love meeting other Grand Canyon-lovers, but am I going to call that dude? Heck, no.

"Guys like that turn me off. At this point, I don't really give a crap about their secret hikes. They can keep 'em. He didn't ask anything about us or what we were doing. It especially bothers me that he didn't ask anything about *you*. It's not often you see kids here doing unusual stuff, you know? Yeah, going down Soap is nothing special, but walking along the river and coming out Rider Canyon is. That's atypical, especially for a kid.

"Anyway, for me, it's about making memories and sharing this place with cool Canyon people, not Canyon nerds like them. Cool people, like you."

He smiled.

Weston and I started at a fast clip to make up for lost time—not only those precious few minutes talking to that guy at the trailhead, but because it was an already-short February day and we were getting started later than I'd hoped. We had driven up from Flagstaff that morning, arriving at the Marble Canyon home of Pam and Clair Quist an hour later than I anticipated. Longtime river runners and part owners of Moki Mac River Expeditions, the Quists lived in a rustic home accented with lots of wood and stone. I'd asked Clair, a friend and expert on the Marble Plateau maze of roads, for a shuttle ride. Too kind to say no, Clair (along with Pam) efficiently led us to the top of Rider, where I parked my 4Runner. Then they shuttled Wes and me back to Soap Creek in their half-ton truck.

For this, our first hike of 2009 and our second lengthwise leg, we intended to hike four miles down Soap Creek Canyon to the Colorado at River Mile 11, traverse along the river for six miles or so, then go five miles out Rider Canyon at River Mile 17.

"I really like this new Osprey pack, Dad. Thank you." The pack had been a Christmas gift, one he'd researched and I'd gladly bought for him. That purchase was his backpacking buy-in.

Soap Creek basically is a larger and longer version of Cathedral Wash, gradually dropping four miles to the river. While the forecast had called for possible rain or snow, neither happened, and we made it to the river in fine shape. The wind kicked up as we began setting up camp on a large sand dune downstream of the drainage mouth. Cold sand blasted us and sent the tent flapping, and we tag-teamed to secure it.

After a quick dinner, we ducked into the tent to warm up.

"It was nice to get out of school a day early," Wes said. "Thanks."

I knew he meant it. Almost overnight, school seemed to have become purely a burden for him. Gone were the relatively carefree days of elementary education. Part of this stemmed from the step-up in course work and increasing expectations from his teachers and us. Adolescent culture changes were noticeable; cliques were forming, and teasing and shunning were becoming more intense, not to mention crueler. With increasing frequency, Wes chose to be on his own.

Making matters worse was baseball. Wes had always loved the game and excelled in Little League. He played spring ball now, with most practices in the gym. Typically, only the best of the city's Little League players moved on and continued to play, and competition got tougher as the kids got bigger. Bigger kids, especially in sports, often come with bigger attitudes. Competitive trash-talking, increasingly profane, had become commonplace with trolling and taunting, especially after any miscue.

"Do you miss spring ball?" I asked.

"No, not really." He got quiet. "But I really love doing this stuff," he added as he climbed into his bag. "Can I tell you something else?"

"Of course."

"It was a fun day, Dad, but I miss Mom."

In the morning, we packed up early. Wes didn't dawdle. I could sense he wanted to get home to talk with his mom; he confided in her, sharing things he wouldn't tell me. He'd seek her out for solace and advice, especially when feeling down. Whenever he asked her, "Can we talk?" we knew he felt depressed. Unfortunately, that request seemed to be coming with increased frequency.

Wes on the Esplanade. *Tom Myers*

We made good time walking on the flats of Supai ledges and arrived at Rider Canyon before noon. There, we looked into the narrow section of Rider Canyon below us, which we'd bypassed. It appeared dark and mysterious. *Could people like those canyoneering guys actually rappel through them and safely make it to the river, then float downstream? If so, how cool!*

We made it out in good time, then headed back to Flagstaff. As we reflected on the trip, we also wondered how the canyoneers at Soap Creek had fared. When we eventually learned the answer, it came as a shock.

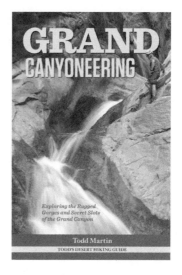

A couple of years later, I received a phone call. The man on the line introduced himself as Rich Rudow and told me he'd gotten my number from a mutual friend. We had an enjoyable conversation, and he told me he had a book he wanted to give me, *Grand Canyoneering*, written by his friend, Todd Martin. In return he asked if I'd sign his copy of the Harvey Butchart biography I'd co-written. Flattered and now on a first-name basis, I invited Rich to come by my house.

When I let him in, I thought he looked vaguely familiar. He handed me *Grand Canyoneering*. This book, it turned out, is one of wicked genius. It expounds on amazing slot canyon routes in the Grand Canyon that can only be accessed via rope, then sometimes egressed only by packraft. It reveals spectacular, stunning, and previously unknown places that hikers of the Butchart and Steck era (including me) would have collectively agreed could never have been visited otherwise. These remote Canyon recesses were—and are—aptly referred to as the "last of the Great Unknown," by Rich and Todd Martin. They are, of course, right. And to make the slots presented in the book "known," required not only brainpower, but bucketloads of sweat equity, nerves of steel, and a passion to explore.

Along with Martin, Rudow took part in a multiyear effort to be the first to lay claim to this premium virgin territory. Then, like Harvey Butchart and George Steck, Todd chose to share the thrill of these shocking discoveries and how to safely traverse them in a guidebook. Rich factored heavily into the book's creation; an engineer by training, he brought critical analytical skills from a sedate field into a physically radical one with extremely high stakes. He assisted Martin in calculating necessary rope links, securing anchors, determining the best rappelling and ascending devices—all essential to safely traversing slot canyons, where one miscalculation or inattentive moment can result in death. When Rich left my house, I still hadn't put two and two together. My jaw dropped when Wes did.

"That was the guy we met at the top of Soap Creek," he said after thumbing through the book, which included a few pictures of Rudow. I was chagrined to realize he was the guy I'd felt rebuffed by that day.

Later, Rich explained the initial secrecy to me. They were concerned that word would get out on the packrafting the group had done earlier during that trip. If the NPS found out, he and his band could be in trouble. In addition, he added, Todd Martin really didn't want to be scooped on the project—to have someone steal the idea and do a similar book. Finally, he reported that when Wes and I stopped by, they were pretty exhausted. And here I'd thought they were just being dicks.

⟅⟆

We finished our hike uneventfully, making it down Soap and out Rider just fine as an overnighter. In May 2009, we knocked out a third hiking leg, scrambling the ten miles from 19-Mile Canyon to Rider Canyon as a day hike. During our drive back, an eighteen-wheeler suddenly veered into our lane. I had only a couple of seconds to swerve onto the shoulder, just barely missing a head-on collision. That instant provided a sobering reminder that often the most dangerous part of Grand Canyon hiking is driving to and from the Canyon.

Often but not always.

October 2009

The third driest Fall in northern Arizona history coincided with our fourth hiking leg. For this one, Wes and I planned on going from Mitchell Canyon (again, the unofficial name given the drainage by George Steck to honor Ron) at River Mile 37, then upstream to South Canyon at River Mile 32. About ten miles total, it would include one night camping down in the Canyon. With both his teachers' and his mom's blessings, I took Wes—who again seemed thrilled—out of school a day early. For this hike, I also invited Eric Gueissaz, John Thybony's old buddy and former best man, and a current, longtime friend of mine from the South Rim who'd been hiking the Canyon far longer than I.

Born in 1940, Eric grew up in a small town north of Lake Geneva in Orbe, Switzerland. He came to the US in the late 1960s, finding work as a chef in San Francisco. Quickly fed up with the big-city lifestyle, he contacted a friend who suggested he call someone at the Canyon about a job. He ended up in Arizona working for the Fred Harvey Company as a sous-chef at El Tovar Hotel.

A wiry, gregarious, philosophical, and fiercely opinionated man, Eric had more Canyon friends than anyone I knew. He and I had talked for years of teaming up for a Canyon hike, and we were finally making it happen.

The three of us drove to Marble Canyon and met Russell Sullivan at his house at the little development of Badger Creek. We needed another shuttle driver and Russell, a seasoned Grand Canyon river guide for Hatch River Expeditions, obliged. Like the Quists, he knew the roads of the Marble Plateau well and had an equally picturesque home, complete with a flagstone patio configured so ancient ripples in the sandstone ran in the same direction. As we loaded up on water at his house, he asked, "Are you guys sure you don't want more water?"

"I think we're good," I declared. "I have eight liters, Wes has seven."

We looked at Eric, whose unique appearance has always fascinated me.

Stubbly whiskers—like little white cactus spines—poked out of his chin and cheeks. A thick gray Walrus mustache dangled below a somewhat bulbous nose. His leathery, wrinkled face perfectly matched his weathered hiking boots. Adding in his shoulder-length gray ponytail, a dated-looking flannel shirt and faded blue jeans, he collectively appeared to be a cross between an old hippie and grizzled prospector.

"I'm good, too," Eric confirmed. "I have plenty."

"We should be able to resupply at Starship Camp," I told Russell, referring to a breathtaking spot on a Supai slickrock cliff, framed with sandstone hoodoos. "There's a big pothole there."

"Yeah, but it's been a dry fall," Russell countered. "I'm talking really, *really* dry. We haven't had rain in three months." Concern edged his voice.

"I know, but there's also a water cache there. I've seen it. We should be fine."

We banged over intermittent washboards on an otherwise fairly smooth dirt road for fifteen miles into House Rock Valley, where I dropped off my GMC Yukon at the South Canyon trailhead. Then we hopped into Russell's rig and veered farther east into no-man's land near a stock tank referred to by local cattlemen as "Tank Seven."

"Well, good luck, you guys," Russell called out his truck window, waving as he drove off. Clouds of dust billowed high in the air as his vehicle bounced down the dirt road. The plumes, confirmation of what Russell had told us about the parchedness, could still be seen long after the truck had passed from view. Packs on, we wasted no time walking about a half-mile to the south, to the apex of Mitchell Canyon and a navigable break through the cliffs.

"There's Starship," I informed Wes and Eric, pointing to a flat peninsula of Esplanade Sandstone, projecting to the southwest out in the distance, about 1,200 feet below. In a direct line, it seemed about a mile away. "I'd like to camp there if we could. See that dark, oblong thing near the edge? That's the huge pothole I've been talking about. Last time I came through here, the water was a foot deep. It's about six feet wide by twelve feet long, I'd guess. I'm talking big. To me, it looks like it has water," I assured them, staring at the dark shadow that clearly stood out against the pink-red of the rock. "What do you guys think?"

Both Wes and Eric agreed it looked full.

"There's also a cache of water under one of those big boulders," I added, pointing next to large rocks nearby. John Azar, a hiking friend, had told me about it. Azar named the spot "Starship" because the surrounding hoodoos and blocky boulders reminded him of the bridge of *Star Trek's* USS *Enterprise*, prominently featured in the popular 1960s television show about futuristic space travel.

I had emailed Azar and another friend, Ken Phillips, to confirm the water cache's status before we left, but hadn't heard back. On my previous (and only) visit to Starship Camp with them during November 2003, the pothole had been full, almost to the brim. "We should be good on water," I echoed for a second time, mostly attempting to convince myself.

Harvey Butchart wrote about the very hike we were doing in his logbook. In an April 19, 1975, entry, he specifically addressed the issue of water in this area:

> I would agree with Mitchell that the best way to go from there into South Canyon would be along the top of the Supai. I believe that this loop could be done in one day.... Without stopping to camp, water would not be a problem. [36.8 Mile—South Canyon Loop]

I knew the walk along the top of the Supai to South Canyon and back out would prove tedious, probably a very slow ten miles total. Like Harvey, I believed it could be done in a day. But I elected to make it an overnighter to avoid rushing—to make the trip less of a grunt and more enjoyable.

In hindsight, I managed to ignore the sage caveat within Harvey's summary: "Without stopping to camp, water would not be a problem."

We did, however, stop to camp.

CHAPTER SEVENTEEN

Dirty Little Secrets (Part Two)

37-MILE ROUTE (MITCHELL CANYON) TO SOUTH CANYON

To really experience the desert … you have to imagine what it would be like to drink blood from a lizard or, in the grip of dementia, claw bare-handed through sand and rock for the vestigial moisture beneath a dry wash.

Marc Reisner
Cadillac Desert (1986)

October 2009 (continued)

Thirst can be viciously powerful, even merciless. Like a torture device, intense thirst can drive people to do just about anything—even potentially deadly things, such as drinking antifreeze, sea water, urine, or blood—to relieve their agony.

In the Grand Canyon, people have tried to tear open cacti with their bare hands; or, risking certain injury or death, attempt impossible downclimbs or jump off cliffs to get to water. Ruthless and unrelenting, thirst builds much like the need for oxygen when your head is held underwater. It spurs the same desperate terror, only in slow motion.

An important aside, one that particularly applies to those who hike in the Grand Canyon: It's okay to be a little thirsty. Thirst is generally a friend, not a foe. Think of it like pain, a bodyguard in the literal sense. When you heed its signals, which are mostly gentle, it protects you from harm by keeping your body's water and salt levels safely balanced long before its nudging turns to vicious lashings.

Most people understand that low water intake is bad and leads to dehydration. Unfortunately, what many don't know is that *too much water* can also be dangerous. Drinking more than what your thirst tells you to, or "overdrinking," introduces excessive water into the bloodstream and dilutes your body's blood sodium (salt) level. This may result in the development of a serious illness called hyponatremia. Also referred to as "water intoxication," its symptoms include disorientation and confusion—similar to being drunk on alcohol. In severe cases, hyponatremia causes brain swelling that can result in seizures, coma, and death. Currently, about 90 percent of those with heat illness who end up being admitted to hospital ICUs from the Grand Canyon are there as a result of overdrinking and hyponatremia, *not* underdrinking and dehydration.

Fortunately, hyponatremia, like dehydration, is easily prevented by drinking according to the dictates of actual thirst. Another way to think about this is to consider thirst as an irrigation valve for your body's water needs. When you're thirsty, the valve is open (drink); the tissues in your district need water. Conversely, when that thirst is quenched, the valve is closed (stop drinking); don't flood the system. Continuing to drink after thirst has been quenched is like ongoing skin scratching after an itch has been relieved. It can create a far bigger problem than the symptom you alleviated. Finally, while it's okay to fill your belly with water (like a canteen) at the onset of a hike or after a long break, it's not okay to keep doing so. Instead, if you're feeling really hot but not thirsty, pour that extra water over your body to cool yourself down. It's artificial perspiration, sweat you didn't have to earn.

⌒⌒⌒

We didn't make Starship Camp, even though Wes practically ran down the Mitchell Canyon break. Eric lagged behind, and me in between. We decided to dry camp on a Supai ledge about a half-mile from Starship, using our water to prepare dehydrated meals. Believing we had two potential sources for resupply, we drank our fill and then some through the warm evening, washing down salty meals and snacks with no regard for water rationing.

Up at 6:15 the next morning, we were hiking at a leisurely pace by 7:45. As we closed in on Starship Camp, the words of *Star Trek's* iconic intro popped into my head, which I kept tweaking to fit the day's objective, as well as Weston's and my long-term goal: *Grand Canyon, the Final Frontier. We are the voyagers to the starship Enterprise. Our mission? To boldly go where few have gone before...*

We reached Starship about forty-five minutes later. There, staring into the empty pothole, I took my first (dry) gulp of nervousness. The sculpted pothole's blackened discoloration, which had presented the visual illusion of water from the rim, made the geologic feature look like a burned-out bomb crater.

"Hey, Dad?"

"Yeah?"

"This is a pretty bad sign, isn't it?"

Weston in the bone dry Starship pothole, October 2009.

"Yup."

Wes and I immediately began hunting under boulders and small ledges around Starship looking for the water cache that had been here when I passed through six years earlier. Despite the sense of urgency, per usual, I found myself fascinated by the intricacies of the Esplanade Sandstone. It is the top tier of four different rock types that form the Supai Group. Its stratum erodes into sculpted hoodoos—weird balanced rocks and mushroom-like pedestals—wonderful to explore and, if time allowed, perfect for peekaboo or hide-and-seek. Zipping along at relative warp speed, reaching the Esplanade also shot us 275 million years into the past. Although fun distractions, thoughts of final frontiers, time travel, and peek-a-boo didn't help in the search. A half-hour's worth in the warming air yielded nothing. We sat and waited for Eric to catch up.

"No water?" he asked.

"Nope."

After a short rest, we decided to get moving, which at times became incredibly slow. Unlike western Grand Canyon where the Esplanade lives up to the meaning of its name, "level and expansive" (up to two miles wide), here it's skimpy, sometimes pinching down to two- to three-foot-wide ledges. Landslides frequently obliterate these ledges, leaving sheer gutters filled with loose, unstable rock. Negotiating the gutters is slow and painstaking; each step has to be precise. My hypervigilance on safety now seemed ironic compared to how relatively cavalier I had been about water availability. Using such caution, however, cost us more time and water, all under an unrelenting sun. Again, Wes and I walked with urgency, pushing our pace.

While veering up a break in the cliffs, we stumbled upon evidence of ancient reptiles. Frozen-in-time tetrapod tracks—perhaps of a dozen animals—covered a large slab of Coconino Sandstone. The triangular boulder, about fifteen-feet-tall, sat on edge, the tip of the triangle pointing to the sky. Each five-toed print appeared clawless and about four to five inches in size. They all ran in the same direction, the scramblings of a small herd of pre-dinosaurs. A couple of tracks on another rock were almost as big as my foot.

Called "Diadectomorphs," these terrestrial vertebrates are believed to be an arid-adapted cross between an amphibian and a reptile that roamed the earth at least 30 million years before the first dinosaurs. Indeed, this area—their old stomping ground—was once a massive windblown sea of sand, just as dry or drier than it is now. Finding the site, one worthy of a photo-op, then imagining the short-legged, pigeon-toed, leathery-hided creatures waddling through Sahara-like sand dunes served as another brief but fascinating distraction from our water dilemma.

Reptilian tracks on 15-foot tall boulder. *Anne Miller*

We moved on. Eric followed, catching up with us at rest breaks. This pattern repeated several times. At one rest break, we could hear rushing water. The sound came from the sheer cliff face probably two hundred feet directly below us, tantalizingly close. Vasey's Paradise, as it is known, is a stunning one-hundred-foot waterfall that gushes from the Redwall. It is a must-see for river runners and easily accessed from shore. Knowing that bees or boaters could buzz there within seconds, yet for us to reach it would require climbing gear or a death wish, seemed to mock our predicament.

After sipping parsimoniously, Wes and I inventoried our water supply. I had a liter; Wes had about a half. We were still miles (and hours) from water. Making my anxiety worse, Eric was somewhere behind us. The first real wave of panic jolted through me. I whistled several times. Finally, Eric appeared.

"Tom, we need to get water!" he yelled.

"I know!" I shouted back. "We've been waiting for you!" He eventually caught up, looking grim and sweating profusely. "I'm almost out of water," he said.

"So are we." I could hear the edginess in my voice. "Look, Eric, we need to just get this over with and get out of this sun. We need to get to South Canyon and either head down to the river for water or head up to the rim. There's water in my car. It depends on which option ends up being closer." A few seconds later we headed out again, and like before, in our haste, Weston and I quickly but unintentionally distanced ourselves from Eric.

Reptilian tracks in the Coconino Sandstone. *Tom Myers*

At about five in the afternoon, we reached another large side drainage. We stopped and waited. I could feel myself losing patience; Wes and I could've been nearly out of the Canyon by now. Eric

156

finally appeared. I yelled at him. "Eric, we really need to keep going!"

"Wait there!" he shouted back. He limped over, groaned, took off his pack, then flopped it and himself to the ground. "I'll tell you what we're going to do," he gasped, "and I'll be frank. I can't go any farther. I'm dehydrated and my knee is acting up. I'm going to stay here and set up my camp. You'll hike out and let Ken Phillips know he needs to come get me." (A mutual friend, Ken headed GCNP's Emergency Services.) "He can fly me out of here tomorrow."

I had mixed emotions. Eric was a good friend in bad shape. I felt responsible. For the first time, the thought of one of us dying from dehydration and heatstroke entered my mind, and it nauseated me. So did the thought of leaving Eric, but I knew he was right.

"I'm counting on you guys. I know you still have to hike and will need more water than me, so I'll give you what water I can," he panted.

He emptied about a third of a liter into my bottle. He also drained off some water for himself from beans he had been soaking in a water bottle. I guessed that at most, he had maybe a cup-and-a-half left. It needed to last him all night and at least part of the morning. Wes and I now each had the same, about one-third of a liter. Unfortunately, we still had at least three to four miles yet to hike, plus elevation. We would all be out of water very soon.

In the hot, still air, Wes and I hugged Eric, then marched out. We walked in silence. Thirst began to consume all cognition. In the throes of intense thirst with limited available water, the immediate and seemingly logical remedy is to ration what's left. Resisting the urge to drink, unfortunately, only prolongs the inevitable and allows thirst to build. Yet hoarding, even a little, seems to provide a psychological safety net. There's a terrible reckoning when the last drop is gone.

"Dad," Wes said hesitantly. I turned to him, and we both stopped.

"Can I get a drink?" We had been walking silently in the twilight, finally scrambling into the bone-dry bed of South Canyon.

"Of course." I pulled out my bottle and handed it to him.

No longer able to keep thirst at bay, we were about to take our last swallows of water. We both drank a couple of mouthfuls, savoring every molecule. Turning the bottle upside down, I shook the last drops onto my tongue. Then I tried to eat a tiny piece of a Pop-Tart, but my mouth couldn't make saliva, a sign of advanced dehydration. Neither of us had peed in hours. We had no water left and we had no bailout.

We slowly resumed walking. An hour or so later, I estimated we were less than two miles from where the Yukon sat on the rim, 1,500 feet higher. It had an ice chest loaded with drinks. We were also at least four miles from the Colorado River. Going up-canyon seemed the most rational choice.

"See the ridge line, Wes?" I asked in the darkness. "That notch is where the trailhead is and where the Yukon is parked," I explained, pointing to the visibly jagged rim silhouetted in the starlight. "If something happens to me, look for the trail immediately below that point and veer up to the rim. Don't keep heading up-canyon. Okay? Stay focused and watch your footing. Breaking an ankle here and now could be really bad."

Staying focused under such circumstances anywhere, but especially in the Grand Canyon, is extremely difficult. All thoughts zero-in on one thing. Kenton Grua journaled about this on day three of his first attempt to walk the length. Far more serious than stepping on cactus spines, on October 3, 1973, while hiking in 90+°F weather, he ran out of water.

> I have about 2 miles to walk yet to go and only a few swallows of water left…My mouth is dry and my tongue swollen. The route down is difficult but there! Swallowing my last few drops of water like a thirsty puppy, I cautiously begin the descent. The most difficult part of it is maintaining caution as the thirst builds in my throat like a prairie grass fire.

Wes heard the stress in my voice, urging him to stay focused. "Okay," he replied softly. We continued to walk in dusty silence.

Then we heard a faint slosh sound. I took another step. It was unmistakable and coming from my pack. We still had some water! I tore into the pack. Buried in the bottom, I found a heaven-sent bottle I had somehow overlooked. I shook it, then guesstimated that we would each get about half a cup.

"Here you go, Wes," I announced, forcing a smile with my parched lips as I handed him the bottle.

He looked at me, his gaze earnest, then handed the bottle back.

"No, Dad. You take the first swallow."

I choked up; I knew he had to be at least as thirsty as me. He was also a kid struggling at times in those difficult and sometimes selfish teenage years, where it's all about you and no one understands. As we both took our final swallows, I suppressed the tears I doubted I could make.

After confirming that our last drop had vanished, we tramped through an oak thicket, probably less than a mile from the switchback ascent.

"With all these trees, there must be water nearby," I told Wes. "Maybe a seep. Let's look around." Hopeful, we crashed between the trees, then scanned the cliff walls, peering through dust in our flashlight beams, looking for cracks with moss and seepage. We found none.

Defeated, we veered back into the creek bed. In a short distance, we came upon a low spot near a bend. Within our lights were deep, hardened, and dry fissures in what clearly had been mud.

I knew that dry creek beds in the desert sometimes hid water, especially in their bends. Thirstier than I've ever been in my life and with nothing to lose, I asked Wes to help me break out a few chunks of the cracking, asphalt-like earth next to a boulder. After we did this, we shined our headlamps into the crater we'd created and peered inside...

Craig Childs, author of *The Secret Knowledge of Water*, wrote an essay titled "The Memory of Water: Life in Ephemeral Water Holes." In this 2009 piece, which appeared in the spring issue of the journal *Wings*, he described the euphoria he felt at finding underground water, hidden by Mother Nature. The life-giving liquid revealed, like a dirty little secret:

> At this empty water hole I was not in my waiting phase. I was very thirsty. I put my back into digging down through sand, spraying it out behind me until I reached a layer of putrid black clay that was slightly damp. At that layer I began digging outward, forming a basin. Black water beaded out of the clay. I quickly gathered flat pieces of sandstone and built up the edges of my basin, holding back the black clay. Clear water appeared through my sandstone cistern, slowly filling a cup in the bottom that I gathered in my palms and drank. It tasted good. After an hour, I had a couple of gallons of fresh water.

While the crater we had created held no water, it did have the tarry blackness of fresh mud. Kneeling, we put our hands in the hole. The earth felt cool and damp. Excited, we tore at the soil like frenzied badgers, painfully jamming dirt under our fingernails, flinging it out, hearing it spatter like rain onto the vegetation behind us. Then, before our eyes, dirty, oily-black water began to pool. Within seconds, it grew to an inch in diameter and a half-inch deep. Then two inches and spreading. I felt beyond giddy. I kid you not, the theme song from the 1960s TV show *The Beverly Hillbillies* popped into my head: *And then one day he was shootin' at some food and up through the ground come a-bubblin' crude. Oil that is, black gold, Texas tea.*

We stared transfixed as the lifesaving, more-precious-than-black-gold commodity oozed from the ground. Within a couple of minutes, it had pooled about an inch deep and six inches in diameter. Lying on our stomachs, we took turns sucking it dry. We looked at each other laughing, flashlight beams bouncing off our faces, water dribbling off our noses, lips, and chins. We slurped for half an hour, then finally ate.

Kenton felt similar elation when he finally reached the life-saving water of the Colorado that hot day in October of '73.

Oh, what ecstasy, to dive naked into the mother river and feel her icy waters against my skin. I drink it in large gulps as I swim. Then I sit on the bank and shiver and laugh. It was a pretty close call, and, in many ways, I am damn lucky to be alive.

After eating, our ordeal over, Wes fell asleep quickly. I looked at him. He still seemed so innocent. Tears previously stifled by intention and dehydration now welled in my eyes. Never as a father have I felt so utterly horrible about something I put my child through. My error could've killed him. And me. I couldn't sleep, thinking about the nightmare of what-might-have-been.

I also thought of Eric, alone, tired, and *very, very thirsty*. I bet he wasn't sleeping either. Yet I knew trying to bring him any water now would be way too dangerous. I closed my eyes, but my mind continued to race. I lay awake nearly the entire night, including two hours sitting up and, spoonful by spoonful, filling our water bottles from the tea-saucer-sized pothole.

I woke Wes up at sunrise the next morning, determined to get help for Eric. We quickly ate a couple of Pop-Tarts and headed out. A nasty thicket of vegetation lay just ahead of us and we were both thankful we hadn't tried to push through it in the dark. Cairns suddenly appeared, then switchbacks. By seven, we were at the rim and the Yukon.

Luckily, Becky had bought me a new phone and we had cell reception—just barely. One bar out of five flickered as I dialed the local emergency number for Grand Canyon National Park. The dispatcher referred me to the Search and Rescue ranger on call for the day. Embarrassed, I then told Clint Calan (whom I knew), our story. And apologized. Next, I spoke to another friend, South Rim ranger and paramedic, Brandon Torres.

"I'm really sorry about this, Brandon. I've never had to call you guys before."

"Hey, it's okay, Tom, really. That's why we're here," Brandon interjected. "For what it's worth, we had to rescue another couple of old-timers last week. Anyway, it'll be nice to see some new territory other than Royal Arch Creek. We've had three back-to-back evacs there."

"Do you want me to wait here?" I asked.

"No, we won't stop on the rim. We'll probably just pick Eric up and take him right to Flagstaff."

"Thanks, Brandon. I really appreciate it."

"You bet."

Wes and I drove away, knowing the NPS would likely reach Eric within the hour. We were at Vermilion Cliffs, eating breakfast mostly in silence, when that hour came.

"You think Eric is all right, Dad?" Wes asked.

Eric Gueissaz. *David Zickl*

"I think so. He's tough," I responded.

"What are we going to tell Mom?" he wondered.

"The truth. I almost killed all three of us. I need to own it," I admitted. Two-and-a-half hours later, we were in Flagstaff. We shuffled quietly into the house. Becky instantly picked up on our somber mood.

"Okay, what's the matter?" she challenged. "I know something happened."

I looked at Weston. He shrugged. Becky looked at Wes, then back at me, frowning.

"I'll tell you, Mom," Wes finally said. He told her his take on the trip, convincing her he wasn't any worse for the wear and it had been a learning experience. Ultimately, I offered my culpability-filled version. She didn't like either one. Then I got a call from Eric.

I respected and admired Eric on so many levels. Thoughtful and private, he always considered his words before speaking. I had once asked him about John Thybony and some of his favorite memories of the man. "I do have some good ones," he reminisced. "But I also think they're best left to be what they are, Tom. Memories. I hope you understand." I did.

"I'm doing fine, a lot better now," Eric told me. He said that he'd been given three liters of intravenous saline for advanced dehydration. He also reported that his knee felt much better after rest and ice packs at the hospital.

I drove to Flagstaff Medical Center to pick him up. Wracked with guilt for getting my friend into a truly life-threatening predicament, I apologized profusely. In his more than forty years of hiking the Canyon, and thousands of miles, he had never before needed to be evacuated. Yet he emphatically declined the apology, saying it wasn't necessary. Instead, the philosopher in him deflected blame to another source.

"Reality, Tom. That's what it is!" he declared in his Swiss accent, grinning and wagging his index finger in the air. "The Canyon is reality, thank you very much. It can kick your ass, but it's more than a pain in the butt. It's a lesson for life. To persevere and go on."

CHAPTER EIGHTEEN

George Gets Burned in Cremation

TANNER CANYON TO PHANTOM RANCH

Hey, George, there's some hulking, gravelly voiced, Popeyed-forearmed Neanderthal asking for you. Says he's going to get even with that treacherous Steck. Said his name is Max, Big Max.

Gary Ladd
Foreword/*Grand Canyon Loop Hikes II* (1993)

December 2009

"Hey, Wes, can I have some of your potato chips?" Alex begged. Wes held out his can of Pringles, then suddenly pulled it back, clutching it close to his chest, guarding it. He tucked down his chin, narrowed his eyes, and looked at his cousin Peter and me.

"She wants it. She's always hungry." His voice sounded high-pitched, raspy, and vile, a near-perfect mimick of the creature Gollum's in *Lord of the Rings* where a giant spider tries to eat Frodo. Fourteen-year-old Wes knew his Gollum impersonation creeped-out his eighteen-year-old sister. Wearing an evil grin, Wes cuddled the Pringles can to his chest, then stroked it, gently.

"My precioussss..." he hissed.

⌒〜〜⌒

Two days earlier we had peg-legged through snowdrifts on the Tanner Trail that sometimes reached our knees. December 2009 had already provided an unusually good amount of snow, with more snow and cold weather predicted for

163

our four-day, sixty-five-mile hike to Phantom. In addition to Alex, my twenty-year-old nephew Peter also joined us; my old college buddy, Mark Crane, ran our shuttle and tagged along for a few hours of hiking that first day. We stopped at the top of the Redwall for lunch and soaked in the spectacular views.

In the distance, the Colorado River made a sweeping bend near Tanner Rapid. Seeing the river brought up memories of my Hermit hike with Mark more than a quarter-century earlier.

"So, Mark, do you think my turd is still bobbing around in Hermit?" I joked.

"No. I think it washed up on shore and it's getting fossilized, like you and me." He winked.

"Ain't that the truth! I wish you were coming all the way, but we'll see you in a few days, right?"

"Yep. I wish I was too, but gotta get back to pulling teeth." For the past fifteen-plus years, Mark had been an oral surgeon (not a dentist) in Flagstaff. "See you New Year's Eve." He saluted, then started back up the trail.

In four days, Mark planned to hike in with his fourteen-year-old daughter, Janelle, along with Becky, our daughter Brittany, and a few other friends. They expected to meet us at The Tipoff, the junction of the South Kaibab Trail with the Tonto Trail; among other things, it had composting toilets, which made it a perfect pitstop. From there, only three miles would separate us from our destination: the trail crew bunkhouse near Phantom Ranch.

The NPS had offered us the opportunity to celebrate the New Year at the bunkhouse as a perk in exchange for my volunteer work as a medical advisor. Compared to sleeping in a tent, it was pure luxury, offering a big living room, kitchen, two bathrooms, warm showers, two bedrooms with bunk beds, games, books, even a guitar—better than The Ritz—and all at the bottom of the Canyon.

The hike down Tanner went great and—by lucky coincidence—we got to share a river runner's camp with boating friends at Tanner. The next day we made ten miles along the Escalante Route to our camp at Hance Creek by early afternoon. After another sixteen miles along the Tonto to Grapevine Canyon on day three, we settled into camp just as the weather turned nasty. Our tents pitched, we ducked inside: Wes and Alex in one, Peter and me in the other. Soon, giggling erupted. The laughter coming from Wes and Alex's tent was far too enticing to miss out on, so Peter and I invited ourselves in. Nestled shoulder to shoulder, we started sharing food, including those Pringles.

❦

"Gimme those, you little jerk!" Alex punched his arm, then grabbed the chips and laughed with the rest of us. The lighthearted mood came as a welcome flip-flop from our previously stressed-out one during the dry and dangerous conditions in Marble Canyon months earlier. Within that perspective, I also embraced the rainy weather.

Sunlight briefly spangled the cliffs when I rousted everyone early the next morning. We needed to make seventeen miles to reach the Phantom bunkhouse. As we stepped from the tents fog settled in, as did a drizzle of freezing rain, which soon morphed into sleet that pelted down on us in waves. Three hours and ten miles into our hike, as we neared Cremation Canyon, the sleet turned to snow. Hiking around Cremation became a sloppy slog. Alex, wearing new hiking boots, developed blisters

Alex and Wes. *Tom Myers*

and started limping. Meanwhile, Wes—wet, cold, and cranky—let the weather get the best of him and stormed off ahead in a beeline trudge, shortcutting the trail. He disappeared from view in the whiteout as Alex, Peter, and I tried to keep up.

"Hey, Wes, wait up!" she and I yelled. He ignored us both.

"Wes is being a little turd," Alex remarked between tears.

Removing her boots, we found a huge, torn-open blister on her heel. I put a dressing on it, then with teeth gritted, she squeezed her foot back into the wet boot, and we started trudging again. When we topped a rise, we spotted Wes, who had finally stopped at The Tipoff's composting toilets near the South Kaibab Trail, taking shelter below the deck attached to the outhouse structure. As the snowy conditions offered no let up, we quickly took cover with Wes.

As luck would have it, Becky, Brittany, Mark, and Janelle arrived fifteen minutes later. For about ten minutes before they arrived, we huddled under the deck. During that time, after I scolded Wes for running ahead and ignoring us, we fired up our cook stove and made hot chocolate and our last freeze-dried meal, a bacon-and-eggs breakfast. Once warm and fed, Wes quit sulking and apologized. It seemed fitting that the apology for his crappy mood came when we were standing next to an outhouse. That got me thinking about a time a decade earlier when, not very far away, I had been a turd myself, a real stinker to George Steck.

March 1998

"Yeah, I was ready to kick your ass when I read that letter!" John Southrey told me shortly after initial introductions were made. He had flown into Phoenix and driven to the Grand Canyon to stay at our South Rim Village house in advance of a surprise party John Azar had masterminded for George Steck in Cremation Canyon. Nearly two years had passed since George's practical-joke letter to Southrey. He and several buddies had tried to concoct a payback, but to date nothing great had presented itself.

Azar, friend and hiking companion of both men, had come up with an idea. In November 1997, he wrote to Southrey, explaining his scheme: "I'm planning a surprise party for George Steck on Saturday, March 14, 1998. It will take a well-organized conspiracy to pull it off and I hope you can take part. Here's my plan…"

Azar and George would camp outside of the park at Red Butte on Friday the thirteenth; the next day, they would hike into Cremation Canyon to spend two nights. Azar would also invite a bunch of George's closest friends. A few of the invitees, however, would "bail" a few days before, leaving (he hoped) George "feeling a little sad."

A forlorn George, along with Azar, would then mope alone into the party spot in Cremation Canyon. Before they arrived, the alleged party-poopers would

Jacek Macias, John Southrey and me on O'Neill Butte. *Jim Ohlman*

have already secretly hiked in and squirreled away food and drinks for the party. Finally, we'd all jump out from the rocks we'd hidden behind and yell "Surprise!" Azar's scheme was intended as payback for the "skeletally disadvantaged" letter to Southrey.

Azar worked as an architect and contractor in Albuquerque. Along with his buddy Billy Driscoll, a microbiologist from Washington, D.C., and Jacek Macias, an engineer from Chicago, Azar had shown up at the house my family and I lived in on the rim the day before the hike. They came for dinner, along with George and Mike Steck. Much to my embarrassment, the "skeletally disadvantaged" John Southrey accompanied them. A CPA from Austin, Texas, he looked fit and every bit like a capable climber.

John told me about receiving George's letter, and his reaction. It couldn't have come at a worse time, he confided, after he'd arrived home from a fishing trip to Canada. "I was really pissed at you when I read the letter," he groused. "I got detained at the airport because they thought my fire-starting kit was a bomb trigger. They harassed me for several minutes. Then, when I finally got into Austin, I was exhausted. It was in the wee hours of the morning.

"My wife, Judy, who was in on the joke, was there to pick me up. She said, 'John, I'm sorry to tell you this but you have a *bad letter* waiting for you at home.' When we got home, I read the letter and literally exploded! I was so pissed at you and the park service! I totally believed it! That's when my wife said, 'Calm down. You need to call George Steck. I think he knows what's going on.' When I called George, he confessed that he was the one who came up with the fake letter. I've been trying to figure out a way to get even with him ever since. He's smarter than hell and not easily fooled."

Another invitee also showed up—Jim Ohlman, the Harvey Butchart protégé. I'd known him casually for several years; we met during my research on Harvey and Ron Mitchell, as mentioned earlier. A lanky guy, Ohlman had hiked multiple times with Harvey, logging nearly as many hiking miles as his mentor (12,000). He had also climbed 150 of the 154 named Canyon buttes, nearly twice as many as Harvey. Along with Ohlman, Southrey, Macias, and me, he would head out for Cremation Canyon in the morning. Azar, Driscoll, and Mike Steck would come in later with George after we'd set up for the party and hidden ourselves away.

When morning came, knowing that George and the others would be lagging behind, and with time to burn, the four of us detoured off-trail to climb O'Neill Butte, Ohlman in the lead. Southrey, harboring no hard feelings, chatted with me. After getting better acquainted, our conversation turned to George.

"So, John," I asked, "Do you think this party is a good payback for George's letter?"

"Oh, not at all! This party will be very cool. Don't get me wrong!—it's awesome that Azar set it up, and I'm sure it will be a surprise, but it's not the same. I mean, it's really funny now and a relief that it was all a joke, but he had me madder than hell with that letter."

I agreed. For George, this party would likely have a feel-good astonishment but not the swing of emotions reflective of a great practical joke: shock-anger-laughter-admiration.

"Yeah, it'd be nice to get him back. I just haven't had any great ideas," Southrey lamented.

After the climb, the four of us stopped at The Tipoff to pick up a stash of beer and food left by a Fred Harvey mule wrangler as a favor to Azar. We still made Cremation by early afternoon. Once there, we dumped our packs and tucked away the party supplies. Knowing George lagged way behind, Macias and I jogged down into the narrows of Cremation Canyon just for the heck of it. An hour later, we returned to see that Azar and others had arrived; they told us that George and Mike—moving slowly—were within minutes of the camp.

"Okay, listen up! We'll all jump out and yell surprise after George gets here!" Azar instructed. "Now, everybody hide!"

George eventually wobbled in, eyes glassy and body teetering. As he did, we all jumped into view yelling, "Surprise!"

At first, George appeared flustered, then his face broke into a huge grin when he found himself suddenly surrounded by many of his closest friends, all saying hello and giving him hugs and back slaps. Then, at Azar's direction, we quickly went to work to set up for the party, gathering the stuff that had been hidden away.

What we eventually laid out was unlike any backpack party I've ever been to, before or since. It even rivaled the best river-trip parties (almost no limits on food and beverages) I'd experienced. First, we arranged an adult beverage bar of beer, wine, and margaritas. Using Tapeats Sandstone ledges as serving tables, we set out guacamole, chips, salsa, and cheese and crackers for appetizers. Azar steadily fried corn tortillas and heated up his precooked taco meat. Finally, he arranged a taco bar: lettuce, tomatoes, cheese, onions, sour cream, salsa, and green chilies.

"Hey, Uncle George, want me to fix you a margarita?" Mike asked our guest of honor.

"I'd love one." He sounded recharged.

Mike handed it over.

"Hey, Uncle George, want some tacos?" Mike continued.

George said yes.

I walked over to Mike.

"Why do you call your dad 'Uncle George,' Mike?" I asked, confused.

"Oh, that?" Mike chuckled. "Yeah, it's kind of funny. When I was a kid and tried to ask my dad a question, I'd be like, 'Dad! Hey Dad!, Oh Dad! Yo Dad! Dad! Dad! Daaaad!?' It seemed like I'd say 'Dad' over and over. I knew he wasn't deaf, but he had tuned me out. Maybe it was because I was always bugging him, asking him questions. Anyway, it seemed impossible to get his attention. Then I noticed one of my cousins walk over and go, 'Hey, Uncle George?' and he instantly turned and said, 'What?' That was when I figured out that to get his attention, I had to call him 'Uncle George.' It works pretty well. Watch."

"How's it going, Dad?" Mike spoke nonchalantly. We looked over at George. Nothing. No reaction. He seemed lost in his margarita.

"Hey, Uncle George," he vocalized with essentially the same tone and decibel level. George instantly turned and looked at Mike.

Mike smiled at him, then turned and grinned at me.

The party buzzed with happy commotion. Conversations and toasts kicked in, mostly laced with funny tales about George and his exploits. Dinner went off without a hitch. As the sun set, the party seemed to gain momentum. Clearly, the bash had successfully met Azar's goal: a big, fun gathering that caught George by surprise.

More than an hour into it, it began to dawn on me that this party didn't even approach what could be considered a balanced retribution for George's dastardly duping of John Southrey, one in which I had been complicit. Now that I knew him a bit, I felt a twinge of guilt. Southrey, clearly a good guy, seemed pretty even-tempered. Yet George's letter agitated him to the point where he'd felt an incredible need to put his boot in my butt.

I pondered that while drinking a beer. Then, suddenly, I had a revelation—a devious, Machiavellian idea to even the score and ease my conscience.

"Hey, Uncle George," I called out.

George quickly turned, just as he had in Mike's demonstration.

"Yeah?"

"Can I ask you a question?"

"Sure."

"So, the disclaimer you have at the beginning of your book, the one that says the author and publisher have no responsibility for any injury that occurs to someone using your book …." I was referring to the legalese included to prevent lawsuits, which George printed in bold at the beginning of both *Loop Hikes* books as a "Warning Introduction:"

Neither the author or publisher assumes responsibility for any injury that may result from taking any treks described in this book. This is a guidebook only; once in the outback you are on your own.

"Yeah, what about it?" he asked.

"Has it worked for you?" I queried.

"Well, I don't know. *Why?*" he probed, now less glassy-eyed.

"I'm asking because I've been working on writing a medical field guide for treating injuries and illness in the desert wilderness and I'm a little concerned about liability."

"I don't know if it works. It's never been tested."

"So, you haven't heard anything from the guy who was in the clinic this summer, after getting in trouble doing one of your loop hikes?" I lied, fabricating the "trouble" and "the guy."

"No, I didn't!" His eyes widened. "What happened?"

"Oops! It's probably nothing, George. Sorry to bring it up during your party," I stammered, trying to sound sincerely sheepish.

"No, no! It's okay!" he blurted, now totally focused. "Tell me what happened."

"Awww, George, this is your party. It's not a big deal. We can talk about it later."

"No, no. Please tell me! Now I'm curious. What happened?" He was practically begging.

Uh-oh. I hadn't thought far enough ahead to invent detail. I didn't think I'd need to. Nearly a decade had passed since the publication of George's first book, and I guessed that a minor mishap or two by someone using it might have come up by now. Gary Ladd had even joked about it in his foreword to *Loop Hikes II*, hinting there would be trouble. Ladd wrote that "Big Max" (see the epigraph at the start of this chapter), presumably feeling misled, was going to "get even with that treacherous Steck."

The intensity of George's interest caught me off-guard and gave me second thoughts. The whole idea of trying to hoodwink him in the middle of his party suddenly seemed a little cruel. But then again, with my help, George had worked up Southrey into a near-frenzy. I knew what Southrey would want. Plus, abetting him could ease my own guilt. A win-win. At George's expense, of course. *But hey, we're in a canyon called "Cremation" and this is a semi-roasting of George. Shouldn't he expect to get a little burned?*

As I continued to vacillate, the final resolution of the decency-versus-deception dilemma came rather easily in the form of a simple question.

What would George do?

"Okay, George," I finally conceded, turning and looking him square in the eye. "I'll tell you what happened." My tone turned serious. "I didn't actually see the guy. The other doctor I work with did. Some hiker, a dude in his forties, was flown out of the Canyon apparently in heatstroke. He was yelling and upset that he didn't find water on the hike like he believed he would from reading your book."

"Really? This is news to me," George remarked, now squinting at me through his spectacles. His face had the same expression I'd seen at our meeting in the clinic, except now his features were firmer and more stony than ever. I thought he might be onto me. *He knows I'm fibbing. He's scanning for cracks, something that will make my fib falter, my corruption crumble.* I tried to stay focused and not smirk. I imagined my face as pothole water in which George saw only a stoic reflection of himself.

He finally sighed, and his features relaxed. "I haven't heard about this yet," George confided, now seeming both vexed and a little sad.

I looked down at my feet and kicked a few stones, my guilty conscience gaining traction over skullduggery. *Poor old George!* For a moment I considered coming clean. *Wait a second! Poor old George? What about poor old John?!* Finally, I reached a mental truce, a two-fold decision. First, I would remain true to the lofty standards of George Steck in practical joke warfare. Second, because I loved the man, I would pull my last punch, ever so slightly, to soften the blow.

"Yeah, well, here's the good news, George," I said. "At least he didn't die. In fact, I know he was treated and released. So, it couldn't have been that bad. We see that kinda heat stuff all the time. People end up fine. Plus, I bet it was his own fault. I also heard he was kinda stupid. You know the type, a dull normal," I added with a wry smile. "He had to be. Your books are great. They really are. Your advice is always accurate. Personally, I don't think it'll amount to anything. *Okay?*"

"Well, okay, good," George responded, looking a little less slumped.

"Honestly, I really don't want you worrying about it, George. I think it'll be fine," I confidently added while slapping him on the back to perk him up. Then with a shit-faced grin (part beer, part glee), I cheerfully announced, "This is such an awesome party! Isn't it? Aren't you having a good time, George?"

He stared at me.

"Here," I smiled, offering him a Coors. "Have a beer, on me."

By morning, much of my smugness had dissipated and guilt had taken its place. Over a leisurely breakfast, I talked to George again but about a different subject: tips on walking the length. His free sharing made me feel even guiltier. I pulled Southrey aside and filled him in on what I'd told George the night before about the fictitious heatstroke patient.

"George seemed a little rattled by it. Now I'm feeling like a rat, John. Do you think I should break it to him today and tell him it was all a joke?" I asked.

"Oh! No! Absolutely not! Don't tell him anything! This is perfect! I work in the medical malpractice insurance field and know lawyer lingo. I'll write a letter to George saying that he's going to be sued by the heatstroke guy! That'll have George shitting his pants, but he's gonna love it!" He laughed.

George received the letter four months later. While George didn't shit his pants, I almost did from laughing when I read a sneak preview of John's "lawyer letter."

Another thing stands out from my memory about the Cremation party: a conversation George and I had about his Ordeal by Rubble. That dialogue, like a defibrillator, jump-started my nearly comatose goal to hike the Canyon's length.

> Tom,
>
> George and I are even!
>
> After George received this fictitious letter that I made up, he immediately went to the kitchen to prepare for himself a margarita. He then sat down again and reread it, and after Helen awoke from a nap, he came into the bedroom with a margarita for her. Helen was surprised it was margarita time so early in the evening, and that's when he said, "Helen, it looks like we are going to be sued."
>
> He learned within the hour it was all a joke.
>
> — John

Bertrand, Jacobs & Hillard, LLP Attorneys At Law

███████████████████

123 La Posada Lane
Suite 302

San Antonio, Texas 78217
210-805-0933
Fax: 210-805-0997

July 15, 1998

Mr. George Steck
8503 La Palomita Ave. NE
Albuquerque, N.M. 87111

Dear Mr. Steck:

This letter is notice to you about this firm's representation of Mr. Jason Kolrec, our client and the claimant in this matter.

Mr. Kolrec suffered serious and permanent injuries while backpacking in Grand Canyon National Park, AZ. on August 3, 1997. Mr. Kolrec relied upon your guidebook GRAND CANYON LOOP HIKES I (specifically your *Circumambulation of Powell Plateau* hike described on pages 69-87).

Our client was a relatively inexperienced hiker, and it was his reliance upon your negligent guidance in terms of hiking times and the reliability of water (sources) that were the direct cause of his injuries. Specifically, on day six of Mr. Kolrec's trip, he was unable to find the "Good Flowing Water" at a place you called "Key Spring" (a water source you stated as being reliable on page 85).

As the result of running out of water, our client suffered severe dehydration and heatstroke resulting in a permanent loss of motor function in his left facial muscles and a 35% loss of vision in his left eye.

Mr. Kolrec had to be airlifted out of this remote area of the park at considerable expense, and he subsequently has incurred medical expenses and lost wages exceeding $78,000 year-to-date. It is expected that he will never be able to return to his regular occupation as a senior computer programmer, and that his anticipated total "loss of wage earning capacity" is well in excess of $1,000,000. It has also been determined by Mr. Kolrec's primary care physician that his future medical and rehabilitation expenses will exceed $110,000 in addition to the $78,000 already incurred.

We want to enter into prompt negotiations with you and your attorney to discuss an amicable settlement to Mr. Kolrec's claim of negligence against you. Please contact me within the next three weeks to resolve this matter. If I have not been contacted by Monday, August 7, 1998, our firm will immediately file suit on behalf of Mr. Kolrec against you in the 139th District Court of Bexar County, TX.

Sincerely,

William Jacobs
Attorney at Law (TX Bar No. 113456)

df

The fake attorney letter that John Southrey sent to George Steck. *Steck family archives*

George Steck, Don Peterson, Adair Peterson, Allen Steck, and Robert Benson at Lees Ferry.
Steck family archives

CHAPTER NINETEEN

The Ordeal by Rubble

START OF STECK-LED THRU-HIKE, 1982

Red exhaustion rips at your throat
And salt sweat spills off your forehead and mats
your eyelids and brows
And drips on the burning ground
And your legs start to turn to rubber and collapse like a balloon.
"Pretty soon I've got to rest.
How much farther?
What's the good of all this God damn work anyway?"

Terry and Renny Russell
On the Loose (1967)

September 1982

Five years had passed since the "Down the Gorge with Uncle George" trip, and now an entirely different group traveled with him in Elmo, his VW van, to Lees Ferry. At this isolated spot on the Colorado River, sound resonates widely in all directions; like a dinner bell, tire-crunched gravel signals a vehicle's arrival to anyone nearby.

When Elmo, with George at the wheel, pulled up, a young man wearing glasses, a backpack, frayed cut-offs, and hiking boots approached the van. For someone who had been backpacking for two months, he seemed amazingly little the worse for wear. Of the four occupants who piled out of the van, only one needed to be introduced to the backpacker—George's brother Allen.

"Al, this is Robert," George said.

"Nice to finally meet you," Al acknowledged, extending his hand. "I've heard a lot about you." The young man had a stiff grip.

"Likewise," he responded.

Al had been hearing George speak about Robert Benson for several years. At twenty-six, Benson had a reputation as an extraordinary hiker, proving himself to be in an elite category. Conversely, Benson was equally well aware that Al Steck was no ordinary outdoorsman. At fifty-six, he had a reputation as a world-class climber and mountaineer. Nearly identical in height and build, Benson and Al likely saw a reflection of themselves in one another, albeit a generation apart.

For George, growing up mostly apart from his brother, he hoped to connect with Al at a deeper level on this trip. He also knew that Robert Benson, a German immigrant, was a somewhat troubled young man. George hoped their trip might serve as a long-lasting, positive inspiration for him.

George, Adair Peterson, Robert Benson, Allen Steck, and Don Peterson at Lees Ferry at the start of the hike. *Steck family archives*

Also hand-picked by George were two other invitees, friends from Albuquerque, Don and Adair Peterson. Like Don Mattox, Don Peterson worked as a researcher at Sandia and Adair, his wife, an accomplished painter, pioneered rock climbs and served as one of the first women to teach technical climbing in New Mexico. In their mid-fifties, both Petersons planned to hike out from Phantom Ranch. Benson was the only young person. They had all gathered to do an eighty-one-day thru-hike of the Canyon. If they succeeded, it would be the first trek of its kind.

George had mulled over this hike for years, at least since his Lees Ferry-to-Lava Falls hike. To attempt this one, far larger in scale, he needed to do two things: first, retire from Sandia labs and second, commit to even more painstaking planning than he normally did.

As thorough as his preparation had been for the '77 trip, he obsessed far more over this hike. Allen Steck later summed up George's organizational efforts for what he called the "mind-bending, 80-day ordeal-by-rubble walk" in his foreword for *Loop Hikes I*:

> We followed along the northern side of the Colorado River, George's
> ingenious route permitting us to spend 52 nights camped by the river

itself. His planning was meticulous, flawless. The requirements of the Park Service necessitated the preparation of an itinerary (which included the placement of 11 caches) that we eventually followed with excruciating precision. Various elements of this imaginative itinerary were a direct result of original explorations by George and his friends … and by Harvey Butchart and others in earlier years.

After last-minute gear-checking and -shuffling, the team took a collective breath so someone could take a group photo. For the three men intending to hike the full distance (the Steck brothers and Benson), it would be the last time they would walk on asphalt for nearly three months.

The trail-less walking below Lees Ferry proved immediately rough and tedious. Exhausted when they arrived at Six Mile Wash, which took the entire day to reach, their enthusiasm drained as reality set in. As a trashed George Steck wrote in his journal that first night:

I was wasted when I arrived at camp and was greeted by hordes of mosquitoes. It was hard to cook or mix margaritas, terrible with no wind to blow them away. The thought of eighty-one days of this is too dismal to think about for long.

Benson, who also journaled, jotted, "It had been quite rough terrain—about as bad as Cataract Canyon," referencing a difficult section about 200 miles upstream. He added: "It sure didn't feel like a promising start on part II of my trip."

"Part I" of his trip had begun two months earlier, on July 4, 1982, in Moab, Utah. After months of planning, researching maps, consulting experts, and methodically placing caches, he walked alone through canyons along the Colorado River and then around the massive shoreline of Lake Powell. By the time Benson reached Lees Ferry, he had already spent fifty-eight days hiking more than 800 miles in the summer heat.

An efficient, steady hiker, Benson knew that alone, he could have covered the distance to Six Mile Wash in far less time than they'd managed that day. But as part of the group, he felt a responsibility to stick with the others and downshifted his pace. They—Adair in particular—still moved far slower than he expected, and his frustration fermented. Benson offered to carry some of Adair's gear, but she declined, blaming her slow pace on lingering bronchitis. She told Benson she thought she'd improve in the next few days as she got her wind and hiking legs.

Still feeling annoyed in camp, Benson confided to his journal that he doubted she would have any fun the first few days. As a result, he bet he wouldn't either.

Nevertheless, he accepted it as a small tradeoff for the most meaningful time in his life.

George met Benson in 1976, introduced by friend and Sandia coworker John Shunny. Unlike Steck or Mattox or Don Peterson, Shunny worked as a journalist, not an engineer or scientist. He and his wife, Paige, hosted Benson in their home. When John discovered that his nineteen-year-old houseguest had a blossoming love of hiking, what to do next came instantly.

> I introduced him to my friends, George Steck and Don Mattox, both of them veteran Canyon runners who do it the hard way, on foot. At first, they were put off by this young man, a recent arrival who talked brashly, even arrogantly, of long forays into the Canyon. They knew that the Canyon record was replete with stories of half-baked expeditions, where an overestimate of resources and an underestimate of the challenge produced disaster. But Robert redeemed himself on backpacks in the Canyon with George and Don. It was clear that he was competent down there among the carnivorous limestone. About this time when someone would ask me what our house guest did, I'd say that Robert was a professional backpacker who took work breaks.

For the next several years, Benson hiked with George, the older man serving as mentor for the younger, who seemed to have a chip on his shoulder. George stoked Benson's fire and confidence for adventuring in the Grand Canyon by including him on challenging loop hikes. Eventually, Benson began to venture out on his own, upping the challenge with each successive hike. Hitting his stride in 1981, the competitive German became determined to do something much bigger and far more challenging to make his own mark.

Benson learned from George about Kenton Grua. He also knew Grua had done his hike entirely on the south side. Benson then told George he wanted to walk the Canyon's length on the north side, sounding determined to become the first to do so.

When Adair Peterson, a serious Canyon hiker, got wind of his goal, she felt concerned. Adair, whom Benson respected, talked him into postponing his objective until 1982 to gain more experience. In the meantime, a man named Bill Ott knocked off the first full traverse on the north side. According to George, when Benson found out, "it bothered the hell out of him." He remained annoyed with Adair until George reportedly helped talk him into something far more stupendous: become the first person to hike the length of Grand Canyon on *both* sides.

Benson initially bought into the idea, but then decided even that wasn't grand enough. To prove his preeminence, he came up with his own version of a Canyon über-hike … not just any hike, but the HIKE-TO-END-ALL-HIKES in the region: he would walk from Moab, Utah, along the Colorado River to the upper reaches of Lake Mead, then turn around and do it in reverse. Colossal in scope, it totaled roughly 4,000 miles, the equivalent distance of flying from New York to Mexico City and back. By comparison, it made George's current trek in Grand Canyon seem trivial. Yet, the first day of that Grand Canyon trek had proven to be anything but.

Fortunately, as Adair predicted, both her leg strength and balance, as well at her respiratory stamina, improved. As she pepped up, so did the group's communal mood. After bumming some beers from river runners on day two, they celebrated. They partied again when Benson found a couple of beers and a bottle of sherry in the sand three days later. Each member enjoyed some alcohol during evenings in camp, especially Benson. Some days, it was the only thing he enjoyed.

For Benson, the honeymoon was over by the end of the first week. Moody and frustrated, with little patience for the others, he sought out ever-more time alone. This change in attitude did not surprise George. He knew Benson preferred solitary hikes, particularly when the trips lasted more than a week. The decision to hike with anyone seemed to involve a mental tug-of-war for Benson. George had known that being in a group would try Benson's patience. He just didn't expect Benson's mood to turn sour so quickly, nor, as he would discover, to have the younger man's frustration directed at him. At first, Benson only complained in his journal, as noted in this entry for day four.

> The day had a bad start. I woke up with George screaming in his rough morning voice, "time to get up." It sounded like a sonic boom in the peaceful Garden of Eden. My world of sweet dreams harshly exploded to be replaced by the cruel environment of reality. I hate to be awakened other than by nature, especially when it's still pitch dark—6:15 a.m. I remembered that George wanted to get an early start.

Benson then announced to the group, "I'm going to sleep as far from George as I can." For George, while the comment stung, it wasn't completely unexpected. Neither were Benson's complaints of stomach trouble on the morning of day nine. Over the years, George and Benson had become as close as Benson would allow, George always considerate of the younger man's depressive mood swings. These could kick in quickly, sometimes without warning, and were often bookended by the abdominal pain that had also plagued Benson for years, long before he saw the Grand Canyon, or even the US.

Robert Benson (whose birth surname was Eschka) was born in 1956 in Weidenberg, Germany, a medium-sized city of about 6,000 located in the Bavarian district of Bayreuth. Eleven years had passed since the fall of Adolph Hitler's Third Reich and the Allied troop invasion of Berlin, four hours away. He was one of three children in a family headed by a Nazi sympathizer who still believed in Aryan superiority—that Germans constituted a supreme race, physically and mentally stronger and intended by Providence to dominate other races.

Though bright, Robert suffered from undiagnosed dyslexia, a condition that fully manifested at age twelve. His grades fell from As to Ds, and his father—reportedly overbearing, bitter, and angry at his less-than-perfect son— frequently lashed out verbally, chastising Robert for his failings. Depressed, anxious, and desperate to escape his father's wrath, Robert dropped out of school and ran away to France. Stressed and alone, he later confided to George that while in Paris, he "lived on the streets, drinking from the gutter and eating out of garbage cans." As time would tell, neither his stomach nor his psyche ever fully recovered.

Robert finally became so sick that he had to return home, where the father- son relationship cascaded from bad to worse. Willful and fixated on a permanent escape, he set his eyes on the mythic landscapes of the American West, having become infatuated with the region from western movies he had seen on television as a child. In the US, he hoped, he would find refuge and a new life. He also realized that once he made the move, he would likely never come back.

In the fall of 1975, at age nineteen, Robert Benson left Weidenberg for good, carrying only a backpack and a visa that allowed him to stay in the US for six months. However, his emotional baggage more than made up for the lack of personal belongings.

After a brief stay with an uncle, Hans Echmann, in Princeton, New Jersey, Robert hitchhiked to California, making stops at Glacier and Yellowstone National Parks to backpack. By early 1976, he reached San Francisco, but quickly lost interest in city life. He yearned for a landscape that could soothe his high-strung psyche and fickle stomach and challenge his fidgety body. Back on the road, he bummed rides from whoever would pick him up. One of those rides dropped him off at the Grand Canyon. Stunned by the landscape, he felt an incredible desire to hike in its depths.

Robert realized, however, that any significant backpacking would require what he didn't have: money. Worse, his passport, the best (and only) form of identification he possessed, had been lost, or possibly stolen, in San Francisco. On the plus side, he could speak, read, and write English extremely well; as a teenager, in anticipation of someday going to the US, he had worked diligently to become proficient in the language and lose most of his accent. Still, he needed to find work. And he needed a little good luck. Fortunately, the two came as a package deal.

Mother's Day, May 9, 1976. John Shunny, his wife, and two of their three sons were surprised to come upon a lone backpacker on a dusty backroad in the high desert of New Mexico. The family was headed for the base of Cabezon Peak, a volcanic dome of columnar basalt sacred to the Navajo people. Climbing its 2,000 feet to the summit had become an

Robert Benson (left) with friends of the Shunny family on Cabezon Peak, May 1976.
Shunny family archives

annual Mother's Day tradition for the Shunnys.

"Where ya headed?" the curious Shunny patriarch asked the young man after stopping.

"La Madera," he replied. Intrigued by what he recognized as a subtle German accent, John next asked the stranger what brought him so far off the beaten path. Robert said that he had attempted to climb Cabezon Peak but couldn't find the route up.

"Why don't you come with us? We're heading to climb the peak right now."

Peter Shunny, then a fifteen-year-old, still remembers the moment well. "Robert had, like, this really huge backpack, the biggest I've ever seen. He was sweaty and pretty dirty. He climbed into the back of the truck and sat on the bed between me and my brother and all this camping gear. I remember thinking, 'Wow! What the heck? Nobody ever goes backpacking out here. This guy is really unusual.'"

John Shunny later wrote that the young German "was collecting visits to New Mexico ghost towns, and La Madera, some 50 miles distant, was next on the list." Sympathetic because their oldest two boys were also avid hitchhikers, the Shunnys offered Robert something else he couldn't refuse. They invited the trail-worn young man to stay with them in their Albuquerque home. Sick of being a vagabond, Robert gratefully accepted. The invitation became open-ended, and Robert eventually took up residence in the eldest Shunny son's former bedroom.

Perhaps it was divine payback for a childhood filled with pain and heartache, but just like that, Robert had a loving family and a home in the US, one he would always return to, for the rest of his life. Another plus: Keith, the middle Shunny son, taught him carpentry, a valuable trade that allowed him to find paying work and contribute his share to the family's well-being.

Robert Benson, Poncho the dog, Pete, John, and Keith Shunny, 1981. *Shunny family archives*

Once his visa expired, Robert was officially an undocumented immigrant, an "illegal alien"—technically, an "outlaw" on the lam. However, he made it very clear to John that he had no intention of returning to Germany, suggesting that doing so would possibly kill him. Hearing this, John became determined to assist Robert in permanently melting into American society.

Despite working in a top-secret research facility, John willingly stuck his neck out in this endeavor—*way out*. In addition to his journalism background, John had expertise as a graphic designer. He used the latter skill to forge a fake social security card, birth certificate, and even phony local high school report cards for the German. But first, John knew that if Robert really wanted to blend in with Americans, he needed a name change.

From an obituary, either John or Robert came up with a Social Security number for a recently deceased man named Randall Benson. Robert then adopted the dead man's last name and the number. To smooth the transition, he kept his first name. Henceforth, Robert Eschka would be Robert Benson. Excising his last name also provided a way to excise his father's legacy.

Then, the two devised a plan to explain away his subtle German accent without raising suspicion. Part of his reincarnation would include claiming that he grew up in the Midwest, raised

John Shunny and Robert Benson. *Shunny family archives*

by a German immigrant grandmother in Minnesota. There, he learned German as his first language. Despite this plausible explanation, he continued to work very hard to disguise his accent.

Collectively, everything seemed to be working far beyond what Robert ever imagined for himself. He had a home in America, was learning a trade, had a paying job, a loving adoptive family, and amazing landscapes to explore. He felt American in so many ways, proud and grateful to be here. The symbolism of his very intentional July 4th starting date (despite the heat) reflects this. His mind and stomach, however, never let him forget his origins.

~~~

Cramps and diarrhea began to plague Benson before the end of the first week of the Canyon hike. He blamed it on pothole water. Yet the others, drinking the same water, never got sick. When episodic vomiting kicked in as well, he became too weak to get up. As the group neared Nankoweap Canyon, River Mile 52, Benson chose to camp alone downstream. He slept miserably. The next morning, he journaled:

> Another horrible night with continued vomiting and diarrhea, my body didn't hold a drop of water. Every time I took a swallow, I threw up a quart causing my body to dehydrate rapidly. The morning looked like the end of the world.

Meanwhile, for the others upstream, the evening couldn't have been more different. A boatman (who happened to be Stan Steck's landlord) floated by and reported that he had a twelve-pack of beer for them, courtesy of George's oldest boy. They gladly accepted. Feeling a twinge of guilt as they drank, George later noted: "So we had twelve beers—and Robert had just left—too bad. I pissed in the river though, to send some beer remnants his way."

Still feeling ill the next morning, Benson urged the group to leave him. Much to his annoyance, they didn't. They also ignored his repeated declarations that they were "individual groups and not responsible for each other."

About mid-morning, an OARS commercial river trip floated past. Trip leader Liz Hymans offered Benson a couple of options: She could take him part-way or all the way to Phantom Ranch; wherever she dropped him off, he could rest and recuperate until the others in his party showed up; or, OARS carried a ground-to-air radio and she could call for a helicopter. Benson declined both offers. In his journal he explained why.

> I felt somewhere between life and death yet the fanatic idea of hiking to Lake Mead overpowered all the pains. I have been on foot for two and a half months now, more than half-way through. I just had to go on even if I had to rearrange my itinerary.

He insisted he wanted to be left where he was. He did agree, however, to have Hymans take a message to the ranger at Phantom that would make the NPS aware of his location, condition, and likely late arrival; he also agreed to take a couple of days of rest. George wrote the note for Benson, in which he specified that Benson would send another status report within the next three days. Both messages would be transported by boat. If the Phantom rangers didn't receive the second message within those three days, they were to assume that Benson's condition had worsened and that he would require an emergency evacuation.

Before she left, Hymans gave Benson penicillin tablets to take, although she doubted it would help much. Her premonition proved correct; he threw them up almost immediately, as well as a Valium (a sedative) tablet that George had given him. Feeling worse, Benson spent the next two days in his sleeping bag as the others hiked downstream.

On day seventeen, the beginning of a third day alone, Benson woke up with his gut feeling like "a 40 psi radial tire." Yet by late-afternoon, he felt amazingly better, well enough to start hiking again. Seeing some rafters, he sent a note with them to the ranger at Phantom, saying an evacuation would not be necessary and he should be arriving at Phantom within three days.

Recharged and intent on reuniting with his hiking companions, Benson pushed down to Unkar Creek at River Mile 72 with new-found ferocity. Eventually, he caught up with his group at the southern end of the Unkar Delta. Like the prodigal son, he received a big welcome. George wrote: "Around 1530 Benson appeared! Joyous reunion! We used up the starter fluid, as well as the margaritas to celebrate. He looks fine."

Four days later, on September 26 and day twenty-two of the hike, they caught the Clear Creek Trail and made it to Phantom Ranch by evening. At the canteen, they indulged in lemonade at $1.10 per cup. They then moved downstream to Bright Angel campground, where they encountered Don Mattox, John Shunny, and Bill Dunmire (superintendent of Carlsbad Caverns National Park and the guy George had pranked with CLF coupons). Dunmire was slated to continue downstream on the big hike while Shunny, Mattox, and the Petersons would exit after two days at Phantom.

Phantom NPS ranger Dave Buccello had arranged for an antiparasitic medication, Flagyl, to be brought down to treat Benson for possible giardiasis. After retrieving this and their Phantom caches, the group moseyed up to the beer hall to celebrate. A jovial George called Helen from the pay phone, and later wrote that "it was a real boost to hear her happy voice."

After a layover day, they rose at 5:30, ready for their $6.25 breakfast at the canteen: orange juice, scrambled eggs, bacon, hot cakes and syrup, and coffee. Benson, whose stomach issues seemed to be mostly in remission, complained of excessive farting. Well aware from the noise and stench, George commented, "Eternal flatulence is the price of puberty."

The first night after Phantom, George, like a true mathematician, noted in his journal how far they had come:

> Today we camp at 94 Mile and 3x94=282 [three foot miles for every river mile], what I list for Pearce Ferry. Also, today is day 27 and 3x 27=81. So we are one-third of the way in both time and distance. In excellent spirits and physical condition.

After an uneventful week of walking, they reached Shinumo Creek, River Mile 109, on day thirty-five. No longer physically ill but apparently—once again—tired of communing with others, Benson told the group he would set out on his own for the next few days to do some exploring and would meet up with them downstream.

George did not try to dissuade him; on the contrary, he thought the time apart would probably do both some good. Plus, George was in no rush. In fact, his plans called for a rest day at Bass Camp on the bank of Shinumo Creek to await the arrival of his sons, Mike and Stan, who would be coming down North Bass Trail. The Steck boys showed up at 9:30 the next morning, just as Benson was getting ready to leave. Mike and Stan brought fresh fruits (including watermelon), veggies, ingredients for a large fondue, filet mignon steaks, and salad. They also brought a liter of 151-proof rum, as well as Mai-Tai mixes. Specifically for Benson, they packed in water-purifying tablets and antacids. With real margaritas and an upbeat evening in the works, Benson decided to delay his solo exploration by a day.

Shortly after waking the next morning, Benson threw up and reported that he had suffered diarrhea during the night. Despite no one else getting sick, Benson blamed his symptoms (yet again) on an infection rather than a hangover or something based in his psyche: "The bugs are back or I caught something new."

The rest of the hiking party planned to take a week to navigate the ins and outs below the southern half of the massive "sky island" of Powell Plateau. Meanwhile, Benson would hike higher up, coming around the back side of the same plateau closer to the rim. Both routes were free of serious obstacles and both factions anticipated days of uneventful hiking, after which they would reunite at Tapeats Creek. Still intent on leaving despite the relapse in his stomach issues, Benson split from the group around nine that morning.

Days earlier, according to George's journal, while camped at Crystal Rapids and drinking margaritas, "Al and Bill told climbing horror stories."

Hiking remote and alone, the German would soon add one of his own.

Self portrait near River Mile 181. *Robert Benson*

CHAPTER TWENTY

Quiet Like a Cemetery

STECK-LED THROUGH HIKE 1982 (CONTINUED)

And ah God's mercy, what a stroke was there!
And here a thrust that might have killed, but God
Broke the strong lance, and rolled his enemy down,
And saved him: so she lived in fantasy.

Alfred Lord Tennyson
"Lancelot and Elaine"/*Idylls of the King* (1959)

October 1982

After departing Bass Camp at the river, Robert Benson hiked two miles up the North Bass Trail. Next, he veered off eastward. For four additional miles, he meandered along, across, and sometimes through the beautiful perennial flow of Shinumo Creek within the Shinumo Amphitheater (*Shinumo* is the Southern Paiute word for "old people" or "cliff dwellers.")

Near the confluence of two deep, vertical gorges, Benson stopped, surrounded by breathtaking scenery: a clear slickrock pool, shady cottonwoods whose golden leaves quaked in the breeze, and a level patio of Tapeats Sandstone. Even by the Canyon's superlative standards, this spot boasted exceptional beauty. Enraptured, Benson dropped his pack and unrolled his sleeping pad.

Eighty years earlier, mapmaker Richard T. Evans had found the area so enchanting that he bestowed names redolent of Arthurian legend, the locale his portal into a Canyon Camelot. The mysterious converging canyons became the Merlin and Modred abysses. Ultimately, Evans labeled a total of nine geologic features within a five-mile radius with Arthurian appellations. One of those

187

features now caught Benson's attention.

The next morning, October 11, Benson left camp; slinging a daypack over his shoulders, he veered right, following the Abyss Creek fork. This decision had him bushwhacking through dense cottonwoods and willows that lined the bank, fording the creek probably a couple dozen times, as well as several hundred yards of mandatory creek walking. For about five miles, he kept heading north, aiming for, then reaching the 7,420-foot summit of Elaine Castle.

According to the folklore, after Elaine of Castle Astolat died of unrequited love for Sir Lancelot, her lifeless body floated downriver to Camelot. Here in the heart of the Grand Canyon, Elaine's "castle," a blocky Coconino Sandstone butte topped by the Toroweap Formation, is overshadowed by Lancelot Point, which looms high above on the Canyon's North Rim.

Standing atop Elaine's Castle, Benson planned to reconnoiter the terrain to the west, specifically for a potential route to Muav Saddle. Situated below Swamp Point one mile down the North Bass Trail, Muav Saddle acts as an isthmus connecting Powell Plateau to the North Rim. Passing across this saddle would take Benson to the western side of that plateau and set him up to eventually meet George, as planned, at Deer Creek.

From Benson's camp at the confluence of Merlin and Modred Abysses via the North Bass Trail, the distance to the saddle totaled close to thirteen miles. Shortcutting along the top of the Redwall or along a band of the Supai Formation could possibly shrink that distance by half. But first, Benson had to ascertain if such a route was feasible.

By early afternoon, he had easily managed the nontechnical scramble to Elaine's summit. Surrounded by spectacular views, he crouched to inspect a climbing register. Only four people had signed in, included someone Benson frequently referred to in his journals using the initials HB: "Jim Sears Harvey Butchart, August 9, 1969."

Benson scanned westward for that possible shortcut. A walk along the top of the Redwall or Supai looked straightforward from here, except for one little-known section. Wondering if it would "go," he needed to get much closer to inspect it. Clambering down the butte into a ravine that sloped south, Benson was soon halted by a cliff band. He needed to downclimb. When he reached a spot that became dicey for his feet, he transferred the bulk of his weight to his hands. Suddenly, both handholds broke off, sending him into a freefall.

Within a couple seconds he hit, then tumbled an additional twenty feet down a slope of sharp rubble. Face-down but still conscious when his body came to a halt, he opened his eyes to see nearby rocks spattered with his blood. Strangely, the thirty-foot plunge onto unyielding talus caused him no immediate pain. Other than his own breathing, his world was as silent as the proverbial grave.

Fleeting thoughts during his fall had included hope that the crash landing would kill him or somehow leave him unscathed. For several seconds, he remained immobile, dreading the worst: something in between.

Then he attempted to move. When his limbs failed to respond, he panicked. This spurred him to try harder, demanding that his arms and legs obey. When they finally did, the psychological relief was instantly nullified by abrupt, searing pain in his pelvis.

As the shock of what had happened ebbed, the severity of the pain in his pelvis seemed to worsen. Scared yet flooded with adrenaline, he tried to stand. Excruciating discomfort in his pelvis dropped him back to his knees. Hiking out under his own power at that moment was clearly unlikely. Signaling an airplane with his mirror and getting rescued before dark also would be an incredible long shot and likely very time consuming. Most urgently, he needed to survive the coming night, which meant getting to water; and getting to water meant descending to a lower elevation. So he started to crawl, creeping along a ledge toward the route he had come up, then back down the drainage.

As the sun set, he stopped at a small water-filled pothole in the Muav Limestone. Four agonizing hours of shuffling on his hands and knees had gained him a mere three-quarters of a mile; unfortunately, his camp, food, and gear were still over two miles away.

Deciding to hunker down near the pothole, he gathered twigs and sticks one by one, then lit a fire and curled up next to it. Freezing, and in severe pain made worse by uncontrollable shivering, he got very little sleep. In his journal, he later summarized the day's events with a short, two-word sentence that was close, but, fortunately for him, inaccurate: *Fatal day!*

In sharp contrast, about the same time, Steck effused about how stress-free and pleasant his own day had been:

> Today was a good day … Stan and I take shampoo … now it's warm clothes time. Huge din din. Before dinner K and I played duets for two soprano recitals—sounded great…. Nice breeze today too, which makes walking a lot easier. Boats came by … and someone waved a beer at us.

The next morning, the start of a layover day, George continued to cozily snooze in his sleeping bag in Hakatai ("Colorado River" in the Havasupai language) Canyon. At the same time, a shivering, pain-consumed, and sleep-deprived Benson forced himself to stand and began a tortuous shuttle over the rough terrain down toward his camp at the Merlin-Modred junction. The hours, like his thoughts, body, and limbs, dragged; his pain nearly intolerable. Re-negotiating the thick vegetation overhanging the banks along Abyss Creek, as

Hikers in narrows of Abyss Creek. *Weston Myers*

well as the inescapable hopscotching of slippery boulders within the creek proved brutal in time and effort. Spent and still in significant pain, he sat down and decided to give his signal mirror a try. After unsuccessfully flashing at "more than a dozen planes and helicopters," he had no option but to resume his shuffle-crawl.

After several hours, he finally reached the junction of Abyss Creek where it collides with the rushing spring water of Shinumo Creek. Here he faced another dilemma: reaching his camp on the opposite bank. Forcing himself to stand, he attempted to wade the now tripled-in-volume creek flow. Almost immediately, he took a misstep on a slick boulder and twisted a leg. He howled a blood-curdling scream, so startlingly loud even to himself, that he hoped it might attract the attention of someone nearby.

It didn't.

When he finished inching to his camp, he gingerly lay down on his sleeping pad to assess his injuries—and his options. Though he wanted to believe he hadn't cracked any bones, the severe pain shooting from his pelvis into his sacrum and hips forced him to accept the diagnosis that he probably had.

He concluded that his survival options boiled down to two choices: one, remain in camp and continue to use the signal mirror for a helicopter rescue, or two, try to navigate the four miles back to Muav Canyon, then ascend the nine miles up the North Bass Trail to Muav Saddle in hopes of recuperating in the cabin there. He decided to sleep, if pain allowed, on this decision.

It, too, didn't.

Still, by morning he had made up his mind about how to proceed. He documented his decision and the reason why in his journal. Prone to melodrama in these writings, his next entry seems exceptionally so: "I finally chose to continue to move as long as I had a breath of life left."

For the next two days, he hobbled along, sometimes reverting back to all fours, hooking his foot through one of the pack's loops so he could drag it along behind him. Predictably, doing so made a slow, agonizing slog even worse. Despite exhaustion, aspirin, and alcohol, camps offered little relief and almost no sleep. On day three, he started drinking earlier in the day to break the pain cycle; frustrated by a body that refused to accomplish the impossible, he intentionally got drunk.

Even so, he knew that if he could reach the Muav Saddle cabin the next day, he had a good chance of receiving medical help. He remembered that Mike Steck planned to hike out the North Bass Trail, along with two doctors who had joined George's entourage after Benson left. While Benson's melodramatic narratives continued, he added some optimism.

Little hope remained that the doctors coming up Saddle Canyon on the seventeenth could fix me up for another forty-day hike. What if they refused to give me any drugs, they probably would want to take me to a hospital, pump me full of X-Rays, and lock me up for days or even weeks. Yet a glimpse of hope for a miracle remained.

About the same time, George Steck remained a happy hiker in a celebratory mood. He had passed his halfway point: forty-one days down, forty to go. That evening, his group shared the gorgeous, sprawling beach at Stone Creek, River Mile 128, with Sanderson River Expeditions. Schmoozing with one of the boatmen, George wrangled a $20 deal to have the guides cache two cases of beer at Whitmore, River Mile 188: one for him and the other for Benson.

Meanwhile, Stan chatted up another boatman. The guide, a small, soft-spoken man, seemed unusually knowledgeable about the canyon, both the river corridor and the downriver routes afoot. Stan shared this conversation with his dad.

"What's the guy's name?" George asked.

"Kenton."

George's eyebrows shot up. Soon, he moseyed back to the river guides' campfire.

"Are you Kenton Grua?" he asked the river imp, a man nearly a foot shorter than himself.

"Yeah," Kenton responded.

George introduced himself and then asked Kenton for details about his thru-hike in 1976, especially the sections that awaited them downstream. Equally impressed by George, Kenton grabbed a notepad and jotted down George's phone number and address, then noted the encounter with his group. He also took their photos.

That night, George confided to his journal that meeting Kenton Grua had inspired him to consider writing a book about walking the Canyon's length. The book would focus on the most significant Grand Canyon hikers, like Kenton, whom he hoped to interview in more detail after the trip. He planned to make Robert Benson's hiking obsession the book's organizing theme.

Less than twenty-four hours later, on October 16, after taking four and a half days to complete the most grueling ten-mile traverse of his life, George's intended protagonist staggered through the doorway of the two-room cabin at Muav Saddle. Nicknamed "Teddy's Cabin" by local Mormons, it was a "snowshoe" cabin built by the NPS in 1925 as an overnight accommodation for backcountry patrols. (Its namesake, President Theodore Roosevelt—who'd camped at the saddle in 1913 during a mountain lion hunt on nearby Powell Plateau—didn't have a chance to stay in it before he died in 1919.)

Benson scrounged the mostly empty cabin for anything that might help him survive. Fortunately, in 1978, Jim Ohlman (who had attended George's Cremation party and had tried to help me track down Ron Mitchell) had stashed food, noting his name and the date. The famished Benson helped himself, despite the staleness of the food. After hauling water from a nearby spring at the base of the Coconino Sandstone cliffs, Benson tossed his pad and sleeping bag on a set of naked bedsprings and tried to nap. He nodded off, hopeful that at any moment he might be pleasantly surprised by the doctors during their hike out.

The following day, October 17, NPS backcountry ranger Mark Sinclair popped into Teddy's Cabin as part of a job detail. He was shocked to find the sluggish,

Teddy's Cabin. *Rich Rudow*

disheveled man inside. Although Sinclair had hiked in to fix the cabin's windows, he quickly concluded that the old building's occupant was in greater need of repair. He not only urged Benson to seek medical attention, but offered to assist.

Astonishing Sinclair, the stoical young man flatly declined. Benson did, however, perk up when Ranger Sinclair mentioned that his itinerary would take him to upper Tapeats Creek the next day—George's current neighborhood. Benson hit up Sinclair to act as a courier for a note to George. In it, he informed George that he would meet him at Deer Creek in two days. Sinclair agreed, then spent the day hanging out and fixing the windows, with Benson enjoying his company.

In the morning, note in hand, Sinclair bade Benson goodbye. After Sinclair left, high clouds moved in, and the weather cooled. So did Benson's mood. That night, consistent with his prior doomsday tone, he wrote: "The 18th was a cold morning, still waiting—very quiet like a cemetery—the graveyard of my trip?"

Fortunately, he spent most of the night pain-free, his first good rest since the fall. Lazarus-like, he rose the next morning, feeling some actual spunk. He also realized how lucky he had been, given the slim chance of walking away from such a fall. The forced R&R, plus alcohol, seemed to have been the perfect medicine. Now, he found himself afflicted by another medical ailment: cabin fever.

> I'm going crazy with all the waiting, especially since I don't know if it will be possible to continue or not. I drank a lot of rum today finishing up the bottle, it helped for mental stability and as a painkiller. It's a beautiful day, I laid in the sun on a bench all day trying to keep my mind off of the big question.

That "big question," whether he could actually meet George and continue downstream, was likely the furthest thing from George's mind when Mark Sinclair met his group at Tapeats Creek. There, he handed Benson's note to George, then described Benson's accident, which provoked stunned expressions and gasps among the listeners. Fortunately, Sinclair reassured the group, the tough German was on the mend and fully intended to rendezvous with them.

That same day, around five in the evening, eight days total after his fall (and day three in the cabin), Benson heard voices. It turned out to be Mike Steck; his girlfriend, Kathy; and another friend, Steve White. Mike Steck recalls how overjoyed Benson initially seemed but how that balloon burst when informed that no doctor accompanied them. Mike told him that the one and only doctor on their trip had hiked out earlier than planned.

Based on the timing, Benson realized that he must've missed the doctor by only a few hours on the day he arrived at the cabin. So, the medical assessment he wanted and needed wasn't going to happen here.

White, Stan Steck's former college roommate, offered Benson yet another opportunity to get that assessment, however. Upping the ante of Sinclair's offer, he was willing to not only give Benson a ride back to Albuquerque (White's vehicle was parked just a mile away at Swamp Point), he'd deliver Benson directly to medical care. Furthermore, he promised Benson—provided he received medical clearance and wanted to resume his hike—he would then drive him back here to Swamp Point. The huge detour back to Swamp Point wouldn't be a problem for White, as he would be on his way back to California anyway.

While Benson appreciated White's exceedingly generous offer, he nonetheless declined it. His traverse had to be continuous, he told him; he had to stay below the rim the entire time. The trek would be ruined if he left the Canyon for treatment.

"I tried to reason with him," White said. "I told him, 'Look, I understand long-distance hiking, but it's not worth dying for.'"

"I disagree," Benson replied.

Benson did, however, enlist White to deliver yet another note, this one confidential, to Helen Steck; what went into this missive is unknown. He also entrusted Sinclair with film he wanted developed.

After his visitors hiked out, Benson vacillated on whether or not he had made the right decision by declining such generous help. He documented his conclusion in his journal: "I had to go on. The trip meant too much."

Determined to link up with George, the next day, Benson took the bulk of the edible food remaining in Ohlman's cache (mostly cereals) and left a note of thanks in the container. Despite his gimp, he made it through the challenging narrows of Saddle Canyon to the bed of Tapeats Canyon, reaching the confluence of Tapeats Creek and Thunder River on the 20th of October.

There, Benson met a hiker named Smith and his son, who had been camping for several days, fishing for trout. Yes, the man reported, they had met a man named George who'd camped here. He'd hiked up toward Thunder Spring. Despite everything, a relieved Benson had fallen behind by only one day.

Smith also showed him George's campsite. Benson knew George's cache had to be stashed nearby. Now low on food—all he had left was a package of soup Mike Steck had given him—Benson hoped something remained in George's cache. Benson ultimately found the cache beneath a boulder, but his *eureka* moment faded quickly. George's bucket yielded only stale cereal infested with maggot larvae. Benson scooped out the grubs and ate the cereal for breakfast. He then used the bucket to wash his tattered cut-offs and other clothing, and then himself, for his first complete bath in more than two weeks.

The next day, Benson followed the well-maintained CCC trail upward past the well-named Thunder Spring and across the bone-dry Surprise Valley, then downslope into the lush Deer Creek drainage. Hoping to intercept George, Benson moved downstream toward the campground under the shade of cottonwoods along the trail paralleling the creek.

A day earlier, George's party had hiked to the Colorado at the confluence with Deer Creek. There, they had hobnobbed with some river runners, who offered them beer and invited them to share their camp and a meal.

Now, while hiking back up to the Deer Creek Campground to retrieve their gear, George and the others speculated on the odds of finding

Benson's shorts. *Robert Benson*

Benson waiting for them there. When they didn't see him, George felt let down. Two-and-a-half weeks had now passed since their separation. Sighing, George and the others began packing. As George laced his boots, he glanced up-canyon and spotted a solitary hiker limping in their direction.

"Who's that?" he asked aloud, not quite believing his eyes. The others looked up.

"A hiker," Stan nonchalantly replied, then went back to packing. Meanwhile, George continued to scrutinize the approaching figure.

"No! It's Robert!" he exclaimed, hurrying in the hiker's direction.

The others followed. For the next several minutes, Benson recounted a condensed version of his mishap. When he finished telling the story and fielding questions, an upbeat George informed him of their luck for the evening. They would celebrate his return with all the comforts of a river-runner's camp: cold beer, good food, a toilet, conversation, and laughs. Benson was elated. Together, the group hiked back to the river, where the boaters ferried them across to their camp on the south shore.

The river trippers included two faces familiar to Benson: Dave Lyle and Ed Hasse, both Cataract Canyon boatmen for the Flagstaff-based river company Wild and Scenic Expeditions. He had met the two back in July, at Spanish Bottom above Cataract Canyon, near the beginning of his epic hike. The chatting, drinking, and laughter around the campfire continued for hours. Although Benson's hip pained him when he limped to bed, the day had been rewarding. He swallowed a few pain pills, lay down, and closed his eyes. Relaxed, almost pain-free, and among friends, he slept the best he had in weeks.

Wes and Connor peering over the 500-foot drop into Saddle Canyon.
Tom Myers

CHAPTER TWENTY-ONE

Beyond the Starship

37-MILE ("MITCHELL") CANYON TO NANKOWEAP

Exploration is in our nature. We began as wanderers, and we are wanderers still.

Carl Sagan
Cosmos (1980)

Walking is man's best medicine.

Hippocrates (460 BC–375 BC)

January 2014

We will die if these bikes are stolen.

"There," my daughter Alex's boyfriend, Ethan, pronounced after writing this message and attaching it to the bikes. "Maybe they'll be here when we get back. If that doesn't work, we're gonna have to walk." He looked into the distance, to the east across the Marble Platform, then north to the road we just came in on. "I don't know which one would be worse. That bike ride is gonna suck."

"You know, Ethan, I'll gladly do the bike ride if you think it's going to be too hard for you," I teased, knowing this subtle dig, purposefully done in front of Alex, so as to nudge him.

"No, I got it," he quickly replied after glancing at Alex, then back at me, not willing to be shamed by a guy more than twice his age.

We stood at the Saddle Mountain entry point to the Nankoweap Trail. À la George Steck, I had created a multi-day Marble Canyon loop hike as a well-deserved diversion from school for four of the participants. The plan called for us to descend at 37 Mile Canyon, aka Mitchell Canyon. It was the same route

Wes and I'd covered before with Eric Gueissaz, only this time, we'd make a right turn and hike in a southwest direction, first along the top of the Supai, then onto the Redwall. At River Mile 50, we would veer down to the Colorado River and traverse the right bank to Nankoweap Creek at River Mile 52.5, finally hiking out the Nankoweap Trail. This, the ninth leg in our lengthwise traverses, would equate to roughly 45 miles, bringing our lengthwise total mileage to nearly 190 in just over three weeks of total hiking.

Five days from now, we would (I hoped) return to where we now stood and find the two bikes still stashed, unmolested, in the trees. While the rest of us waited, Ethan and eighteen-year-old Wes would hop on the bikes and pedal along the rim road to retrieve the Yukon, about ten miles away.

Connor Phillips, one of Wes's boyhood buddies, joined our group. A twenty-year-old college student, Connor had been acquainted with Wes since infancy. Both spent their earliest years together on the South Rim, where Connor's dad, Ken Phillips, worked as a ranger, and his mom, Annie, as a part-time teacher. During the drive to the trailhead, I noticed that Connor—now a broad-shouldered, nearly six-foot tall man—still recovering from a cold, had a bit of a cough.

Alex, who had become interested in walking the length herself (something I encouraged) also joined us on this leg. Her relatively new boyfriend, Ethan, and his twenty-five-year-old brother, Matthew, rounded out the group.

Ditching the bikes, we rattled down a rough, two-track road over washboards and sharp limestone rocks. I wanted to make good time but knew better than to rush. Nearly four years earlier, Wes and I had been out here with the intention of doing a portion of this loop when we had a blow-out. As the June sun beat down, I "let" Wes change the tire, his first. This time, I balanced speed with caution.

Clear, cold, and dry weather greeted us when we arrived in a cloud of dust at Tank Seven. Fortunately, the cloud my Yukon kicked up wasn't nearly as big and ominous as it had been in the fall of 2009, when Wes, Eric, and I experienced our dehydration drama. This winter's precipitation had been near average. Tank Seven, the last in a series of seven concrete watering troughs spaced over a dozen miles (placed decades earlier by House Rock Valley ranchers for their cattle), had water in it. Another good sign.

After parking, we walked the couple of hundred yards to the rim. I gulped nervously as I scanned for Starship Camp, our goal. This time, much to my relief, the pothole was clearly full. Even without binoculars, we could see light glinting off its ice-covered surface. Knowing the day would be short, we hustled down the Mitchell Canyon drainage, and within two hours stood beside the pothole. Its rounded edges and icy water made me think of a backyard kiddie pool during a frosty cold spell.

We broke the ice; lay on our stomachs; and slurped its delicious water straight from the pothole—quite a dramatic contrast to the experience four years earlier at the same spot for Wes, Eric, and me. As the temperature dropped, we quickly set up camp and made hot meals using a variety of dehydrated dinner packets. By 7:30, we were ready for bed. The boys slept in separate bivy sacks, while Alex shared a tent with me. I was pleasantly surprised to see that our sleeping arrangements didn't seem to bother Ethan.

Starship pothole with water. *Tom Myers*

In the morning, Alex and I got up first, followed almost immediately by Matthew, a quiet, somewhat-enigmatic former Marine sniper, who, in perfected stealth mode, began heating water. One by one, the other boys rousted. Uniformly bleary-eyed and groggy, each admitted he hadn't slept well. Their bivy sacks, now covered in frost, had proven too flimsy to keep out the cold. Worse for Ethan, his sleeping pad had deflated. "I didn't sleep at all," he grumbled as he held up his frosty and clearly flat air mattress.

Feeling refreshed and peppy, I tried not to gloat but couldn't stifle a been-there chuckle. To my relief, Ethan also laughed it off, then hugged Alex. I knew that he knew he was in my fishbowl and that I was quietly monitoring his every move and word to my daughter.

My friend, Greg Reiff, a teacher at Coconino High School in Flagstaff, worked as a river guide for Canyoneers, a company his grandfather, Norman Nevills, founded in 1938. I also rowed trips for them once a year. Greg, knowing Ethan to be a humble, salt-of-the-earth-type kid, had urged him to apply for a shop job at Canyoneers right out of high school. With Greg in his backcourt, he was hired. I recalled meeting Ethan as he stood amidst a sea of dirty tents, paco pads, and ammo cans doing clean up and repair work.

Only a few months prior to this hike another Canyoneers guide broke some shocking news. "Hey, Tom, do you know your daughter Alex is dating a Canyoneers guide?" a boatman named Jamie Townsend asked. A gregarious, tobacco-chewing man, Townsend frequently dressed like a homeless person. He punctuated his question with a smirk, a tobacco wad bulging in his lower lip, the brown juice staining his teeth.

I stared at him, trying to look horrified about his comment (which was easy to do).

"Oh my, God! No! No!! *Really?!* ... Ummm, it's not you, *is it?*"

"No," he giggled.

"Whew! Thank God!" I teased.

We both laughed.

"Okay. So, who is it then?" I eyed him cautiously.

"Ethan Dyer."

Hmmm ... okay. Ethan and I worked a few river trips together, and I found him to be an affable and solid crew member, and probably the pick of the limited litter at Canyoneers. But I never imagined him dating one of my daughters (let alone being my future son-in-law, as it turned out).

We made hot chocolate and coffee, ate a quick breakfast, and discussed the plan for the day, as well as for the rest of the week. "All right, let's see what ol' Georgie Porgie has to say about getting to Buck Farm," I thought out loud, referencing our goal for the day. I pulled out a photocopy of George Steck's "Marble Canyon Route Summary." An original work created for *Loop Hikes II*, it included line drawings of side canyons, as well as estimated hiking times between each using three possible routes: atop the Redwall, across the Esplanade, or along the rim.

By George's estimate, our day's goal of walking along the top of the Redwall to Buck Farm Canyon would take about four-and-a-half hours. Out of curiosity, I discovered that George also estimated that walking along the rim from Saddle Mountain, where we'd stashed the bikes, back to where we had parked the Yukon, was eleven hours. Wes and Ethan could likely do that rim section much quicker on bikes, but I thought it best to keep that little "eleven-hour" tidbit to myself.

I did, however, share George's estimate to Buck Farm. "Sweet!" Weston exclaimed. "I bet we hike faster than George and should easily get there before dark, even if we go exploring around here." We took a couple of hours to look around some of the nearby Redwall narrows before heading for Buck Farm Canyon, a half-day beyond Starship. We easily made that goal, and as we had the night before, set up camp long before sunset. In the morning, Connor, still recovering from a cold, began coughing more intensely. It concerned me.

"How're you feeling?"

"Oh, I'm fine, Tom. It's just a little cough," he told me. I remembered seeing him at Grand Canyon Clinic when he was about four years old, so ill with tonsillitis that he couldn't eat or drink. I told his mom, Annie, that he needed an antibiotic shot and she gently broke the news to him. He didn't take it well.

"No shot! No shot!" he had screamed. Seeing me sneak out of the exam room before the nurse gave him the injection, he shrieked, "I hate you, Tom!"

Over the years, I've periodically reminded him of that episode to make him blush. To this day, when I bring it up, he both laughs and apologizes.

"I was a weird little kid," he typically adds. Shy, intellectual, and introverted, he struggled in high school and had trouble making friends. Before we left on this trip, Annie'd told me that he still wasn't in a good head space, and how grateful she and Ken were that we'd invited him along.

Connor with a piece of Starship pothole ice.
Tom Myers

The Redwall bed of upper Saddle Canyon (River Mile 47)— our intended camp—had no pothole water as we had hoped, so Ethan and I headed up-canyon looking for resupply. The others soon followed. Within about 200 yards, we came upon a lone pothole capped with six inches of ice. After breaking through, we gathered about ten liters and brought it back to camp. Because of the cold, we all hit the sack early, but not before reflecting on our great first day.

After another cold but uneventful night, we were on the move again shortly after sunrise.

Throughout the morning we made good progress, stopping only briefly when we stumbled upon a dangling web of rusty wires, scattered decaying boards, and short posts of rebar drilled into the bedrock of a Redwall notch: Leftovers from a bygone and, hopefully, long-gone era of dam building on just about any free-flowing river in the American West.

More specifically, the trash represented the last remnants of a 3,400 - foot - long tramway strung from the Rim to the top of the Redwall. This tram transported men and materials to the site of a proposed Marble Canyon Dam, where between 1949 and 1952 survey crews diligently combed the cliffs and drilled test holes to assess whether the limestone could handle a 380-foot-tall dam and the tremendous pressure from the lake it would spawn. Fortunately, because of environmental activists led by Kenton Grua's old boss Martin Litton, the Bureau of Reclamation's efforts to cram the dam down the throat of Marble Canyon at taxpayer expense went bust.

I saluted Litton and company as I stared at the dregs. I also couldn't help but smirk at the irk this rare win for environmentalists must have been to the Bureau's muckety mucks and regional politicians. *You want another dam? Well, too-damn bad.*

Around lunch time, at River Mile 50, we came across the first signs of regular foot traffic on a social trail near a huge projection fittingly named "the diving board" at the top of the Redwall. Unofficially called the Boundary Ridge trail because it corresponds to the eastern edge of the old park boundary prior to the 1975 expansion, it follows a fault to the beach below. It's a steep and sometimes exposed route with dicey footing, especially when descending while wearing a heavy pack. Still, having a trail was a welcome change from blazing one. Ethan helped Alex at an exposed spot, taking her pack across. *Good boy! Chivalry duly noted.*

As we neared the beach, I spied a river party floating downstream. I immediately started to peel off my pack.

Alex and Ethan negotiating the Redwall.
Tom Myers

"Dad? What are you doing?" Alex asked, puzzled by my hastiness.

"I forgot my beer in the car. I'm gonna try to bum some to celebrate our last night!" I called over my shoulder as I started to run. Once I got to the river's edge, I shouted and flailed my arms at two people in an approaching raft.

"Need some help?" one of them shouted after they spotted me.

"No! We need some beer!" I yelled.

They freely parted with four beers before floating away in apparent tranquility. Meanwhile, we plodded downstream along the bank into what would become relative misery.

Before Glen Canyon dam (and Hoover downstream), the Colorado in flood routinely weeded the Canyon's riverbanks, stripping it of all but the hardiest of plants and draping its shorelines in sand.

Now, the river's tightly controlled and sediment-free flows not only don't rebuild beaches, they also allow some species to explode on the skimpy shorelines that remain. The end result is a nearly impenetrable jungle of unnaturally dense riverine foliage. The way they overcrowd the tiny beaches reminds me of rabid fans at a sporting event. Indeed, within the gigantic Grand Canyon version of the Roman coliseum, these die-hard plants (literally) seem to be fighting one another for the ringside view of the great gladiator—the Colorado River—battling its rocky foe.

Of this aggressive fan base, the non-native tamarisk (*Tamarix* spp.) is one of the worst. "Tammies" are not even close to their fun, cheerleader-sounding nickname. Introduced in the late 1800s by settlers to help with erosion control, they thrive in desert environments and rival the most obnoxious weeds in one's yard.[10] These small evergreens, averaging six to ten feet tall, are also called salt cedars; their "pom poms"—branches loaded with shaggy, scaley, needle-like leaves—are often encrusted with white, salty secretions. Trying to plow through a grove, the branches not budging an inch, is no fun. The fragile needles easily break off, sticking to sweaty skin and hair, and filling shirt collars, boots tops, pockets, and the space between shoulders and backpack.

Their annoying presence comes in addition to clusters of their equally annoying cohorts, such as scratchy catclaw, thorny mesquite, and gnarly hackberry; sticky seep willows; scruffy snakeweed, rabbitbrush, and brittlebush; razor-edged bear grass, rock nettles, and—no surprise here—multiple types of cacti, nearly all of which have very hard and very sharp spines (you feel one deep poke, you've felt them all). The vegetation becomes a can't-see-your-feet, clothes-catching, shin-banging, face-slapping, crotch-whacking, shred-and-poke-your-everything mosh pit. Little did we know, negotiating these river jungles would be a recurring theme as we moved downstream.

We soon discovered that attempting to maneuver along the slopes above the present and old high-water zones—where there is little to no vegetation—was frequently impossible due to steepness and loose rock. That reality kept forcing us back into the jungle. It also became clear that the best way through often required charging like a running back, essentially thrashing with arms and legs churning. Any movement short of that risked a loss of momentum and becoming stuck like an insect in a giant spiderweb.

Wes led the first of many encounters. Lowering his head, he hurtled into the thicket and disappeared. Shaking trees and leaves, cracking branches, snapping twigs, and crunching footsteps marked his progress. Additional clues as to what we should expect consisted of snorts, heavy breathing, grunts, howls of pain, and loud cursing. We all followed, the thick undergrowth doling out this cruel and unusual punishment while being as maddeningly indifferent as a driver who sideswiped your car without noticing, let alone caring.

We weren't alone in this experience. Kenton commented on the same struggles when he hit River Mile 50 on March 5, 1976.

---

10 In 1995, Grand Canyon National Park began a tamarisk-removal project along the river corridor, manually extracting the trees. Unfortunately, they seem to grow back faster than they can be removed.

Gawd, we learn what work is. The tamarisk - arrowweed is impenetrable, growing down to an overhanging the river. Up the talus, the jungle becomes a deadly tangle of mesquite and catclaw, every bit as impenetrable as the jungle below but with thorns and claws, which tear at eyes, clothes, skin, pack, leaving us cut, scratched, and bleeding. Mostly we try to stick to the steep talus slope above the mesquite and catclaw but the going is difficult slow there also, with hardly a stable rock to step on. One is on one's ass as much as feet up here...I think we must have sounded like a couple of Sherman tanks on a search and destroy mission while trudging through that jungle.

We finished the day by taking three hours to force our way two-and-a-half miles downstream through that horrible vegetation, eventually arriving at Little Nankoweap at River Mile 52—scratched, torn, exhausted, but relieved. After dinner, we sat around talking, sharing the beers, and toasting the day. Then Connor began rummaging in his pack. He pulled out a little baggie and held it up.

"Anybody want some jellybeans?" he asked.

We all looked at him. Unruly, short-cropped hair and baby-faced grin above a whisker-free chin made him look about fourteen instead of twenty.

"Sure!" we all echoed, and he passed it around.

"What are these little brown pills?" Alex queried, after spotting a few while sifting through the jellybeans when the bag reached her.

"Oh, that! That's my ibuprofen," he grinned. "You can have some of that too if you want."

"What?!" Wes asked, sounding and looking dumbfounded. "Connor, why do you keep your ibuprofen with your jellybeans?"

"Are you kidding, Wes? It's like the perfect drug combination for hiking Grand Canyon. I take them both for dessert."

That brought down the house with laughter. For my part, I especially enjoyed seeing Wes and Connor together again, happy in each other's company—something that had been absent for several years, and that I had sorely missed.

⌒⌒⌒

Once upon a time, Connor and Wes had been best of buddies, brothers from different mothers, a bond fostered by the outdoor adventuring our families had done together, including several Canyon hikes and multiple river trips. But during their early teens, the bond frayed. Neither Wes nor Connor showed any interest in one another, drifting apart despite our attempts as parents to keep them close.

When I'd initially asked Wes if he'd be okay if I invited Connor along on this Nankoweap hike for old time's sake, he hadn't gushed with enthusiasm. He said it would be fine but added that he doubted Connor would go. Ironically, I had been wondering the same thing about Weston.

Becky and I were blindsided when Wes began to hate high school and thus, his life. Prior to that, in grade school and middle school, he had thrived, enthusiastic about academics, about sports, about relationships. He also coaxed me into learning new things with him, things I previously had no real experience with, like hard-shell kayaking, snowboarding, and baseball.

While Wes quickly became proficient at all of these, he really excelled in academics and as a baseball player. Striving for perfection in both, he lived for baseball, defining himself by how well he performed. A big, strong kid, Wes could both throw a ball incredibly hard and hit home runs. He excelled through Little League and middle school.

Entering high school, he received a call to try out for the varsity team, despite the fact that he was a freshman. Unfortunately, when he didn't make varsity, his confidence tanked. Stuck on the freshman team, both his self-esteem and pitching nose-dived; then he quit baseball altogether.

Going into a dark place, he refused to talk, and gave up on counseling after two sessions. Sometimes, he went for days without changing his clothes or showering. When one of his old teammates, a boy Wes had grown up and played Little League baseball with, committed suicide during their junior year, Becky and I went into panic mode. A year later, another Little League teammate did the same. All of us—Becky, me, Wes's sisters—were scared to death. He stopped hiking with me, stopped doing anything with me, or for that matter, with any of us. We couldn't reach him, and his rejection cut like a knife.

Now, as we ate those jellybeans, I felt tickled beyond belief, enjoying one of the best feel-good, down-in-the-Canyon buzzes I've ever had. It came close to compensating for the nearly two lost years. The biggest thing was having my boy back, and like his old self.

I also knew part of it came from a different kind of "drug combination." Back to the concept of addiction …

I never fully appreciated the incredible power of dependency until a patient with emphysema (aka COPD) explained it to me. Despite experiencing what equates to slow-motion suffocation, she was hopelessly addicted to nicotine and continued to smoke. Early into the visit, I had reflexively rattled off in standard doctor-speak, "You need to quit smoking."

With tears in her eyes, her gaze earnest, she sniffled, "Doctor, you don't understand. Cigarettes are my best friend. Unlike people in my life, they've always been there when I needed them most, during the stressful times. And they never judge me." She told me she got hooked on cigarettes as a teenager.

Instead of a snarky, "Well, with friends like that, you'll never need an enemy," I stayed silent, digesting what she said. It made an impact. In that empathetic moment, with similar gratitude, I thought of one of my own "best friends."

Wilderness, like nicotine, is nonjudgmental. Similarly, wilderness asks no questions and welcomes all comers. But unlike nicotine or heroin or alcohol, it holds no one hostage, nor (barring accidents) does it damage the body. While it cares not a whit for any individual and is incapable of reciprocating kindness or respect or love, wilderness can be a neutral "friend with benefits." As a smoker does with cigarettes, I routinely seek out this "friend" when times are tough.

A few more thoughts on this natural, healthy way of coping with stress. Humans are meant to move, from cradle to grave; and it's innate. Look at infants: Even on their backs, turtlelike, they wiggle their arms and legs around for no apparent reason except for movement. Then, once they're old enough, most babies instinctively crawl, then toddle outside, suggesting that humans intuitively seek nature. Together, movement in the outdoors promotes good health in mind and body.

How? Physical activity conditions our heart, lungs, muscles, and so forth while keeping our bones dense and strong. Physical exertion also releases endorphins, the body's natural antidepressants, and sunlight stimulates the release of serotonin—another natural antidepressant—in the brain. Combining the two, as in hiking or backpacking, is metaphorically like Connor's ibuprofen-and-jelly bean mix: the perfect drug combination. It helps thwart depression and anxiety while fostering fitness.

Trying to practice what I preach (and vice versa) throughout my medical career, I have routinely suggested to my patients, even those confined to wheelchairs, that incorporating time for movement—especially outdoors—is an essential part of optimal health. In many ways, it's the ultimate medicine. Doses are free and limitless, and can be titrated to the patient's size, age, fitness, and desires.

Is outdoor physical activity a cure-all for emotional stressors? Of course not. But to boost self-esteem and get out of a mental rut, will yourself to walk out of one of the biggest ruts on earth—the Grand Canyon—or do something similar in a favorite landscape. Even better? *Do it with someone you love.*

I took a small handful of jellybeans and smiled at Wes and Connor. They mirrored that smile. Through the evening, a happy mood and laughter dominated. It was clear: Not just for Wes, Connor, and me, but for all of us, the drug combination was working.

CHAPTER TWENTY-TWO

River Mischief, and the Birth of Death

NEAR THE LITTLE COLORADO RIVER

I maintain that Rio Colorado is masculine, powerful, cunning and cruel,
a Moloch of the Canyons.

Oscar Jaeger
The Great Grand Canyon Adventure (1932)

Vanity working on a weak head produces every sort of mischief.

Jane Austen
Emma (1815)

June 1970

To Ron Mitchell, writing a vague description for his planned river crossing seemed the best way to keep the Grand Canyon Backcountry Reservation Office (BRO) from rejecting his hiking permit. *Divulge as little as possible; don't draw unusual attention.* If the BRO actually knew the unsafe technique he and two friends intended to use for the crossing, the permit would probably be rejected. So, all he wrote was "cross the river." Fortunately for them, Mitchell's ambiguity worked.

Permit in hand, Mitchell and his two buddies—Motorola coworkers Ken King and Dale Graham—hiked down the fourteen-mile-long Nankoweap Trail from the North Rim to the river during intense but not unexpected June heat. Reaching the Colorado just before dark, they set up camp.

A reprieve from the sweltering temperature eluded them until well after midnight. Lying uncovered on their sleeping bags, the men collected blowing sand, an entomologist's delight of bugs, and other debris on their sweaty skin. With daybreak came the intense sun and cicadas crowing like roosters. Walking downriver along the Colorado's right bank, the trio periodically dipped into the frigid water to prep for their river crossing.

By 1970, seven-year-old Lake Powell had become so deep that water released from behind its dam ran about fifty degrees, more than twenty degrees colder than the typical pre-dam days. For their crossing, Mitchell had chosen swift flatwater well downstream of the tailwaves of Kwagunt Rapid near River Mile 56, where—other than a few small riffles—the Colorado offered smooth sailing for at least a couple of miles. He knew this from the handful of Canyon trips he'd worked for Sanderson Expeditions over the previous three summers.

A Hatch river trip pontoon boat motored close to him and his two friends. The pilot, surprised to see hikers in the torrid heat, offered them a ride to the other side. Ron flatly turned it down; a ride, he felt, would be "cheating." He wanted to cross the river like Colin Fletcher and Harvey Butchart had: under his own power.

"Suit yourselves," the boatman replied, shaking his head.

Ron then gave his buddies a tutorial on how they would cross—a concept he'd devised and practiced in a Phoenix swimming pool but had yet to try in the wild on the river. First, he inflated his air mattress. Next, he wrapped his backpack, boots, and other gear burrito-style with a large plastic sheet. Then, he lashed this bundle onto his inflated air mattress with rope, leaving a twelve-foot loop of slack. Per Ron's plan, they'd hold this loop between their teeth (like a horse holds a bit), allowing them to swim while towing their air mattress cargoes behind them.

No one brought a life jacket; they wouldn't need them, Ron advised. Instead, they would mimic what he had practiced in the swimming pool and use their Ensolite sleeping pads as personal flotation devices. Ron went first. He fastened his pad around his torso and secured it with nylon cord, then waded waist deep into the river. Biting down on the tow rope, he pushed off into the current.

Using steady, even strokes, he started swimming for a sandbar on the other side, about a hundred yards downstream. The river, however, zipped him past this target before he made it even a third of the way across. Realizing he had greatly underestimated the effort he'd need to reach the opposite bank and beginning to panic, he started swimming as hard as possible, taking a much more aggressive upstream ferry angle.

Alas, the tethered air mattress remained in the grip of the current. The opposing forces yanked the rope in his mouth, twisting his head back—like horse and rider fighting each other for control.

About three-quarters of the way across, Ron ran out of steam. As he was

Ron Mitchell. *Ron Mitchell archives*

catching his breath, he glanced downriver. Dead ahead was a little rapid with two- to three-foot waves, plenty enough to capsize his rig. Fueled by another burst of adrenaline, his thrashing stroke propelled him to the other side, although far beyond his initial goal. He flopped onto the bank, took a few deep breaths, then waved the others over.

Seeing Ron's intense yet nearly futile effort, Graham and King began their paddling in a relative frenzy. They made good progress until an unavoidable hydraulic caused King's air mattress to buckle and capsize. Air mattress now upside down, its strapped-on cargo instantly waterlogged into the equivalent of a sea anchor. Making matters worse, King's feet became tangled in the tow rope.

Meanwhile, Graham, who had remained upright, successfully ran the riffle that had flipped King. Paddling as frantically as Ron had, Graham reached the left shore, but about a half-mile below Ron. At the same time, King, hobbled and at the mercy of the current, funneled downstream.

Ron watched in horror. The moment seemed to be a replay of one of Harvey Butchart's all-too-real nightmares. In May 1955, Harvey led twenty-two-year-old Arizona State College student Boyd Moore, a non-swimmer, into this same stretch of river after also hiking down the Nankoweap Trail. Moore tried paddling across the river on an air mattress while wearing his backpack. He immediately capsized, then panicked. Struggle as he might, he was unable to remain upright. Ultimately, he locked his arms and legs around the air mattress as if it were a log. Holding on for dear life, he managed to keep only his nose and face above the chilly, spring-runoff water; his backpack and the bulk of his body dangled iceberg-like, beneath him. His position and the convection of the current quickly sapped his strength and lowered his core temperature. Harvey chased Moore for miles on his own air mattress in what turned out to be a vain rescue attempt. Ultimately, Moore couldn't save himself, nor could Harvey save Moore. The five-mile ordeal finally ended with the weakened and hypothermic Moore drowning in Lava Canyon Rapid.

Ron took off downstream in a rock-hopping, cactus-dodging sprint, hoping for a different outcome for King. For the next hour and a half, he searched for the man, looking behind boulders, under cliff ledges, and within vegetation along the bank. He dreaded finding him floating face down. This worst-case scenario seemed to materialize when he spotted King's pack bobbing by itself in an eddy.

Then nearby, he saw King sprawled on a beach. He lay motionless except for intermittent air gulping, like a fish in the same situation.

Ron ran over and shook him, hard. He yelled King's name. Semiconscious, pale, and hypothermic after his long-distance dunking in the cold water, King's eyes briefly opened, then rolled back in his head. Ron kept shaking him. Seconds later, King began coughing and spitting up river water as he came out of his near-drowning delirium. When he could finally speak, he told Ron he couldn't remember crawling up on shore, let alone how long he'd been lying there. What he was *quite* sure about, however, was that he wanted to kill Ron for nearly killing him.

Graham, exhausted and also hypothermic, eventually caught up to the other two. The three dog-tired men spread their soggy gear out to dry and warmed themselves in the sun. Then they began a slow walk downstream. Twenty minutes into the trudge, King suddenly sat down; shivering violently, he began to retch.

When they reached a small beach below the Little Colorado River, they made camp. King, who had been mostly silent, seethed about the disaster that had almost happened. The next day, they rimmed out by midday and made a somber drive back to Phoenix. All three were husbands and fathers.

May 2014

"That's so sad about Boyd, Dad," my twenty-two-year-old daughter Alex remarked after I told the story of Boyd Moore. Wes, Connor, Alex and I stood on the riverbank close to where the tragedy took place.

For Weston and me, this was hiking leg #11; the plan was to go from Saddle Mountain down the Nankoweap Trail to the river, walk along the Colorado downstream to the confluence with the Little Colorado. Unlike Mitchell, we'd bum a ride across, then hike the Beamer Trail to the Tanner Trail for our way out, a total of about 45 miles over three days.

In that moment, to further emphasize the river's danger, I would've added Ron's misadventure had I known about it at the time, which I didn't. But I did mention a tragic day five years earlier, when fifteen- and sixteen-year-old boys and the twenty-two-year-old brother of one of them tried to swim across the river after hiking down the South Kaibab Trail. The swimming feat had been on a bucket list of to-dos for the oldest of the three. After reaching the Canyon bottom during a church group hike, he talked the other two, reportedly also good swimmers, into the risky venture. Confident of success, none had lifejackets. All

Wes, Alex, Connor and me at Nankoweap trailhead.
Phillip Bremer

three drowned within less than two minutes.

I told the kids about these heartbreaking incidents to illustrate how the Colorado River also plays a role in the Canyon's potentially lethal Grand Deception. Just as its rims' cooler temperatures and eye-deceiving views entice the unwary into its depths, so too does the river exert an irresistible pull on hot, exhausted hikers desperate to cool off. Far swifter and much colder than most imagine, the river has caught way too many intentional waders or swimmers off guard, sweeping them into oblivion. The shocking cold has also been known to trigger heart attacks in older individuals who became unintentional swimmers after an accidental fall-in from shore or a boat flip.

Personally, I've never tried to swim across. Nor will I. However, on countless occasions I have waded or swam in a relatively calm, I'll say it again—*relatively calm*—eddy to enjoy a watery reprieve from the heat. These moments have never failed to be frustrating as the shocking cold becomes intolerable after just a few seconds. *How can water be so damn cold in a blazing hot desert?*

One reason. A big, ugly one fifteen miles upstream from Lees Ferry.

The water in the Colorado River within Grand Canyon comes from deep within Lake Powell, through turbines near the base of the massive Glen Canyon Dam. Hundreds of feet down, this water receives no solar warming and thus is always frigid.

For years, I've considered the dam's reincarnation of the Colorado the equivalent of Frankenstein's monster. Prior to its completion in the mid-1960s, the Bureau of Reclamation argued that the dam would make the Colorado safer through small, controlled-release flows and eliminating floods. Like Dr. Frankenstein in the novel, they did not seem to consider that their "creation" would turn deadly. Or that it would actually increase the danger. Cold rivers kill more people than warm rivers, simple as that. Rapids are dangerous, but without floods to flush them, they get bigger. Add shock and hypothermia to the equation and the combination suddenly becomes much more deadly.

I've also tried to make light of this irritating irony as a joke perpetrated by a cold-hearted government agency. Water is released through Glen Canyon Dam's turbines almost exclusively for power generation and to fulfill downstream water obligations to the Lower Basin States. Over the decades, little to no consideration was given to the effects of near-glacial temperatures and unnaturally fluctuating flows on the downstream ecosystem and the hikers and boaters who explore it. I've imagined dam operators laughing maniacally and saying, "That'll get 'em, boys!" as they sent icy water hurtling downstream toward someone like me. In silly retaliation, I've been known to wave a fist in the direction of the dam a time or two and shout, "You guys suck!"

All jesting aside, the river's hazards are no joke. Wear a firmly secured life jacket whenever you enter beyond knee-deep in water with current, and only swim in the calmest of eddies.

⌇〜⌇

When that interlude ended, we got back to business. We started hiking downstream along the riverbank, mirroring both Mitchell's and Harvey's trips except for, again, one major difference: we'd definitely be bumming a boat ride.

Near the Little Colorado River (aka, the Little C), we happened upon some boaters (a circumstance I bet on) camped on River Right, our side. They not only treated us to a late breakfast, they also shuttled us across the river, dropping us about 100 yards upstream of the Little C's confluence with the Colorado. During that ride, another river hitchhike I'd made came to mind. It led to what I frequently refer to as the "Birth of *Death*," which is the answer to what seems to be a burning question for many, based on how often it gets asked.

In April 1998 during a busy spring at the Grand Canyon Clinic, I challenged myself with an epic day-hike down Tanner to the Little C and back, nearly thirty-six-miles, round-trip. Becky frowned when I told her my plan.

"Sounds like a bad idea, if you ask me," she warned. "Promise you'll be careful."

The next morning, as I snuck out, I glanced in my kids' bedrooms. All were sleeping soundly. *Yes, Daddy will be careful.* Leaving our Grand Canyon Village home, I drove to the Tanner trailhead, starting down shortly after five. Half-jogging, I arrived at the river before nine and took a brief break. Then I started hiking upstream along the Beamer Trail. At Lava Canyon, River Mile 66, I saw a river trip parked on the opposite shore. They appeared to be in the middle of breakfast. I convinced myself they were bored and in need of some entertainment.

I frumped my shirt—part of it tucked, part hanging—turned my hat cockeyed, and held my *Trails Illustrated* map by one corner, then shook its two by three-foot size hard. It popped open, like an unfurled flag. I stepped out of the bushes...

"HAA-LOO! HAA-LOO!" I hollered across the river while waving my map. No reaction. *Hmmm ... Be louder. More visible.*

"HAA-LOO! HAA-LOO!" I bellowed, now frantically waving both arms, flailing my map overhead.

"Hey!" someone yelled back after finally spotting me. "Do you need something? Help?"

"Oh, Oh! HAA-LOO! HAA-LOO!!" I shouted back, excited at having been noticed.

"Do you need something?" someone yelled again, louder.

"Zank you! Zank you! How FARR to FAN-TUM Ranch?!" I hollered back while pointing upstream. I knew Phantom was more than twenty river miles *downstream*. I intentionally pointed in the wrong direction, portraying myself as a disoriented clown of a foreign tourist, ridiculously far from his goal.

"What?!" the person shouted back.

"How FARR to FAN-TUM Ranch?" I yelled again, deliberately slower, louder, "How FARR to FAN-TUM Ranch?" I gesticulated again, pointing *upstream*.

Someone yelled something back that I couldn't make out. I convinced myself the garbled reply sounded like "two."

"OOHH! OH-KAY! OH-KAY!" I nodded in understanding, continuing to fake a European-ish accent. "I go TWO MILES to FAN-TUM Ranch!" I kept pointing upstream. "TWO MILES! GREAT!" I held up two fingers like a peace sign. "ZANK YOU! ZANK YOU!" Smiling, I bowed politely several times.

Commotion exploded in the river party. Several jumped up. One guy ran to the river's edge, arms frantically crisscrossing.

"What?! NO! NO! Wait! Dude! Phantom Ranch is that way!" he barked, then pointed downstream in the correct direction. More people came to the river's edge. "Phantom Ranch is that way!" several shouted. With that announcement, they also pointed—dramatically, unequivocally—downstream.

"WHAT?! NO!" I screamed back. "You are RAW-UNG! You are RAW-UNG! I go to FAN-TUM Ranch!" Defiantly, I pointed back upstream. "I have ZEE MAP! I have ZEE MAP!" I slapped it with my other hand. "I go to FANN-TUMM Ranch! FANN-TUMMM Ranch!" I intentionally drawled the words. *Zeez dumb Americans obviously don't understand Ingleesh.*

"TWO MILES!" I shouted once again. Then I shrieked like a maniac, "*ZAT WAY!! ZAT WAY!*" In my rebellion, I thrust my pointer finger yet again upstream in a dramatic bayonet stab.

The whole river party stood and formed a line. *All of them.* "PHANTOM … RANCH … IS … THAT … WAY!" they yelled in chorus while simultaneously extending their arms and pointing downstream like a version of New York's Radio City Rockettes.

"NO! NO!!" I shouted back! "You are CRAY-ZEE! YOU ARE ALL CRAY-ZEE!!" I shoved the map in my pocket and steamed off. Upstream.

I snickered to myself as I disappeared over the dunes and into the tamarisk.

At that point, I assumed that they would let me learn the hard way. There is no Phantom Ranch upstream, bro. I wouldn't get an ice-cold Lemmy. Or Tecate. Or snacks. Or any "I hiked the Canyon" tee-shirts.

But I would get what I deserved.

I peered back. A guy was getting ready to row across the river to my side. *Uh-oh!*

I didn't expect this at all. A heroic effort to save me from my own lunacy.

I popped back out of the bushes and ran to the river's edge.

"HAA-LOO! HAA-LOO!" I happily hooted, waving.

"Hey, he's back!" someone shouted, pointing at me.

The boatman, just getting into the current, stopped and turned to look at me. Gasping, he panted, "Hey, dude! Wait! Wait!! You're going the wrong way!"

I looked at him, then at the rest of his group on the beach.

"I knew that," I calmly announced in perfect, unaccented English. "I was just testing you guys." *Ta-da! See? In other words, I'm not really a confused foreign tourist. I'm just an asshole pranking you.*

"You all did great, by the way!" I cheerfully added.

Groans erupted from shore.

"Fuck you!" the boatman yelled.

"Awww … it was just a joke," I offered contritely. "It'll be really funny tomorrow. Trust me! And thanks for trying to come save me. I really appreciate it!"

"Yeah, right," he spat.

"By the way, can I have a ride?"

"Hell no!" he yelled as he rowed back.

I heard some laughing and some cursing from their camp.

"Remember!" I shouted. "It was just a joke, a little Canyon humor! Nothing personal! Okay?" Now ignoring me, they resumed eating and futzing.

"You guys have a great trip!" I waved goodbye. The interlude had cost me about ten minutes. But in the end, that ten-minute delay would gain me something far more valuable.

To meet my goal and return to the rim before dark, I needed to make it to the Little Colorado, pronto. Hustling upstream, I had covered eighteen miles by the time I saw the Little C's turquoise waters. With no time to dawdle, I ate my lunch and rested for thirty minutes, then reversed my tracks to begin the grueling hike out.

Huffing and puffing along the Beamer, I hit my wall. I looked back upstream thinking, *I need to hitchhike this river section.* A fleet of bright yellow rafts with OARS painted in red on the side tubes would've been particularly welcome. Years earlier, when I told Kenton Grua I wanted to experience rowing the Canyon, he had introduced me to the OARS/Dories manager, Regan Dale, who put me on several trips rowing baggage. I now knew many of the guides.

Lo and behold! Yellow OARS boats actually appeared, as though sent by the Fairy Godmother Department. *Sweet!* I jogged toward a clear area where I could be sighted and picked up.

My timing was perfect. The boats were within a hundred yards when I reached the river's edge. I hunkered down among the willows. As the gap closed, I instantly recognized the lead boatman in his yellow lifejacket. Ha! Another bonus.

"Hey, Michael!" I yelled to my friend and longtime OARS river guide, Michael Ghiglieri, the trip's leader, who was rowing the first raft. He steered toward my vicinity, scanning the bank. Then he spotted me.

"Tom? Is that you?" He looked bewildered.

I tried to appear nonchalant, as though the serendipitous meeting was no big deal.

"You're late," I teased.

"I'm what?"

"Late." I smirked and pointed at my watch as he rowed over. "You were supposed to be here ten minutes ago, remember?" Michael laughed, then invited me aboard. Next, he handed me a cold soda and a candy bar. Despite my intrusion, his four passengers seemed more curious than annoyed. Michael, who had seen me jogging, primed them for my boarding by saying that I was a hiker who was likely in trouble and needed something.

Following updates on his family and his various trips, Michael told me he'd completed his seminal book, *The Dark Side of Man: Tracing the Origins of Male Violence.* It had consumed him for several years. He then asked me about the status of my monograph, *Fateful Journey: Injury and Death on Colorado River Trips in Grand Canyon.* Like him, I had been working on this project for years and publication was also close. We discussed these deaths for several minutes, me highlighting some of the major incidents and conclusions. All on his boat seemed intrigued, especially Michael.

"You know, Tom," he proposed in a moment of obvious revelation, "we should do a book together on all the deaths in the Canyon."

"I don't know, Michael," I sighed. "It was hard enough just doing the ones with river runners. I think the entire Canyon would be really difficult, if not impossible." *Fateful Journey* had been tough work. Fitting it in while working more than full-time as a doc had been brutal. And frustrating. Not to mention the surprising roadblock I'd run into: the NPS kept no complete database on deaths.

"I bet between the two of us, we could do it. I know it would sell," he countered.

I pondered that. For me, getting *Fateful Journey* into print would be anticlimactic. Despite the catchy (in my opinion) title, its mostly lackluster scientific prose made it a tough read. The only ones I knew who'd read it in its entirety besides Michael and me were my coauthors, Larry Stevens and Chris Becker. Even Becky couldn't choke down the finished product.

Yet it contained a lot of useful, potentially injury-preventing and life-saving lessons for river runners. *How could the information save a life,* I mused, *if no one reads it?* Knowing this and having been told by the publisher, the Grand Canyon Association (now, Grand Canyon Conservancy), that it had become an "editorial rat's nest," at one point I suggested that we dump the scientific approach for one that was more readable. "Let's make it a popular work for the lay person, and just tell the stories. Then slip in the life-saving lessons," I had recommended.

"That'll never sell," came back, followed by an equally flat, "River stuff never sells."

"Yeah, but death does," I challenged. "Look at T.V. and movies. Plus, I know that *Death in Yellowstone* just came out and it sold out its first edition in one summer." Indeed, this book had proven a huge success.

"Nope. Your book will be a monograph or nothing." The editor didn't offer much room (or hope) for further debate.

I made Michael aware of that, then said, "We'll probably have to self-publish. I know nothing about that. Do you?"

"No, but self-publishing is common these days. I'm sure we could figure it out."

Michael dropped me off at the foot of Tanner Trail around two in the afternoon. Giving me a few snacks, he pulled back into the current; as they floated away, he called back to me: "Think about what we talked about, Tom, and let me know."

I did just that. I also discussed it with Becky, an accountant naturally averse to chancy financial propositions. The time and monetary commitment could be huge. And self-publishing would be chancy. Plus, she knew that thus far, all the work on *Fateful Journey,* my time and my dime, had returned us nothing. So, she was skeptical. Once, in the thick of the project, she had asked me, "Why do you do this stuff, anyway?"

"It's a hobby. Plus, it might save a life."

At least I wasn't out carousing, I added. I also reminded her that doing the study happened to be her fault anyway. Years earlier, I had told her that eventually, I wanted to take our family down the river.

"Over my dead body!" she'd declared.

"Why?" I asked.

"Because it's dangerous."

"You don't know that."

"You don't know that it isn't."

"What if I prove it?"

"Maybe."

Our study did prove it: The risk is low. (And yes, I eventually took the whole family down the river.) The study clearly revealed ways risk could be mitigated. I also reminded her of promising interest in the subject, including phone calls I'd received from *Outside* and *Time* magazines as well as *The New York Times, Arizona Republic,* and *Los Angeles Times* newspapers.

Still dubious, Becky sighed, "Well, if only you could make your hobby pay for itself."

Make my hobby pay for itself? Yeah, right.

She knew I was several hundred hours, and we were several hundred dollars, in the hole with *Fateful Journey.* There was no way I'd ever break even with that project. Still, making money had never been a goal. What was? I reminded myself of the ten-year-old boy I saw in the Clinic two years earlier. He died from heatstroke. His devastated grandma, who had been well-intentioned in organizing, then leading the inner-canyon July hike that took her grandson's life, admitted to me she didn't fully appreciate the danger the Canyon's intense summer heat poses.

Shortly after Michael got off the river, I went by his Flagstaff home.

"Let's do it," I said.

Three years, thousands of research leads, and multiple rewrites later, in 2001 we finished the first edition. Ultimately, we decided on the title *Over the Edge: Death in Grand Canyon.* Our first printing of 6,000 copies sold out in six weeks; over time, print runs and sales multiplied. The book even won a National Outdoor Book Award.[11] Besides fulfilling our goal of potentially saving lives, it has created steady income for Michael and me, freeing up my time for Canyon trips like rowing a boat or walking the length.

---

11 *Over the Edge: Death in Grand Canyon* won the "classic" 2016 National Outdoor Book Award.

So, there you have it. The answer to how *Over the Edge: Death in Grand Canyon* was born. Its genesis owed to a chance—but fateful—encounter that probably wouldn't have happened were it not for a faux confused, loud-mouthed tourist in search of Phantom Ranch.

CHAPTER TWENTY-THREE

Cheating the Grim Reaper

STECK-LED THRU-HIKE 1982 (CONTINUED)

Today is the day of revelation.
George Steck
Journal Entry, Day 52

October 1982

George paused. Looking over his shoulder, he saw sunlight reflecting off the Colorado River, 200 feet below. A deep green ribbon with silver highlights, the river's slow and silent movement mirrored George's own. As he inched forward, he realized that the Muav Limestone ledge under his feet was shrinking: handholds to fingertips, footholds to toes. His progress stopped when he arrived at a waist-high bulge in the cliff face. Keeping his weight over his feet, George sucked in his gut while arching his back, and tried to slink past. Suddenly, the foot ledge gave way.

The jolt tore his hands free, and he began to slide down the cliff face. With freakish luck, his clawing hands encountered a knob of limestone and he abruptly halted his plummet. George cried out for help as he dangled in space. His brother Al, only steps behind, rushed over; bracing himself, he reached for George. Frantic, gasping, George clasped his brother's hand.

Al leaned back, straining. "I can't lift you! I can't lift you!" he shouted.

Robert Benson, who had trailed the two men, quickly moved alongside. He steadied himself and grabbed George by the wrist.

"I got you," he assured.

Benson heaved upward and back, attempting to lift a man who outweighed him by thirty pounds. It worked. He hoisted George back to safety. When it was

Hikers in the Muav Gorge near 150 Mile Canyon, September 1989.
From closest to farthest: Lee Steck, George Steck, Dick Long, and Brooke Long. *Gary Ladd*

over, George stared at Benson, then started to tremble.

The shuddering woke George up.

The dream, although terrifying, didn't completely surprise him. He knew it reflected a potential scenario at a very real and dangerous ledge in a cliff just downstream from where he slept. As anxiety-provoking as Lava Falls is to river runners, so too, is this ledge to would-be hikers.

The ledge in question lay at River Mile 149 within the towering 1,200-foot vertical cliffs of the Muav Gorge, again, created by stacked formations of limestones. Specifically, this foot ramp—dubbed the Impossible Bay—hung high above the river, similar to the bighorn ledge that Kenton Grua and Ellen Tibbetts walked in 1976, but only on the opposite side. It had taken George's group fifty days and nearly 400 miles of hiking to get within striking distance. While the others were confident about negotiating the ledge, in George's mind, it was a death wish.

However, with faith, focus, and friction, he had been told, it *was* possible to cross it. George had confided his apprehension about the spot to Benson as they moved ever closer to it. Benson, who had done the traverse before, coolly responded, "You shouldn't have too much trouble," then forged ahead to scout it out.

When George arrived at the spot, he found Benson waiting, perched like a bird just past the crux point. That in itself gave George butterflies. Benson rarely stopped, preferring to blaze out front.

George stared at the traverse. "I don't think I can do that," he blurted.

"Of course you can," Benson reassured him. "It's easier than it looks." He then coached George on the moves needed to make it across the fifty-foot section.

Benson turned out to be right. George found it relatively easy and far less scary than he'd imagined.

Feeling like they were home free, they continued downstream. Then Benson began to struggle after a minor stumble caused a flare of pain in his hip. As they neared the mouth of 150 Mile Canyon where they planned to camp, his pace slowed drastically. Lagging a half-mile behind, he finally dropped to his hands and knees to rest. George was concerned; he knew it bothered the hell out of Benson to not be in front.

The mouth of 150 Mile Canyon is the terminus of one of the Grand Canyon's deepest, steepest, and narrowest side canyons. Entering the river gorge from the north, this drainage has experienced enormous, powerful debris flows, some with garage-size boulders. Over eons, many of these boulders have dropped thousands of feet and several miles through this side canyon's constricted confines, ending up in a nodular pile at its mouth and creating the huge, Class 8 (on the Grand Canyon rapid scale of 1-10 in difficulty) Upset Rapid.

This rapid's thundering booms can be heard for up to a mile or more in every direction.

George, Al, Stan, and Benson dropped their packs and set up camp in a flat sand and gravel area along the bank at the base of the cliffs. In addition to the ominous roar of Upset, the massive cliffs—ancient eroding skyscrapers of rock and as tall as the Empire State Building—plus foreboding clouds overhead, made the alleyway feel gloomy, dungeonlike. Passing storms had hammered the area over the past few days. All were nervous as they thought about the next day's goal—climbing up the canyon.

From the river, it's two-and-a-half miles to the top of the Redwall through 150 Mile Canyon—a difficult and dangerous two-and-a-half miles. Local legend has it that Mormon cowboys in the area nicknamed the canyon "SOB" (or "SB") because it was a "son of a bitch" to get cattle down its upper reaches to the Esplanade level for grazing. Part of the Redwall dilemma for hikers attempting to navigate it is that most of this canyon's debris flows don't reach Upset Rapid. Instead, rock chunks jam up in the drainage, creating chokestone barriers, many with very hazardous, exposed drop-offs.

George knew what they were up against. So did Al. Three months earlier, in July, they had made an exploratory hike down this canyon to the river and back. They found six major obstacles, drops over chokestones. All were close to fifteen feet high, the highest being twenty-five feet. Two could be bypassed fairly easily, but the others were far more dangerous. Using a portable drill, they secured anchor bolts at the lips of several of the bigger drops, then clipped in carabiners. Nylon cords were threaded through each carabiner, then fastened to the wall below each chokestone. If all went according to plan, in October they would ascend by rope, pulling it through the carabiner from below using the nylon cord.

Part of the motivation to ascend 150 Mile Canyon included retrieving a cache placed in its upper reaches, but traversing its narrows was not essential for their trip to succeed. They had the less risky but tedious alternative of walking roughly eight miles back upstream to Kanab Creek, up Kanab Canyon for several more miles to the Esplanade, and then over to the cache. This would mean repeating the Impossible Bay in reverse, which George

George Steck watching Don Mattox crossing Impossible Bay. *Gary Ladd*

opposed. Plus, it would add at least a couple more days.

Fortunately, despite the threat, it didn't rain during the night. At some point, the clouds broke and George noted seeing "benevolent stars" within the blackness. A good omen. It helped him sleep.

Benson, however, didn't. He had chosen to camp up-canyon away from the others and seemed glum in the morning when he came down for coffee. Matching Benson's mood, dark, low-hanging clouds began to gather, but the threat of rain appeared to be minor. No one was concerned, or eager to break camp early. Instead, they enjoyed a leisurely breakfast.

Before packing up, George wrote in his journal: "Today is the day of revelation—are our ropes still in place, or did a flash flood wipe them out?"

From the river, the initial entry to 150 Mile Canyon's mouth is gravelly and flat. Within a couple of hundred feet, it narrows to about thirty feet wide, then abruptly dead-ends at a fifty-foot dry fall. From there, Muav Limestone walls immediately rise another forty vertical feet to sloping ledges. About a thousand more feet of limestone close in from above.

After finally breaking camp, the group made a moderately exposed, Class IV free-climb on the east side of the drainage to the ledges above. Gray skies and the walls' steely sheen evoked a wintery feeling. That, the cold air, and his nerves gave George chills.

Then it started to drizzle.

The possibility of a flash flood occurred to them. Yet from having hiked through the drainage once before, George and Al knew that within 150 Mile's confines multiple life-sparing sanctuaries existed, as well as places where they could potentially scramble up and away from a flood. Furthermore, George believed it was far more likely a flash flood would come with a slow rise rather than a sudden wall, giving them time to seek safety.

It was a demonstration of their lack of immediate concern that, despite the ongoing drizzle, after an hour of hiking they stopped for a break to make hot coffee. The gray-white walls, now glistening wet, created an even greater sense of gloom and confinement.

Soon after their break, they discovered another bad sign: a catclaw root torn loose by a flash flood, probably weeks earlier. The light nylon lines Al and George had placed earlier to ascend the chokestones had likely been ripped away as well. Al picked up the foot-long root and tied it to his pack. He thought it might come in handy.

The first chokestone they reached validated their worry. The nylon cord was gone. Worse yet, the bolt, hanger, and carabiner had also disappeared. Without these, climbing the slick, exposed cliff face to place a rope would be more difficult. A fall would be deadly. Yet, someone needed to make the risky climb.

They all turned to look at Al.

◦〜〜◦

George always introduced Al with pride. "This is my famous brother," he would say, referencing Al's reputation as a world-class climber and subject of articles and books on climbing. George also took pride in the fact that he'd played a small role in his kid brother's climbing success. Tagging along with George on climbs in Yosemite had whetted Al's appetite for the soon-to-be-wildly popular activity. In 1946, after a year in the navy, Al joined the rock-climbing section of the Sierra Club and began climbing in earnest in places like Yosemite Valley and the Sierra Nevada.

Influenced by climbers like David Brower, Al learned the use of pitons through trial and error. In 1949, he made his first climbs in the Alps. With a friend, he completed the first ascent by Americans of the north face of the Cima Grande in

Sentinel Rock, Yosemite.

the Italian Dolomites. What solidified his place in climbing history, however, happened the next year.

Over five hot days in late June 1950, twenty-four-year-old Al Steck teamed up with a fifty-one-year-old Swiss blacksmith for an epic climb in Yosemite. His climbing partner? John Salathé, the man known as the "godfather of Yosemite climbing" and credited with forging the first climbing piton. Together, this unlikely duo completed the first ascent of what is now known as the Steck-Salathé Route up the 1,600-foot north face of Sentinel Rock in Yosemite Valley. It was a seminal moment for Al Steck and climbing became his way of life.

Al went on to participate in the first major American mountaineering expedition to the Himalayas in Nepal and made a first ascent in Canada's Saint Elias Mountains on the Alaska/Yukon border. That climb took thirty-five days and has never been repeated.

In 1969, Al co-founded Mountain Travel, America's first true, outdoor adventure travel company. Nicknamed the "Slim Fox" because of his lean build and stealth-like climbing, Al also served as long-time co-editor of the mountaineering journal *Ascent*. With Steve Roper, he cowrote the book *Fifty Classic Climbs of North America*, first published in 1979. Al's autobiography, *A Mountaineer's Life*, was published in 2017 by Patagonia Press.

By the time of the 1982 hike, no one questioned Al's climbing credentials. George, on the other hand, freely admitted to his awkwardness using ropes for canyoneering. He described his skill level in *Grand Canyon Loop Hikes II*: "On my own, I can handle 15-foot rappels—maybe even 20-foot ones—and with a gun to my head I could do 25. But 50 or 100 feet? Shoot me."

George also confessed that he didn't invite Al along to make up for climbing abilities he lacked. Early in the thru-hike, he had asked Al, "Do you know why you're here?" Both knew—having grown up apart after their parents divorced, George living with their dad and Al with their mom—they weren't as close as they would've liked. They also had different personalities: George, mainstream with a career and a family, more closely resembled their father, while Al was somewhat of a black sheep.

Allen and George Steck. *Gary Ladd*

Wanderlust and adventure travel intrigued him far more than settling down. Unfortunately, it took a toll on his personal life, including a painful divorce in 1977.

Al pondered George's question.

"Well, first, to make a trip with you," he finally said. "And to do something audacious and to see the Grand Canyon." This response pleased George. Al then turned the same question on his brother. George responded similarly. "To make a trip with you, Al. To do something physically demanding. And to bathe in Grand Canyon splendor." They also agreed that completing the first continuous thru-hike of the Grand Canyon had tremendous appeal. Beyond these motives, George knew that having Al along came with other potential benefits, one of which now presented itself.

Al studied the exposed, dangerous ascent. Besides rock-climbing skill, Al brought with him two climbing tools: a "Friend" and a Chouinard "Crack 'N Up." The Friend is a spring-loaded camming device that attaches to a rope. It can be collapsed and inserted into a crack. When released, it expands and wedges itself tightly in the space. The Crack 'N Up, a metal device about four inches long, looks like a flat, miniature boat anchor; once the hooks take hold in a crack, a rope can be looped through a hole on the tool's opposite end. Using the Friend, Al inched up this first chokestone. Fortunately, once at the top, he found the previously placed hardware hidden under debris. He set the rope for the others to climb, and they soon followed.

As the light rain continued, they picked up the pace. Their relative sprint came to a screeching halt at the second chokestone. Besides the missing nylon cord, a new pool of water, thirty feet long and several feet deep, blocked their ascent. Getting across without submerging their packs would be a challenge. George suggested that they pendulum the packs across.

Al swam to the other side, took out a rope, and, holding one end, threw the coiled remainder back. Still holding the rope, he climbed to a high point. Benson then crossed the pool and situated himself so he could assist by yanking on the rope once a pack was attached. After connecting his pack, George stripped to his underwear and waded into the frigid pool, holding his pack over his head as his bare feet slithered across the unseen, slimy rocks. Suddenly, he began to slip under.

"Hurry!" he cried, hoisting his pack as high as he could. "It's all yours!"

Benson pulled hard. The pack skimmed the water, then landed on the other side, below Al. George swam through the pool, then climbed out, soaking wet, shivering, and exhausted. But he had a dry pack.

Some adjustments to the technique were clearly needed. Al climbed to a higher point, squatting on a tiny, sloping ledge before repositioning the rope. After that, they hauled other packs across with no dunkings. Slowly, they passed packs and climbed up, the barest of friction securing them to the slippery limestone. It worked, but it ate up precious time. Meanwhile, the drizzle became a steady rain.

Wet and cold, wearing only a shirt and shorts, George donned Stan's poncho to try to stay warm. Once past the second chokestone, they negotiated the middle section of the Redwall narrows, about a mile of slot and bathtub pools, with efficiency. Only one required wading. They made up time until they encountered another large and unbolted chokestone.

Al and George stared, puzzled. Given the absence of a bolt—and the fact that neither remembered it—the chokestone was likely new. In front of it lay a big, muddy pit of water, about ten feet in diameter and five feet deep. Its stony bowl appeared stuccoed with a stinky, gooey layer of red mud. Al suggested they bypass it by climbing left using the Crack 'N Up. One by one, each man navigated the barrier, leaving a slathering of slippery mud in his wake that increased the difficulty for the one who followed. The last person, George, needed a hand at the top.

Fortunately, a third chokestone turned out to be easier to navigate, but as luck would have it, the fourth sent them back to the drawing board. The nylon cord? Gone. The Friend or the Crack 'N Up? Useless. Why? No cracks. Even under dry conditions, the polished vertical walls were unclimbable. Making matters worse, the cold and damp had taken a toll; all the men were physically drained and borderline hypothermic. Al, who had done most of the rope work, felt his hands begin to cramp, curling into uncooperative fists. The ropes were soaked and heavy, as were the Prusik loops they had attached to the rope as footholds for climbing. The wet loops tightened, becoming increasingly harder to loosen and slide up the rope. Yet for this fourth chokestone, they would need them, as well as something improvised. But what? Then Al remembered what he had attached to his pack.

After prying his hand open, he dug out the catclaw root and tied a rope around it. Double-checking his knots, he took a deep breath and lobbed the root over the chokestone. It landed out of sight. He tugged on the rope. It stuck. With a few vigorous pulls, it wedged even tighter. The setup functioned as a perfect anchor and handline for the climb. Al repeated this for the fifth chokestone obstacle as well. An hour later, only one climb remained.

Descending these Redwall narrows back in July with Al, George had been vaguely terrified. Now, staring at the last chokestone, a sense of contempt surged through him. Determined and defiant, he tore through the climb "as though the demons of the pit were after me." Once at the top, he felt like a conquering gladiator, tasting rain and salty sweat in his mouth but likening it to blood. The last treacherous slot behind him, George found a smooth ledge under a nearby overhang, flopped down his pack, then himself.

He looked at his watch: Four in the afternoon. It had taken them eight hours to traverse only two-and-a-half miles. They would camp here. As George watched the rain, the others wandered in, one by one. Benson, dragging, arrived last. The

George and Allen ascending the last of the redwall narrows in 150-Mile Canyon. *Gary Ladd*

downpour became steady and the wind began to blow.

After choosing sleeping spots and a place for their kitchen, the group shared a dinner of green chili stew and margaritas made from Everclear (a high-octane, pure grain alcohol) and Crystal Light, consuming more than usual in self-congratulation and relief at ending the day with everyone in one piece. They chatted about the harrowing moments, but mostly about Al's heroics. While Al downplayed his efforts, George didn't. He wrote: "Al was the hero and I gave him a big hug. We felt that we had cheated the Grim Reaper once again."

Somewhat surprising, even Benson, who almost always preferred to be in front, was pleased at the way they had gotten through. His pleasure derived from a strangely selfish reason. Initially, he had made it clear that he didn't want to come up 150 Mile Canyon because of the pre-placed bolts. The bolts, he lamented, "spoiled the purity of the venture." Rather, he felt, "success should depend on one's own abilities, not hardware." When Al was forced to climb all the chokestones, Benson's objections, like the nylon cords, vanished. The trip became "pure" again.

By early evening, the skies briefly cleared and sunlight reflected on the distant wall to the east. But the uplifting moment ended quickly as the clouds reappeared and the rain resumed with even greater vengeance. Tucked under the shelter and still jazzed, George didn't care one iota. Instead, he wrote, "We gleefully thumbed our noses at the storm."

In the waning twilight, they heard a tremendous roar, then floodwaters gushed over the wall opposite their overhang. The thirty-five-foot waterfall drew them out for a better look. Walking to the edge of the narrows, they peered down into the Redwall slot below. The foot-deep water hurled into the gorge with an enormous, thundering noise. They flashed their feeble headlamps into the terrifying, murky cauldron. The scene gave George the impression of "a pack of wild brown and white dogs in a feeding frenzy."

Returning to their shelter, George had the very real sense that the journey would be all downhill from there. As he later wrote in *Loop Hikes II*, it was the "most extraordinarily intense day of my canyon life." Unable to contain his ecstasy, he shouted obscenities into the darkness at the top of his voice. Then, smiling, he listened as the sound bounced off the cliffs, a mix of wind and echo.

CHAPTER TWENTY-FOUR

Ruby Slippers and Situational Awareness

SOUTH BASS TO HERMIT

I also wish to acknowledge a debt to the Great Facilitators—the staff of the
Backcountry Reservations office who have, over almost two decades, been
uniformly friendly and helpful. Among these, I need to single out Tom Davison,
Mark Sinclair and **Ken Phillips**. *[emphasis added]*

George Steck
Acknowledgments/*Grand Canyon Loop Hikes I* (1989)

October 2014

Dust poofed into little clouds as I pulled the Yukon to a stop in the dirt parking lot for the South Bass Trailhead. Late summer, and now fall, had been exceptionally dry, similar to the arid conditions in 2009 when Eric Gueissaz, Wes, and I had run out of water and nudged ourselves a little too close to being entries in *Over the Edge*. A couple of months earlier, we had aborted an attempt to trek this forty-five-mile leg from South Bass to Hermit Canyon for two reasons: too hot, too dry. The weather was cooler now, but the relative dry spell had persisted, evident by the thick layer of dust covering the Yukon, even filling the cracks between doors.

Despite these conditions, we laughed in anticipation of a fun evening while we unloaded pizza, sodas, beer, and camp chairs. Although preoccupied, we noticed two men sitting in the shade of pinyon trees. Their grim faces, slumped shoulders, and the backpacks lying nearby suggested defeated hikers. With no other vehicle in sight, they also appeared to be stranded many miles from pavement. Ken Phillips, Connor's dad and an NPS ranger, walked over to them. I followed.

"Are you guys okay? Do you need help?" Ken asked, shifting naturally into ranger mode.

Both men appeared to be in their middle fifties. One seemed especially glum.

"I'm not feeling that great," he reported. "We were going to hike from Bass to Boucher this week but decided against it. We got down to the Tonto and saw there was no water at Serpentine. It's really dry. I started feeling sick, getting heat-exhausted. We thought it was better to hike out than risk it." He went on to say that their vehicle had been shuttled to the Hermit Trailhead, where they were originally supposed to exit.

"We're waiting for a ride from the park service to our car. What are you guys doing?"

Ken and I looked at each other.

"Same thing you were gonna do," I confessed.

Seconds later, an official-looking white NPS SUV drove up. We watched as our friends, ranger-paramedics CJ Malcomb and Emily Pearce, stepped out. Malcomb, in his mid-thirties, and Pearce, in her mid-twenties, both worked under Ken in Grand Canyon's Emergency Services.

"Wow! Fancy meeting you two here," CJ quipped, glancing from Ken to me. CJ headed up the Canyon's Preventive Search and Rescue (PSAR) program. "What are you guys up to?"

"Same thing those guys you're picking up planned to do," Ken announced. "Hiking Bass to Boucher."

"Really?" Emily chimed in, eyebrows raised as she gazed from Ken to me. "Well, be careful. It's really, really dry down there."

Once out of earshot of the two would-be backpackers, CJ sighed, "Yeah, we're basically here as taxi service because one of those dudes conveniently got a belly ache. Their car's at Hermit's Rest. They bailed and hiked back out just after getting started. They have no ride back. Rather than walk, he called us on a sat phone. I think the guy with the belly ache just got a case of bad nerves because he didn't find water at Serpentine." CJ looked at us, then at our group standing beside the Yukon.

"Are you all going?" CJ probed.

"Yep. All but the driver," I replied.

CJ's face turned pensive.

"You guys think you'll be all right?"

"Well, we're betting on finding pothole water. Plus, we have Sapphire and Boucher creeks, and we can always go to the river. I think we'll be fine," I said.

"Well, alrighty then. You guys take care." He smiled and turned, but then looked back over his shoulder and smirked at Ken. "We'd hate to have to come rescue our boss."

Within the NPS Ken Phillips was a living legend. A leading expert in search and rescue (SAR), he spent thirty-two of his thirty-five years with the agency at Grand Canyon National Park. He'd worked his way up the ranks, starting in the Backcountry Office in 1983, making reservations for hikers, including George Steck. He became a backcountry ranger/EMT, then paramedic, and ultimately Chief of Emergency Services.

Conservative and calculating by nature, Ken avoided risky situations and was proficient in "situational awareness," a skill that emphasizes being constantly attentive to potential dangers while making decisions during emergencies. It stresses the use of good judgment rather than wishful thinking as the primary driver for prevention. Ken taught classes in situational awareness around the US, and even overseas. Frequently he started his presentations by passing out a laminated card. The card captured "Situational Awareness" founder Karl Weick's philosophy for communicating during emergencies:

Here's what I think we face.
Here's what I think we should do.
Here's what we should keep an eye on.
Now talk to me.

Ken had asked to join us so he could spend more time with his son Connor, who again, had been Wes's buddy since they were toddlers, only recently becoming his most frequent hiking companion. I liked having Ken along. For one thing, his extensive experience and many NPS connections made him a great safety net. Second, he had a satellite phone. (Becky and Annie—Ken's wife and Connor's mother—had become increasingly concerned about our hikes, to the point of insisting we carry one.) Third, I liked Ken bookending me as another old guy; he was fifty-five, I was fifty-one. We'd likely bring up the rear. A bonus, Ken was affable, a great conversationalist, and had an excellent sense of humor. True confession: my primary reason was that I was grateful to count him among my closest friends.

I wasn't the only one.

George Steck had become acquainted with Ken during his early days as a ranger in

Ken Phillips with George. *Gary Ladd*

the park's NPS Backcountry Office. After issuing George multiple hiking permits, they had advanced to a first-name basis. They'd even hiked the Canyon together. In 1991, Ken and Annie bestowed on George the honor of being godfather to their daughter, Chloe.

CJ and Emily loaded the stranded men's backpacks into the SUV. All four climbed aboard.

"Good luck," the man with the stomachache called out to us. "We hope you find water." Now looking relaxed, he smiled and waved.

I waved back. *I wonder if you know what a sweetheart deal you just got?* His smile suggested he knew all too well.

We finished unloading. The roof rack had been piled high with backpacks and several juniper logs. We built a fire, set up chairs, then grabbed slices of Fratelli's pizza purchased in Flagstaff. Ken and I popped beers.

"Hey, Uncle Tom," Peter asked. "Do you think we'll be all right?"

A biomedical engineer, Pete also had Canyon experience. He'd hiked with Wes, Alex, and me on our snowy Tanner-to-Phantom leg in 2009. He'd also joined us on several of our New Year's family hikes and river trips.

"Yeah, I do," I told Pete. "There should be pothole water in most of those drainages. We'll just have to be vigilant and plan on doing a little searching. And we always have the river for backup."

For this trip, my other nephew, Phillip (Pete's brother), once again served as our chauffeur. In addition to those who had become the "trip regulars"—Wes, Connor, and me—a couple other hikers were on board.

Nineteen-year-old Thomas McCullough had graduated with Wes from Flagstaff High School. Six feet, four inches tall with short, dark hair, Thomas went by his first initial, T. As had Wes, T attended NAU. I found it pleasantly coincidental that T also happened to be a great-nephew of Bruce Babbitt.

Happy-go-lucky and quick to smile, T worked for Babbitt's Backcountry Outfitters, a longtime family-owned business in downtown Flagstaff. Five months earlier, in May 2014, he had completed one leg of our mega-hike, a Marble Canyon section from Rider to South Canyon. During a long, dry stretch atop the Redwall, he'd located critical pothole water, an impressive feat for his first-ever overnight backpack in the Canyon.

Our other new invitee was a twenty-two-year-old from California named Vince Sutherland. A *Star Wars* fan with a cross country runner's build, Vince aspired to write science fiction. He and Wes had worked together three summers as landscapers. With only one previous hike in the Canyon, a rim-to-rim crossing, he seemed especially jazzed to be coming on this one.

Between Connor, T, and Vince, it was hard to say who was more baby-faced. All three could've passed for high school sophomores. These three would also accompany Wes and me on the remainder of our length-hike. Henceforth, I started referring to the fledgling foursome as "the boys."

When the wisecracks and firewood dwindled, we began a serious discussion about the water situation for our hike. Weatherwise, late October in the Canyon is typically perfect. Days are usually warm but not hot, nights are cool but above freezing, and there's enough daylight to allow for making serious miles. But for natural water sources, October is almost always riskier than September or March. Monsoons typically end by mid-September. Potholes run dry. Springs flow minimally, if at all. No springs existed in the immediate area of Bass Canyon.

George Steck had once suffered a serious water problem here. On a blazing hot Fourth of July after hiking to a scenic inner-Canyon feature called Royal Arch, he and Stan, along with Don Mattox, sidetracked into the wrong ravine and ran out of water. In the heat, a dehydrated George became weaker and weaker, flirting with early heatstroke. When Stan, who had rimmed-out first, didn't see his dad following him, he grabbed extra water from their car, doubled back, and found George collapsed, his skin hot and dry. Stan immediately started pouring water over George's body to cool him and also encouraged him to drink it.

That rescue had come in the nick of time. Hours later George had hobbled out, exhausted but alive. Later, in *Loop Hikes I*, he wrote, "If I made the same mistake again, I'd be dead."

This hike would be new territory to everyone except me. The one and only time I hiked this section, fifteen years earlier, had been in early December. Water had been plentiful. For this trip, with the punishing summer heat now ended, we hoped the seeps in the drainages had started trickling again. My anticipated worst-case scenario would require us to detour to the river for water via a side canyon we'd be crossing. Such detours could cost hours but did offer a potential bailout if the springs were dry. After discussing all this in the firelight, we took a vote on going ahead with the hike or aborting. All were in favor of hiking. We toasted the verdict.

In the morning, omen-like, a fire on the North Rim poured smoke into the Canyon's depths. I asked Phil to park my Yukon in the Backcountry Office parking lot, next to Ken's 4Runner. Then he and the Yukon disappeared in another big cloud of dust.

Each of us carrying about two gallons of water, we started down South Bass Trail, engulfed by hazy, gray-white smoke. Two hours and four miles later we reached the Tonto Platform and turned right, eastward, onto the well-defined Tonto Trail. Within three hours, we had arrived at the apex of the massive, snakelike side canyon appropriately named Serpentine (it's actually named for the mineral, not its shape). Contouring around it required four miles of walking to net one river mile. Just as the belly-acher at the trailhead had reported, this drainage was

Filtering pothole water. *Tom Myers*

bone dry. We searched for water pockets several hundred feet up-canyon and down-canyon from the trail but turned up nothing. So, we continued onward. Two miles farther east, we reached a canyon called Emerald. It, too, was dry. So was the next drainage, Quartz.

As may now be apparent, tributary canyons in this section of the Grand Canyon are known as "the Gems" or "the Jewels" and named (most officially, a few unofficially) after semiprecious stones: Crystal, Jade, Jasper, Slate, Topaz, Agate, Sapphire, Turquoise, Emerald, Ruby, Quartz, Serpentine. Few to none of these namesake minerals are actually found in these side canyons. John Wesley Powell reportedly started this naming trend, beginning with Sapphire. Mapmaker Richard T. Evans and then the USGS followed suit for others. River runners know the Gems are responsible for some of the Canyon's biggest and best rapids. For example, the massive Crystal Rapid, formed by Slate and Crystal Creek Canyons, comes with a reputation of being as badass as Lava Falls. Far more important to us, however, the Gems normally contain hidden water.

While it goes without saying that it is potentially dangerous to hike in a hot, dry desert world, it may be less obvious that the scarcity of water is a huge part of the appeal. Why? Simply for the thrill of searching for and finding it. It's even better when you don't expect it. Indeed, for a backpacker in Grand Canyon, or in any desert for that matter, discovering water is like finding gold. And Mother Nature frequently offers this treasure in dramatic fashion: in lush, secretive oases or within sculpted stone goblets, shallow rocky saucers, and deeply incised clefts. Some of the pothole pick-me-ups are formed by trickling water on cliff faces and can be spotted by the colorful streaks of mineral deposits the dribbles leave in their wakes. Bands of rusty red, tangerine orange, avocado green, and abalone white—rainbows in stone—often signal the watery reward.

Luckily, the next canyon we reached, Ruby, finally served up what we wanted, albeit with no dramatic flair. Two bug-infested potholes had somehow survived the heat, hidden in the shade at the foot of a small cliff located upstream of the trail crossing. We stared into these deep, dark puddles, their scummy water twitching with life. Brushing the insects aside, we gratefully filled our bottles. We designated Ruby as camp for the night.

By eight the next morning we were up and at 'em. Within an hour we crossed two more canyons unofficially called Jade and Jasper. No surprise, both were waterless. Fortunately, the next canyon, Turquoise, offered a large, cone-shaped pothole close to the trail crossing at the base of a fifteen-foot cliff. After clearing away its sprinkled layer of dead bugs, leaves, and other debris, we tanked up. This proved a wise move. The next three drainages—Sapphire, Agate, and Slate—were dry.

As a sidenote, while researching our hike online, I found a website that claimed, "Slate Canyon is a perennial water source." This had been reassuring news. Turns out, however, it was false advertising, like so much to be found on the internet. Buyer beware!

Usually in the lead, Weston had been limping since before reaching Slate. He had dropped back to walk just ahead of me. He now sat on a ledge. Clenching his teeth, he removed each boot and sock in slow motion, as though he were peeling a really stuck Band-Aid off freshly burned skin. His bare feet had several blisters. I inspected them and found myself wincing. One blister on his heel looked exceptionally bad, angry red skin at its base. From a medical perspective, a foot blister has long reminded me of an infected tooth, partly because of its white, lumpy appearance but mainly because pressure on either one causes god-awful pain.

His new hiking boots were to blame. Personally, I'd switched several years earlier from heavy boots to cheap running shoes for hiking the Canyon to avoid Weston's very scenario. My reasoning was that circumventing blisters (a problem common with new, stiff, or poorly fitting boots) could be done with a comfortable running shoe, worth their relative lack of support and protection. So far, it had worked. I'd buy $30 to $40 running shoes at Big 5, use them for a few hikes, then throw them away. Wes, on the other hand, had researched and purchased top-of-the-line hiking boots. Now, he wanted to toss them off a cliff. After removing his socks, he sighed, then happily wiggled his toes.

Unfortunately, his reprieve was temporary. Just as people with bad teeth eventually have to eat, Canyon hikers, despite blisters, have to hike. Also, I had to be at the clinic the next morning; Peter and Vince also had to work; and Connor, T, and Wes had to be in college classrooms. And to reach the rim from our current location on the Tonto Trail, we still had more than a half-marathon of miles to walk and 2,500 feet to ascend—all in one, slow, painful bite.

Wes changed from boots to slippers. Fortunately, the slippers, while falling short of a Novocain injection, did ease the pain.

"I think I'd rather wear these for the hike out," he sighed. "Those boots hurt too bad."

"Fine. Let's tape the slippers on," I replied as I dug in my bag for duct tape.

In a reverse of Kenton Grua's crippling moccasin episode, Wes

Wes's taped on slippers. *Tom Myers*

ditched his boots for moccasin-like slippers. He looked into the distance toward the rim as I taped them securely.

"You know, Dad, it's one thing for the Grand Canyon to be a hot desert. It's another thing to be a vertical treadmill. This hike is gonna suck."

At that moment a recurring Canyon hiking fantasy came to mind. During my more than 300 inner-Canyon hikes, when I'm deep in its depths, the idea of being teleported to the rim or somehow levitating out has never failed—not even once—to force itself into my consciousness at some point. Usually, it's "Beam me up, Scotty" from *Star Trek*. This time, as Wes put those slippers on his tortured feet at Ruby Canyon, it was "Ruby slippers." *Too bad I'm not Glinda the Good Witch from the Wizard of Oz. I'd have Wes tap his slippered heels together and say, "There's no place like home."*

Wes stood, grimaced, then teetered as he shifted his weight to the least painful spots on his feet, grunting as he slung on his pack. Hobbling with a peg-legging gait, he began what clearly would be a slow trudge out. I followed. As Wes's limp became worse, he fell further behind. I matched his slower pace while the others charged out of sight, Connor in the lead.

⌒⌒

Six hours later, just before sunset, Wes and I gratefully reached the rim: our twelfth hiking leg complete, about half of the Canyon's length done. Over three hundred miles down and about three hundred to go.

We walked from the trailhead to the Hermit's Rest curio shop. Clean-looking tourists gawked at us, eyes zeroing in on Weston's funky footwear. We heard a few chuckles. For me their stares evoked a sense of pride; our trail-worn appearance and Weston's beat-up, taped-on slippers made it clear that we'd been down in the Canyon on an "adventure."

We scanned for our other five hikers. *Surely, they had to be here.* Still, we hadn't seen them for six hours, since back at Slate Creek. Unblistered, hiking stronger and faster, they'd left us in the dust. Now, when they failed to materialize in the patio area or gift shop or parking lot or bus stop, Wes looked at me. "This is really weird, Dad. You don't think they're behind us, still in the Canyon, do you?"

I glanced at him and sighed. "Yup."

We began to discuss how such an illogical flip-flop may have happened ...

Two miles and almost an hour after leaving Slate Canyon (where we'd taped on his slippers) we arrived at Topaz. We found neither water nor buddies. We assumed they'd blown by rather than waiting for us. In fact, I told Wes I was annoyed, reiterating what he had heard me say on all of our trips: never split up, hike only as fast as the slowest person, and stay within eyesight of one another. For safety, it's imperative. Next, we shuffled past Topaz. When we reached a large oxbow bend in the trail, we made what turned out to be a pivotal decision: shortcut.

Shortcutting trails in Grand Canyon, or elsewhere, is generally a bad idea. All too frequently it's a cookie-cutter error made by people who end up in trouble when they do it.

At this point for Wes and me, however, lagging behind and feeling stressed, a shortcut proved just too darn tempting. We decided to veer upward above the actual trail for about ten minutes or so, eliminate the oxbow, and intercept the speeders on the far side. Even if we failed to spot them, we figured we'd likely see them hanging out by the refreshing waters of Boucher Creek where surely they'd stop and wait for us.

After bisecting the oxbow we dropped back down onto the trail. We looked in all directions. And saw no one. We whistled and yelled. No response. I became even more annoyed.

Our section of the Tonto Trail was mostly hard-packed and dry. Even so, tracks of various vintages still showed. Were any of them left by our group? It was too hard to say. So we continued on—maybe they'd be waiting ahead. Two hours later a view of the greenery of Boucher Creek gave us a great morale boost. Not only had we put another five miles under our belt since Slate Creek, we now had access to unlimited water. Plus, Ken and the others would be there. *Wouldn't they?*

We descended to the creek bed. Fresh boot prints were scattered everywhere. But no humans were in sight. As Wes rested his feet, I walked upstream and down, whistling and yelling. Again, silence.

During a quick lunch, I vented to Wes about my frustration over the apparent lack of responsibility by the others—especially Ken. Of all of us, he should know better. As we headed onward, I continued grumbling. In the warm 85°F heat, it took us four hours and four liters to cover the final ten miles to the rim. As we neared the top, I bet Wes our missing guys would be hanging out at Hermit's Rest, relaxing and chowing down. I fully intended on delivering an earful to go with every mouthful.

After we failed to find them at Hermit's Rest, we hopped on the shuttle bus to Bright Angel Trailhead. Then we walked to the Backcountry Office parking lot, our fingers crossed. *Maybe, just maybe they'd be there...* They weren't. Both the Yukon and Ken's 4Runner sat empty.

As the sun set and the air temperature plummeted, we hopped into the Yukon. I planned to crank the heater. I turned the ignition key. Nothing happened. Not even a cricket click. *Shit!* I popped the hood. We cleaned the battery connections. I tried the key again. Still stone-cold dead. *Damn it!* (We only later found out the reason: Phil had accidentally turned on the interior lights when he had shut off the headlights.)

I phoned my Grand Canyon Village friend Bryan Wisher, a retired inner Canyon ranger. He picked us up, took us to his house, fed us, then drove us back to give my dead Yukon a jumpstart. When it finally fired up, we thanked him and kept the engine running to recharge the battery and warm up with the heater. A few minutes later, I shut it off. We closed our eyes until a sharp rap on the window brought us back to alert. Two shadowy figures wearing backpacks stood at the driver's window.

"What the fuck?!" a shocked Ken, arms extended and palms up, said as Wes and I stared out at him and Vince with a mixture of relief and concern at only seeing the two of them.

"Where are T, Connor, and Pete?" I blurted, although I already suspected the answer.

"I sent them back to look for you," Ken groaned. "They're still down there."

"How'd you guys get ahead of us?" Vince asked, flabbergasted.

"We decided to shortcut that big bend just past Slate," Wes said.

"Ahhh! Figures! That's where we stopped to wait for you!" Vince added with astonishment.

"We waited and waited, thinking your feet must have been in bad shape, Wes," Ken added. "When you didn't show up, I sent the others back to find you."

"Bummer," was all I could think to say. "Where do you think they are now?"

"Oh, shit. I don't know," Ken announced with another groan. "Who knows how far they went back? I'm sure they've turned around by now, but they're putting in a long, long walk. It'll probably still be a few hours before they reach the rim." He shook his head and sighed. "I need to get something to eat."

We drove to the Maswik Lodge cafeteria. Silence dominated as Ken and Vince ate. Finally, we decided that Wes and Vince should return now to Flagstaff in the Yukon. They had work and school in the morning. Meanwhile, Ken and I would take his 4Runner to the Hermit Trailhead (Boucher Trail intersects the Hermit

Trail about a mile from the rim) and wait. On the drive, Ken didn't make a peep.

"Sorry, Ken," I eventually offered, "but I can't take all the heat for this one. You guys left us. I know we shouldn't have shortcutted, but we were trying really hard to catch up. I always tell the boys we have to stay in eyesight of each other. It's a rule."

Ken remained silent. His lack of response suggested that he owned some of what had transpired. We parked at the Hermit Trailhead around nine, and he shut off the engine. We sat quietly, alternately dozing, sulking, and star-gazing. About eleven, we spotted flashlights bobbing near the trailhead sign. Pete appeared first.

"Hey, Uncle Tom! Great to see you!" he was cheerful and seemed little worse for wear after a more than thirty-mile hiking day. "Where's Wes? How's he doing?"

I updated him. Then he reported that Connor and T weren't far behind, and sure enough, T arrived within minutes.

"Hey, Tom!" T gasped when he reached the rim. "Glad you guys are okay."

"Thanks. So, how far did you go back?" I asked.

"All the way to Slate."

I grimaced. I knew that "detour" equated to about five miles one way.

"Dang. Sorry, but thanks for doing that."

"Yeah, sure."

Seconds later, Connor showed up.

"Hi," he announced. He wasn't even breathing hard. "How's Wes? Where is he?" he added, looking around. "And how are his feet?"

"He and Vince are headed back to Flag," I replied. "His feet are pretty sore, but he's doing okay."

"It's my fault," Connor sighed. "I was leading and walking pretty fast. Sorry."

"It's not your fault, Connor," I said before explaining our shortcut. "And as they say, 'All's well that ends well.' You guys are all awesome … thanks for making the extra effort to rescue Wes and me."

After sharing hugs, we all loaded into the 4Runner. I sat shotgun as Ken drove. In the back seat the boys immediately dozed off. Most of the tension was gone, but Ken remained quiet.

While the silence between us in that moment was bad, it was not the worst we'd shared. On what would be the hottest day of the year in 1996, Ken medevacked a ten-year-old boy suffering from heatstroke from the bottom of the Canyon to the clinic. I was covering emergencies. When they arrived, I learned that although the boy's body had been cooled, he remained unresponsive and pulseless. Ken and another medic were alternating chest compressions on his small, comatose body. But despite those efforts, and the cardiac shocks and drugs we administered, we watched as the monitor captured the final beats of his little heart. Not wanting to accept the final flatline when it appeared, it took several seconds before I could force out my choked-up pronouncement of his death and "call the code," directing cessation of resuscitation efforts. What followed was horrible silence. *The silence of death.* Few things are more dramatic than the contrast between the desperate emergency-room pandemonium that goes with trying to save a life followed by the sense of defeat, despair, and silence when those efforts fail. When the patient is a child, that sense is torture.

Often what follows is an equally overwhelming sense of sadness. I'll never forget the tears in Ken's eyes, which I know matched my own. *No child should ever die this way.* I put my hands on the gurney and hung my head.

Then Ken walked over and hugged me.

Now, nearly twenty years later, I knew Ken didn't need to be reminded of that moment from the past for perspective. What he needed was one from the present.

"Hey, I think it's pretty cool that Wes and Connor have reconnected. Plus, they seem really happy again. Isn't that awesome?" I turned to look at him.

Ken glanced over at me, flashed a brief smile, then turned away.

With that, I began thinking of the Situational Awareness mantra he likes to quote, and applied it to the moment:

Here's what I think we face: Long drive, late night, elk on the road. Ken tired and grumpy.
Here's what I think we should do: Keep Ken awake and get him in a better mood.
Here's what I think we should keep an eye on: One eye on Ken, one eye on the road.
*Now Talk to Me...*Get Ken to speak.

"It's all good, Ken," I offered. "Look, we're all out safe and sound. That's all that matters. Right? And now the boys have an adventure to talk about. Their first night hike. I bet it won't be their last. Plus, we all learned good lessons."

Ken sighed, then turned to me. "Yeah, you're right," he finally said. 'It is really cool."

We chitchatted the rest of the way to Flagstaff. Neither of us fell asleep, and for bonus points, we did not hit an elk....

CHAPTER TWENTY-FIVE

Near-Mutiny and Early Christmas

STECK-LED THRU-HIKE 1982 (CONTINUED)

Oh God! By tonight we'll all be invalids again.

George Steck
Journal Entry, Day 79

November 1982

Filet mignon was on the menu for the night of November 3, 1982. Sara Steck, Al's twenty-seven-year-old daughter, had backpacked it down the ultra-steep Lava Falls Trail. Here she met her Uncle George, Robert Benson, her father Al, and cousin Stan at the rapid. Sara also brought a friend, a newbie to the Canyon, twenty-eight-year-old Marcy Olajos.

After years of summer family backpacking trips together in the Canyon to Thunder River, George and Al knew that Sara was more than capable of completing the hike to Lake Mead when they invited her along. She in turn vouched for Marcy's ability to do the same.

As a favor to George's group, NPS ranger and pilot Mike Ebersole had flown Sara and Marcy from Grand Canyon Village to Tuweep, then drove them to the Lava Falls trailhead. The young women also brought wine, bread, and cheese for an evening fondue, as well as a pound of Peet's coffee and coffee filters.

For the Steck brothers and Robert Benson, it was their sixtieth night below the rim. With seventy-five percent of the Canyon behind them, they were entering the homestretch. Yet despite this, as well as the addition of the two young ladies and an evening meal of steak paired with wine and a cheese fondue, not all were in a celebratory mood. Benson complained that he wasn't feeling well, blaming

Sara Steck.
Steck family archives

the usual culprit, his stomach. Marcy, too, seemed a little subdued; while shyness and being new to the odd group contributed, the Lava Falls Trail had proved a sobering introduction to the Canyon. Sara's cheerful chattiness, however, more than made up for Robert and Marcy's relative dreariness.

The next day, Marcy struggled in the rough terrain below the rapid and twisted her ankle. When she limped into camp later that day, exhausted and stressed, the men were concerned. Especially Benson.

Stan taped up Marcy's ankle the following morning while Sara brewed the coffee. The slow start meant that making it nearly ten miles to Whitmore Wash, George's goal for the day, now seemed unlikely. Even without Marcy's ankle injury, they expected that hiking the steep and tedious lava-strewn terrain would prove exceedingly slow. Benson, the only one who had hiked through this stretch before, had warned them about it, especially the sheer, potentially dangerous 400-foot lava dike obstacle near River Mile 184.

Benson led the way, Al following immediately behind him. The others hiked in no particular order. After several hours of painstaking but relatively straightforward hiking through lava scree and jungley riparian vegetation, they arrived at the dreaded dike. Benson and Al ascended a steep ravine, then looked back. Stan and Marcy were nowhere to be seen. Annoyed, Benson sat with Al and waited. Thirty minutes later, the two showed up, with Marcy clearly struggling. Benson would later write in his log: "I realized that our new hiking companion wasn't ready for this terrain and our pace."

A dangerous downclimb followed. Benson and Al wore their packs while negotiating it without a problem. While this helped restore Benson's confidence since his fall at Elaine Castle, unfortunately the route spooked the others. Stan set up a belay, then they lowered their packs and inched down. Benson climbed back up to help guide Marcy's feet along the steepest section. This position left him vulnerable, but his assistance was critical to getting her down.

The route next incurred another steep drop. The hikers contoured to the right, then descended 200 feet to a narrow shelf 300 feet above the river. Benson told everyone that a gully dropping just beyond a nearby pinnacle would be their final descent.

Exhausted after completing this nerve-wracking down-climb, George announced that they would camp there, three miles short of their goal, despite the fact that it was only mid-afternoon.

George said he'd found the day's hiking both physically and emotionally exhausting. He also let Benson and his brother know that he didn't appreciate them moving ahead so quickly, disappearing from view, leaving the others behind to fend for themselves. Once that was laid to rest by an apology from Al, George's disposition improved. Meanwhile, Benson secretly fumed. As he noted, "I wanted to talk to George about my discontent tonight but I had already jammed down two beers before I had a chance—didn't want to spoil his good mood."

For the next five days, the hikers labored downstream, Marcy limping with every step. George became more territorial about the day's goals. Like a stubborn general he seemed resistant to input from his underlings. Benson's resentment and frustration grew. On November 8 (day 65 for the original group), at Parashant, he confided his smoldering irritation with George, adding yet another reason, in his log:

> Tonight seemed to be a good opportunity to straighten out the discomfort that I've been experiencing under his leadership and being second fiddle.
>
> I let him know that I felt like I was being pushed into the background, but not as much the last few weeks as in the beginning. Every time we meet a boating party he introduces himself as the head honcho. My role was just one of the companions, and soon I realized that this was a "Steck" party—no more a "Benson" party.

Benson had spent a lot of time and effort to make his portion of this trip possible. He had done his own exploring, preparation, and caching. He knew he could've easily done the entire trip on his own, and that they needed him far more than he needed them. Yet, despite his efforts and expertise, he felt marginalized and pushed to the background. Down in the mouth, he started to isolate himself, and continued to complain in his journal, his insecurities clearly on display.

> When people speak about the Grand Canyon they will remember this dude George guiding a group of people through the entire length of the Canyon. "Benson? never heard of him." It sort of bugged me in the beginning but I got over it. George can have all the credit as long as I'm accepted as a member of his group. But later on I realized that I was not part of his crew either. I had my own food and gear. I wasn't sitting with them at the dinner table, I didn't eat out of the same pot. I noticed that a certain social distance was kept. I also didn't seem to get any part in making decisions. Others didn't either, I guess they didn't care, but I did.
>
> Being part of a group, I concluded, meant having the right to some influence on when to stop and where to go. "If you don't like it you can

leave," they have never said that but I felt that attitude towards me. I joined up with George for the company; I found it a lot more fun and entertaining. But I didn't dream that I'd have to give up my complete individualism.

The next night, Benson decided to confront George. He suggested making the rest of the trip a "corporation," [*sic*] but presented it to George as an ultimatum: "Either that or split up."

Clearly it bothered Benson that George had relegated him to hanging on George's coattails. Yet Benson's contradictory nature came into full view here;

Allen and George on the Esplanade in western Grand Canyon. *Steck family archives*

his words seemed in direct conflict with his actions. For example, at least twice he made triumphant, Herculean efforts to rejoin George and the group, the first being early in the trip after his bad stomach symptoms cleared, and the second, after the fall that possibly fractured his pelvis. He could've easily split from the group for entirely justifiable reasons.[12]

But despite what he wrote or said, his actions demonstrated that he wanted, even *craved* companionship. His need for attention and to create his own legacy were also clear.

George, hurt and again taken aback, reacted as Benson likely expected. He told Benson he didn't feel he had been acting as a monarch and was "willing to consider a partnership" and to be more diplomatic. He humbly asked Benson to stay. His ego assuaged, Benson noted that he felt "a lot better just getting it off my chest!"

On the morning of November 13 temperatures dropped near freezing. The hikers cleared the frosty dew off their sleeping bags and dried them by a fire. When they headed downcanyon later that morning, Benson—who, uncharacteristically, seemed to be in a good mood, cheerful and smiling—let the others go ahead of

---

12 It is unknown if Benson ever had xrays or other imaging of his pelvis to confirm if he had sustained any fractures from his fall. Given the fact he was able to finish the hike, it is suspected he didn't.

him. Except for one. Sara. He suddenly stopped, causing her to do the same. He turned and looked into her eyes. Then, after some hesitation, he spoke.

"Will you marry me?"

For a moment, Sara was speechless. "I didn't know what to say. There had been no romance, no flirting, no hint of attraction. While he was reasonably good-looking, physically fit, and about my age, his moody, sometimes abrasive and melancholic personality was a turn-off. So was all his profanity. (Benson's friend Stan Jones said Benson could "out-cuss a mule-driver.") Plus, he drank too much. Anyway, there was no way I was going to marry him. So, I told him no." Speculating as to why he would even ask such an absurd thing, Sara concluded it had less to do with love than it did with Benson becoming a naturalized US citizen through marriage

The following day the group made good time traversing downstream of Diamond Creek on the Tonto Platform. Even Marcy was moving faster. Following a well-defined game trail upstream of the junction with a large canyon entering in from the north named Separation, near River Mile 240, their steady clip continued. Unfortunately, their pace petered out about one mile before they reached Separation. (It had been named for three crewmen who, in 1869, separated from John Wesley Powell's group there only to be killed by undetermined assailants.) Less than a quarter-mile upstream from the mouth, they scrambled down a near vertical, 200-foot chute of broken slabs of gray schist to the canyon floor. Here they retrieved some cached food and beer and set up camp for a planned layover. Shortly after arriving, Benson began drinking beer, heavily. He also seemed to go out of his way to pick a fight with Sara. After arguing, he wrote: "She didn't like my leadership."

The next day most people lazed around, napping or reading. The mood was somber and George seemed deflated. He freely admitted to the others that he was counting the days until the end of the trip. So were Marcy and Sara. Benson, on the other hand, was unusually active. He did laundry, showered, and wrote that he felt content and didn't want to leave the Canyon. Yet he made it a point to squabble again with Sara, perhaps still stinging from her rebuke to his "marriage proposal." That evening Sara lit candles around the camp to cheer up the scene. Benson brooded. Seeing this, but trying not to embarrass him, the two went out of earshot of the others. Here she confronted him.

"Is there a problem? Aren't you glad you are here with us?"

"It's personal," is all he said. But in his journal, he was more forthright.

I had an argument with Sara in the morning. I had carried all the extra food and she had only two days' worth. I asked her to carry some beers for dinner and she got upset and refused—she's starting to get on my nerves.

On November 19, the hikers reached Surprise Canyon at River Mile 248 by mid-afternoon. Here they retrieved two more caches, Benson's and George's. George's included a full case of beer. The men got drunk. Tensions temporarily lifted and laughter circulated around the campfire. Benson, however, shocked even himself with his vulgarity and bad manners. Most of it was aimed at Sara. Yet he felt he "caught himself" before it got too out of hand.

Braying feral burros woke them the next morning, along with spotty clouds and sprinkles of rain. George and Al rigged a tarp. As the day turned sullen, tension once again mounted. Even Al had a long face. He, too, now seemed to be counting down the days, ready to be done. Marcy, in pain from repeated stumbles, felt frustrated and fed up, and wanted to be out of the Canyon more than anyone. She admitted this to Stan, and when he saw a boat passing by, he yelled and asked if they would take Marcy out. They agreed. The others, both saddened and relieved to see Marcy leave, called it a day and camped on the spot.

That night, Benson suggested they share his hot buttered rum to improve their spirits. He asked someone to heat the water for the hot drinks while he set up his camp. Upon returning, much to his annoyance, he saw they had not done so.

> Nothing seemed to turn them on except getting out of here. I can understand Sara saying that she hasn't had any fun on this trip. She said the only fun was when everybody got to camp and had the margaritas. She said that Marcy had not had any fun. Sara kept saying that they had a lot more fun on the trip five years ago. Stan was the only one that I couldn't read an opinion on.
>
> Nobody ever said anything about their feelings and opinions, just let it be known by being grumpy. I was the only one to tell George about it but it didn't change anything. George is in charge which meant follow without questions or go your own way.

The next morning, George's mood seemed to improve. With the giddiness of a school kid anticipating a holiday break, he wrote in his journal: "Four more days of hiking til Christmas. Day eighty-one will never come. It will be day seventy-nine, day eighty, day eighty, day eighty, etc."

On November 23, 1982, day #80 of their journey, they arrived at their final cache, hidden in a shallow cave of a nearby travertine bluff below the Bat Cave at River Mile 267. The cache included an inflatable raft and three PFDs left by a friend, NPS ranger Don Forester. They now had two options: One, they could inflate the boat and exit via tedious paddling, or, two, they could lounge in the cave and wait for Forester, who left a note saying that he would be passing by at

3:30 that afternoon as part of his patrol. They voted for the cushier choice, kicking back and waiting for Forester. George, who helped make his prediction come true, wrote: "So, it looks like day eighty is the end and day eighty-one never did come. ... As soon as our decision was reached, I ate the eighty-first lunch."

When Ranger Forester showed up at 3:45, they hopped on his boat. Cold wind blew as they motored into Pearce Ferry Bay. Helen and Ricia stood waving and smiling on the boat ramp. They brought champagne to celebrate.

As George, Al, and Benson stepped on shore, they became the first three people to thru-hike the Grand Canyon in one fell swoop. Sara and Stan, completing this portion and combining

Allen popping the champagne cork. *Steck family archives*

it with the "Down the Gorge with Uncle George" hike in 1977, now also had completed a continuous hiking line through the Canyon. Collectively, the five finishers ranked as the third through seventh (depending on arrangement) of those to walk the total length, a number that instantly more than tripled the total of those who had done it before them (Kenton Grua and Bill Ott). More significantly, Sara became the first woman on the list of hikers who had completed the length of the Canyon. They celebrated, popping the corks of the champagne Helen and Ricia brought.

The "Ordeal by Rubble" was over.

Benson and Allen sharing a toast. *Steck family archives*

Hiking in the thick of it. *Tom Myers*

CHAPTER TWENTY-SIX

Into the Jungle

LAVA FALLS TO DIAMOND CREEK

But far and away, the hardest going—not the most dangerous or anything—but the hardest, most difficult going, was where you had to go through jungle....

Kenton Grua
Interview with Lew Steiger, 1997

March 2015

"Tom, can I talk to you?" John Azar whispered.

We stood in the entry of the "Morning Star," Azar's Fredonia, Arizona, home and future bakery. Sunlight came through the tall east-facing windows of the stone-walled, 120-year-old, two-story building. Remnant of an early Mormon settlement, it was constructed from rock quarried nearby and had been abandoned for years before Azar bought it in 2005. Shortly afterward, he left his home in Albuquerque and moved to Fredonia for good.

Azar gave me and the boys (Wes, Connor, T, and Vince) a tour.

He had plans to turn the first floor into a small restaurant, complete with a commercial-grade kitchen and bar. The second floor would have rooms for rent. Now, more than ten years into the project, it remained far from complete. Building materials and tools cluttered the kitchen. We found a rusty, six-foot chain stuffed into the oven. On the walls hung old pictures of local logging crews and wildland fire fighters. Nameless faces of Kaibab National Forest hot-shots in 1970s garb stared at us. A shelf above a 1950s-vintage dining booth displayed old hiking boots—worn out and shriveled—like trophies. Azar explained how each pair had once belonged to a serious Canyon hiker. With pride, he pointed

John Azar. *Sally Underwood*

out a pair that had been George Steck's.

The boys and I had spent the night as Azar's guests. Besides my wanting them to meet him, I knew the proximity of his place to the North Rim made it an excellent springboard for the biggest and most challenging hiking of our fourteen legs to date: Lava Falls to Diamond Creek, River Mile 179 to 226, a trek for which we'd allotted six days. Finishing it would push Weston's and my total mileage to more than four hundred.

The east side of Azar's upstairs featured the four bedrooms he rented as part of a hostel. The west side served as his man cave. It held a tiny kitchen nook, a living room dominated by a big-screen television, and two large wall-length shelves. Books about the Canyon lined the shelves, along with big white binders that held John's years of research on historic Canyon characters and local cabins. Most intriguing, however, was a massive map of northern Arizona's huge Kaibab Plateau (including Grand Canyon). It covered the entire north wall of Azar's upstairs living room and emphasized the importance of this landscape in his life.

John Azar is a serious Canyon hiker, though at first glance you wouldn't be able to tell. He prefers wearing sweatpants and moccasins. Combined with a beard, pony-tailed hair, and a wool beanie, he looks more hippie than rugged-outdoorsy. He also sports a little paunch on his five-foot, seven-inch frame.

"I'm a hiker in a boatman's body," he jokes.

Somewhat of an eccentric, Azar moved to Albuquerque from California in 1978. Ten years later, he worked his way into a position in Steck's Army and made several hikes with him. (It was Azar who set up George's surprise party at Cremation Canyon in 1998.)

In 2002, he completed a sixty-eight-day hike from Lees Ferry to Diamond Creek that included the section along the river we five were about to tackle. Seconds before he whispered that we needed to talk, he had meandered among us, scrutinizing our cargo. He picked up each pack, tested it for weight, then sized it up against its intended carrier.

"Sure, John. What's up?" I asked.

"Look, I think you'll do okay and probably Wes, but I have some real concerns about these other boys.

I stopped my own packing. "Okay. Like what, John?"

"Well, that kid, Vince, he's hardly done any hiking *and* he's wearing tennis shoes!"

"John, we're all wearing those kinds of shoes, including me." I showed him my footwear, a cheap pair from Big 5. "What you see is what I got. We started wearing running shoes way back in Marble. Sure, it's a trade-off for sturdiness, but they're light and we have yet to get blisters. Anyway, Vince is a really strong hiker. He had zero problems on our Bass-to-Hermit leg, and he's in great shape."

"Hmmm. Well, I still recommend against tennis shoes. That lava will tear those shoes to shreds. But whatever. Okay. Now about Connor there," he said tipping his chin in Connor's direction. Azar was a friend of the Phillips family and well-acquainted with Connor. "He's just wearing shorts. His legs are going to get shredded. It's a nasty jungle down there along the river."

"He always wears shorts, John." I explained. "That's his choice. He gets scratched up but he never complains. So, he wears what he wants."

"Well, still a bad idea. He'll find out the hard way. Now, that other kid, T." We both looked toward T, who appeared to be cramming yet more stuff into what looked like the mouth of a hippo's head, the green fabric overstretched and bulging.

"I know that kid's big but his pack weighs, like sixty pounds! He's got a three-pound tub of peanut butter in there and a five-pound sausage! And Wes's pack is just as heavy! I think they're carrying way too much weight."

"Sweet! I was hoping T'd bring sausage. That stuff's great!" I said, intentionally going off-topic. "It's homemade elk sausage with green chiles in it. You'd love it, John. His dad makes it."

Azar looked at me, his face scrunching.

I sighed. "Look, I appreciate what you're saying, John. I do. But I let them bring what they want. T and Wes are young and strong. I'd rather have them bring too much food than not enough. Plus, the way I figure it, there'll be extra for me." I grinned.

Azar shrugged. "Fine, but I'm telling you this hike is going to be really, *really* rough. Far worse than anything you've done yet. Here, at least take these boots for Vince." He handed me an old, beat-up pair that looked like he pulled them off his display shelf.

"Okay, thanks. I'll offer them to him."

"Also, do you have any duct tape?"

"Well, yeah, a little, for equipment repair or medical stuff. *Why*?"

"You'll find out soon enough when your shoes fill with sand and sticks and cinders and shit when you're bushwhacking along the river," he declared. "You all should be wearing pants, by the way. Then you need to tape your pant legs to your ankles and shoes to keep that crap out. Here, take this." He handed me a big roll of duct tape.

"Anything else, John?"

"No, I guess that's it, but I'll be surprised if you guys make it."

We left John's and headed for Tuweep Valley (also called Toroweap) and the Lava Falls trailhead, nearly two hours away from Fredonia. *Tuweep* is the ancestral land of the Paiute; the word means "the earth." *Toroweap*, another Paiute term, means "dry or barren valley." Nowadays, people use "Tuweep" when referring to the valley and "Toroweap" for the rim. In all of Grand Canyon National Park, Toroweap Overlook offers one of its most spectacular views.

The road from the state highway AZ 389 to Tuweep is an unpaved sixty miles. Graded and wide, it's like a backcountry freeway, and it's tempting to speed across it. But hitting a section of hard-packed washboard littered with sharp gravel risks a slide-off or flat tire. While so far I'd never ended up in a ditch out here, twice I've ended up with flats.

The last time I'd seen the local ranger station here was nearly twenty years earlier, when Becky and I brought our kids to the "Tuweep Fest," a fall celebration started in the early 1990s by former Tuweep ranger Ed Cummins and his wife, Cathy. Ken and Annie Phillips also made the trip with their kids. Connor had been a toddler then, Wes an infant.

Todd Seliga. *Don Lee Brown*

The setting seemed unchanged. I hoped to see my friend, Tuweep ranger Todd Seliga. Seliga had a reputation as an astounding Canyon hiker. Indeed, he'd hiked the length of the Canyon, not once but *twice*, including a relative sprint in 2013 when he logged the fastest time ever: a mind-blowing twenty-four days, like he was on steroids, but in reality he was fueled only by dates and macadamia nuts. He crushed Kenton Grua's thirty-seven-year-old record by nearly two weeks. Seliga also was known for his unique patrolling of the Tuweep District: on the rim by motorcycle and below by canyoneering rappels.

We stopped at the entry gate. An older guy wearing an NPS uniform approached us. I had heard that this ranger covered for Todd on his days off. Off, too, were the scheduled dates on my permit. We were one day early. Feeling much like I do when a cop asks to see my driver's license, I showed him the permit. He studied it for a span that seemed far too long. *Is there a problem, officer?*

"Have a great hike," he finally said as he handed it back to me. He apparently didn't notice the discrepancy in dates, or at least, wasn't going to be a stickler about it. I sighed in relief as we waved goodbye.

We drove past Vulcan's Throne, a dramatic volcanic cone rising nearly 600 feet above the Tuweep valley floor. The Throne formed when lava squirted upward

Connor, T, Wes, and Vince hamming it up at the start of the hike. *Tom Myers*

through underground cracks more than 70,000 years ago, during the Pleistocene Epoch. Even earlier, as far back as 830,000 years, lava from the nearby Uinkaret volcanic field had oozed through nearly a dozen subterranean vents and into the Grand Canyon. As the molten rock started to cool, more lava pushed past, piling higher and jutting out farther until, ultimately, it crossed the river and created dams.

The river has long since breached all of them. Still, remnants of the dozen lava dams remain. At Toroweap Overlook, we stared down at the dark black, sooty-looking leftovers of one estimated to have been 1,200 feet high (twice as high as Glen Canyon Dam and backing water over a thousand miles upstream). After admiring the spectacular views, we drove the rough two-track road to the remote section of the rim for our planned descent down the Lava Falls Trail. The "trail" is unmaintained. It is also shadeless, steep, and dangerous. Following a nearly vertical ravine of loose, broken rock, it drops 2,500 feet in 2.8 miles, or 893 feet per mile (again, for comparison, the maintained South Kaibab Trail drops 700 feet per mile). Within the last decade, two deaths had occurred here, one from a fall and the other from heat. I was determined to keep our group from adding to the number. As we unloaded and checked our gear, I also grabbed the two items John insisted were essential for success.

"Hey, Vince, you want these?" I held up Azar's clodhoppers.

He looked at them and wrinkled his nose. "Ahh, no."

I also pulled out the big roll of duct tape for his recommended "ankle taping." "Any takers?"

Nope. I tossed both back into the Yukon.

Shouldering and fastening my pack reminded me of securing a life jacket before running a big rapid. What the intimidating Lava Falls Rapid is to river runners, Lava Falls Trail should be to hikers. Although the trail is only a little over two-and-a-half-miles long, its shortness comes at a steep price (pun intended): precipitous footing. A couple of steps down this route are all it takes to realize how easily your feet could shoot out from underneath and send you careening to serious injury or death. Besides the gradient, which sometimes angles up to sixty degrees, a thin layer of pebbly cinders and other rocks often blankets the underlying basalt bedrock. Standing upright on it, let alone traversing down it with a heavy backpack, the ball bearings set a hiker up for a hazardous slide. One additional hazard here is knocking loose rocks down on those below. This danger presented itself immediately.

I brought up the rear as the boys bypassed a basalt boulder about the size of a kitchen stove perched on the edge of a sheer gully. They all passed to the left of the boulder. Like Wes, T, and Connor before him, Vince put his right hand on it for balance as he passed. When he did this, the probably close to one-ton boulder shifted and, in an instant, toppled into the chute on Vince's heels. Before I even could yell, Vince, who had heard or sensed the rock's movement, made a Peter Pan pirouette, then jumped aside with only a split second to spare. Fortunately, the others below were out of the line of fire as the boulder crashed downward and exploded through the chute.

"Wow! That was close! You okay, Vince?!" I blurted.

"Yeah, I'm fine." His tone was surprisingly nonchalant.

I thought of Azar's comments and Vince's thankfully nimble feet, abetted by the lightweight footwear. *Hah! See, John? Those "tennis shoes" were worth it.*

We reached Lava Falls Rapid by midday and took a break next to the mesmerizing pounding of whitewater. Almost instantly the route behind us became an afterthought. We ate lunch then headed downstream along a small, well-defined trail tramped by river runners. The trail didn't last long; within a half-mile it faded away. The river's edge transformed into a riparian rat's nest of overgrown vegetation, worse than anything upstream.

Fortunately, using Weston's damn-the-torpedoes, battering-ram approach like we had done in the jungles upstream above Nankoweap, we succeeded in breaching section one of this desert-jungle. Unfortunately, during the rest of the afternoon—all four hours of it—the riverbanks dished out more of the same, with no end in sight. In all, we made a total of three river miles—not even close to the ten I'd set as our goal for the day.

Feeling vanquished, and evening approaching, I slumped onto the sandbank at River Mile 183, called Upper Chevron by river runners. I told the boys we were done. I yanked my shoes off and dumped out what seemed like a cup of sand, cinders, bark chips, and tamarisk needles from each. *Okay, John. You were right. Lots of shit in the shoes.* Next, I struggled to yank off my sweaty socks and tee-shirt. Suction tight, I gritted my teeth and pulled hard—I'm talking really hard. When I finally succeeded in peeling them off, all three looked like over-stretched, inside-out snakeskins. Then I wiggled my aching toes and feet into the cool sand, hot spots rejoicing as I did.

Meanwhile, the boys kicked off their own shoes and waded into the river. Within minutes, they were flinging mud at each other, splashing water, laughing. *My gosh! Where do they get all this energy?* After playing, they dug out the food in their packs and started comparing it, like school kids who'd moved from recess into a lunchroom. With no oomph or appetite, I merely watched.

"Aren't you going to eat, Tom?" Connor finally asked.

"Oh, not right now. Probably in a bit. I'm feeling a little nauseated." Actually, I felt a lot nauseated, which I chalked up to worrying about those damnable jungles, more hideous lava, and other dangers downstream. I kept staring at the boys. Thinking of *Lord of the Rings*, they turned into innocent Hobbits. And me? I became Gandalf, an inept and incompetent version, leading them into Mordor… *to mortal coil and their doom.*

I leaned back and closed my eyes.

"Tom, you want some of this?" I sensed something close by and opened my eyes. What I saw was a huge wedge of elk-and-green-chile sausage pinched between a knife and thumb. T, the guy holding it, had a huge grin. Again, this sausage was gourmet, made by his dad after their last hunting trip. T also brought his dad's elk jerky. Even better were his mom's coconut chips and cookies. Generously he always shared these delicacies.

Another bonus that came with having T along was his consistently easygoing, affable nature. For example, during a different hike, Wes found a unused tampon in an abandoned daypack. When T stepped away, he plunked the tampon into T's water bottle. "A tea bag for T-Bag," he quipped. T took a drink before noticing it, but then laughed hardest of all.

"Sure!" I grabbed the sausage and took a bite. It tasted delicious. Just what the doctor ordered, it cured my doldrums and abated my nausea.

"This stuff is awesome," I sighed between bites.

T smiled. "Have some more."

I did, and at the same time, decided to fret about tomorrow, *tomorrow.*

Morning came with packrafting across the river, hoping to save time and to avoid the dangerous dike near River Mile 184, the one known to give hikers

fits, including Steck's army. We inflated each raft, slid in a pack, then the intended paddler wedged himself in. Two at a time, we negotiated across 200 feet of swift current. This whole enterprise took two hours and probably cost us more time than if we had scrambled over the lava dike. Fortunately, as a pleasant surprise, the hiking on the south

T McCullough. *Tom Myers*

riverbank proved easier. Because of cliff shading and facing away from the sun, it doesn't receive near the blasting as the south-facing shore on River Right. Less desiccated, grasses flourish, their root systems stabilizing the soil and thus, footing. Almost immediately we discovered much of the jungle could be safely and swiftly avoided on the slopes above.

Right then and there, we ditched our initial plan to packraft back to River Right. Instead, we decided to take our chances going permit-less on Hualapai land all the way to Diamond Creek (this long section is part of the Hualapai Reservation).

As expected, the easier travel didn't last long. Talus became treacherous, forcing us back into the jungle. We weaved through it mostly uneventfully until we neared River Mile 187. There we encountered a dead-end tangle. Taking off our shoes and socks, we tried to follow a partially submerged sandbar at the river's edge. Soon it disappeared underwater. Gambling that the shallow sandbar would last until we passed beyond the shrubbery snarl on shore, we continued to wade downstream, clinging to vine-like vegetation overhanging the bank. *Finally, that damn jungle was good for something!*

Going barefoot felt more painful than not. Our heavy packs exacerbated foot jams and risked worse rock- and stick-pokes. But it was better than being whipped and beaten by the jungle.

The water became deeper, the current swifter. Soon the river lapping at our packs. T, Connor, and Vince immediately abandoned the river route and veered back into the jungle to take their licks; Wes and I continued to wade. When the river deepened, we slithered back onto the bank, then army-crawled through a low hole in the vegetation. After about twenty feet, further tunneling became impossible, and we erupted into standing positions. We found ourselves trapped, with no obvious way out.

Like an honest version of Br'er Rabbit who *really* didn't want to go back into the briar patch, Wes picked a random spot, lowered his head, and charged into the coppice. A tamarisk branch hooked the top of his pack. Then, like a mantrap, it flung him backward. Wes pushed forward, harder yet. The branch stuck in his pack acted like a bungee cord, boinging him backward again. He tried a third time, gritting his teeth and grunting like a mule pulling a stubborn plow. This too, failed. Spinning around angrily, he finally tore himself free, then grabbed the culprit branch to exact revenge, something I had also been fantasizing about. He tried to break it with his bare hands. No luck. He yanked the branch across his knee. Straining as hard as he could, he finally cracked it. He let go, sighed, then turned to me.

Dirty, sweating, scratched, and covered with tamarisk needles, broken twigs, and an assortment of leaves both living and dead, he said, "Dad, remember how you've told me hiking the length is like finally getting a little monkey off your back?"

"Yeah."

"Well, I feel like this pack," using his thumb, he gestured over his shoulder, "is a big, sweaty, fat guy. And he has ADHD. He's super-annoying. He leans right when I want him to lean left and left when I need him to go right. Then he intentionally tries to knock me off balance by hitting the trees and rocks. The worst part, though? In jungle like this, he's always grabbing at the tree branches that we pass. He sees one and goes, 'I want that one! I want that one!' He reaches out and grabs it, knocking me off-balance again. Then, with some of them, he just won't let go. I yank and yank, trying to pull his hands off. When I finally pull him free, he does the same thing to another tree. He's been doing this to me all day. He's driving me nuts!"

Wes then took a deep breath, turned, and leaned toward the thicket. Just before he started to move again, he looked over his shoulder at me. "I'd rather have your little monkey."

Feeling imprisoned during a similar bushwhack here in April 1983, a frustrated Robert Benson wrote: "What this place needed was a match." Seven years before that and sounding more like Wes, a *really, really* pissed-off Kenton Grua raged in his journal about the unnatural undergrowth and who deserved blame.

I curse the god-damned Bureau Wreck the Nation once or twice or maybe more. It's hard to hold one's temper while trying to crash through heavy jungle, which wasn't here before that damn dam upstream. I'm having nightmares already about what jungle horrors I might encounter and have to push through down in the lower canyon on lake Mead. Those fuckin' redneck horses-assed turds who built the damns [sic] had about as little foresight as possible. And still going on. Gawd it's a monster—

eating the land, ruining it for all who follow. What turkeys. Not worth the pile of burro shit that they came from…We need, instead of construction companies, destruction companies to come in and take out these stupid dams which have cost us all so much in time, money, lives, and beauty. Return the canyons to the Rivers, so men's minds can rest in peace on the living banks. We need to hang some greedy bloodthirsty men by the balls.

We finally emerged from this particular thicket just as evening arrived. Taking that as a sign, we flopped our gear and tired selves on a flat spot just above Whitmore Rapid near River Mile 188 for camp, miles short of our goal. A foodfest lifted our deflated spirits, as did a river party's attempt to fling us three beers from the opposite shore. Unfortunately, all the beers fell short and were swept downstream. While those boaters got an F for flinging, we gave them an A for effort.

As we ate, we discussed our scheduling dilemma. Was there any chance to still make Diamond Creek on time? If not, where could we meet my nephew Phil, who was shuttling the Yukon? Parashant Canyon ten miles downstream seemed like our best bailout; we could try to call Phil on the satellite phone to arrange a rendezvous. Yet that option also seemed fraught with logistic pitfalls. Whether or not we pulled the trigger on a bailout would hinge on our next two days of progress. Or lack of it.

Luck finally seemed to be on our side the next day as we were able to bypass another huge thicket, known as "Hualapai Acres" near River Mile 194, by climbing up and following an inches-wide bighorn trail. It bracketed along a small, exposed ledge with no obvious downclimb. Hoofprints faded but the ample sheep poop kept us on-track. Fingers crossed, we followed it. Fortunately, it turned out to be a fantastic route, switchbacking down to a beach near the mouth of 196 Mile Canyon, where we camped.

I told the boys about Froggy Fault, a shortcut up 196 Mile Canyon. I had

Benson fighting his way through the jungle.
Robert Benson

learned from my friend Tom Martin that Froggy Fault would take us to the Esplanade level, where we could cross its open expanse, then descend 205 Mile Canyon. Though steep, it theoretically could save us miles and hours.

Again rising early, we traipsed up the drainage. Within the Redwall Limestone, we came to a slot with a deep plunge pool that had to be packrafted. Despite this delay, by midday we were atop the Esplanade. Stunning views of this formation's slickrock and fascinating hoodoos extended in all directions. This region could easily pass for southern Utah. The terrain, however, proved more chaotic and confusing than anticipated. We debated which drainage to descend. If we

Using a packraft to navigate a deep pothole.
Tom Myers

guessed right, we could reach the river by dark for camp. This would provide a tremendous psychological uplift. But if we guessed wrong? I didn't want to go there.

Inspired, we practically ran down our chosen drainage, boulder-hopping and tree-dodging in anticipation of a big win. Cruelly, our dash abruptly ended about a mile from the river, at the lip of a cliff. The drop, at least seventy-five feet, proved impassable. As the sun set, we scanned and probed for a safe way to bypass the cliff. Finding none, we retreated in disappointment a few hundred feet back to a large, bug-infested pothole in the Muav Formation, the sole water source.

We were now "zero-for-three" on our daily hiking goals. Defeated and bushed from our mad dash to nowhere, we sat in silence. T lay down near Wes, his head on Wes's thigh.

"Do you remember the Shire, Mr. Frodo?" Wes whispered as he stroked T's forehead. "It'll be spring soon. Do you remember the taste of strawberries? I wish the Ring had never come to me," he said softly, mimicking more lines from *Lord of the Rings*. "I wish none of this had happened."

We all laughed, something we needed. We also needed a plan. And more inspiration.

Hmmm … but what?

"So, guys, you need to know that John Azar gave me a bunch of reasons why he didn't think we'd make it." I proceeded to relate Azar's concerns and comments on our chances. My intent was not to throw John under the bus, but instead to provide a get-pissed-off-and-do-something-about-it pep talk. As hoped, the boys were annoyed by what Azar had said, but also motivated.

"Hmmm…yeah, well, we'll show him," Connor said. "And after we're done, remind me to sock him in his beer gut the next time I see him," he playfully added.

Just like that, the mood changed.

Early the next morning, refreshed and eager, we immediately went into route-finding mode. Connor explored the left side of the drainage below us for a descent. He returned saying the exposure was terrible. Deciding to follow map advice Vince provided, we ascended back up the drainage to the top of the Redwall, then walked south. Thankfully, we soon found a steep but passable chute. We descended it to the bottom of the 205 Mile Canyon drainage near the head of the rapid bearing the same name. Feeling a rush of adrenaline, we realized we now had an excellent chance to make our original goal of Diamond Creek, only twenty-one river miles downstream, during our remaining thirty-six hours. We were off to the races.

We shifted into a relative glide as we neared River Mile 207. An amazing delta of ancient sand dunes (sans jungle) exists here and gave us a sense of walking on a gentle, rolling carpet. It felt glorious. Then, after a whopping thirty minutes of this bliss, the terrain reverted to the usual.

At River Mile 209, the popular river-runner camp and ancestral Puebloan settlement area in what's called Granite Park came into view. We spotted boats moored along the bank. Tents, chairs, and tables covered the shore.

We approached the camped boaters with one thing in mind.

CHAPTER TWENTY-SEVEN

Mr. Potato Head

LAVA FALLS TO DIAMOND CREEK (CONTINUED)

As I see it, there are four ways to experience the Grand Canyon [first three: rim, air, river].... The fourth way—walking—is the most intimate ... snail-like you carry your house and the universe of your needs on your back, the umbilical cord is cut out last and traded for a state of complete intimacy and total freedom. You and the Canyon are conjoined here, at home, in the company of the ancient ones who viewed their world in a similarly earthy, sweaty, connected, and clean way.

Dr. Ivo Lucchitta
"Letters from the Grand Canyon: First Things First"
Boatman's Quarterly Review (2000)

Let them eat cake.
—Attributed to Marie Antoinette (1755–1793)

March 2015 (continued)

Standing on a tall sand dune just upstream of Granite Park beach, we gazed down at the river runners. They didn't seem to be preparing to launch, despite it being mid-morning. They also didn't appear to notice us. Spying on them felt a little weird, like living a scene from a movie. I imagined an old Western: American Indians had chanced upon a party of white immigrants: *These pilgrims are quiet. They show no signs of hostility. Smoke curls from their firepan. They must be lingering. This is good. Very good...*

Instead of a defensive circle of wagons, their many boats were lashed together in an arc within the 200-foot long, crescent-shaped lagoon. Their setup did, in fact,

261

seem a perfect match for an intended goal. We reviewed our strategy one more time.

"Okay, can you be sure you ask them for some chips?" one of the boys instructed me.

"I plan on it."

"And powdered Gatorade, Tom," another chimed in.

"Copy that."

"Crackers would be great if they don't have chips, but can you ask for both?" someone else added.

"Sure."

"You don't mind?"

"Nope."

"Cookies would also be great."

"Right."

"Don't forget to ask about the powdered Gatorade."

"I won't."

"Or other snacks."

"Okay! Okay! I got it, you guys!"

Taking point, I strolled toward their camp. The boys followed me in single file. The first person we approached was fussing with his tent, pitched uphill from their kitchen set-up.

"Hi! Sorry to barge in," I announced.

View approaching Granite Park camp with 209-Mile Rapid in the distance. *Gene Couch*

"Whoa! Where'd you come from?" the surprised boater responded. He gazed at the new faces surrounding him.

"Lava Falls," one of us answered.

His face switched to befuddled. "Huh. I hiked the Bright Angel Trail once," he proclaimed, then lowered his head and again started fiddling with his tent. "Do you need some water?" he asked.

I cleared my throat. "Well, we've been hiking along the river for five days. We've had plenty of water, but thanks. We're actually hoping to maybe get some snacks from you guys." I heard a subtle cringe in my voice. "That is, if you have any extra to spare."

"Ah, well, I don't know. Ask the guys at the boats." He nodded toward the lagoon, then went back to working on his tent.

We followed a little path to their kitchen. Roughly a dozen people in their late twenties or early thirties lazed in camp chairs. About a dozen empty beer cans were scattered on the sand nearby.

"Hey, sorry to interrupt," I said as we wandered in.

They looked at us with a mixture of surprise and annoyance.

"Where'd you come from?" someone asked, echoing the first guy.

"Lava Falls."

Another flat, unimpressed "huh" followed. None of the other boaters seemed impressed either. *They have zero clue—zilch, nada—about what a grueling hike we've done.*

"Where are you going?" someone else asked.

"Probably the same place as you, Diamond Creek," I replied.

"No. We're actually going to Pearce."

"Gotcha. Cool," I nodded. "Are you having a good trip?"

"Yep," several responded.

"So, where you guys from?" a boater asked.

"Flagstaff. How about you?"

"Mostly Colorado, Durango area."

I suddenly felt confident about our goal. *People from such an outdoorsy state and town would surely relate to us. They gotta know what it's like to be a hungry hiker!*

"Cool place," several of us acknowledged, nodding, doing our best to develop rapport.

"Do you need some water?" another from their group queried.

"No, but thanks. We're good on water. We've had plenty from mostly hiking along the river," my third reply to the same question. Then I hesitated. Several seconds earlier I had spotted a half-eaten chocolate cake perched on one end of their kitchen table, a likely remnant from the previous night's dinner. *One final appearance before it ends up in the trash.*

263

A thick, creamy-looking chocolate frosting smothered it. I glanced at the boys. Their eyes were also fixated on the cake. I could sense them salivating, like me.

"Uh … this hike's been pretty brutal. What we'd really like is some extra snack food, if you could spare any." My eyes intentionally shifted to the cake.

One of the guys fidgeted in his chair. "Sorry, but we're running low on that stuff."

My eyebrows raised. "Really?" Most river trips are food-fests, "float and bloat," as they say. "You guys have nine boats and you're almost out?" I could hear the hint of frustration in my voice.

"Dude. We still got, like, five days to go." He sounded annoyed.

"Okay. Well, no harm in asking," I replied. "Thanks anyway. You guys have a nice trip." We started to leave.

"Wait a minute," another man finally sighed. Young, lanky, and sporting a scraggily beard, he stood up. He sauntered to the kitchen table, hovering briefly by the cake.

Sweet. He's gonna give us the cake.

"Here you go, dude. You guys can have this," he announced. He had picked up a large raw potato and held it out toward me like a farmer's market vendor.

The boys and I stared at each other in disbelief. I had no doubt that their flummoxed looks matched my own. Before we could speak, Potato Man picked up a second spud. "You can have this one, too." He wore a big grin as he proudly hefted the proffered taters.

We were stunned, speechless.

Then he added, "And you can have what's left of this, too." He pointed at a gerbil-sized serving of hash browns left in a frying pan. "Oh, dude! You can also have these!" he said with equal enthusiasm. He lifted a small can of diced green chiles, then tilted it so I could see inside. The remainder barely covered the bottom of the can. Flies buzzed nearby.

Over the years, I've found the dynamics between Grand Canyon hikers and boaters to be mostly harmonious. The majority of boaters are friendly, welcoming, and generous. They typically share camping spots, food, beer. They also help hikers when needed. I believe it's because they realize we're in the Canyon for the same reasons: love of adventuring in the scenic wilderness. Many river runners are also hikers who understand how grueling backpacking can be. Most commercial guides in Grand Canyon, whether they backpack or not, comprehend this reality.

Then again, the dynamics between boaters and hikers can turn weird, uncomfortable even. For starters, a minority of river runners project a vibe of superiority or snobbery or territorialism. First, because boaters are wedded to the river, some consider it exclusively their domain. Also, boating Grand Canyon safely and efficiently usually takes skill and experience and expensive equipment, whereas anyone can hike the place. Further, by comparison, backpacking can seem relatively boring. Plus, you suffer while doing it. It lacks the sex appeal and heroism of rowing a boat through rapids. So, in their eyes, why backpack? Their answer is simple: You don't have the talent or courage or money to boat. That mindset makes it easy for some boaters to become gloaters.

❧

My eyes shifted from scraggily Potato Man to the leftover chocolate cake. It beckoned like a Siren. Potato Man stared at me, waiting for me to accept his spuds. The silence felt awkward. My eyes quickly abandoned the cake to look at him again. Then I intentionally flashed them back to the cake. Back and forth. *It's a hint, dude.*

He obviously didn't get it. Instead, he continued to display his taters, which framed the smirk on his face. Maybe he thought his offer was funny. Or maybe it resulted from getting stoned by one too many beers or joints that morning. Or perhaps he was really that oblivious and stupidly ignorant. Either way, it didn't matter.

Okay. Let me get this straight, dude. You've probably already eaten (and drunk) twice as many calories this morning sitting around than the hundreds we've burned hiking, and you want to give us those two huge, delicious-looking raw potatoes, a nibble of hash browns, and a spoonful of slimy green chiles a fly was about to lay eggs in? Wow! How generous, dude! Maybe you could throw in your big pot for boiling some water, your propane bomb, and cookstove? We could then carry all that heavy shit until we get to camp and then take forever to boil the potatoes into delectability! How could we turn down such amazing generosity?

"Ahh, thanks but no thanks," I ultimately sighed. "I guess we'll be going. You guys have fun for the rest of your trip." We started to walk off.

"Wait a minute," an older guy, probably in his fifties like me, interjected. "I have a couple of chocolate bars you can have." He hustled to retrieve them from his tent.

God bless you! Jesus loves you! You have a spot in heaven! I almost blurted this out loud when he handed me the candy bars. Instead, a simple, "That's awesome. Thank you so much!" came out.

Still, before we left, I decided I needed to ask the unthinkable. It was a "speak now or forever hold your peace" moment. If I didn't ask, I would kick myself later. So, I threw it out there.

"Umm … do you guys have any beer you can spare?"

They looked even more put out. One guy nervously shifted in his camp chair. Another's bare feet kicked empty beer cans. Finally, one of them said, "Sure." He stood up, went to his boat, and clambered across the deck to the stern. He yanked up a drag bag that had been dangling in the river, reached in, and pulled out five beers. Carrying one in each hand, he stuffed the other three into an elbow crook.

I was stunned. *This is so awesome! One beer for each of us. These guys are all right after all!*

The beer man stepped off the boat and walked to me.

"Here you go." He handed me one of the beers. Then, bypassing the boys, he delivered three to his buddies lazing in the chairs. Keeping the last one for himself, he then plopped into a chair, popped open number five's top and took a swig. His three buddies did the same. I shrugged my shoulders in more disbelief as I looked at the boys.

We headed downstream. We stopped opposite 209-Mile Rapid, about a hundred yards from their camp. The rapid's big hole thundered, smothering our conversation from eavesdroppers.

Heading downstream below 209-Mile Rapid. *Tom Myers*

I don't remember who said what, but a slew of comments and curses then erupted from our group: "I can't believe it! That really sucked! Those guys were assholes! That dude with the potatoes is Mr. Potato Head!"

The "icing on the cake" commentary came from Wes. "I really wanted to go up to that guy and take his potatoes in my hands and stare at them for a second. Then, I wanted to turn and chuck them as far out into the river as I could and yell, 'Are you friggin' kidding me?! We don't want your stinking potatoes! We want your friggin' chocolate cake! That's what we want! That friggin' cake! We know that cake's going to go in the trash!'"

For me, both bemusement and annoyance from the incident lingered well into the afternoon as we headed downstream. *Mr. Potato Head! What a jerk! And if they didn't eat it, what a waste of a cake.* I thought that our interaction had to be up there for the most ridiculous of its kind in the history of Canyon hiking—taking the cake so to speak.

That smugness changed when I learned of another hiking episode that, ironically, also involved a cake and, not to mention, George Steck. This trek, done by a husband-and-wife couple, still stands as one of the most remarkable in the history of the Southwest and makes ours look like, um, a cakewalk. It also included one of the earliest traverses of the Canyon's length. Luckily, no one died, but it had a sad ending, nonetheless.

Bec Kiel collecting pothole water, 1985. *David Kiel*

CHAPTER TWENTY-EIGHT

Walk the River Grand!

THE STORY OF BEC AND DAVE KIEL

*Endless talus—jumping from boulder to boulder to boulder to boulder—
concentrate, think ahead, fight to maintain balance without losing the forward
momentum, never pausing. Keep up, keep up, maintain concentration. Every so
often the stress builds and blows my concentration into a whirlwind of dizziness.
Slip, crash, bang, ouch; try not to get mad. Regain composure, don't slow down.
Concentrate, concentrate.*

Bec Kiel
Journal Entry, Day 204

It is a great art to saunter.

Henry David Thoreau
Journal Entry (1841)

May 1985

No amount of reassurance or pleading could nudge Dave Kiel's wife Bec into
risking the exposed traverse. To her credit, in the hours preceding she had
made steady progress, just as she had done during the days, weeks, and months
since they had started the Canyon portion of their trek. She let neither the harsh
terrain nor a backpack that weighed nearly half as much as she did stop her.

Until now.

The lava dike near River Mile 184—its rough surface radiating a blistering
150°F—was covered in pebbly rock that shifted unpredictably under her
feet. Despite sweat stinging her eyes and despite knowing better, she could

Bec Kiel at the start of the "Walk the River Grand!" hike, high in the Rocky Mountains. *David Kiel*

not help looking down. Several chunks of lava kicked loose by her boots slid into a seconds-long free fall before explosively cracking into shards against the ledges below. The sheer drop had to be at least 200 feet.

She knew she wouldn't survive a slip here. No one would. Heart racing, she began to hyperventilate. After eight months of nearly nonstop, physically—and emotionally—exhausting backpacking that had begun high in the Rocky Mountains, she had become far tougher and more resilient than she'd ever imagined possible. But now, here, above this exposure, Bec began to tremble. Tears flowed, then quickly evaporated in the still, oven-hot 105°F air. She looked at her husband Dave standing in front of her, face grim, arms folded, saying nothing. The stark contrast between this moment and the one that had begun their endeavor couldn't have been more dramatic.

Ten months earlier, in July 1984, they had stood high above a small stream called the North Fork below the summit of the 12,945-foot-high Mount Richthofen in Rocky Mountain National Park's Never Summer Range. The ground beneath their feet then had been soft. A cool breeze rustled the bunch grass and understory of Rocky Mountain fescue and fool's huckleberry. Whitebark pine, western larch, and subalpine fir stippled the landscape. The snow-capped summits of Colorado's famous Rocky Mountains gnawed at the horizon. The crisp, clean, high-elevation atmosphere had felt grand, the mood perfect.

Eyes bright, delight evident on his face, Dave ceremoniously filled a quart bottle with melting snow water—the "source" of the Colorado River. This modest flow fed rivulets on the ground that funneled into the North Fork. In turn, the North Fork fed into what ultimately becomes the Colorado River. Taking a long drink, he handed the bottle to Bec. She took a swig, then they embraced. After years of fantasizing about this hike and spending the previous year in planning and preparation, their dream of following the Colorado River together "from source to sea" had finally begun. At that moment Dave and Bec Kiel may have been the happiest couple on earth.

In high school, Bec was a shy, self-described "wimpy, asthmatic, book nerd." However, her aversion to seeking fitness and exploring the outdoors reversed just before she graduated from high school. The catalyst? Her father, John Reed. "We're going hiking today," he announced while the family camped in Kings Canyon during her senior year.

Nervous at first, she found exploring Kings Canyon on foot with her dad to be physically and emotionally exhilarating. So much so that hiking had become her favorite outlet and her dad, her number one enabler.

As a young man David Kiel (pronounced Kyle) lost his father to cancer. Uninterested in pursuing higher education or indeed, any specific occupation, he instead tapped into the small inheritance from his father, eking it out via a meager monthly budget and spartan lifestyle so he could pursue what he really loved: hiking in wild places. In 1973, for example, he became one of the first people known to have completed the 2,650-mile, Mexico-to-Canada Pacific Crest Trail. Then, twice, he hiked from the salt pan of Death Valley (282 feet below sea level) to the summit of the Sierra (Mount Whitney's peak, 14,495 feet), a route known as "Lowest to Highest." By choice, he made each of these treks alone.

Bec and Dave met in 1974 and married in 1979; shortly afterward, they accepted a friend's invitation to live rent-free on his densely wooded, Oregon parcel. During this time, Dave, who harbored an ever-increasing fascination with the Colorado River and the iconic western landscapes it bisected, pored over maps of the river's profile within its quarter-million-mile watershed. Despite being only the fifth largest river in the United States, it drains an incredibly expansive, mostly arid area that encompasses parts of seven U.S. states and two Mexican states. The river's name, "Colorado," Dave knew meant "colored reddish" in Spanish. He also knew the name reflected the river's historically heavy silt loads. Particularly appealing to him was the mysterious canyon country from whence these fabled silt loads came. Mapping out a potential backpacking route that followed the river through these convoluted canyons, as well as the country above and below, became nearly all-consuming. When the mapping was finally completed, he estimated that his idee fixe—the first of its kind following the Colorado's entire 1,450 mile length—would equate to about 3,700 foot-miles. He also calculated it would take almost exactly one year.

His plan called for the two of them to backpack the six-year-old Continental Divide National Scenic Trail from Rocky Mountain National Park southward past Colorado's highest "Fourteeners" (peaks towering at or above 14,000 feet elevation). They would then veer eastward near Independence Pass, penetrate picturesque Maroon Bells above Aspen, and trek onward across Grand Mesa. En route, they planned to summit at least eight of Colorado's fifty-eight Fourteeners. Essentially, they'd spend the summer in Alpine splendor exploring the many high-Rockies headwaters that feed the Colorado River.

From Grand Mesa, they would descend into Grand Junction and rejoin the Colorado River in nearby Colorado National Monument. Continuing southward, they'd veer toward Moab, Utah, and enter the heart of the Colorado's world-famous canyon country.

For this latter portion of their walk, Dave allotted eight months—the majority of their trip. They'd traverse several river gorges: Stillwater/Labyrinth; Cataract; Glen Canyon; and, of course, Grand Canyon among them. Then the pair would hike downstream, the bulk of it around the shorelines of six reservoirs formed by dams on the Colorado, five in the US and one in Mexico. Finally, they'd walk through the Mexican desert following any remaining river remnants or streambed to the Gulf of California. They set mid-July 1984 as the start date of their year-long hike, hoping to get beyond Grand Canyon before summer 1985 and its predictable heat.

Financing the trip proved challenging. Both Dave and Bec found work locally, but what they earned barely allowed them to meet living expenses, let alone sock away funds required for their yearlong expedition. Dave then had a eureka moment: Outdoor food and equipment companies might be willing to sponsor their trip. He queried a number of companies, explaining how the company's generosity and donated products would be hyped later in the book he planned to write. It worked. Donations came in from Roman Meal, Marmot Mountain Works, Moss Tents, Danner Boot Company, and others.

While Dave took the lead on planning their complex logistics, Bec headed up the laborious job of preparing a year's worth of backpacking food. Because they couldn't afford (nor liked) commercially prepared meals, she took a nutrition course, bought a food dehydrator, then devised and tested dinner recipes prioritizing nutrition. In their little trailer, the dehydrator ran 24/7 as she cooked, dried, and stored beans, rice, vegetables, even beef jerky.

In late 1983—most of their research, map study, promotional work, equipment orders, and purchases complete—the couple moved into Bec's parents' house in Redondo Beach, California. They brought all their personal items and a year's worth of dehydrated and bulk food with them. All that remained was the tedium of packaging the food into daily servings. Following Bec's direction, up to four people—Dave and Bec, John Reed, and Dave's younger brother, John Paul—worked assembly-line fashion in the Reeds' garage. By early June 1984, with dozens of packed-to-the-brim pails of food, extra clothing, boots, and winter gear, they began an equally challenging job: placing their caches. This enterprise required a series of its own expeditions.

A happy Dave Kiel after retrieving a Grand Canyon cache. *Bec Kiel*

Their cache-placing excursions took seven weeks, during which they ferried supplies to remote wilderness spots along their route. This necessitated traveling an estimated 3,000 miles by vehicle, much of it over rough backcountry roads; 300 miles by boat on Lake Powell; and approximately 180 miles on foot. They also planned to mail additional caches to Grand Junction, Colorado; Moab, Utah; Leadville, Colorado; and Grand Canyon Village. Fortunately, Bec's parents helped with all of this.

None of their caches included water. Dave planned on them finding water, even in arid canyon country. It was part of the challenge, he said. Because he thought the territory would be best savored when newly experienced, he also convinced Bec that they didn't need to make any reconnaissance hikes or training trips beyond those for cache placement. After more than a year of planning and preparation, they were ready to start.

On July 12, 1984, Bec's dad shuttled the pair to Rocky Mountain National Park. For six weeks they lumbered through the Rockies, each carrying a forty- to fifty-pound pack, averaging nearly ten miles a day. They resupplied every seven to ten days, often in Colorado ski towns such as Breckenridge, Leadville, or Aspen. In town, Dave would mail a written summary of their just-completed segment to Bec's parents. The Reeds would then type those notes on custom letterhead which had "Walk the River Grand! From Source to Sea Down the Colorado" bracketed by a canyon logo emblazoned atop the page. Colorado proved idyllic, but Dave and Bec knew the most difficult stretches lay ahead in the rugged, dry canyon country. Even so, they were far less intimidated by this terrain, especially Grand Canyon, primarily because of one man, and not Harvey Butchart.

In 1984 Stan Steck lived in Moab and worked as an NPS ranger at Arches National Park. Dave met Stan during one of Dave's permit- and information-gathering visits. "You need to talk to my dad," Stan told him after Dave had filled him in on their goal.

Between phone calls and letter writing, the Kiels got to know George and were encouraged by his easy-going demeanor, knowledge, and incredible willingness to help. He practically spoon-fed Dave his unique knowledge of off-trail hiking through Grand Canyon. Of George, Dave would later write, "a finer coach would be hard to find." Playing matchmaker, George also urged Dave to contact Robert Benson and Harvey Butchart for yet more information, and gave him their mailing addresses. In shades of Colin Fletcher but exponentially better, just like that, Dave had access to a perfect trifecta of Canyon backpacking experts.

⌒〜⌒

On October 7, 1984, as the Kiels approached the Dewey Bridge just upstream from Moab, excitement tempered their exhaustion: They would be meeting George Steck face-to-face for the first time. He showed up on cue, appearing older than they anticipated, and less rugged looking. But he also proved to be youthful in spirit, funny, friendly, and consistently generous. That evening, he bought them dinner in Moab; afterward, Dave and George discussed the next phases of the Kiels' hike: the Colorado River's daunting canyon country. Along with a six-pack of beer, George produced Benson's giant bound volume of topo maps. On his series of 7.5-minute maps, Robert Benson had inked-in his route and notes. To Dave Kiel, receiving Benson's treasure trove felt divinely inspired, "like the parting of the Red Sea."

Three weeks after leaving George and resuming their trek, the Kiels descended 2,000 feet down a jeep trail to Queen Anne Bottom on the Green River. From there, they hiked and floated past the confluence of the Green and Colorado Rivers to Spanish Bottom in Canyonlands National Park. After traversing Canyonlands, they entered Glen Canyon National Recreation Area and began the tedious ambulation of the outermost reaches of Lake Powell. From communication with Robert Benson, the one and only person known to have traversed the area using the same goal, it would be the most complex of their entire journey. In the letter he let them know that unlike the Grand Canyon or Canyonlands, the stratigraphy "is totally unpredictable."

Indeed, walking around the lake proved to be, as Dave predicted, a "logistical nightmare." By mid-December, they had arrived at Bullfrog Marina, having completed only about a third of the distance along the 185-mile-long lake's northern shoreline. Their hike had consumed close to 150 days, but at this point, they had scheduled a well-deserved, month-long break. Flying from Bullfrog to Page, they boarded a bus to Los Angeles, where they relaxed with the Reeds over the holidays.

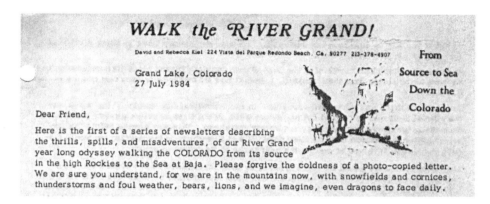

In mid-January they returned to Bullfrog Marina to once again take up their hike around the north side of Lake Powell, following in Benson's footsteps and using his maps. This proved far more difficult than they had imagined; the route veered high on the slickrock, up and away from lake water. Most of the slickrock potholes had dried up and any water they did manage to locate was frequently capped by several inches of ice. Retrieving their caches also proved difficult; one required a sixteen-mile round trip to the edge of the lake.

Zigzagging in and out of hundreds of twisting, arthritically fingered drainages in the badlands-like, salmon-colored slickrock framing Lake Powell consumed January and half of February. On February 19, 1985, day 189 of their journey, exhausted and filthy, they finally touched pavement in Page. By this time, they craved first-world comforts and conversation with others. After checking into the Empire House Motel, they phoned Bec's parents; the Reeds told them that a man named Gary Ladd, who lived in Page, had offered his assistance.

Ladd, who would later befriend George Steck, was an accomplished Glen Canyon hiker with over a dozen years of experience in the region. He knew the serious challenges presented by the country's broken topography. A few weeks earlier, while out on an excursion, he had found an addressed and stamped envelope and a note in a hiking trail register. The note said: "Hi—We are hiking the length of the Colorado from its source to the Sea of Cortez. If you could please mail this letter, it would be greatly appreciated. Thank you. —David and Rebecca Kiel"

Ladd mailed the Kiels' letter and also included correspondence of his own, writing: "Besides being the guy who picks up mail at NP registers, I'm a photographer who lives in Page. If you need any help and a place to stay, please look me up." He added his phone number and address.

After four days in the motel, Dave and Bec met up with Ladd, who turned out to be both affable and a valuable resource. Not only did he escort them to Antelope Canyon, a stunning nearby slot canyon, he also offered a tour of Glen

Bec and Dave Keil, May 1985, *Lake Powell Chronicle.*

Canyon Dam. That night over dinner at the house of one of Ladd's friends, he put on a slide show of his outdoor photography. While the beautiful images amazed the audience, most of the twenty-five attendees seemed more curious about the unusual couple's adventures.

On February 26, after a week's respite, Ladd dropped them off on the barren slickrock south of Page. Before the day's end, they arrived at the Spencer Trailhead along the rim of the Vermilion Cliffs. The 360-degree views were spectacular. To the northeast—as far as the eye could see—lay sculpted Navajo Sandstone. Off to the west, the magnificent cliffs jutted at least ten miles into the distance. In the foreground, a reincarnated but eye-pleasing version of the Colorado River—unnaturally deep greenish blue—moved lazily through the panorama. Most breath snatching for Bec, and not because of its beauty, was what lay two miles and 1500 feet immediately below. She journaled: "We are poised on the edge of the Grand Canyon, entering a major turning point in our trip. But the joy of my anticipation is overshadowed by the dark cloud of worry ..."

CHAPTER TWENTY-NINE

Lava Monsters and to the Sea

THE STORY OF BEC AND DAVE KIEL (CONTINUED)

There was nothing I could do, she had to get across this slope on her own. I couldn't carry her, drag her, or even coax her on. She was face to face with herself, with her own limits, with the lava monster.

Dave Kiel
Walk the River Grand! From Source to Sea Down the Colorado

May 1985

George Steck had specifically warned them about the sheer, nearly 400-foot-high lava dike near River Mile 184. The footing would be treacherous and the exposure terrible, he'd said. Now, with clenched teeth and tears streaming down her face, Bec knew that had they heeded George's words, this terrifying moment easily could have been avoided.

Compounding her regret, less than twenty-four hours earlier, a Moki Mac boatman named Roger Murphy had offered them a ride downstream to beyond the dike. Bec had immediately accepted. Dave, however, just as quickly declined. "Thanks, but our goal is walking the length of the Colorado the whole way," he declared. "From source to sea. We need to do it under our own power."

That evening a discouraged Bec journaled: "I am very sad to see Roger's empty raft pull away from us out into the river, knowing what a bitch that buttress is going to be."

Bec slept poorly that night but began hiking without protest in the morning. Six hours later, by mid-afternoon, after enduring relentless heat and "forced crossings through thick jungles of mesquite and other flesh ripping plants," they

277

had logged less than two river miles. Next, on the initial ascent of the buttress, Bec stumbled, deeply abrading most of one thigh on the sharp lava cinders. Despite this, she limped along, following Dave up the cliff's increasing exposure. Suddenly he stopped.

Feeling rattled, Dave later wrote that the cliff face at that spot, "dropped off at a ridiculous angle." He managed to cross it, however, but admittedly was, "swallowing hard, not looking down, not thinking of the consequences if I would slip."

Once beyond the crux, he looked back toward Bec. She, too, had stopped, having walked as far as she dared. Seconds ticked by. Despite having seen him successfully navigate the exposed portion and despite his coaxing, she couldn't will herself to move. Increasingly distraught, tears flowed. Breath-holding morphed into hyperventilation and soft crying into sobs. Of that moment Dave wrote, "She broke—falling, not down the cliffs, but over the emotional edge." Bec ultimately turned around and headed back down. Sighing, he reluctantly followed her zigzagging descent back down the slope they had ascended. No words were spoken until Dave accidentally kicked loose a bowling-ball-sized chunk of lava.

"ROCK!" he hollered.

For a second time, Bec froze. An instant later the careening boulder whizzed past, missing her shin by inches. A direct hit would have shattered her leg and likely sent her into a death plunge. She shrieked, then, according to Dave, "let loose a torrent of a year's worth of hardship and toil and began weeping uncontrollably, spasms convulsing her frail-appearing frame." Bec eventually calmed, and anger and resolve took over. Machine-like, she descended to the river.

Getting back to the banks of the Colorado in one piece did little to offset their overall feeling of despair and frustration. It became all too clear that they had grossly underestimated both the difficulty of the terrain and the heat, mistakes that could cost them their lives. They also knew they had no one to blame but themselves.

Weeks earlier, absent any pressure to make miles to beat the summer heat, they had taken their time reaching Phantom Ranch. After arriving on April 3, they hiked out the South Kaibab Trail to Grand Canyon Village, then frittered away six days there. As they relaxed in the rim country's coolness and enjoyed visits from Bec's parents and George Steck, temperatures within the Canyon's depths predictably cranked up.

When they finally reshouldered their packs and hiked back down, inner Canyon highs were hitting the low nineties. Still in no rush, they relished the chill of Bright Angel Creek and the swamp-cooled air of the Phantom Ranch canteen for two more days. Their nonchalance would prove to be a mistake.

Temperatures were soaring to near 100°F when they reached Lava Falls in mid-May, more than two weeks after leaving Phantom. For a brief reprieve they hiked out the Lava Falls Trail to spend a week at the Tuweep Ranger Station as guests of NPS ranger Mike Ebersole. On a seasonally hot Memorial Day weekend, they once again donned their packs, bade goodbye to Ebersole, then slogged back into the Canyon.

⌒⌒⌒

Dave and Bec had been sitting in silence near the river for nearly an hour after retreating from the dike when some rafters led by a professional river guide named Mark Thatcher floated into view. Bec flagged them down and asked for a ride beyond the lava dike. They said yes, and to her surprise, Dave eagerly jumped on board. Within minutes they were beyond the buttress, Thatcher's group dropping them off just downstream.

After two days of walking, they neared River Mile 191. Neither hesitated to wave over another boat, this time a commercial motor rig, and ask for a ride thirty-five miles downstream to Diamond Creek. They needed a break, not only because they were wilting in the heat, their boots disintegrating, but they also knew Dave's grandmother was recovering from a broken hip and he wanted to see her.

At Diamond Creek, they scored a ride on the river trip's bus heading to Seligman. Once there, they phoned Bec's dad to inform him of their impending visit. Taking a Greyhound bus to LA, they were picked up at two o'clock in the morning by a cheerful John Reed. Dave's grandmother appeared to be on the mend, and Dave and Bec rested in Redondo Beach for a week.

Despite the summer's ongoing heat, both felt they were too close to finishing the Grand Canyon portion of their hike to quit. So, on June 8 John Reed drove them to the Parashant area. He also paid for Dave and Bec to take a commercial helicopter ride from Whitmore Wash on the rim to the helipad along the river back at River Mile 183 (a frequent departure spot for river runners) where they could pick up their hike close to where they had left off.

Resuming their walk, the heat felt just as oppressive, and the steeply angled walking, just as monotonous. David described the latter in a newsletter:

> *Sidehilling - continuous sidehilling. Always walking a slope...*
> *We are turning into the proverbial hobo (granted a canyon country version) whose one leg is shorter than the other from continually walking one foot on the curb and one in the gutter in an endless hunt for that next cigarette butt.*

With early July temperatures sizzling around 120°F, they maneuvered downstream to below Diamond Creek. High and dry on the exposed sprawl of the Tonto Plateau, they drank the last of their water. This wasn't the first time. Only days earlier they had similarly run out. Luckily, they found water within a deep cleft between boulders but just beyond arm's reach. Decomposing lizards bobbed on its surface. In a sad irony, they apparently drowned in their attempt to reach it. Using a pot dangling on a string to collect what they could, they retrieved enough to buy them time. They dubbed the water "lizard tea."

Bec Keil on ladder at the bat guano mine, River Mile 267. *David Kiel*

Now, desiccating within the waterless pressure cooker, they openly discussed dying. But fate proved, yet again, to be on the Kiels' side: a freak monsoon storm rolled in. Dave set out a plastic tarp and they collected about three cups of rainwater, just enough to make it back to the river, then continue downstream.

On July 18, 1985, a few days after the one-year anniversary of having begun their mega-hike and two months later than Dave had predicted, they reached River Mile 267. With the official end of Grand Canyon still eleven miles downstream, further walking seemed both pointless and perilous. Dangerously weak, Bec had lost weight she couldn't afford. Dave, too, was spent. After 84 days in Grand Canyon, the majority under a blazing sun, the two called it quits and hitchhiked a ride with Hualapai River Runners to Pearce Ferry.

Seventy-eight-year-old Harvey Butchart was there when they arrived. He had corresponded with the Kiels by mail, as well as Bec's dad, who informed him of their estimated arrival. Harvey had been skeptical about their epic endeavor and wanted to meet Dave and Bec in person. The Kiels were awestruck meeting the Canyon legend. Harvey had similar feelings about the Kiels, especially Bec, but for a different reason:

The thing that really amazed me was to see how light Bec Kiel is, about 110 pounds, and to think that she can carry a pack weighing more than half her weight. They said that she often started with a pack weighing more than 60 pounds.

On the heels of near-death misery upstream, they concluded that backpacking along the river to the gulf was neither appealing, nor wise. Instead, with John Reed's help, they devised a plan B: use a canoe. Within days, they had the boat they needed, courtesy of Mr. Reed. Ironically, completing their "Walk the River Grand!" journey now required them to paddle nearly 500 miles.

⌒⌒⌒

In his book *A River No More*, Philip Fradkin chronicled his experience attempting to kayak the Colorado through Mexico to the Gulf of California (aka, the Sea of Cortez) in 1978. He wrote: "To follow the river from Morelos Dam to the gulf is tricky business. First, it's there, then it isn't, then it is, then it isn't. Its presence depends on when the toilet is being flushed." More specifically, in 1975, Bureau of Reclamation surveyors had reported that the great river's existence came to an anticlimactic end in the Mexican desert about fourteen miles short of the sea.

Because of dams, running the Colorado through Mexico had fallen into folklore; perhaps only a handful of people in history could make that claim. Unlike traversing the lower Canyon during extreme heat, for this portion of the Kiels' journey, however, the timing couldn't have been better. Beginning in 1983, exceptionally wet years and deep snowpacks resulted in high-water runoffs that filled reservoirs. In a domino effect, water released from behind the river's dams temporarily resurrected the Colorado beyond its last shackle (Morelos Dam), the flow enough to breach the dried-up delta and push the river into the Gulf of California for the first time in years. By the time the Kiels arrived, these unusually high flows were still driving the Colorado into the gulf.

On October 30, 1985, sixteen months after their start high in the Rockies, the Kiels' paddled into the estuary east of Isla Montague, the mouth of the pre-dam Colorado River Delta. They stared in awe as the tidal bore gently pulled them into the sea. Dave poetically captured the moment, as seen through his eyes.

It is a world of bent and reflected light, the mirage and its deception. A world of flaming sunsets and pastel hued sunrises. A lonely land of mirrored reflections on the Rio Colorado's tranquil surface. Distant horizon so flat and true, it must have been scored across the earth

Bec paddling into the Sea of Cortez. *David Kiel*

with a ruler … A searing sun, shifting tide, endless space—nothing to anchor one's mind to.

Back in Southern California a few days later, engulfed by smog and traffic, the couple's reentry proved rocky. Within two years, despite the generous support of Bec's parents, they separated, then divorced.

And here's where cake comes in. When I think of the Kiels, both envy and irony pop into my mind—envy of their one-of-a-kind hike and even rarer float, and irony when I think about backpacking and cake.

When George Steck met Dave and Bec for the first time at the Dewey Bridge above Lake Powell, he had a large, glistening-white sheet cake just for them. Despite their weeks of brutal hiking, the nutrition-conscious Kiels found the sight of it repulsive and declined what the boys and I would have practically killed for.

I also think of their divorce. How could they split after enduring so much together? George Steck believed the Canyon itself was partly to blame; specifically because of the Kiels' story, he sometimes referred to it as the "great separator."

In my own experience, the Canyon is more of a "great uniter," welding loved ones closer together. Certainly, this has been the case with my family and my marriage. But I also know where the Canyon ranks in my life relative to them.

They do, too.

In his 1984 letter to Harvey Butchart, whose marriage and family also suffered because of Harvey's Canyon hiking obsession, Dave Kiel wrote: "For me, backpacking is my greatest love in life." Dave's words easily could have been attributed to Harvey himself. Maybe for both men, when it came to their closest personal relationships, *that* was actually the problem.

CHAPTER THIRTY

Meeting the Mad Man

LAVA FALLS TO DIAMOND CREEK (CONTINUED)

If people persist in trespassing upon the grizzlies' territory, we must accept the fact that the grizzlies, from time to time, will harvest a few trespassers.

Edward Abbey
A Voice Crying in the Wilderness (1989)

March 2015 (continued)

The boys and I weaved among the jumbled boulders lining the south side below 209 Mile Rapid in the same tedious ambulation we had grown accustomed to. A drizzling rain made the slickrock even slicker and reduced our slow progress to sluggish. By mid-afternoon, we plopped our exhausted selves onto a lovely, sloping sand bank above a rapid called Little Bastard near River Mile 212—ending another hell day in paradise.

The next morning came with more shoreline rock-hopping. As usual, I fantasized about the pre-dam, Grand Canyon world. The free-flowing, rusty-brown river, coursing with pulverized silt, would have carpeted most of these rocks with sediment. The riverbanks would have been akin to sidewalks of dried mud. Now, the pale green, sediment-depleted, anemic Colorado fails to make deposits; it only erodes, stripping away the final remnants of what little sediment remains, exposing the bank's underlying boney cortex. For walking, it's a boot-slipping, foot-jamming, toe-tripping pain in the butt.

Fortunately, by mid-morning, boulder-hopping madness yielded to temporary sanity on the level Tapeats Sandstone. When it comes to the personalities of rocks, the Tapeats is Grand Canyon's sweet, sedimentary grandma. The only problem is that you have to get past grumpy Grandpa Redwall, the Canyon's mean old man, to get to her. But she's worth it. I found myself metaphorically kissing that gal with every step.

Before long, we five reached one of the most aptly named features in Grand Canyon, also one of the coolest: Pumpkin Spring at River Mile 213. The lone "pumpkin" doesn't occupy a patch. Rather, it rises right out of the river's left bank, nestled in a cove of 550-million-year-old polished Tapeats. Twenty feet or so long, bulging vertical bands of yellowish orange stains from warm-water-loving bacteria decorate its exterior. Here, the Tapeats projects about fifteen feet above the river during typical flows. Viewed from river level, this travertine spring's resemblance to a pumpkin is so striking that Canyon aficionados affectionately refer to it as "Charlie Brown's Great Pumpkin." Looking down on the pumpkin from above— its hollowed interior, brimming with murky, green-yellow algae-festooned water—you gaze into a witch's cauldron. Perfect for Halloween, Pumpkin Springs is a one-of-a-kind, whimsical, rocky jack-o-lantern without a face. And its spooky water, loaded with heavy metals—arsenic, lead, and zinc among them—is as dangerous to one's health as it looks.

With smug pride, I told the boys that I had never seen a snapshot of backpackers here. So, we took a group photo with the pumpkin as a backdrop. But all too soon, as we moved downriver, the enjoyable Tapeats ended and the damnable sidehilling resumed. Then the river trip from the previous day floated into view. *Mr. Potato Head and his gang.*

The boys (Connor, T, Wes, Vince) and me at Pumpkin Springs.

"Hey! Do you need anything, any food?" one guy cheerfully yelled.

Annoyed, my first mental response was *Yesterday you couldn't spare anything because you were "running low," remember?*

"No," I shot back and kept walking. "We're good."

Uncool backpackers or not, we still have our pride. I walked faster. Another of their boats drifted by. Someone else shouted us the same question. Maybe they felt remorse for dissing us the day before. I barked out the same answer. The boys also declined. I hoped our vibe spoke loudly: *You guys suck.*

I recalled George Steck's hexes for stingy boaters. In *Loop Hikes II*, he wrote about "clever ways to cadge beer from passing boats." These included his sophisticated LAST CHANCE TO DISPOSE OF EXTRA BEER BEFORE ENTERING RAPIDS banner. He called the process "The Science of Beer Cadging." He explained what to do if unsuccessful: "If your best efforts go unrewarded, you show your darker side. For this, we have several curses:

•May your beer bags rot.
•May your oars go limp.
•May your propeller cavitate.
•May your bilges putrefy.
•And (for extreme cases) may your boat flip."

We veered high when we neared 217-Mile Rapid, hiking in the rising cliffs of schists and the Diamond Peak granitic pluton in what's called Lower Granite Gorge. As Vince contoured above a big drop, he surprised a rattlesnake tucked into a crack two feet from his nose. Vince didn't flinch, and luckily neither did the snake.

The Canyon's venomous denizens fuel another aspect of the Grand Deception. Blame this on books, Hollywood, and other media. These critters, especially snakes and scorpions, have been villainized for decades. In reality they are non-aggressive, and trust me, they are not motivated to waste their venom on something they can't eat, like a human. Leave them alone and they'll typically leave you alone.

Historical records support this. Indeed, how many documented Grand Canyon deaths to date are directly related to rattlesnakes or scorpions? Zilch. Nada. The only documented death even tangentially related to a rattlesnake happened in 1934, when one lunged at a prospector. The poor bastard (the prospector, not the snake) was supposedly so scared that he keeled over and died from a heart attack without having suffered a bite.

Rising ever higher above the Colorado, we contoured until descending to the mouth of Mile 220 Canyon. Having been high and dry for hours we were more than ready to tank up and eat lunch. I took a siesta while the boys debated the relative merits of *Game of Thrones* versus *Star Wars*.

A two-boat river trip chugged toward us. We all perked up. For me, as with George, it presented an opportunity for scientific study dependent on multiple repetitions: Time for another try at beer-cadging.

"Got any beer you can spare?" I shouted.

Lest I be labeled a lush, let me explain: I don't drink daily, nor have I ever had a problem with alcohol abuse. But after hiking or rowing all day in Grand Canyon, especially when it's blazing hot, nothing on this planet tastes better than a river-cold beer. *Nothing.* On this, George Steck and I were pretty much in sync.

In *Loop Hikes II* George includes tips on where to discover errant beers when hiking along the river. "Look for cans of beer and pop in eddies below a rapid. Look also where driftwood has collected at higher water. I have probably found 99 cans of beer, and once, a friend found a can of Tuborg Gold high up in a tamarisk."

Taking his own advice, George once sought out and found the "mother lode"—a cache of about 30 beers—during his 1982 thru-Canyon hike. A note attached to the cache declared, "Hi, Steve, Ralph, Bill et. al., this is for you." This discovery presented a mini-dilemma for Steck and company. Should they raid the stash or not? Resolution came through classic George Steck, guilt-erasing logic: "Since my brother, who was with us, is named Al, it was obvious we were included in the invitation."

After I yelled, the guy at the oars of the second boat hopped up from his rowing seat. Lickety-split, he flung open the lid of his cooler, grabbed a couple of beers and lobbed them like hand grenades in our direction. The first kerplunked into a nearby eddy. I snatched it up. Sadly the second, in true grenade fashion, exploded when it hit a rock near Connor, blasting Michelob into his face. As the beer, sputtering and flopping like a fish out of water, sprayed Connor, the other boys roared with laughter. To save Connor's honor and to put the injured beer ... well ... out of its misery, I immediately grabbed it, popped the top, and guzzled.

By the time we made camp near River Mile 222 we were euphoric. Diamond Peak, a looming 3,512-foot tall sentinel three miles to the southwest that signaled the end of this leg of our trek, dominated the western skyline. Of our entire trip thus far, today was the first day we had made excellent time, exceeding what we had hoped for in miles. Diamond Creek, our destination at River Mile 226, now appeared pretty much in the bag.

We consumed almost all of our remaining food. Still hungry, T offered to head back to boaters we had encountered upstream and ask for snacks. An hour earlier, we had been too gun-shy to inquire as we scurried through their camp, our only words being apologies for the intrusion. T wanted volunteers to go with him, but Connor, Vince, and Wes all shook their heads no. After the Mr. Potato Head experience, I thought, who could blame them? I considered this for several seconds, *Hmmm...what the heck?* I then agreed to go with T.

This river party turned out to represent more the norm. They welcomed us graciously. All seemed in good spirits (partly

My shoes.

from having imbibed good spirits, as evident by beer cans and a whiskey bottle) as they celebrated their last night on the river. I cringed when T announced that I was one of the authors of *Over the Edge*, but this gang seemed impressed. Someone even produced a copy they wanted me to sign. Without us asking, they offered us beer and ginger snaps. *And* ginger cake. Their wonderful hospitality more than made up for our earlier encounter with Mr. Potato Head and his crew.

The boys cheered when we returned with the spoils. In turn, T and I were thrilled to hear that Wes and his mom had chatted on the sat phone during the interlude; Becky promised she would have my nephew Phil bring pizza and drinks when he picked us up the next day at Diamond Creek on Hualapai Nation land.

On our last morning we arose early to allow plenty of time for the final assault. Before starting, I sliced V-shaped notches in my running shoes at ankle level. The off-kilter sidehilling we'd been doing had created painful abrasions on the inside of my downhill ankle and the outside of my uphill one. They had been torturing me—red hot branding irons poking my ankles with every step. I only needed these shoes to last one more day. As a joke, I thought I'd offer them up to John Azar, who doubted we'd ever reach Diamond Creek, for his nostalgic shoe shelf.

With visions of pizza dancing in our heads, we blitzed over to the next drainage, then bombed down the slope toward the glittering water of the creek that clearly fits its name. Wes moved out front at a near breakneck pace and soon disappeared. When the rest of us reached Diamond Creek Road, he was still MIA. *Did he go to the outhouse? Ah, whatever. He'll appear soon enough.* Now was the time for jubilation, for foot-loving flatness. For being done with our hardest leg!

Then a white four-door sedan roared up. After slamming to a stop next to us and kicking up a dust cloud, the driver, a scowling, middle-aged Native American man, bounded out and charged over to us. He looked mad. *Really mad.*

"You're trespassing!" he barked, pointing at us. "You were hiking and camping illegally on our land!" The badge on his shirt identified him as a Hualapai tribal ranger. (I'll call him Wilson, though that wasn't his name.)

"I waited in my car all night for you guys!" he bellowed.

Although I knew he was right about our trespassing, my first instinct was sarcasm. *Really? You waited all night in your car? For this? Jeez, you need to get a life, bro.* However, guilt trumped snark.

"Sorry about that," I apologized. "How'd you know we were coming?"

"Some river runners said they saw you! They said you were out of food and water!"

Shit! Mr. Potato Head! Those bastards!

"Uh, that's not actually true. We had plenty of water. We also had food. We only wanted snacks and powdered Gatorade."

"Well, it doesn't matter!" Wilson snapped back. "You were trespassing and you're in big trouble! Now where's the other guy?" He scanned around. "I know he's here, somewhere. They said there was five of you!"

"I dunno. I think he got here before the rest of us."

"Well, get in the car! We're going to go find him then."

Wilson yanked open the back door on the passenger side and motioned for me to go in. As I obeyed I noticed a thirty-something-year-old Native American woman sitting quietly in the front passenger seat. When she glanced back at me she looked just as serious and official as Wilson. He thumped the door closed behind me, then hustled around the car and into the driver's seat, slamming his door, too. Despite all this, I found myself secretly smirking. *Hah! Wes likely saw the ranger coming and hid. Good boy!*

Then reality set in: We were in big trouble. And I knew that big trouble with the Hualapais meant *big* fines. A hiking buddy came to mind, a herpetologist named Andy Holycross. He has walked the length of the Grand Canyon not once, but twice. I vaguely remembered him telling me that his first attempt resulted in huge fines with Hualapai. As in *gigantic* fines. A $2,000-per-head price for his violations came to mind. Sitting in the backseat, I did the math then broke into a cold sweat. For five of us…$10,000! *Holy shit!*

As Wilson drove the three of us away, I looked back through the rear window. The boys stood as still as Canyon hoodoos, staring at me. They looked much like I now felt, bewildered and worried. As we rumbled away, the boys disappeared in the storm cloud of dust.

CHAPTER THIRTY-ONE

The Hualapai Spanking

LAVA FALLS TO DIAMOND CREEK (CONTINUED)

*A mistake that makes you humble is better than an achievement
that makes you arrogant.*

Anonymous

March 2015 (continued)

Still fuming, Ranger Wilson craned his neck to scan back and forth through his windshield as we barreled down Diamond Creek Road. Moving at a speed higher than prudence would dictate, his vehicle bounced hard over several rough spots. Though his head bobbled from side to side and up and down, his gaze remained steady.

Before the hike I had forked out nearly five hundred dollars to the Hualapai tribe to use the road, a hefty sum, so my nephew, Phil, could drive my Yukon down to pick us up then drive back out. Yet as Wilson bounded us over the washboards, that $500 road-use fee I paid would likely prove a pittance compared to the fine I now imagined I would get slapped with.

Diamond Creek Road is not just any road. Aside from being the Grand Canyon's only remaining toll road, it's one-of-a-kind in another way: After Lees Ferry (226 miles behind us), it's the only road in the entire Grand Canyon that provides access to the river and a convenient entry or exit point for river runners. The Hualapai Tribe owns and maintains the road, and they charge

Diamond Creek road with Diamond Peak in the distance. *Jane Mintzer*

non-Hualapais per head and per vehicle to use it.

The Hualapai, "People of the Tall Pines," are an impoverished tribe; despite nearly 80 percent adult employment, their mostly low-paying, service-industry jobs mean that more than 40 percent of the tribe's 1,650 members live at the poverty level.[13] For critical income generation, it's no surprise that fees are assessed for road use by non-tribal members. It's about twenty miles one way down Peach Springs Wash to the river, the last two miles being in the bed of the perennially flowing Diamond Creek. Portions of the fees are used for endless road upkeep because of flash-flooding washouts, rockslides, and wear-and-tear from daily vehicle travel.

So what's a "fair" price to drive on this road? The answer? Whatever the market will bear. And who can blame them? Anyway, this currently translates to "not cheap." (In fact, use fees have increased four-fold in the last two decades.) *How ironic that a "diamond creek" turned into a "gold mine!"*

---

13 *Demographic Analysis of the Hualapai Tribe Using 2000 and 2010 Census Data*, completed by Arizona Rural Policy Institute, W. A. Franke College of Business, Northern Arizona University, Flagstaff.

"Who are you and what were you guys doing here?" the Hualapai woman in the front seat asked. Far more professional, not to mention calmer, than Ranger Wilson, seconds earlier she had introduced herself to me as the general manager of Hualapai River Runners, the concession the tribe ran that launched daily from Diamond Creek. Having the head honcho show up made it clear they meant business. I gulped.

"My name is Tom Myers. We're backpacking the length of Grand Canyon in pieces," I explained. "This was our longest, hardest stretch. We went from Lava Falls to here. We've been backpacking for six days."

"How many days were you on our land?" she queried.

"Four."

"Four?! You were trespassing and camping illegally for four days?" Wilson shouted as he turned and scowled at me.

"You should have gotten a permit from us," the woman manager added matter-of-factly, ignoring her colleague's rage.

"I was told you don't give out hiking permits."

"That's not true. We do. You just have to apply for them."

"Well, I didn't try to get one because we honestly didn't plan on being on your land. We were going to do all our hiking on River Right, on park land."

"Do you have a permit from the NPS to prove that?" She looked skeptical.

"Yes, I do." I handed her my permit. She glanced at it, then me.

"So why did you come over to our side?"

"It was mostly a safety issue. We wanted to get around a dangerous cliff, a huge buttress of lava about forty miles upstream. So, our plan was to packraft across to the other side, get downstream, then packraft back to the park side once we were past the cliff. The crossing was harder and riskier than I thought it'd be. I made the decision to stay on your side for safety reasons. I'm sorry. It was my mistake. I'll pay whatever fine or fees I need to."

"Who are the other guys with you?" Her voice remained calm and steady.

"My son and some of his buddies."

"Who's the guy who came to pick you up?" she asked, referencing my nephew Phillip, whom I later found out had been approached and interrogated by Wilson.

"That's my nephew."

"How old is your son?"

"Nineteen. We've been hiking down here for several years. I started him hiking in the Canyon when he was little," I told her. "My wife and I even took him and his sisters on a Diamond downriver trip when he was seven. By the way, does Donita still work in the office?" I asked, name-dropping. "That's who I always got permits from to use the road for river trips," I added, trying to sound as sincere as I felt.

Group shot (a la *Down the Gorge with Uncle George*) sitting on Diamond Creek Road.

"No. She retired and has since passed away. I took her place. So, tell me again what you were doing?"

"We were hiking from Lava Falls. It's about fifty miles upstream from here."

Silence.

"Again, I apologize. I honestly would have tried to get a permit had I known you gave them to hikers. I've always respected the Hualapai. I've paid the fee every time to use your road. I've bought over half a dozen permits from you for river trips. I always try to respect your rules. Walking on your land was more circumstance than choice. It was a judgment call. Again, I'm sorry about this. I'll pay whatever I owe you, and next time, I'll absolutely make sure I get a hiking permit."

I sensed her mulling things over. Meanwhile, Wilson still had his eyes peeled for Wes.

"Your land is beautiful, by the way," I commented. I meant it. "We certainly enjoyed walking on it, and we did it respectfully."

"It *is* beautiful," the manager concurred as she gazed into the distance. Then added, "I have kids myself. I think I'd like to get them out here and do some hiking and camping."

"How old are they?"

She told me they were all pre-adolescents.

"Well, I think getting them doing this stuff is a great idea. They'd love it." I suddenly felt a connection, one parent to another. "The way I figure it, parenting is front-end loaded. If you make time for your kids on the front end, they'll be there for you on the back end. I'm really glad my son still likes to hang out with me. I think it's because my wife and I took time to haul him into places like this when he was little. Same with his sisters. In my experience, kids are naturally drawn to wilderness, and your land is gorgeous and worth spending time in as a family. You won't regret it if you do."

After several more minutes of fruitless searching, Wilson made a U-turn and we drove back to the boys. Seeing us they sprung to bolt-upright attention. Wilson jerked the car to a halt, kicking up yet another cloud of dust.

"Okay, look," the manager said, turning and peering over her shoulder at me. "I believe you. I'm not going to fine you, but here's what you'll have to do. You need to pay for the permit and camping fees for the days you were on our land. Go to the Hualapai Lodge after you drive out. That's where my office is. I'll meet you there and we can go over what you owe us."

"Absolutely," I nodded as I exited the car, elated that she didn't throw the book at me. I nodded politely at a scowling Wilson, then at her. She smiled back. "Thanks. See you in a bit."

They drove away.

Beyond curious, the boys clambered to know what happened. I explained as we walked down the creek to where the Yukon should be parked. Suddenly, Wes popped out from behind a bush.

"Yeah, I saw that car coming and figured it wasn't the welcome wagon," he announced. "So, I hid."

We met up with Phillip, who looked frazzled. Wilson had grilled him hard about our identities and our intentions, and Phillip had truthfully claimed he knew nothing. Otherwise, he had made it down the road without a hitch. Better yet, he had hauled in Becky's promised pizza and sodas. We gorged ourselves during the car-rattling drive to Peach Springs.

In the Hualapai Lodge parking lot, I took a deep breath before walking in. I introduced myself to a young woman behind the counter and explained I had come to see the manager and pay my fees.

"Just a minute, I'll get her." Several minutes later the clerk returned, alone. "She says your bill comes to $1,000—$500 for the permits and another $500 for the fine," she declared.

I handed her my credit card. No questions. No comments. Just relief.

Sometime after getting home, I called my friend Andy Holycross, the herpetology professor who had been hiking with a group (including a Hualapai tribal member) on Hualapai lands and got slapped with fines. For two of them (Andy not being one) the fines amounted to about $10,000—*each*. The ensuing weeks were very stressful for Andy and his group, but the fines were

293

eventually dismissed when prosecutors for the Hualapai failed to show up on the scheduled court date. Admirably, Andy harbors no grudge against the Hualapai Nation. Indeed, months later he went out of his way to respectfully meet with their Tribal Council to obtain permission to finish a lengthwise segment through their land, which was granted. In the years since, he has continued to maintain relationships within the Hualapai community, participating in prayer ceremonies and burials.

Far more inspirational to me on a personal level, however, is Andy's resiliency and his ongoing, unwavering love of the Grand Canyon. This is despite having endured a devastating, nearly unfathomable loss within its depths—that of his wife in a horrible accident.

Like David Kiel but nearly three decades later, Andy partnered with his wife Ioana to complete a lengthwise Canyon hike. And while the Grand Canyon may have played a minor part in ending Kiel's marriage, for Andy Holycross, however, the Canyon's role was unequivocal.

Akin to a Shakespearean tragedy, Andy and Ioana's Grand Canyon love story is the most beautiful and heartbreaking of any I know.

CHAPTER THIRTY-TWO

Prep Work for Holy Ground

THE STORY OF IOANA HOCIOTA AND ANDY HOLYCROSS

South Bass Trailhead... Is it possible to get there w/o going through the Indian Toll booths? Thought I read somewhere that it was.... Was thinking about a Mt Huethawali summit day hike; parking my 4-Wheel Drive/Trailer somewhere and taking my motorcycle to the SB [South Bass] Trailhead.

LR/Message 1 of 127, Nov 5 1:11 PM

November 2010

"LR" posted the above message to the Grand Canyon Hikers Yahoo group. The group (now defunct) was an online forum for swapping tales, advice, and generally geeking out on Canyon hiking. LR also mentioned he had been contemplating a day hike off the South Bass Trail. His simple query started a firestorm of controversy within the group, triggering an astounding 126 follow-up messages over three weeks.

A few hours after LR's post, another member, John, responded by mentioning a possible "sneak route" via the old, now-off-limits, NPS Boundary Road leading to South Bass. LR checked the NPS website, then complained about the NPS directions for driving to the South Bass Trailhead and about the $25 toll he'd have to cough up to drive two miles of Havasupai road.

That's when Rich Rudow (the canyoneering guy Wes and I had met at Soap Creek) chimed in, sharing his altruistic view on the subject of paying to hike. "Such is life," he posted. "The Navajo Nation is the exception. They have a reasonable permit process.... I pay it and I'm just grateful for the privilege of visiting that wonderful area."

Besides his covert work in helping create the *Grand Canyoneering* book also mentioned earlier, Rich, a then forty-five-year-old native Californian and software engineer, had a side gig as an inventor. This led to his development of specialized GPS tracking software, the sale of which allowed him to retire early and do what he loved: explore the Grand Canyon.

Rich's post elicited another from one of Rudow's other Canyon buddies, Chris Forsyth: "For most backpackers, that rate compares favorably to the Navajo Nation and GCNP bargains of $5 per night per person, and even more favorably to the ridiculous entry fees the Hualapai charge at Diamond Creek."

Calling Grand Canyon National Park's $5-per-night/per-person camping fee a "bargain" riled Yahoo subscriber Andrew Holycross. Like Rudow, Holycross (who went by Andy) had transplanted to Phoenix, only he came from Omaha, Nebraska, in 1986 for his PhD fieldwork in herpetology. He eventually taught herpetology at Mesa Community College and was also an adjunct professor at Arizona State University (ASU). "I'm not sure I'd call $5/day a bargain when it comes to hiking in the wildest parts of the canyon. What exactly are we paying for?"

Holycross and Rudow then had a digital duke-out in front of their online audience, but eventually called a truce. While they couldn't agree on permits, the two men could relate on their mutual, and *serious*, love for the Grand Canyon. Armistice prevailed and evolved into email correspondence.

The two also shared an interest in Robert Benson. Rich told Andy that he'd transcribed copies of Benson's logs, which he would happily share. Holycross took him up on it.

In 2011, Andy and his primary hiking partner and soon-to-be-wife, Ioana Hociota (ee-WAH-nah Ho CHO tuh), perused Benson's journals. Captivated, the couple set themselves a goal of walking their beloved Canyon end-to-end, together.

Andy resolved to gradually acclimate Ioana to trekking in the Canyon. To prepare for the physical and emotional challenges that lay ahead, the couple first trekked the well-established Tonto Trail and Escalante Route. Next they tackled off-trail sections. Within a year of reading Benson's logs, Andy and Ioana hopscotched section hikes together, one after another on the left side of the river. By fall 2011, only a third of their goal remained undone. Most lay in the remote and relatively inaccessible western Grand Canyon, on Hualapai land.

The rim country in that region offers only a few primitive and generally unmaintained roads, limiting accessibility. And the Hualapais want to keep it that way. Their motive is spelled out on their website. "These canyons are sacred and should be so treated at all times." In other words, it is their holy ground.

Rather than trespass (as I had done with the boys), Holycross wanted an official tribal permit before setting foot on their turf. In March of 2011, as a participant on a Grand Canyon River Guides boatman training river trip, he had met several Hualapai tribal members. Holycross hit it off with one, Joshua Gordon.

They talked hiking; Andy explained his goal to walk the entirety of Grand Canyon on River Left, lamenting the challenges of obtaining Hualapai permission. Gordon, who went by Josh, offered to help, but with one requirement: Could he come along? Josh appeared to be a fit guy, about thirty, affable and energetic. As a tribal member, his presence would nullify the need for a permit because Ioana and Andy would be his guests. Andy agreed to Josh's request without a second thought. Having a Hualapai tribal member along seemed to guarantee any non-

Josh Gordon flipping-off Kanab Creek's "Flipoff" point. *Rich Rudow*

Hualapai a harassment-free journey through the tribe's land, and Josh could be a conduit to learning more about Hualapai culture. Ioana expressed equal enthusiasm when he told her about Gordon's offer.

Both eager, they set aside ten days of their 2011 Christmas break to hike from Hualapai Hilltop to Diamond Creek. Two other friends and longtime Canyon hikers, Bill Burger and Matthias Kawski, also received invitations, as did Josh's little brother, twenty-two-year-old MacGregor, specifically at Josh's request.

Half Hualapai (on their mother's side), the Gordon brothers inherited their other half and last name from a Scottish father. Neither brother, however, had Grand Canyon backpacking experience. Still, the way Holycross saw it, having not one, but two, Hualapai tribal members would double their odds of success on Hualapai land.

On December 28, 2011, Andy Holycross and his group drove to Peach Springs for a rendezvous with the Gordon brothers and their maternal uncle, Pat Mahone. Years earlier, after their father abandoned his boys, Pat took on a paternal role in raising them. He paid particular attention to Josh, somewhat of a wild child. A hike like this would be good for the boys, Pat told Holycross. Pat also offered his assistance, which Andy accepted with gratitude. Pat not only drove Holycross's FJ Cruiser down to the mouth of Diamond Creek, but also shuttled the group to the

MacGregor Gordon, Josh Gordon, Andy Holycross, and Ioana Hociota at the start of their Supai to Diamond Creek trip. *Bill Burger*

start of their hike at Hualapai Hilltop in his own truck. There, feeling psyched, they hugged Pat goodbye, then started down the Supai Trail.

A week later, their route along the Esplanade level veered close to the rim at Prospect Canyon. Here they met Pat again. He'd somehow managed to bounce and bang his rusting old truck down a barely passable road leading into the Prospect drainage, a side canyon that forms Lava Falls Rapid. A spectacular Esplanade overlook rewards those who reach the road's end. A month earlier, Andy had cached water here.

Pat had brought fixings for a barbecue. He also brought another Hualapai man unfamiliar to Holycross, who Pat introduced as a relative. While they enjoyed food and Canyon views, Andy noted Pat's friend mostly watching, then commenting on, the only female present, Holycross's young wife. Afterward she told Andy that the man had creeped her out.

On day eleven of their hike, bushed and leg weary, the group lumbered into Diamond Creek, more than ready for a comfortable drive home. When they reached the parking area, however, Andy's Toyota FJ Cruiser was nowhere to be found. Did Pat not leave it? Did somebody steal it? Josh called his uncle on the group's satellite phone and learned shocking news: The tribe had impounded the truck. Pat didn't know why but promised he would immediately pick them up.

After nearly two hours of slamming around in the back of Pat's beater truck as it bounced along Diamond Creek Road, they arrived at the Hualapai Lodge and River Runners office in Peach Springs. Josh and Andy spoke to the manager of the Hualapai's commercial operations, who also happened to be Gordon's boss.

She said the vehicle had been towed because the group had been hiking illegally on Hualapai land. She refused to elaborate on how she knew about their trek, but Josh and Andy suspected "creepy" had reported the vehicle, which resulted in it being impounded.

Upon hearing this, Gordon blew his top. He and the manager argued. Josh insisted that tribal members could hike on tribal lands with guests and didn't need permits. Nope was the manager's response. With or without a tribal member present, nontribal members always needed a permit, she claimed. Gordon knew of times when other tribal members had exercised the liberty he mentioned, so he took his boss's stance on their situation as a personal offense to him and his brother. He doubted this would have happened if they had been full-blooded Hualapai. Unsympathetic, she doubled-down on her decision.

Demoralized, they paid the $350 towing and impound fee to recover Holycross's vehicle. After paying, Andy asked the manager how he could obtain a permit to finish the section they still needed on Hualapai land from Diamond Creek to Lake Mead. She advised them to submit their proposed hiking itinerary to Hualapai Cultural Resources for review. If approved, they could purchase a permit from the Hualapai Game and Fish Department.

Andy and Josh debriefed their companions, then they all vented. After calming down, the group initiated the application process that day. Josh Gordon said he could help. With Andy, he marched to the office of Hualapai Cultural Resources. For the permit inquiry, Gordon told Holycross it would be best if he spoke to the office manager alone. When minutes passed without an apparent result, Holycross became antsy and went into the office.

The manager gave both men explicit instructions: To avoid the fate of their last trip, the group would need to submit a trip proposal for review showing the "exact route" they intended to take, including a signed agreement to respect and not disturb any sensitive cultural and archeological sites they may encounter. If their application was approved, they would pay a permit fee at the Game and Fish office and be granted access.

After returning to Phoenix, Andy quickly drafted a detailed proposal, including a map of their intended route and dates of travel. Within the week he sent copies, written under Josh Gordon's name, to Gordon and the Hualapai Cultural Resources office.

Andy phoned Josh several times regarding the status of the review. Josh reported he still had no firm response from Cultural Resources, but their office anticipated no problems.

Feeling optimistic, and with the Diamond down-hike still more than a month away, Andy and Ioana scheduled a couple of interim hikes over the 2012 Valentine's Day weekend in Marble Canyon. After completing these, Ioana would be caught up with Holycross with respect to lengthwise legs except for one: a several-mile section below the tip of the Great Thumb. It was the same segment that Harvey Butchart—for justifiable reasons (as noted earlier)—had also saved for last in his length-of-the-park hike in 1963. This crux lay below a cliff face with the innocuous nickname of Owl Eyes.

Andy Holycross and Ioana Hociota.

CHAPTER THIRTY-THREE

Just Like Bogie and Bacall

THE STORY OF IOANA HOCIOTA AND ANDY HOLYCROSS (CONTINUED)

To love is nothing. To be loved is something.
But to love and be loved, that's everything.

Themis Tolis (2017)

February 2012

Just as Andy Holycross started to drift off, he heard a voice. *Her* voice. "Andrew," Ioana called in her Romanian accent. He sat bolt upright. She never called him Andrew. Usually she called him Andy or *Iubi* (pronounced YOU-bee), Romanian for "my love." She reserved his full name for spats or serious conversations. Yet that's what he heard, a melancholic sound in her voice bordering on ominous. His skin prickled.

He checked his watch. Three-thirty a.m. *Jesus, are they coming up with headlamps on at this hour?* For several seconds he listened intently. Nothing. Lying down again, Holycross tried to dismiss the entire incident—*Just a dream, you fool. Go back to sleep.*

Less than two hours earlier Andy had rolled his vehicle to a stop at the rim near Great Thumb Point, one of the most remote places in the lower forty-eight states. Horn intentionally blaring and headlights flashing, the untoward commotion created by Andy made an already freezing Rich Rudow shiver even more. Rich, who had followed Andy on a Polaris ATV at high speed, knew they lacked a permit to be on reservation land.

Fourteen months had passed since the two men had jousted in their petty Yahoo quibble, one that both now found embarrassing. Since then, they'd become friends, even hiking together. For Andy, more worried than he had ever been in his life, having Rich with him now was a testament to how far that friendship had come.

⌒〜⌒

The Great Thumb is well-named. This iconic Canyon geologic feature about thirty miles west of Grand Canyon Village projects north into the Canyon for about twenty miles. Arcing eastward, its configuration on a map resembles a bony human digit, the skeletonized thumb of a hitchhiker seeking a lift from Arizona to New Mexico. Its outermost portion, nearly five miles long by one mile wide, is called Great Thumb Mesa. This geological phalanx is flanked by the apices of two side canyons, which on the map look like creases in the thumb's joint— Fossil Canyon on the east and 140 Mile Canyon on the west. At this isthmus the drainages are less than a mile apart. Holycross and Rudow parked near the apex of the 140 Mile Canyon arm.

Snow and ice had melted off the section of road that longitudinally bisects the Thumb to its tip. Also lucky, when the two exited their vehicles, an absolute stillness seemed to confirm that there wasn't a soul, let alone a Havasupai official, for miles. Even if there had been, they'd arguably done their due diligence with the Havasupai and left their $25 access fee at the empty toll station, more than an hour behind them. On the flip side, the silence also meant that the people they'd hoped to find here weren't there either. The two walked to the rim and peered over the edge into pitch blackness. No flickering headlamps. No firelight. Nothing.

Seeing no need to stay up any longer and gripped by the bitter cold and fatigue, Andy grabbed Matthias Kawski's sub-zero sleeping bag and threw it down on a level, snow-free spot between junipers, then crawled in. He knew his friend wouldn't mind; he'd intentionally left the heavy bag behind with Holycross for this very reason. Matthias certainly didn't need it for himself in the warmer conditions on the Esplanade below during the two-night, three-day traverse with Ioana. Rich set up a tent near Andy and fell asleep almost instantly.

For Andy however, sleep remained distant, as thoughts of Ioana and their life together flooded his mind.

⌒〜⌒

On September 4, 2006, nearly six years earlier, forty-two-year-old Andrew Holycross took a coffee break between lectures at the ASU Memorial Union. His academic assistant, Ernie Nigro had tagged along. Andy pulled out a cigarette and asked Ernie if he had a light. "Sorry, but no," Ernie replied. Suddenly, a cute nineteen-year-old freshman nearby blurted, "I have one." The young woman's

302

smile caught the recently divorced Holycross off guard. They began to chat and she introduced herself as Ioana Hociota. Andy noted her subtle European accent and asked her where she called home. Her answer surprised him.

In 2002, as a fourteen-year-old eighth-grader, Ioana and her family had immigrated to the United States from Romania after winning a visa in a national lottery. In May 2006, she graduated with honors from Desert View High School in Phoenix, Arizona, then enrolled at ASU. She told Andy she wanted to get a mathematics degree while minoring in biology, and harbored an interest in research and possibly teaching. Then she planned to pursue a PhD in math.

<hr />

"So, what about you?" she asked. The pretty undergrad—five feet, six inches tall, athletic build, wavy auburn hair—seemed eager to hear about the middle-aged academician. Sensing this, Andy put it front and center that he was divorced and a father. He had two boys, one close to her age at seventeen, the other eleven. He also confessed his love of herpetology, especially snakes.

Walking to his office, their conversation continued. Several minutes later, clearly relaxed, Ioana played music on her iPod and began to dance. When the song finished, she smiled, waved goodbye, and left her professor's office with Ernie. Ten minutes later he found the pair chatting outside his office building.

"Hey, really nice meeting you," Andy called to Ioana as he walked past. "Don't be a stranger," he added.

"*You* don't be a stranger!" she teased in response. "I'm serious! Call me. Here's my number," she said, handing him her phone number which she had written on a piece of paper. "I'd love to chat." She smiled.

"Deal," he said, grinning back.

Later, keeping his promise, Andy used the phone number Ioana had given him. Soon, undergrad and professor began having coffee, lunch, walks. The intelligent young woman who spoke four languages and had a great sense of humor impressed Holycross. It didn't take long for him to invite her on a trip to his favorite landscape. She had never hiked Grand Canyon before and admitted being both excited and intimidated by the prospect. Andy vowed to himself to make the hike different

Ioana in high school.
Courtesy of Andy Holycross

from his own first attempt, something he calls an "epic fail."

In 1996, inspired by Edward Abbey's *Desert Solitaire*, Holycross concocted his first Canyon trip—a relative whopper, even for a Canyon-savvy hiker let alone a newbie. He planned to descend the North Rim at 150 Mile Canyon and then, over the course of a week, walk the Esplanade to Tuweep, about seventy-five miles. He invited other equally enthusiastic (and equally inexperienced) backpacker friends to join him, including his outdoorsy dad and his athletic stepmom. As so often proves to be the case, he overestimated his group's hiking abilities and underestimated the Canyon. Whipped and in over their heads, after two days they aborted the trip and hiked out.

For Ioana's first Canyon hike, Andy chose something far tamer. They descended the South Bass Trail and camped overnight at the river. He provided her with hiking boots, a backpack, and plenty of encouragement. She didn't need much of the latter, and according to Holycross, "took to the Canyon like a fish to water," absorbed by its beauty and the physical challenge.

When Hociota became a US citizen, Holycross attended the swearing-in ceremony. She stood during her ceremony, then stepped forward and cleared her throat. She spoke with pride about her Romanian heritage, and said how thrilled she was to officially become an American.

Over time, despite the nearly two-decade age gap, their romance blossomed. To skeptics, Ioana loved to say, "We're just like Bogie and Bacall," referencing Humphrey Bogart and Lauren Bacall, movie stars of the 1940s and 1950s. Bacall had been nineteen, like Ioana, when she first met the forty-five-year-old Bogart on a set. Bacall and Bogart had twelve years of marriage and two children together before Bogie's premature death at fifty-seven in 1956.

On June 11, 2011, Andrew Holycross and Ioana Hociota exchanged wedding vows on the remote but stunning Marble Viewpoint near Grand Canyon's North Rim which overlooks the expansive Marble Canyon Platform. More than a hundred attendees danced away the evening on an imported dance floor from which Ioana rarely left. She informed her new husband that it was the happiest day of her life. He felt the same.

Their Romanian guests greeted the bride and groom with the phrase "*Casa de Piatră*"—or "house of stone," a Romanian wish for a strong marriage. The newlyweds began calling Grand Canyon their Casa de Piatră, their home away from home. They hiked on weekends and during holiday breaks. As their experience together grew, so did their goal to try more challenging Canyon hikes.

After obtaining Robert Benson's journals from Rich Rudow, Ioana proposed that they, too, walk the entire length, sharing the experience. Andy Holycross needed no convincing. Slowly they began piecing together hiking sections in links, Andy repeating some of what he'd already done. As newlywed gifts to one another,

Ioana and Andy's wedding at Marble Viewpoint on the North Rim. *Courtesy of Andy Holycross*

they hiked from Lees Ferry to Navajo Bridge and from Tatahatso Canyon to Eminence Break—their first hikes alone as a couple in the Canyon since having descended the South Bass.

On their last night they camped near a beautiful pool in Tatahatso Canyon and snuggled as the setting sun reflected Canyon walls on the water's surface. The next day they traversed a Redwall bench just wide enough to walk side by side. They held hands. Clouds appeared; cold winds signaled a winter storm. Within the cool breeze, as light and shadows danced around them, Holycross embraced his new wife. Her eyes twinkled. "I'm so happy, Iubi. This is perfection. Being here with you."

Two weeks later, the completion of yet another leg would catch her up with her husband in connected links. Having previously hiked the section she needed and not able to take a break from work, Andy arranged for close hiking friend, Matthias Kawski, to accompany Ioana. Kawski had hiked a dozen multiday trips in remote Grand Canyon locations under all types of conditions; moreover, he shared their goal of completing a lengthwise traverse of the Canyon.

The section the two needed to complete included a five-mile portion below the distal end of Great Thumb, the stretch from Fossil Canyon on the east and 140 Mile Canyon on the west. They would go down the former and come out the latter. Once completed, like Andy, Ioana and Matthias would have a continuous hiking line from Lees Ferry to Diamond Creek, leaving one leg: Diamond Creek down to Pearce Ferry. They planned on knocking that off over spring break, two months away.

On February 23, the weather forecast called for sunny, mild temperatures and no precipitation. Perfect for hiking. Andy shuttled Ioana and Matthias out to Great Thumb. They parked on the east side atop the Fossil Canyon route. Several inches of snow still covered the ground when he helped them set up a tent. He'd be back in two days to pick them up. Before hopping back into his truck, Andy added one piece of advice.

"Be careful at Owl Eyes Bay, Iubi. Stay high."

Owl Eyes.

CHAPTER THIRTY-FOUR

Owl Eyes

THE STORY OF IOANA HOCIOTA AND ANDY HOLYCROSS (CONTINUED)

I was born when she kissed me.
I died when she left me.
I lived for a few weeks when she loved me.

Humphrey Bogart
In a Lonely Place (1950)

February 2012

In the Kaibab Limestone cliffs below the northern tip of Great Thumb Point loom a matched pair of gigantic, shadowy concavities that suggest massive eye sockets. Each is about 200 feet high by 100 feet wide and are so obvious from the bottom of the Canyon that every river guide points them out to passengers. A large, beak-like projection of rock below the sockets suggests a Mount Rushmore version of the face of an owl. Perched high in the Canyon wall, this owl lords with stoic indifference over the landscape below and all who pass by.

∞

"It was an impressive place," wrote Colin Fletcher in *A Man Who Walked Through Time* about the Owl Eyes Bay (aka, amphitheater). Before Harvey Butchart became the first person in recorded history to hike across it, he had warned Colin Fletcher about its steepness as well as the hazards of two adjacent amphitheaters. It was no coincidence that Harvey had yet to hike this segment, his last, to complete the length of Grand Canyon National Park in 1963.

Harvey told Fletcher, "They're steep, those amphitheaters. Very steep. But I'd guess they're both passable. Still, you can never really tell with these things until you give them a try."

Yet, in his logs written after he had completed the section, Harvey says nothing about the amphitheaters. Fletcher, on the other hand, didn't mince words when describing how spooked he felt staring into the bay of Owl Eyes:

> The Esplanade tapered abruptly to a narrow terrace that hung between two cliffs as if it had merely paused there, waiting for a heavy storm to send it crashing on downward. The scrub-covered talus sloped at a horrifying angle. And below its lip the rock plunged almost sheer for fifteen hundred feet. Now that I have seen the place I understood why the far side of the amphitheater was bighorn sheep country.

Feral Havasupai horses avoid Owl Eyes Bay. Still, as Fletcher noted, bighorn navigate them. So, rarely, do humans. Like Fletcher, Ron Mitchell (the third man known to pass through) remembers the spot well. After reading *The Man Who Walked Through Time*, Mitchell prepared by having his hiking companion Dale Graham bring a hundred-foot climbing rope just in case they needed to belay each other.

On day ten of a fourteen-day trip that began in late April 1971, they turned the corner below Great Thumb Point and headed east. Almost immediately they encountered the first bay: Owl Eyes. Mitchell stopped and stared at it. He knew the rope was useless. Nervous, he looked at Graham, then at what lay before them.

"Where are we supposed to walk?" he asked.

Lugging sixty-five-pound packs, they inched forward, side-hilling on the loose, angle-of-repose talus. They double-checked, then triple-checked each rock they stepped on and each foothold scraped into level notches by their hiking boots in the sloping dirt. Stable footing was critical to avoid a death plunge. They also clung to low-lying vegetation. The first quarter-mile took an hour of creeping and panic control. In his journal Mitchell later wrote:

> Left camp at 8:45. Arrived at start of 1st and most terrible amphitheater at 11:30 and went 20 min. more. Ate lunch and started again at 12:15. Finally came out at 2:45—3 hrs to get through!

Of the three large bays Ioana and Matthias would encounter, Owl Eyes' Supai ledges pinched down the narrowest, sometimes only two or three feet wide above a 400-foot drop. Here, steeply sloping, erodible Hermit talus angles to the edge of the drop, leaving very little space for level walking. Rockslides make for even more precarious footing. Scrub vegetation dots the steep slope above. Traversing higher where there is something to grab in the event of a slip is a tedious, but possible, alternative, allowing a slightly wider margin of error for survival.

～～～

Twenty-four hours after dropping off Ioana and Matthias, Andy was sitting at a table in the Campus Coffee Bean in Flagstaff. He received an unexpected phone call. The number revealed its source to be the satellite phone the hikers had borrowed from Rich Rudow. Andy tensed. He knew Ioana carried the phone. Had something gone wrong?

"Hello?"

"Hi, Iubi!"

He sighed with relief. She sounded cheerful. Other than a minor hiccup with their cookstove, Ioana reported, their hiking day had been perfect.

"Where are you?"

"We're at a great spot, below the tip of Great Thumb, slightly east of Specter Chasm. There's a big pothole full of water. You'd love it. Can't wait to see you the day after tomorrow!"

"Can't wait to see you either. Get some sleep. And remember, be careful at Owl Eyes."

"We will. Love you, Iubi!"

"Love you, too."

The next morning, Holycross was in a nostalgic mood. Thumbing through photos on his phone of his life with Ioana, he felt both blessed and overwhelmed. But by noon those feelings had shifted to an uncharacteristic worry. He knew the two hikers would be approaching Owl Eyes Bay. He told himself that, while steep and tedious, the route was otherwise straightforward; he had done it, as had several others. Besides, Ioana and Matthias had

Ioana on last hike. *Matthias Kawski*

Rich and Andy. *Bill Burger*

hiked through as bad or worse places many times before. Still, Andy knew this spot presented the biggest risk.

Ioana wasn't supposed to call him until the next morning. This would give him the several hours of lead time he needed to arrive to pick them up at the top of the 140 Mile Canyon route, their exit point. Still, he hoped she might surprise him with an unscheduled call to inform him that they had successfully passed Owl Eyes. As the hours ticked by with no phone call, Andy's sense of dread escalated. Around eight that evening, his phone finally rang. Again, he held his breath, but this time his phone identified the caller as Rich Rudow.

"Are we still on for tomorrow morning's pick up?" Rich asked.

"Yeah, we're on." Andy then told him that although he couldn't explain why, he sensed something was wrong because he hadn't received a satellite call from Ioana.

Rudow downplayed it. For one thing, he said, no call had been scheduled. Second, maybe she left the phone turned on in her pack and the battery ran out. That had happened to him once before.

These explanations didn't assuage Holycross's misgivings.

"Well, you wanna go out to Great Thumb now?" Rudow's offered.

"Tonight?! Like right now?"

"Sure. If you're that worried, let's go."

The offer floored Andy. He knew leaving now would mean arriving in the middle of the night. Rudow, he also knew, had just driven back to Phoenix from an extended trip. He had to be exhausted.

At any rate, even knowing it meant missing sleep that night, Holycross took Rudow up on his offer. Rich hopped into his truck, trailering his four-wheeling Polaris, and drove to Flagstaff to rendezvous with Andy. They caravanned to Great Thumb and arrived at two a.m. near the apex of 140 Mile Canyon, where Ioana and Matthias would exit.

Holycross slept fitfully, waking before dawn on Sunday morning. Both he and Rudow awoke bleary-eyed. Rich also distinctly heard Ioana's voice calling "Andrew" and assumed that she'd hiked out in the dark. Dog-tired, he'd fallen back to sleep. Now he was surprised not to see her with Andy. Chalking up the voice in the darkness to a dream, he kept it to himself. That morning—February

26, 2012—marked the ninety-third birthday of Grand Canyon National Park.

Once the sun had fully risen, the two men scanned the Esplanade below the 140 Mile route with binoculars. Ioana and Matthias should be camped down there somewhere. They saw no one.

The men jumped onto the Polaris and sped to the rim above Owl Eyes Bay. Using the binoculars, they scanned the route the two would have taken, focusing more intently at the crux point. Rich thought he saw footprints at the back of the bay but couldn't be sure. What he *was* sure of was seeing no sign of the hikers. Both men checked their cell phones, and both showed no missed calls.

By ten-thirty, the phone call Ioana had promised was hours overdue. A dark feeling gnawed Holycross's stomach as he and Rudow headed back to the top of the 140 Mile route. Again, they glassed below. Again, nothing.

Andy shouted. Suddenly, he and Rudow heard a single voice. It was faint but unmistakably a man's. Using the binoculars, Rudow spotted Kawski standing within the upper Coconino Sandstone cliffs a couple of hundred feet below the rim. And he was alone.

Andy's heart raced. "Where's Ioana?" he shouted.

"She's down!" Matthias yelled back, his voice unsteady.

Andy swallowed hard.

"Down where … below you?"

"She fell!"

Holycross felt his heart blow out of his chest.

"Where?!"

"Below Owl Eyes."

With those words, one of the worst nightmares of Andy's life—one he had feared and prayed would never happen—was confirmed. Frantic and knowing that Ioana had the satellite phone, he pulled out his cell phone and pecked 911. No service.

"FUCK!" He turned, his eyes boring into Rudow's. "We need a plan! Now!"

Rich looked down into the Canyon.

"Matthias!" he yelled. "Do you have the GPS waypoint where she fell?"

"Yes!"

Rich turned back to Andy. "I'll hike down and help Matthias up. I'll get the GPS waypoint and send a satellite text with the coordinates to my brother-in-law. He can relay the message to NPS Dispatch."

"Okay. Okay. While you do that, I'll drive to the last place I was able to get a reliable cell signal and call 911."

As Andy accelerated away. Rudow scrambled down to the distraught Kawski. They briefly hugged, then climbed back up. After reaching the rim Rich typed in several text messages to his brother-in-law, Dale, using a prototype DeLorme satellite tracker. As he gave Dale the coordinates and accident details so he could relay them to the NPS, Matthias dropped to the ground, curled into a fetal position, and started to sob.

About a half mile away, Holycross's cell phone began showing a signal. Slamming on the brakes, he bolted out of the vehicle and climbed atop its roof. His 911 call connected with Grand Canyon's NPS dispatch. Trying to steady his voice, he reported his wife's fall and requested immediate emergency Search and Rescue assistance. When the dispatcher soberly repeated the information back to him, Andy lost control. "Pick me up! *Please!* Take me with you! I know where she is!"

The dispatcher said no. Instead, the NPS official instructed him to drive back to Grand Canyon Village to the Emergency Services headquarters. He would be met there. The call ended.

Clambering off the roof, he jumped into the driver's seat and gunned his truck back to Rudow and Kawski. Skidding to a stop, he jumped out of the vehicle and charged over to Kawski.

"What the hell happened?!"

Although both men were on the ASU faculty, it was Ioana who actually introduced them to one another. Matthias, a native of Germany and professor of

mathematics, had taught one of her classes. During this class she discovered that he, too, was an immigrant who had fallen in love with the Grand Canyon and a dedicated hiker who had started backpacking the Canyon during the late 1980s. Kawski had nearly twenty years of Grand Canyon backpacking experience by the time he met Ioana. After her introduction, the two men, along with Ioana, began hiking together and had a couple of years of Canyon hiking under their belts by this trip.

In 2004, doctors diagnosed Kawski with multiple sclerosis, a potentially crippling and sometimes fatal disease.

Andy, Ioana and Matthias. *Courtesy Andy Holycross*

Matthias's doctor told him he had to keep moving, to stay active in mind and body as long as possible to stave off life in a wheelchair. This proved to be far easier said than done. He needed inspiration, and much of it came from Ioana. Not only was she a fellow European taken by the Canyon, but her energy, cheerfulness, and unwavering optimism were infectious. "Ioana brought me back to life," Kawski said.

Matthias told Andy and Rich that he and Ioana had experienced a great first day-and-a-half, easily traversing two of the three bays. They slept well the first night next to a pothole, then started early in the morning, making steady progress to the final bay, Owl Eyes. After negotiating the bay's snowy, shadowy east side with no problem, they stopped for lunch in the sun near the back of the bay. They both felt good, confident. Matthias took a photo of her at

Ioana. *Matthias Kawski*

their last lunch spot, grinning and playfully holding a bread stick in her teeth as if smoking a big cigar.

They reached the crux spot by one p.m. Kawski, always ultraconservative in his routes and reluctant to chance exposure, chose to traverse the higher, more tedious line on the Hermit slope where he could use vegetation for support and balance when needed. Ioana had opted for the more straightforward lower line, the one most hikers, including Holycross and Rudow, have taken. Matthias hiked out front and above. Suddenly, he heard a short scream and the clatter of rocks, followed four or five seconds later by a muted thump. Then silence.

During this account, Rudow and Holycross only listened.

"Why did you separate?!" Andy finally snapped.

Matthias's face fell and his eyes welled with tears. In his heart, Andy knew that separating was not the critical issue. He walked over to his distraught German friend and embraced him. Both men cried.

An instant later, he shifted back into frantic mode. "We need to go! Now!"

He and Matthias jumped into the FJ and floored it. Desperate to reach Grand Canyon Village before the helicopter, he drove like a madman. Rudow, driving the smaller, more agile Polaris, could barely keep up. At one point, Holycross struck a tree and tore off part of his bumper. He also repeatedly tried to phone dispatch for updates. Finally, his call connected.

Yes, the NPS chopper had spotted his wife at the base of the Supai cliffs directly below Owl Eyes. The terrain made it impossible for the pilot to land close enough, so the NPS would return with personnel and equipment for a short-haul extraction using ropes and a gurney suspended from the helicopter. Based on the 400-foot drop, her position, and the lack of movement, the dispatcher warned Andy that he needed to prepare for the worst.

Within two hours, the three men arrived at Fire Station One, the park's EMS facility. While pulling in, Holycross spotted two female rangers standing solemnly in the parking lot. He jammed on the brakes, stumbled out, and rushed over to the women.

"Have you heard from the chopper crew?"

Grief flooding their eyes, one of the rangers faltered, "I am so sorry …"

"No! No! You're a liar, a fucking liar!" Andy heard himself shout before his legs gave way. He collapsed onto the pavement and pounded his fists. Heaving sobs overwhelmed him.

As the rangers tried to console him, Canyon District Ranger Debbie Brenchley, first on the scene, shared details on how and where Ioana's body was found. Collectively, they surmised that she had lost her footing, or the ground had given way just above a sheer, nearly vertical, and mostly hidden rocky chute. She slid and rolled down a thirty-foot ravine, which—lacking vegetation and ledges—failed to arrest her fall before she tumbled over the edge of the cliff.

Andy asked to see her body. The rangers agreed but informed him he'd need a chaperone, because the incident was still under investigation. One of the rangers, a grief counselor, accompanied him. In the ambulance bay she unzipped the body bag. Other than appearing uncharacteristically pale, Ioana's face exhibited almost no damage. But her wonderful animation, vivacious personality, and dynamic spirit were gone.

In that moment and for the first time in his life, he fully appreciated the reality that our bodies are merely shells, containers for our spirits. That spirit is the essence of who we are, and the body carries it only for a short time. Within this apparent truth, he felt no special bond to the body in front of him. It was no longer his wife. Everything that mattered, everything he loved about her, everything they hoped and dreamed for in their lives, had disappeared.

Then Andy closed his eyes. In his mind she came alive.

"I'm not going to live long, Iubi," she had once told him.

"What?! Why would you say that? Don't be ridiculous!"

"I don't know why. I just feel it. I always have. But I never want to die in a stupid accident, like my uncle." Her uncle had perished in a fiery gasoline explosion. Ioana shuddered every time she recalled the memory of losing him.

And Andy would hug her and say, "That's not going to happen."

He opened his eyes, then turned to the ranger.

"Can I be alone with her?"

Despite protocol, she complied. Holycross talked to her body, touching her face, kissing her lips. This triggered another memory.

Whenever either was about to do something risky, the other would say, "Remember how I like you?" and the recipient would respond, "I know, Iubi. You like me warm."

Now the playful phrase, contrasting so sharply to her cold skin, became an unspeakable horror for Holycross. *How could we have been so flip?* he chided himself.

He returned to the parking lot. There, the NPS handed him Ioana's pack, which had been retrieved during the recovery. Rummaging through it, Andy found her hiking journal, her first; usually, he wrote about their hikes. From her handwriting, Andy sensed she had written her last three words while she was drowsy, maybe just before falling asleep on the final night of her life: "I miss Iubi."

Andy handed Rich his satellite phone, which had survived unscathed. Rudow took it home and stowed it away. Weeks later, when he pulled it out and pushed the power button, it came to life.

⌒⌒⌒

With the loss of a son in 2020, Andrew Holycross endured another personal tragedy. Nonetheless, he admits life goes on. With Matthias Kawski, he created an endowed scholarship in Ioana's name. He also found love again with his high school crush, Sonya Sass. They have been happily married since 2013. Andy is still teaching and loves talking about snakes. But even more, he relishes teaching his students about life, emphasizing the importance of making time for dreams, pointing out that tomorrow may never come.

He is also still hiking Grand Canyon. Indeed, three months after Ioana's death, he and some friends completed the Diamond-down section of his lengthwise hike on River Left. A year later, he finished a length-of-the-Canyon thru-hike on River Right.

In an article by Scott Seckel in *ASU News*, "Love and Loss in the Grand Canyon" (February 2019), Andy responded to an interview question about why he keeps going back to the Canyon after Hociota's tragic death.

> "My first inclination … was a visceral hatred of the canyon because, in my mind, that's what took her," Holycross said. "But I realized that feeling doesn't make sense; it's not rational.

"That feeling didn't last long. It was sort of a fleeting thing. Later, the more I thought about it, that was the place where Ioana and I were at our best. As a couple we were peas in a pod down there. She loved it...

"The canyon transcends ... all of the horrors of our lives and everything else. It's there and waiting for you. You accept it on its terms. Part of it is—what would she want? Would she want me to stop going there? Would she want Matt to stop going there? She would have kept going, I'm reasonably sure. She was passionate about the canyon, passionate about its conservation and wild places, passionate about challenging yourself more than anything else.... Why walk away from that?"

Ioana and Andy in Havasu Canyon. *Courtesy Andy Holycross*

CHAPTER THIRTY-FIVE

Diamond-Down (Part 1)

WESTERN GRAND CANYON

If you want to hike Grand Canyon to be on some list, you're going to fail. If you're not motivated by the beauty that you see along the way, the incremental suffering and pain is going to catch up to you.

Rich Rudow
Hidden Grand Canyon (2018)

January 2015

It happened in slow motion. Pete's pack rested upright at its angle of repose about twenty feet from a cliff edge. Its nearly fifty-pound load included sleeping gear, food, clothing, a tent, an iPhone, camera, headlamp, extra batteries, and water bottles. Even a boomerang. The pack teetered.

Several days earlier the area had received a dusting of snow, yet potholes along our route turned up dry, and any surviving snow now only existed in shady nooks. I told the boys to pack their water bottles with snow in case we didn't find water at our planned camp, 232 Mile Canyon. We set our packs on the thirty-degree slope above a cliff edge and the snow-stuffing began.

"Pete! Your pack!" someone shouted.

We all turned to watch the pack somersault backwards once, then twice. Then it did so again. And again. And again. With each tumble it picked up speed. We watched, fascinated but dismayed, as it cartwheeled right over the cliff…

Earlier that day we had climbed aboard my raft and launched from Diamond Creek. Part of our novel idea was to tackle our Diamond-down section combining backpacking with a river trip. Over the next four days, we would

Tom Martin.
Courtesy of Tom Martin

hike as much as we could of the roughly 120 walking miles needed to parallel the 54 river miles to Lake Mead. Then we'd boat the rest of the way out, leaving what still remained for a second trip.

My friend Tom Martin volunteered to assist us by chauffeuring my eighteen-foot Domar raft. After rigging the boat, we rowed across the Colorado to the north bank (River Right) above Diamond Creek Rapid. Tom dropped us off at a tamarisk-willow-arrowweed-and-cat-claw-choked sandbar at the base of a small side canyon. He'd row downstream while we hiked atop the cliffs above. Our plan called for a rendezvous in two days at Separation Canyon, near River Mile 240, thirteen miles downriver. We carried walkie-talkies to communicate.

After yet another hellacious bushwhack, we breached the sandbar's jungle to a cliff face with a break. Then we scrambled up it to the Tonto Platform to find ourselves amidst a Terracotta Warrior army of jumping cholla cactus that covered several acres. We zigzagged through the pokey obstacle course, dodging the three-to-four-foot-tall plants. Evading these platoons of cactus midgets wielding spikey little maces was challenging; we all suffered an impaling or two while doing our crossing.

Once beyond, things went smoothly as we maneuvered around a cliff edge of 231 Mile Canyon via a game trail. When pothole water became nonexistent, I voiced my concerns about dry camping and snow stuffing…

Now, holding our collective breath, we heard Pete's pack whistle through the air in a free fall. Seconds later a muted "poof" drifted up. We looked at each other. A few nervous chuckles broke out.

"That was crazy!"

"Holy cow! Did that just happen?"

Pete began to scurry after his pack, heading toward the cliff's edge, which was covered in loose, ball-bearing rock.

"Peter! Don't!" I cautioned. He stopped and looked back, frowning.

"Look, Pete, we'll probably be able to get to it from below. If not, we'll figure something out to share gear and food."

"Yeah," the others chimed in.

But we all knew no one had a spare sleep kit. Plus, Pete had several hundred dollars invested in his gear. Retrieving the pack, not snow-stuffing, now became our priority. Pete hustled out front, determined to locate, then retrieve his pack.

"Hey, cool! There it is!" he excitedly pointed several minutes later. "And it looks like there's a break in the cliff that I can get through to go get it!"

"Great! Just be careful!" I yelled back.

The pack had fallen about 100 feet. Velcro-like, the spiculated rock it landed on had snagged it. Anything that had blown out of the pack likewise stuck to the slope. We watched Peter scramble to it and cheered as he gathered his gear. After another twenty minutes, he stood beside us, breathing hard but wearing both his pack and a big grin.

"My camera's busted," he panted. "But it wasn't too expensive. The only other things that broke were a couple of water bottles," he cheerfully added. Energized by this victory, we resumed the hike, picking up our pace to make up for lost time.

At 232 Mile Canyon a hand-written note greeted us: "Hi guys! Glad there is water here!" Tom had walked up the drainage and penned the message after noting a water-filled pothole. We made camp and toasted the day and Peter with that pothole water, thankful that he had his own tent and sleep kit.

Looking down-canyon in the twilight toward the river below, grateful for our good fortune, I pondered what lurked at the foot of this drainage: 232 Mile Rapid, also known by the more alarming name of "Killer Fang Falls." This rapid most likely killed newlyweds Glen and Bessie Hyde after their sweepscow hit the rapid's "fang" rocks, which at certain flows poke up like jaw canines. It is speculated this collision flung one or both into the river. Or perhaps one jumped in to save the other. Either way, neither was seen again. Glen's grieving father, Rollin, trudged almost 90 percent of the approximately 120 foot-miles westward from Diamond Creek to Grand Wash in a heartbreaking search for his only son and daughter-in-law—a sad footnote in the history of lengthwise Canyon walks. (In *Sunk Without a Sound*, Brad Dimock examines the couple's mysterious disappearance and details Rollin Hyde's search.)

It now occurred to me that Wes would be walking around the "fangs" for the second time, only this time from much higher up. The first time had been thirteen years earlier in May 2002, when I took my family on a Diamond-down river trip. The trip had a three-fold purpose. First, to pick up John Azar and his buddy Billy Driscoll at the end of their sixty-eight-day Canyon hike from Lees Ferry to Diamond Creek. Second, to scope out the setting for a potential film documentary based on *Over the Edge*. Michael Ghiglieri's screenwriter friend from Newburyport, Massachusetts, joined us. He had contacted Michael and me about a collaboration between the British Broadcasting Company (BBC) and the US-based company that produced *American Experience*. And third, to have a great excuse for a fun family-and-friends outing.

Michael brought his seventeen-year-old son, Cliff. George and Mike Steck joined us, excited about picking up Azar and Driscoll. Besides my family, I invited our friend Sandy Nevills-Reiff, daughter of Canyon river legend Norman Nevills and mother of my buddy Greg (the Canyoneers' guide who introduced me to Ethan).

The two men were waiting when we arrived at Diamond. Not surprisingly after nearly two-and-a-half months of walking, both were thinner, not to mention weary. They mostly lounged around, resting and watching as we rigged boats. George, then seventy-seven, was also a little sluggish; he hung out in the shade during the rigging marathon for what would be his last river trip.

A couple hours after launching, we pulled in above 232-Mile Rapid to scout potential runs. Becky, having heard the Glen and Bessie Hyde story, immediately insisted that seven-year-old Wes walk around the rapid with her. While I agreed, he immediately protested. It didn't surprise me when Becky reported that he'd been hopping mad throughout the boulder hop.

❧

"Hey, Tom. Heading your way," Connor broadcast over the walkie-talkie. We knew Tom Martin was floating somewhere below us out of sight. If he had been nearby, he would have been easy to spot. At six feet, six inches, Tom—gangly, garrulous, and animated—is one of the most knowledgeable people alive on the subject of traversing the Grand Canyon on foot and by river. Coauthor of the successful *Rivermaps: Guide to the Colorado River in the Grand Canyon,* he also wrote *Day Hikes from the River.* A veteran of nearly a hundred river trips and thousands of Canyon hiking miles (including the length in pieces), Tom is also blessed with a photographic memory.

While he's generally a cheerful guy, you don't want to argue with Tom about protecting the Colorado in Grand Canyon, or historical events, or about the merits of the do-it-yourself boater. He does not hold commercial rafting in high regard. He also dislikes motors on the river and goes nose-to-nose (or usually neck to nose, given his height) with anyone who thinks otherwise. But we remain good friends, partly because we follow the "agree to disagree" philosophy.

Connor's walkie talkie crackled. "Copy that. I'll see you in a bit," Tom confirmed.

In the late afternoon of day two we arrived at the foot of Separation Canyon, River Mile 240, and downclimbed a steep chute a couple of hundred feet from the mouth. (Steck and company had used the same chute in 1982.) From there, we waltzed into the luxurious river camp Tom had set up. Way beyond the call of friendship, he had not only provided a table full of appetizers, but had also prepared a spaghetti dinner. We slept great that night.

Up at first light, and after a quick breakfast, we set out carrying only daypacks to walk to 242 Mile Canyon. Around noon, we again met up with Tom. This time, God love him, he'd hauled lunch fixings up the drainage. After lunch, we swapped daypacks for our big backpacks, intending to camp up and away from the river. After loading up with water, we headed out for our goal of Surprise Canyon, about fifteen miles away.

The massive, limestone-capped Spencer Towers to the south, rising 1,200 feet from shoulder to summit, dominated the scene throughout the afternoon. Despite our quick pace, we seemed to be getting nowhere. Yet some fascinating archeologic finds offset our frustration. Evidence of Ancestral Puebloans, as well as earlier and later Native Americans, was everywhere: roasting pits, flint lithics, pot sherds. Thoughts of meandering down here wearing nothing but yucca sandals and a breechcloth made me cringe. What single word best describes them? Gnarly. Even now, hiking off-trail in the Canyon almost always comes at a price to human flesh, usually paid to limestone. Wes reminded us of this when he took a tumble and shredded his arm on a chunk.

George Steck noted the uncanny attraction this Karst layer seems to have for human skin in *Loop Hikes I*:

> Another unlikely villain, this time mineral, is the "carnivorous" limestone. When limestone weathers in rain a sinister two-dimensional sawblade effect is produced not unlike a rock's being covered in shark's teeth. Throw your hand out onto this rock and you'll live to regret it.

We fell short of making Surprise Canyon by several miles. Low on water, we stopped anyway and dry camped in the cliffs. Much to my relief, Connor pulled a dromedary bag filled with four liters of water out of his pack and passed it around. He didn't say a word, just politely smiled. In return, we tag-teamed him with hugs.

As the night wound down, the Canyon's indomitable silence took over. Within that silence I reflected on Connor's selfless act and that beautiful bag of water. It got me reminiscing about another poignant Canyon moment I'd experienced nearby.

In October 2013, after camping at a remote area on the Shivwits Plateau with Rich Rudow and Josh Gordon, I'd hiked down Trail Canyon near 214 Mile with Josh to meet Andy Holycross. Josh—who amidst shots of whiskey the night before, had us laughing so hard that I strained my stomach muscles—was giddy during our hike. He almost pranced down to the Esplanade. Despite being a member of the Hualapai Tribe, he had been forbidden to finish Andy's earlier south-side hike, and was denied the "Hualapai guide" job Andy needed for his Diamond-down portion. Being shunned yet again, possibly from being only half Hualapai, had crushed him. Andy wanted to change that.

Our meeting, coordinated by Rich via satellite text messages, turned out to be perfectly timed. Within ten minutes, Andy and another friend of his, Chris Forsyth (part of the 2010 Yahoo group permit dispute), came into view. Andy was nearing the end of the continuous north-side thru-hike that he and Ioana had begun planning two years earlier. Chris had hiked in to join him for a ten-day segment, and Andy had invited Gordon to come along as well. When Holycross saw Gordon, he gave him a great big bear-hug.

The gesture's obviously mutual sincerity made me smile. As they hugged, I couldn't help but notice the changes in Andy's appearance from the last time I saw him. A thick beard came as a dramatic contrast to a thinner body. He had often joked that the way he prepared for prolonged and demanding lengthwise Canyon hiking was "to get as fat as possible." Clearly, he'd burned through that fat reserve. I offered him an extra sandwich, which he gratefully accepted and immediately started eating. As he did, he began rummaging through his own pack.

"I have something for you, too, something I'd like you to see."

Pulling out a small baggie, he handed it to me. After studying it, I found my own self swallowing, hard. I looked at him.

"It's her hair, you know," he said softly.

The strands were auburn, like my wife's.

Sometime after Ioana's death, Holycross shared with me what she had written on her last Christmas card to him.

> If I could, I would redo it and record every kiss, smile, making love, playing and loving you so that if someone will ever be in search of proof that love exists, they will find our love.

"Her sleeping kit is in here, too," Andy told me, laying his hand on the pack beside him. Both items had also accompanied him on the Diamond-down hike the previous March, a month after her death.

"She's gonna finish this hike, Tom, and she's finishing it with me."

～～

Recalling that moment, the Canyon's quietness—a symphony of it—became almost overwhelming. I listened hard, telling myself to embrace it, to understand and learn from it. Balanced by Weston's and the boys' soft breathing, it reinforced what I already knew: Live in the present, appreciate and love the here and now—*but especially the who*—for tomorrow everything could change. I also knew that when it came to the Canyon's glorious silence, tomorrow everything would, indeed, change.

CHAPTER THIRTY-SIX

Diamond-Down (Part 2)

WESTERN GRAND CANYON (CONTINUED)

The First of the Ninth was an old cavalry division that traded in their horses for helicopters and went tear-assing around 'Nam looking for the shit.

Capt. Benjamin Willard
Apocalypse Now (1979)

May 2015

Four months had passed since our first Diamond-down expedition. For this second leg—Weston's and my fifteenth segment—we intended to knock off the last twenty-four river miles to Grand Wash Cliffs by once again combining hiking with a river trip. Also once again, Tom Martin would be providing logistical support.

After launching at Diamond Creek and running thirty river miles, we camped on a beach at what's called Devils Slide at River Mile 255.5, the terminus of our last walk. Morning saw us up at sunrise, picking our way downstream.

The sun had been up for a little over an hour when the day's bombardment of sightseeing helicopters began. Apparently dispatched in salvos of twos and threes and at roughly four- to five-minute intervals, their deep-throated whupping shattered the silence, and their presence dominated our vision. Shortly after, commercial motor rigs and jet boats began adding to the cacophony. Loaded with river runners, the watercraft intermittently thundered by, engines typically at full throttle. Some created large wakes that crashed into the river's silt banks and caused chunks to calve off, sending clouds of dust into the air. In that moment, I tried to reconcile what my vision relayed, but in my mind's eye, things were different. *Very different.*

What I saw was Grand Canyon turning into dense rainforest, the cottonwoods and tamarisk morphing into mangroves and palm trees. The onslaught of touring helicopters became a blitzkrieg of military ones; and the river boats, now navy assault vessels—not on the Colorado but on the Mekong. Those dust explosions? Napalm detonations. Next, the soundtrack from *Apocalypse Now*, Francis Ford Coppola's 1979 epic Vietnam war film, cued up, and Wagner's iconic *Ride of the Valkyries* played in my head. All-out warfare seemed to have descended into lower Grand Canyon. Chaos reigned.

So, what happened? The answers to that question are essentially simple. First, dams happened: Boulder (renamed Hoover in 1947) in the 1930s, then Glen Canyon in the 1960s. Before being "managed" by these concrete barriers, the high-spirited Colorado had raced through here, transporting a daily average of close to 30,000 dump-truck loads of silt. But once Boulder Dam's gates were shut in 1936, the river began snowplowing its silt-laden water against the dam's concrete back. Fine sediment settled in the pooling water and in-filled the canyon's contours. This process continued ever farther upstream, packing the river corridor and its side-canyon junctions with silt for miles and miles. For almost thirty years, the progression went unmitigated, the Colorado discharging a payload of about *one billion* dump trucks of silt into the doomed portions of Black Canyon and lower Grand Canyon. In 1963, the process moved upstream behind Glen Canyon Dam, dooming the enchanting canyon that gave it its name. Both dams, for all intents and purposes, also killed the river in their respective canyons. And both remain nearly tourniquet-tight in their lethal stranglehold.

The corpse of the Colorado here (a.k.a., Lake Mead)—the 110-mile-long, nearly one-trillion-gallon reservoir behind Hoover Dam—had dropped by more than 100 feet by the time we arrived in 2015, the result of repetitive drought years. Massive, high-walled silt riverbanks stretched for miles on both sides of the river as far as we could see. The river oozed through the gray-white sludge which coated the cliff walls like atherosclerotic plaques in the artery of a diseased heart—the clogging severe. This was where the *Fantastic Voyage* through the Canyon came to an abrupt and pitiful end.

Again, thick silt chunks haphazardly break off and fall off into the river. Most come with a rumble, followed by a loud splash, an expanding cloud of dust, and a plume of billowing dirt in the water. At night the sudden calving can be startling. During daylight, the entire scene is nothing short of depressing. The once proud, beautiful, boisterous Colorado River—liquid conqueror of stone and creator of canyons—barely whimpers through here. Feeble and forlorn, it looks utterly humiliated.

While hiking through the same area in 1976, Kenton Grua journaled even stronger emotions about the damage done:

> It's an awful silence, heart rendering quiet. The canyon mourns the death of its maker, the river. And in this death silence, the canyon sleeps, awaiting its rebirth on some distant morning, eons away one man's puny fallacies of a dam crumbles away into nothingness from whence it came. It's murder, by God, and I pray we don't kill more of it. Not just the river, the whole Canyon...I've never felt such sadness, the death of a friend. Why do men do such things? I dry my tears and move forward, ever forward. There can be no doubt the mood of the hike has changed. I cannot mourn for the Canyon. I shall probably not see its living being in my short lifetime. I must carry on.

The farther we maneuvered into the "war zone," a.k.a. "Helicopter Alley"—a roughly ten-mile stretch beginning near River Mile 257—the greater the melancholy. The unrelenting helicopter barrage is the worst part of the second answer to what happened down here: commercialization. For me, with that reality the helicopter imagery morphs from military to monetary. The choppers become flying cash cows, herded into the Canyon to trample the stillness, pollute the

Weston traversing along a silt bank. *T McCullough*

sky, feed on tourists, then get milked—all on "sacred" soil. Which provokes the next question: How—*for God's sake*—did this happen?

Starting in 1987, a year after the tragic mid-air collision in which John Thybony and twenty-four others lost their lives, Grand Canyon National Park and the FAA began implementing the National Park Overflights Act (Public Law 100-91). The act's purpose was two-fold: To study ways to improve safety and prevent future accidents like the 1986 disaster, and to restore a substantial level of "natural quiet" to the Canyon environment. As a result of this study, scenic flights (airplane and helicopter) were limited and below-rim flights (other than administrative or emergencies) were banned. In 2000, these conditions were lifted for Hualapai lands abutting or part of the Grand Canyon. Known as the "Hualapai exception," this decision was intended to boost the tribe's air tourism industry and help raise its people out of poverty. Currently serving about 200,000 tourists annually and generating $50 million in yearly revenue, it has exceeded expectations. But as economic gain often does, it comes with a tradeoff. In this case, the obliteration of the natural quiet that had defined the region and Hualapais' ancestral lands for eons.

Apropos of our battle scene, at a side canyon with the military name Quartermaster, T dropped his drawers. Like a true tail gunner, he aimed his naked butt at an incoming chopper and its gawking occupants. His lighthearted mooning made us laugh, but the realities of the setting quickly shifted our mood back to annoyance and disappointment; the sounds around us waxed so loud at times that we felt like we were paralleling a freeway. We had to shout to be heard. The auditory assault went on all day. *The entire day. Dawn till dusk.* Photographer and filmmaker Peter McBride, who, with writer Kevin Fedarko, finished a lengthwise Canyon hike in segments, sat in the area in 2016 and counted 367 helicopters during one eight-hour stretch. The record is reportedly more than four hundred. We couldn't struggle past the five-mile, flight-sanctioned war zone fast enough.

Nearly as depressing is another change that adds to the combat-zone vibe here. This one reflects the Southwest's water wars and drought. When lake levels were high, vegetation sprawled on the saturated silt benches. Similar to an invasion of weeds in a yard, willows, tamarisk, and cottonwood trees increased exponentially. For three decades they thrived, ever taller, ever thicker. Then came the arid years of this century's first two decades, exacerbated by big cities like Las Vegas, Phoenix, and Los Angeles fighting for their share of the water. Lake levels dropped and these silt beds dried out; the trees soon died en masse. Now only their leafless and lifeless gray-black carcasses remain. Acres and acres of arboreal skeletons stand or lie scattered across the silt banks by the tens of thousands. Their broken, helter-skelter appearance reminded me of the trusses and girders in a bombed-out city , the fallout from having been nuked by a dam.

Navigating this deciduous death on foot turned out to be far more dangerous than traversing the living jungles upstream. Some sections required a weird balancing act and a bit of a gamble. We had to tiptoe atop a dead tree trunk or slink across a lattice of pointy branches and risk being impaled by a misstep or unintentional post-holing. Trying to get beyond this seemingly endless rat's nest of punji sticks proved not only painful, but also excruciatingly slow and anger-provoking. Wes had brought a machete, but it proved of limited use; a chainsaw would've been only a little better. *What would be the best weapon for such a battle?* A flamethrower. Burn it all down and start over.

The helicopters quit flying when the sun set. Yet around us, deadness remained. To me this damaged section of the Grand Canyon is extra depressing when you consider that prior to Hoover Dam, the area would have rivaled any of the Canyon's best for scenery and adventure. How? First, breathtaking vistas, as good or better than anywhere upstream. Second, stunning side canyons—Surprise, Salt, or Burnt Spring—which stretch for miles but are now so barricaded by silt and jungle that most would-be hikers don't give them a second glance. Third, Lava Cliff and Separation Rapids, as big or bigger than the best rapids upstream, including Lava Falls. Combined with other significant rapids, the whitewater from Diamond-down would have been fantastic prior to 1936. River runners would have been blown away. Nowadays most just blow by.

When we entered Dry Canyon to camp at River Mile 265, however, our spirits lifted. Tom and a young man we invited along named Caleb Cordasco had already set up a kitchen, toilet, and fire pan. More thrilling than the camp setup, however, was watching twenty-four-year-old Caleb, a family friend and T's cousin, walking on shore. Five months earlier, an accidental fall had paralyzed him.

How Caleb's parents, Billy and Fon Cordasco—as well as other family and friends, including me—received the tragic news of his fall remains intensely vivid. During what was—hands down—one of the most fun New Year's Eve celebrations of my life, we heard abrupt, very firm knocking on the Havasupai Garden bunkhouse door. The opportunity to use the bunkhouse for a New Year's party came in return for work I'd donated as an EMS instructor and medical advisor for the NPS. Upon hearing the knock, iPod music, conversations, and laughter immediately ceased and all eyes focused on the door. Cold air and snow blew in when we opened it and saw Betsy Arnou, the NPS ranger on duty that night, someone I knew well and respected. While I anticipated a "Hey, keep it down" reprimand, her solemn demeanor suggested something far more serious.

"Who is Billy Cordasco?" Her voice was uncharacteristically serious.

"I am," Billy answered.

"I have an important phone call for you. It's about your son."

We assumed that whatever might have happened to Caleb had to be related to the hazardous weather, like a car accident. Billy left with Betsy, then returned looking shell-shocked; he reported that Caleb had fallen forty feet while ascending a wall at the local climbing gym in Flagstaff where he worked. The fall had crushed several vertebrae in his lumbar spine and left him paralyzed from the waist down. He was undergoing emergency surgery.

Flagstaff neurosurgeon Steve Ritland, a close friend of the Cordascos and McCulloughs, had been relaxing at home when he received the phone call from a mutual friend about Caleb's injury. Ritland immediately drove to Flagstaff Medical Center and reviewed Caleb's X-rays and CT scans. In addition to a crushed spine, Caleb had severe fractures of both heels. "Well," the hospital's radiologist, sighed to Ritland. "It's not going to matter anyway," commenting about the heel fractures. "He's never going to walk again."

Ritland spent the entire night extracting splintered bone from Caleb's spinal cord. Miraculously, the impact had not severed it. After months of physical therapy, and with Ritland's blessing, Caleb joined our Diamond-down trip. We cheered as he shuffled around the sandbank.

The next morning, we trudged with daypacks along the river's very edge below the omnipresent silt banks now looming thirty to forty feet overhead. We also waded in the river, lighthearted and barefoot, like Huck Finn and Tom Sawyer. As usual, silt bank chunks randomly broke off; thank God, none of the big ones landed on us. By early afternoon, we reached Grand Wash Cliffs. Here we hopped aboard the boats with Tom Martin and Caleb.

Our last night's camp, festooned with cow pies and mud, was about a mile from the takeout at Pearce Ferry. Unloading the boats and stepping into the sandy muck was like post-holing in snow. Feet quickly disappeared. Then ankles. Then shins and knees if you stood in the same spot.

For laughs we wriggled around to see how deeply or seriously we might get stuck. I wrestled myself free before reaching knee deep, while Tom and Caleb avoided it entirely. The other boys—Wes, T, and Connor—did not. Instead, they took turns laughing at each other as they wiggled ever deeper. Soon their thighs and waists disappeared. The intense suction of the wet, dense sand had each one stuck like a finger in a bottle. Yanking around only seemed to make things worse.

Contrary to Hollywood, however, it's almost impossible to die by suffocation in quicksand. Once chest-deep, an animal—or human—will float rather than sink; aerated lungs and body tissue's lower density will keep the head above the quicksand. That doesn't mean it isn't dangerous; its capacity to trap victims can be deadly, especially if predators are lurking nearby.

Speaking of potential predators, we noted the river lurking ever closer to the boys. While they eventually dug themselves out, for the time being they were trapped. In an otherwise carefree moment, the rising river's predator-like movement reminded me of another, yet far more deadly, canyon country scenario: being trapped in a slot canyon at the mercy of a flash flood.

CHAPTER THIRTY-SEVEN

Old Dogs, the Red Wolf, and Monsoon Gambling

WESTON: SWAMP POINT TO KANAB CREEK

*Nobody can fully understand the meaning of love unless he's owned a dog.
A dog can show you more honest affection with a flick of his tail than a man can
gather through a lifetime of handshakes.*

Gene Hill (1928–1997)

*Now come the floods. They charge down atavistic canyons drinking furiously out
of thunderstorms, coming one after the next with vomited boulders and trees
pounding from one side of a canyon to the other, sometimes no more than hours
apart. Sometimes a hundred years apart. Sometimes a thousand.
The floods always come.*

Craig Childs
The Secret Knowledge of Water (2000)

August 2015

Wes's boyhood dog, Mya, had her own backpack. This black Labrador entered
our lives shortly after Weston turned eight. And as is often the case with dogs,
she aligned herself primarily with one person. Wes.

From puppyhood onward, Mya slept next to Wes in his bed. Each night, he
dutifully carried her there. When she became physically able, she hopped onto
his bed herself. This situation lasted for a good decade. When with advancing
age it became too difficult for her, Wes built her a ramp. When she became too

frail for even that, he would carry her 100-plus pounds upstairs to his bedroom and lay her on his bed.

At twelve, Mya developed cancer and died about a year later. We buried her on our property. Wes and I dug the grave. He sobbed. And sobbed. And sobbed.

It may sound odd, but to see him cry, to pour out so much emotion and love, gave me great joy. That's because emotion was mostly absent for more than a year during his late teens. As we laid her to rest, I couldn't thank Mya enough. Her unconditional love for Wes had helped him through his darkest of times. It also nudged him back into hiking the Canyon with me.

Indeed, several months after Mya's death, Wes seemed particularly excited about an August 2015 hike. Part of his enthusiasm emerged from the possibility of walking in the footsteps (and paw prints) of another historical Canyon figure and his dog.

⟳

In the fall of 1925, Red Wolf—given name, Willard Dale—set out on a long walk below the Canyon rim, from Bright Angel Creek to Kanab Creek. If successful, the roughly 130-mile walk basically paralleling fifty-seven river miles would be the longest known continuous trek on foot below the rim at the time. (Emphasis on *known*. Again, we have no records of indigenous peoples' travel below the rim.)

I first learned of Red Wolf in the early 1990s from Canyon historian Dove Menkes. Like an old bloodhound himself with an incredible nose for Canyon history, Menkes (now deceased) had sniffed out the "Red Wolf" a few years earlier and shared his story with me.

Turns out that when Dale made this walk, his big dog—big enough to tote its own saddlebags—had accompanied him. Envisioning the dog (breed and gender unknown), saddlebags and all, boldly going where no dog—and few humans—had gone before, intrigued me as much as Ron Mitchell's explorations with his young son, Randy. This canine connection made it even more fitting that Weston's first solo hike in the Canyon be in dog-loving Dale's footsteps, and into Kanab Creek, no less.

As an aside, of Dale's self-reported long walks, this one could not be chalked up as his grandest in Grand Canyon National Park. Not even close. That is, *if* you could believe him. Another Grand Canyon historian, P. T. Reilly, didn't. Like Menkes, Reilly also had a great knack for digging up obscure Canyon history. He wrote this about Red Wolf, the man with the adopted lupine moniker:

330

He wore dirty buckskin, thick glasses, was a prodigious walker, a fine shot. Poached deer and lived off the country.... Claimed to have walked the entire North Rim from Grand Wash to Lee's Ferry—obviously a lie.

In his research, which predated Menkes', Reilly also discovered Red Wolf's given name and that he'd been born in 1868 in Missouri. In the 1890s, Dale headed west and somehow ended up at the Grand Canyon, most likely to prospect. Along the way he acquired (or gave himself) other nicknames, including Wild Jim, Red Angel, and Golden Jesus (because of his long, reddish-blonde hair). For a while he lived in the so-called Outlaw Shack near Lees Ferry.

Whether Dale actually walked the entirety of Grand Canyon's North Rim (a potentially massive feat) cannot be substantiated. Nor is there definitive proof to the contrary. Still, Reilly may well have been correct. The Grand Canyon-loving Dale apparently had no problem grandstanding; he credited himself with originally suggesting the motto "Grand Canyon State" for Arizona when it became a state in 1912. (Arizona eventually adopted the motto, a good choice given the other options, among them, "the Baby State.")

While there's no proof that Dale did or didn't walk the entirety of the North Rim, there *is* proof that he at least walked below the rim into Kanab Creek: an inscription in Chamberlain Canyon, one of Kanab's tributary canyons. Chiseled in Supai Group sandstone are the words "Red Wolf" and dates: 1902, '17, and '25. These inscriptions, found by hikers in 2003, also show a scratched-in arrow pointing downward adjacent to the pecked-out numbers, which suggests that Dale may have been in and out of Kanab Canyon over a span of twenty-three years. The '25 date also suggests that he in fact completed his long walk below the rim from Bright Angel Creek to Kanab. Sadly, Red Wolf's walk reportedly came at a significant cost: his big dog died along the way.

"You know, Dad," Wes once commented sometime after we discussed Red Wolf and his dog. "I think being

Red Wolf in full regalia.
Courtesy of Dove Menkes

a hiker in the Canyon is kind of like being the dog of a cruel master. The Canyon beats the crap out of you, but you lick your wounds and always come back for more, tail wagging."

True to his word, Wes cheerfully and repeatedly returned for more of the Canyon, despite taking several brutal licks from it on trips with me. The next one came with a condition: He wanted to go alone.

Red Wolf inscription in Kanab Creek Canyon.
Arnie Richards

On August 22, 2015, Wes and his then girlfriend, Patricia McCullough (T's sister), and I camped on the rim. This followed an all-day shuttle to drop off my Yukon in Hack Canyon, an arm of Kanab Creek and the planned exit point for Weston's solo hike. We arrived at Swamp Point just before sunset. Mostly clear sky loomed overhead. Yet scattered here and there were billowy white clouds with splotches of grays and blacks. *Rainclouds.*

Since I've been in medicine, a water-laden cloud's appearance has always reminded me of a fluid-filled human lung as seen in a chest x-ray: blotchy gray and white. "Wet lungs," we call them. They commonly present with pneumonia or heart failure. As wet lungs can be life-threatening to humans, so too can "wet clouds" be to a canyon hiker.

❧

Called "monsoons," these summer storms frequently offer welcome reprieve and a big drink to the Southwest's dry and thirsty land. The afternoon thundershowers are the result of a gradual buildup of moisture-laden clouds. Unfortunately, most of the water that reaches the ground during these storms departs as quickly as it arrives.

Sometimes quicker.

With nothing to hold it back, rain falling on rocky terrain in Southwest canyon country makes a frenzied sprint toward the lowest point. By the time it gets to the bottom of a canyon drainage, it's often a debris-choked tidal wave of mud, rock, cacti, cow manure, basketballs, tires, and other gobbledygook from the high plateaus and surrounding reservations. The largest and most dangerous flash floods gather the disrupted earth—sometimes to the consistency of a concrete slurry—and like a blast from a bazooka, annihilate anything in their path. These hazardous flows can be triggered by a single storm cell over a relatively minuscule area. Yet just a few miles away, the setting can be blue-skied and bone-dry. Therein lies the problem—and the danger of yet more Grand Deception—exploring desert Canyon Country during potentially stormy weather.

On plateaus, monsoon activity can be seen for miles. Within the confines of a canyon, however, a limited sliver of sky is often all that's visible. The deeper you are, the narrower your view. Thus, entering slot canyons between July and September, aka monsoon season, is a bit of a gamble—the monsoon gamble. When is it a safe bet to enter? When is it not?

For starters, if it's already raining, or if ominous black thunderheads plainly announce an imminent downpour, the decision about entering or not entering should be obvious. Stay out. Fold. Mother Nature just showed her hand and she's holding a Royal Flush (literally).

August monsoon storm at Kanab Creek. *Rich Rudow*

But suppose she's wearing her poker face and that limited slice of sky is invitingly blue, or the clouds are fluffy-white? In other words, benign appearing, like the blackjack dealer showing the three of clubs instead of an ace. Then a hiker's decision is clearly tougher, but there exist some other important "tells," as they say in Las Vegas.

First, by definition and atmospheric physiology, monsoon storms are afternoon events. To wit, fifteen of the Canyon's sixteen flash-flood victims, as well as all eleven victims of a flood in nearby Antelope Canyon in 1997, died during the afternoon. Additionally, more than 80 percent of flash floods recorded in the depths of Grand Canyon at Bright Angel Creek between July and September occurred during afternoon or early evening.

Second, in Grand Canyon, it usually takes large flash floods from one to four hours to reach the river because many originate far up side drainages, on the plateaus, or even on the rims (the closer the flood is to the river, the smaller and less lethal it tends to be). All that being said, flash floods can arise year-round, but are often more frequent and intense when the ground is already saturated, such as during late summer after consistent monsoons.

Fortunately, the third and most important tell is that flash floods are often telegraphed. Alert hikers can perceive a flood's impending arrival before they actually see it. For example, subtle clues are a tip-off: the sudden muddying of a creek, water trickling in a previously dry drainage, animals or birds scurrying downstream or out of the drainage bottom, the muddy smell of clay and other minerals, a sudden shift of wind to downcanyon.

The best and most blatant warning though, especially with very large floods, is the sound that precedes them. Often, a steady hissing sound coming from upcanyon can be heard before the flood appears. This gradually increasing hiss then morphs into a deep roar as the flood approaches. Similar to the thundering of a train, the ominous noise warns people to get out of the way or face the consequences. Sometimes the flood's sound precedes the torrent by a minute or more.

Yet, as loud as this roar may be, if one is near or in a creek, it can be masked or muffled by stream babble until the approaching flood is mere seconds away. Staying up and away from creeks may be helpful in perceiving an oncoming flood. Also helpful is noting potential escape routes in a hike's narrowest sections; many floods can be outmaneuvered by side-scrambling out of the drainage bottom—if the walls aren't too steep. Sometimes, only a few seconds are all that's needed.

Better yet, if you find yourself in canyon narrows when a flood might be imminent, avoid anything you can't sprint through or climb out of in a hurry. And never—*ever*—camp, nap, or linger in the narrowest sections during potentially wet weather. Finally, appreciate that rushing water is deceptively strong. It can seem to defy physics by floating boulders, some the size of small houses, and carry them downstream. In fact, it takes only a couple of feet of water to move cars and trucks.

So, what does playing the monsoon flash-flood gamble by entering a narrow canyon during potentially stormy weather and living to tell the tale come down to? As in Vegas, your best guess, based on the hand you're dealt. *And luck.*

~~~~~

Weston's solo plan included a descent off Swamp Point into Saddle Canyon. From there, he would traverse through Tapeats Amphitheater to Thunder River before hiking over Surprise Valley to Deer Creek. Then, he planned to hike down to the river and along the right bank downriver to Kanab Creek. Finally, he would exit via Kanab to Hack Canyon, then up. An ambitious endeavor, the route of this sixteenth leg amounted to about fifty miles over four days. When finished, he would've not only caught up with me in a lengthwise line but, pushing his total mileage to close to 600, surpassed me in distance. I was all for it.

Becky, predictably, wasn't. A self-described "helicopter mom," she opposed the idea. "Wes will be fine," I assured her. "We need to let him off the leash."

After reiterating that his Canyon experience now exceeded that of anybody his age whom I knew, that he would carry a satellite phone, that he'd likely run into other hikers or river runners at Tapeats Creek and Deer Creek, as well as Kanab Creek, and that I had done much of the same hike twenty years earlier, solo no less, she finally, reluctantly, relented.

As the sun set on Swamp Point, we stared at the clouds. Wes and I discussed how a flood might happen and what he should do if it did. Part of this discussion involved George Steck and a flash flood he encountered in precisely the same area where Wes was headed.

Fortunately, no one in Steck's party got injured or died. But George had lost everything he'd been carrying. Luckily, his group eventually found all of his gear scattered downstream, except one boot. For the rest of his trek—out of necessity and for laughs—George wore that boot on one foot and a tennis shoe on the other.

Twenty-five years after George's misadventure, nearly to the day, I woke Wes at sunrise. He needed a few hours to get through the narrow confines of the Redwall Formation in Saddle Canyon by late morning, well before the typical monsoon rains of mid- to late afternoon. This section seemed like the crux of his entire trip. After Wes had eaten and packed, Patricia and I shooed him on his way.

After negotiating the Redwall narrows in Saddle Canyon, Wes would likely be home free. When he got to Kanab Canyon, a bigger corridor with an average width comparable to a two-lane highway to a four-lane freeway, it would take a really, *really* big flood, *a river-sized one,* to pose danger. *What were the odds of that?*

Kanab Creek flash flooding, water still rising, August 24, 2015. *Weston Myers*

CHAPTER THIRTY-EIGHT

Out of Dark and Flooding Water

WESTON: SWAMP POINT TO KANAB CREEK (CONTINUED)

Far beneath the rim of this canyon grim
Speeds a river wrought with woes.
And the shadows are deep, and the light is dim
Where the wild water froths and flows.

Vaughn Short
"The Ballad of Belle Zabor" / *Raging River, Lonely Trail* (1978)

It was the possibility of darkness that made the day seem so bright.

Stephen King
Wolves of the Calla (2003)

August 2015 (continued)

In darkness on the boat ramp at Lees Ferry, I phoned Becky.

"Heard anything from Wes?"

"No."

Wes had promised to make regular call-ins each evening using the sat phone.

"What should we do?" she asked next, knowing I would be mostly out of contact for the next two weeks while on a river trip scheduled to launch in the morning.

"Nothing yet," I answered. "But if you don't hear from him in the morning, call Ken Phillips and ask him to start a search."

Hanging up, I felt at least as anxious as she had sounded. I forced myself to look away from the night's gathering storm clouds and tried to focus on my best memories with Wes in the Canyon. One that came on the heels of Kenton replacing Weston's baby booty kept replaying.

Just after Wes's first birthday, my close friend, Grand Canyon backcountry ranger Bryan Wisher (who had jumpstarted the Yukon after our South Bass to Hermit hike), invited our family to stay with him at the Havasupai Garden ranger station. Unlike his sisters, who were walking by age one, Weston had yet to take his first steps unaided. Once Bryan found that out, he seemed determined to change it.

"Come here, Weston. Come on. Come over here! You can do it!" Bryan coaxed, smiling at Weston as we sat in the ranger station's living room.

"Nice try, Bryan, but that ain't happening," I said. "He's not gonna do it until he's good and ready. We've been trying the same thing for a couple of months."

"No, he's gonna do it, and he's gonna do it right here and now," Bryan insisted. "Come on, Wessy. You're down in the Grand Canyon. This is the coolest place on earth to take your first steps. Come here. You can do it! Come on!" he sweet-talked.

Weston, an index finger hooked in the crux of his mouth, eyed Bryan suspiciously. Then he lunged forward, wobbling a half-dozen baby steps before landing in Bryan's arms. We all cheered.

Nineteen years later, after sleeping terribly, and less than an hour before our scheduled Canyoneers launch, I used my final opportunity to phone Becky again. With tremendous relief in her voice, she announced that she had heard from Wes only minutes earlier. He told her that Kanab Creek had flashflooded while he was traversing it.

"He's feeling pretty shook up."

Here's Wes's version.

❦

I hadn't slept great the night before hiking in from Swamp Point. Anticipation and eagerness to prove myself on my first solo Grand Canyon hike kept my mind stirring and sleep at a distance.

After the goodbyes, I began my descent into Saddle Canyon. Sliding, splashing, jumping my way down the Redwall narrows made for a fun morning. At one point, however, I twisted my knee during an awkward landing, which left me limping for the remainder of the trip. I also had my first revelation regarding solo hiking: *Hiking breaks and rest stops are boring. A half-day in and I'm already missing my hiking pals.* With no one to converse with nor share snacks with, continuing to hike had more appeal. So, I pushed on.

I arrived at the Deer Creek Patio a day earlier than I anticipated. I found this iconic feature, a popular spot for river runners, eerily absent of people. I soaked my tired legs and sore knee in the creek as I ate dinner, then went to bed shortly thereafter. Again, I felt lonely. The grandeur of the Grand Canyon is usually enough to conjure powerful sentiments. Yet, I found the majestic vistas and striking landscapes less meaningful because their stunning beauty wasn't being shared.

In the morning, I rose early, packed up, and immediately began hiking. Around midday, as I approached the mouth of Kanab Creek, a river party floated by.

"Hey! How's it going?" someone shouted.

"Good!" I shouted back, waving.

"How long you been hiking?"

"A couple of days."

"Want a beer?"

"Ahh, no. But thanks!"

"Oh, okay! You can have this then, son!"

The boatman stood on his cooler, turned his butt to me, then dropped his trunks to his ankles. The glare off the man's white behind almost caused me to trip. *What the hell?* I chuckled, shook my head, and kept walking.

At the Kanab and Colorado confluence, I sat down and ate lunch. Water trickled clear in the little creek, running near its usual 3 cfs (about 22 gallons per second). I looked up at the sky. A mixture of blue and white, mostly blue, dominated. I called my dad, and we chatted.

"All right, Dad, I'll talk to you tomorrow." I shut off the satellite phone feeling a little apprehensive. I knew that the colossal walls of the Kanab drainage would most likely make another phone connection difficult, if not impossible, for the remainder of my journey. Alternating between trudging and wading through small pools up the beautiful creek, I made camp for the night just shy of Whispering Falls side canyon, three miles from the mouth of the creek. A few raindrops woke me around two a.m., but being totally exhausted, I rolled over and fell back to sleep despite what became a continuous sprinkle. Rising with the sun at five a.m., I found that the previously tranquil creek had transformed into a frenzy of froth and mud.

A sense of panic crept up my spine. While not really narrow as canyons go, the belly of the Kanab drainage tapered to about eighty feet wide at my campsite. It continued to rain, and I faced a dilemma: Do I commit to the long walk to my car in Hack Canyon (over twenty-five miles away), potentially filled with unknown obstacles, in hope that the water recedes? Or do I retrace my steps all the way back to the Colorado and let the storm pass? As any seasoned Grand Canyon hiker knows, you fight for every inch of backcountry terrain you cover, and backtracking is perhaps the most infuriating decision you can make. With headstrong obstinacy and driven by an urgency to get out, I chose to journey farther in.

Staying ashore became my primary objective as I clung to the cliffs above the water or dove through mesquite-tamarisk tangles to avoid entering the current. This strategy, I hoped, would keep me up and away from the torrent if the flood surged. Yet, too often, the terrain's steepness forced me back into the creek, where I had to wade through roiling water that was sometimes up to mid-chest. Occasionally during those moments, as I floated my pack out in front of me, I felt chunks of debris bouncing off my shins and prayed no ankle-fracturing rocks were coming my way.

For a while, I made some progress in the shallower portions along the bank, but just as quickly, my luck would run out. At one point, I found myself facing a narrow section where the creek deepened. I waded in, but with the next step, I couldn't touch bottom. Rushing water covered my head, then shoved me downstream like flotsam. Meanwhile, the rain continued to pour down.

The cold-water immersion helped me gather my wits. Once I got my footing again, I backtracked, then searched for a higher route above in the Muav ledges. I eventually found what I needed and carefully bypassed this crux section. Unfortunately, the walking bench petered out, the walls too sheer and vertical to proceed. After much deliberation, I committed to a precarious butt-slide to get back down for more creekside walking.

All the while, my alter ego, Platoon Sergeant Myers, who happens to be Scottish, kept hounding me. "You best hike up those panties and quit splashing around in that flood like a Girl Scout at summer camp, son! Otherwise, you'll be on latrine duty for the rest of your worthless, natural-born life, you stinky, soggy poor excuse for a backpacker!" Oddly, the sergeant proved quite motivating. *Hey, in situations like that, what else is there to do besides talk to yourself?*

The clouds broke briefly near Shower Bath Spring, a beautiful dripping spring draped with a hanging garden of moss and ferns. About ten miles up Kanab Creek, it's one of the Canyon's most beautiful Shangri-Las. I chugged some of the fresh water coming off the moss, then sat in the sun, warming myself and resting up after seven hours of fighting the flood. Watching the creek's water level inch downward, I got my bearings, then continued up the drainage to the intersection with Jumpup Canyon, twelve miles from the Kanab Creek mouth.

That's when I felt it.

A huge gust of wind hit me. With this came a sudden and serious deluge of rain. The spate bucketed down, creating astonishing, terrifying waterfalls. Enormous cascades plummeted off the Redwall several hundred feet above, meeting the Kanab Creek floor with unbelievable power. With the waterfalls came rocks. A lot of rocks. At the bottom of the canyon, I felt like a sitting duck waiting to be hit as they crashed down. Sprinting for cover, I ducked under a minuscule overhang within a jumble of boulders.

Then, I watched with amazement as the waterline that had been some forty feet away from me now lapped about two feet from my heels. It happened in a blink of an eye: The flood I had battled all day had erupted into a torrent the size of the Colorado.

Literally backed into a corner, I watched in amazement and horror as a full-grown Douglas-fir, torn loose from somewhere upstream, crashed into the opposite wall. With multiple loud cracks, it splintered into pieces. A second later, it careened around a bend and disappeared, lost in the tempest. I shivered at the thought of what could've happened if this massive surge had come upon me as I pushed through the flooding water earlier in the day. I probably would have been crushed and impaled, not to mention drowned.

I sat there for hours, the flooded creek a mere three feet from my hidey spot. Any more water and there would be no more me. I never felt so alone in my life. At the same time, I never felt so guilty. The only thoughts tumbling around in my head were of my loved ones and how I might let them down in the ultimate way.

I had never contemplated my own mortality and my place in this world as harshly as I did that day. This pondering included a serious consideration of what kind of man I would aim to be if I somehow lived through this, and how I could correctly prioritize what's important to me.

As the rain continued to pour and the flood thundered by, my knowing that the water level might spike again without warning and wash me away was mental torture. Though I felt guilty about it, I didn't want to suffer alone. *God, if only I had another person here with me!* Maybe to hold and talk with before our last moment. Instead, I had to settle for a tear-filled conversation with the pile of rocks I erected to serve as a marker for where my twenty years on this earth had ended.

Equally tormenting, I thought I heard an NPS chopper cruising overhead. For several seconds, I could hear its whup-whup-whup over the roar of the flood. Then it faded away. I dug out the sat phone and tried to dial out. Twice. Three times. Four times. Nothing. I stuffed it back into my soggy pack.

I buried myself as far back under that ledge as I could; there was nowhere else to go. *Any second, the water could rise and wash me from existence.* In that moment, I did one of the weirdest and most gut-wrenching things I have ever done: using my cell phone, I recorded a goodbye video message to my family in preparation for the worst-case-scenario.

What on earth do I tell them besides I love you? Do I try to look strong and composed so they won't know I died in fear? Or do I speak with sincere emotion, knowing this might be the last time they ever hear my voice? I chose the latter. (Needless to say, I deleted that video the moment I knew it was unnecessary.)

After the sun went down, the deep canyon's darkness felt overwhelming. Lying in that pile of boulders was also physically agonizing. Intermittently, I flipped on my headlamp to check the water level. The light's beam reached only about halfway across the rushing slurry. Beyond that, there was unnatural, quivering blackness.

It wasn't just the sight of the flood that I found disturbing. The water invaded every sense. A wet-earth smell filled my nose and sinuses. Mist sprayed my face and soaked my tarp and sleeping bag, and I shivered under a cold film of slimy silt. Worst was the unrelenting rumble. The roar reverberated so loud that sleep became impossible. Boulders tumbled down the streambed, cracking into one another with a ferocious intensity. Despite earplugs, I heard the rumble the entire night.

When morning came, I was ecstatic to see that the water had completely dropped. The knee-deep mud it left behind would require a lot of trudging—but still, a most welcome change. After half a day, I made it to the Hack Canyon junction and tried the satellite phone again. Hopeful, I swallowed hard as I pushed the send button.

When I heard my mother's voice, I dropped to my knees. When you've had seemingly eternal time (minutes that passed like hours) to contemplate your own mortality, it becomes infinitely clear that victories or triumphs pale in comparison to relationships.

During that long night, my life threatened by the flooding creek, I had also found myself flooded by memories of my mom. One that I'm more ashamed of than any other stands out: I was sixteen and watched from the doorway as she sobbed uncontrollably into a pillow. I have never—before or since—seen my mother that distraught, and yet, in that instant, I felt nothing. I was emotionally inert. I had been fighting severe depression for most of that academic year. After mandated counseling sessions, I had been deemed a suicide risk. And in fact, I had formulated multiple methods of taking my life. (The irony isn't lost on me that years later, facing a flash flood in the recesses of the Kanab drainage, I looked for every possible way to save it.)

Existentially, I had hit rock bottom, dragging my mother down with me. I still shudder when I recollect the depth of my heartlessness toward the woman who brought me into this world and loved me so unconditionally.

This memory pains me more than any other, but as often is the case, pain is the best teacher.

In retrospect, I know that part of my depression stemmed from the realization that I was, quite simply, mediocre. In a world of billions, to expect to be truly exceptional is almost delusional. But it can be very hard to swallow, especially when you're inundated with social media feeds suggesting that extraordinary individuals are all around you. It was hard for me to accept that I just lacked the capacity (genetic or otherwise) to become, say, a gifted athlete or a ground-breaking thinker in quantum theory.

Furthermore, the social isolation that took root in my life around middle school gained an even stronger foothold during my years in high school. As many teenagers do, I struggled to find my place amongst my peers. As a shy and straitlaced kid with acne, whose best friend was his dad, I didn't feel like I fit in anywhere. My insecurities were further compounded by the hazing I got from several classmates during my sophomore-year. Taken together, it had been enough to push my fragile teenage headspace into a desolate and all-consuming depression.

But, as with any case of depression, there comes a crossroad that demands a choice between action or inaction. I had discovered my bottom level, my lowest rung, and felt left with a simple choice: I could either roll over into weakness and succumb to taking my life or I could fight to live it.

I deliberated for months, but then, slowly, began to climb out of my self-pity and selfishness. Suffering can be a powerful introspective tool, and empathy, true empathy, for those around me is what brought me back. I learned to care about myself by caring about others.

People became my lifeline.

I started small, reforging the fractured relationships with my immediate family first. I began hiking with my father again in the Grand Canyon. Nature had always been an integral part of me, and that relationship became another that I lost in my turmoil as a teenager. I felt like a soft and insecure boy when I stepped back into the Canyon, but over the course of hundreds of brutal and testing miles, I emerged stronger, confident, and more resolute than before. The Grand Canyon became my healing ground. More importantly, my father once again became my closest confidant.

The Grand Canyon also taught me another invaluable lesson, one that seems obvious now, but to that emotionally vacant young man I used to be, I had to discover one boot step at a time. No one can fight your depression for you. Much like the fact that your own two feet are responsible for getting you back to the rim, you can only do it yourself. And similar to facing an uphill talus slope, you must claw and inch your way up and out of those dark places. It's easy to want to stay safe and secure at the bottom of the rubble and succumb to apathy. The difficult choice is confronting the harrowing journey to the top. But with every footfall, you begin to feel more human.

After we spoke, I hustled the ten remaining miles for Hack junction to my truck, then immediately headed to rendezvous with Mom and my sister Alex at Marble Canyon. They met me there with hugs and a Fratelli Route 66 pizza. My appetite had finally returned, and I gorged myself as we sat at the Navajo Bridge overlook and chatted.

I have never felt so grateful and alive as during the drive back home. I realized that, despite the near-fatal turn of events the Grand Canyon had served up, my reverence and love for the landscape remained just as strong, and I vowed to myself to return as soon as I possibly could. I wanted to finish the length more than ever. Kanab Creek also taught me one other thing: If I never do another remote solo hike in the Grand Canyon, I'm good.

⌒〜⌒

According to USGS data on water resources, the flow in Kanab Creek on August 24, 2015 (the day Weston entered) shot up from its average of roughly 3 cfs to 1,100 cfs around noon. It dropped back down to 90 cfs before a second surge around four that afternoon when Wes noted, "the waterline that had been some forty feet away from me now lapped only about two feet from my heels."

On the USGS website for Kanab Creek at that moment, the gauge deflection for flow blasted straight up. Within seconds, the stream increased to 3000 times its usual size, its whopping peak at just over 9,000 cfs. At the same time, the Colorado River flowed at 11,000 cfs. Less than a month later, twenty people died in flash floods in southern Utah canyons near Kanab Creek.

I have long since given up questioning myself about the wisdom of encouraging Wes to do that hike. Also, from decades practicing medicine during which I've seen the horrible things Mother Nature—or worse yet, other people—can do to humans, especially innocent children, I tend not to subscribe to the "everything happens for a reason" philosophy. In this case, however, Weston and I both know the reason: a life-changing one. For that, I am forever grateful.

CHAPTER THIRTY-NINE

Closing the Last Loop

THE PASSING OF GEORGE STECK

And there sat Sam, looking cool and calm, in the heart of the furnace roar;
And he wore a smile you could see a mile, and he said: 'Please close that door.
It's fine in here, but I greatly fear you'll let in the cold and storm –
Since I left Plumtree, down in Tennessee, it's the first time I've been warm.

Robert W. Service
Last stanza, *The Cremation of Sam McGee* (1907)

I think [Grand Canyon] is a jalapeno pepper and Glen Canyon is the honey.

George Steck
Interview with Elias Butler, 2003

September 2002

"Why do you do this? Wandering around such a challenging place?" writer Craig Childs had asked George Steck while tagging along behind him, a notebook in hand.

"I like it," Steck answered.

"But why here?" Childs probed.

George and Childs were part of a group making what would be George's last loop hike in Grand Canyon. Knowing that his hiking days were fast dwindling, George planned a final loop and invited some family and a few close friends to join him. He and his companions dubbed this last hurrah "the old geezer hike."

Over an ample four days, they would lumber about ten miles from the Tuckup trailhead down to the Colorado River at River Mile 165, march seven miles downstream to Stairway Canyon, ascend five miles up Stairway back to

345

Tuckup, and then loop back to the vehicles at the trailhead.

The "old geezers" included George (seventy-seven), his brother Allen (seventy-six), and Don Mattox (seventy). George also invited several younger, stronger men for the companionship and to serve as sherpas. Childs was one.

After rendezvousing at John Azar's place in Fredonia, they headed for the Tuckup trailhead. While descending Tuckup Canyon, Mattox, two years post open-heart surgery, began struggling, having trouble catching his breath. But he soldiered onward to the river. There, a paramedic on a river trip evaluated the exhausted Mattox. Concerned, he encouraged Mattox to consider getting flown out as a medical emergency. Mattox emphatically declined. As a compromise, however, he allowed the river runners to give him a ride five miles to Stairway.

The rest of the group caught up with Mattox and camped. The next morning they headed up Stairway Canyon. Later that day, under full sun, they began their slow ascent through the Redwall. Both George and Mattox ran out of steam. At slightly faster than a crawl and utilizing their sherpas' help, however, they completed the climb through a crack system to reach the top of the limestone. There they camped near a full *tinaja*—a water pocket in the rock surface. Happy hour included the usual Steck margaritas, with ham and potatoes also on the dinner menu. Afterward, one of the hikers serenaded the group with flute music, which Allen accompanied with a few yodels. Exhausted, bellies and minds content, they all slept well.

The next morning saw them up at first light and on the trail early. When they reached the Esplanade, they encountered another hiking group. After exchanging typical pleasantries, they discussed their respective hiking itineraries.

"We're doing a Steck Loop," a guy from the other group reported. "But we can't find our way into Stairway by Steck's description." He sounded annoyed.

"Oh, really?" Azar asked. He turned and looked at the oldest person present. "George, do you think you can help them out?"

The annoyed man's face flushed as maroon as the rock around him when he put it together. He immediately apologized. George took the criticism in stride, which was easy to do given the man's obvious awe at meeting the Canyon hiking legend in person. Then he cheerfully answered their questions and cleared up misunderstandings.

Like the hiker, a deferential Craig Childs also wanted answers from the Canyon legend.

"Why such a unique task, George?" Childs queried for some explanation for George's avocation.

"It's not unique. I just put one foot in front of the other."

"That's not what I'm asking. Why do you walk for eighty days and find satisfaction with some boulder-filled chute that gets you from one place to the next? It must not have been a common hobby among people at the lab. Why, George?"

Not to be pigeon-holed, George replied, "Because I want to, Craig. Same for you, right? We're driven by what we want."

Childs knew George's deflection had been deliberate. From prior hikes together, he also knew George sometimes turned a question around or spoke in mathematical riddles. He occasionally even borrowed Child's journal to scribble out geometric calculations. These habits inspired Childs to begin developing his own evidence-based hypothesis about George's hiking motivations.

Childs knew George as a man of logic and science. Unequivocal evidence of this existed in nearly all of George's endeavors, including hiking the Canyon. The common dominator, Childs believed, was math.

In 2006 Childs summed up his theory about George's hiking in a tribute he titled "The Mathematical Elegance of the Grand Canyon."

His routes were theorems. The pages of equations that he wrote were handholds, boulders, and cracks. He had starting places and destinations, and his body found the way between. All that hullabaloo of canyons came down to the perfect answer to the equation.

As it turned out, the Old Geezer Hike wasn't George's grand finale after all. Thirteen months later, on November 14, 2003, George tottered into the Canyon for a "garden party," thrown at Havasupai Gardens. NPS ranger Bil (nicknamed "One-L" for the spelling of Bil) Vandergraff had arranged it, just as he had done for an evening celebration the night before on the rim which was held at the Kolb Studio. Friends, family, hikers, river runners, and community members were invited for the evening celebration where tales were told and toasts made in George's honor. For ease and accessibility, water and comfort (use of the ranger station/bunk house amenities), and—heaven forbid—quick access to emergency medical services, he had garnered a special use permit for Havasupai Gardens for the second, more intimate party beginning the following day. Besides George and his children—Mike, Stan, and Ricia—about thirty others, all friends of George, were invited. Becky and I felt honored our whole family was included.

After dinner and amidst the continuously flowing margaritas, we huddled around an evening fire. Once again, we roasted and toasted George. This evolved into one of those delightful and unforgettable evenings you hope will never end but sadly does.

An Evening With George Steck
Thursday, November 13, 2003

GRAND CANYON NATIONAL PARK

Reception
· Kolb Studio, 4 pm-6 pm
· Come by to say hi and share a story with George.
· Get your Loop Hikes Guidebooks signed.
· Refreshments provided

George Steck
Backpacker
Canyoneer
River Runner

Audio-Visual Tribute
· Grand Canyon Community Building, 7pm
· Slide show presented by Photographer Gary Ladd.
· "Worm Hole" a film by Tom Myers.
· Assorted historical video & film footage.

Join us for this memorable evening!

Presented by
· Grand Canyon Association
· Grand Canyon National Park
· Friends of George Steck

Refreshments provided by Xanterra Parks & Resorts

Three months later, in January 2004, George suffered a stroke. Several years earlier he had developed high blood pressure and started taking medication, including a blood thinner. He also underwent a procedure to open a clogged carotid artery. The stroke partially paralyzed his left hand and left him unable to play the piano. When it became apparent that the residual left-hand paralysis also affected his ability to drive, George voluntarily turned in his driver's license. To keep his now mostly homebound buddy from going stir crazy, Don Mattox picked up George every Thursday for breakfast at Annie's Soup Kitchen in Albuquerque.

George managed a final road trip in 2004 to the Canyon to attend the Grand Canyon River Guides training seminar in Marble Canyon and speak on the topic of remote Canyon hiking. On March 27, the day before his talk, he premiered his slide show to family and friends at Marble Canyon Lodge. I made sure my kids and I had front-row seats.

I remember it well. Clearing his throat, George had gazed out at the small audience. His voice had its usual raspiness, and his 78-year-old eyes still had that old familiar pothole twinkle but had lost much of their luster. Certainly, some of that was related to age. But most of it, I knew, could be attributed to the loss of Helen. After fifty years together, she had died three years earlier, in April 2001, of complications from kidney failure. I hoped and prayed George's own death was still years away.

Less than a month after his Marble Canyon presentation, John Azar phoned George to say he wanted to drop by for a visit.

"Well, you better hurry," George replied.

Within a couple of weeks, George underwent surgery to repair an aneurysm in his abdominal aorta. The operation considered a success, George went home.

Yet on May 2, 2004, four days after surgery, his daughter Ricia found him dead in his bedroom. His blanket had fallen off. He had one foot on the floor as though about to stand. An autopsy revealed no obvious cause of death, suggesting a fatal heart rhythm. A week later at George's house, his family held a celebration of life.

Helen and George on their wedding day. *Steck family archives*

In 2003, the year before George died, Gary Ladd asked him to write the foreword for his new book, *Canyon Light*. In it, George compliments Ladd, then describes his first experiences in Glen Canyon and Grand Canyon. Perhaps inspired by Craig Childs' questioning, he also poignantly listed five reasons "why he did it," why he planned yet another trip in the Grand Canyon before recovering from the previous one.

> First, the trips challenge body and spirit. I find doing a difficult hike more rewarding than having had done it.
>
> Second, the hikes glorify the essentials—water, in particular, and the individual in possession of a well-functioning body. People sometimes ask me whether I feel insignificant in the midst of such beauty and wonder. In fact, I feel the opposite. When I survey that wonder, I feel magnified by knowing that without my brain there would be no sense of wonder, and without my feet I wouldn't even be here.

Third, the canyon represents a sublime contradiction. The fossilized beds of ancient oceans surround me; the sculptings of long-ago wind and rain envelop me, yet water is basically absent. Oh, there are a few trickles here and there, a few springs in secret places, and a substantial flow in the center. But that flow is often inaccessible, and the canyon carved by water is now a desert. That is the contradiction. I love it.

Fourth, I appreciate the appearance of wildness, and I thank the National Park Service for that.

Fifth, there is overpowering beauty.

Without question, George Steck's legacy as a Grand Canyon explorer and teacher is unique. In 1995 interviewer Mike Quinn mentioned George's guidebooks and asked him if he felt concerned about getting inexperienced people traipsing into the backcountry. Specifically, he referenced about nine college kids who reportedly did one of his loop hikes despite having no Canyon experience whatsoever. George's answer reflected classic, playful Steck humor: "So what? A heavy rain is going to wash away all signs of them. And if it comes at the right time, it can wash them away too."

George ended Ladd's foreword with his final, most important tip for those who follow in his footsteps: "And don't forget the fun."

George Steck. *Steck family archives*

CHAPTER FORTY

Seeing Ghosts

INDIAN HOLLOW TO KANAB CREEK TO SOWATS POINT

One day your life will flash before your eyes. Make sure it's worth watching.
Gerard Way (2016)

October 2015

It felt strange not having Wes along. Since he'd already completed the Deer Creek to Kanab Creek section, a stretch that I still needed and the one that had trapped him with its vicious flashflood, he had zero interest in a re-do. When I asked the other boys in the regular foursome if they wanted to go, T and Connor declined. Vince felt differently.

"I'd love to go."

"Vinnie the Pooh," as Wes sometimes called him, had only one Canyon hike under his belt, a rim-to-rim, when he had started hiking with us a year earlier. Now, a half-dozen or so hikes later, he had proven himself more than capable. Seasoned in route-finding, water-finding, and map-reading, he also happened to be great for philosophical discussions and laughs.

I also invited Joe Stringer, a buddy near my age. Joe had never before hiked, let alone backpacked, the Canyon. Still, he was in good shape and had a lot of backpacking experience elsewhere.

We took Joe's Chevy truck out to the Indian Hollow parking area on the North Rim. From Indian Hollow we would descend off the rim into Cranberry Canyon, then diverge into Deer Creek (River Mile 137) to the river. From there we'd hike downstream to Kanab Creek (River Mile 144), as Wes had done, then up Kanab to Jumpup. Instead of going to Hack like Wes, we'd veer out Jumpup,

Ghost Rock. *Rich Rudow*

then trek out to Indian Hollow and the truck, racking up about forty-five-foot miles—tough miles—to net seven river miles.

Our descent off the rim went quickly. Dropping onto the expansive Esplanade, we looked for an east-facing, forty-foot Supai Group sandstone overhang, the ancient archeological site called Ghost Rock. Here, according to George, we would find a mysterious 4,000-year-old monochromatic painting that supposedly resembled a spooky apparition.

In *Loop Hikes I*, George says the ghost is "at or near the small sock-shaped bit of 4,800-foot contour, with a benchmark of 4,807 feet, about 0.9 miles below the S in FOREST on the quad map." We veered over to the area that corresponded to the "S" on the map and within an hour, stumbled upon ancient drawings that, sure enough, appeared ghost-like. Two large white figures, about six feet tall and looking more alien than human, seemed to float on the back wall, far above the reach of any human arm. Had they been drawn while the artist was standing on something? Or had the ground been higher? Probably both, we concluded.

White spikes, like lightning rods or antennas, protruded from each bulbous head. Arms and legs were absent, and their lower torsos faded into wispiness, like Casper the Friendly Ghost of cartoon fame. Unlike Casper, who wore a perpetual smile, these figures were faceless, making them more nebulous, even eerie.

Nearby in the overhang lay the rusty remnants of an abandoned cowboy camp. We'd begun to notice a pattern of both ancient and more recent use in shelters below the North Rim on the Esplanade level. It contained the trash typical of early 20th century cowpunchers: corroding metal pieces, broken glass, weathered wood, fencing, rusty cans, and barbed wire. With the ghost-like figures staring down on us, we left the remnant junk alone.

Our rather quick success in finding Ghost Rock had us hoping for an early camp. Alas, I inadvertently steered us down a drainage that fed into the neighboring Deer Creek Canyon, not Cranberry Canyon, our goal for the night. After being sidetracked for more than an hour, we finally arrived at the top of

Cranberry. Ominous black clouds moved in about the same time. None of us carried a tent.

With the Ghost Rock overhang far behind, we searched for another natural shelter, finally settling for a small one that left us partially exposed. After our evening dinner a minor drizzle blew in, forcing us to wedge deeper into the overhang. We toasted George Steck with whiskey shots, grateful for his guidance in finding Ghost Rock.

As I sipped my whiskey, I also savored more memories of George. He had died more than a decade earlier. Fittingly for me in the moment, George's own ghost, friendly like Casper's, popped into my consciousness. Just as abruptly, another ghost appeared beside him: Harvey Butchart. For years I fantasized about backpacking off trail with both men down the Canyon, something I never did. Now, the two greatest hiking legends in Grand Canyon history were sharing camp with me, albeit only in my imagination.

Despite knowing Harvey, an evangelical Christian, was a teetotaler, I offered him some of our whiskey, as well as some food. A considerate man, he respectfully declined both. Besides foregoing alcohol, he didn't smoke, cuss, laugh at or tell crude jokes; indeed, throughout his life, he worked hard, went to church, and was honest to a fault. Knowing all of this and feeling suddenly sheepish, I coughed uncomfortably on my last sip of whiskey before setting down the bottle and watching as Harvey prepared his sleeping spot. When completed, he pulled out a can of sardines and some gingersnaps, and quietly nibbled away. At the same time, he began reading a copy of the *Time* magazine he'd toted along.

I glanced from Harvey to George, who looked at me, eyebrows arched, and shrugged. "Thirsty?" George asked, offering me a yellow Prestone antifreeze bottle.

"Ahhh... thanks but I don't know, George," I cringed as I stared at his bright yellow bottle that once contained toxic fluid.

"Oh, don't worry, the bottle

Harvey taking a break, late 1970s. *Scott Baxter*

353

is partly for shock value," he chuckled. "It's clean. Works perfect for carrying water."

"Sure." I took a swig from the bottle.

"Want a margarita?" he offered next.

"I'd love one."

"Hand me your cup." George, who was agnostic, began mixing Crystal Light in it, then he poured in some Everclear. As he did, I noticed his visor. It read *Schlitz*, a beer company. He passed me the margarita. It tasted surprisingly good. Then George started making his own dinner.

"Hungry?" he asked.

"What are you having?"

"Pasta with corned beef in BBQ sauce and spiraloni salad."

"Sounds delicious."

Meanwhile, Harvey had rolled onto his side and pulled his sleeping bag over his head. Within minutes, we could hear him softly snoring.

For Harvey, camps had only one purpose: to recharge after a mentally and physically exhausting day. Yes, he and companions did have conversations (when Harvey wasn't absorbed in *Time*), but the genius was hard to talk to. Plus, he typically didn't share meals or drinks. He made a point of going to bed early because he got up early. For Harvey, time mattered. Speed mattered. Partners mattered. What mattered most? Miles. The best guarantee for this? Go alone. For half of his Canyon hikes that's what he did.

For George, however, a slow but kindred companion was better than none. He soloed a total of once. On trips he led, he de-emphasized the push (averaging about five miles per day compared to Harvey's ten), making his trips far less uptight. If George Steck was the laidback military man, Harvey Butchart was the serious drill sergeant.

Forsaking self-centered goals, George—also a genius—sought and found a family life that enhanced balance. He made the choice early to accommodate his family during Canyon trips. Over the years, they supported George's Canyon obsession, even encouraged it. Celebrated it. Most importantly, they participated in it. Again, for George it wasn't about the miles; it was about the memories. Individual memories may be fascinating, but shared memories are magnetic. They pull family and friends together and remain a lifelong binding force.

In my mind's eye, a sleeping Harvey seemed to quickly fade away. George and I, however, kept a quiet conversation going until he, too, was gone. I sighed to myself. Both men were incredibly kind to me, freely sharing their stories and Canyon experiences. And while I revered Harvey Butchart, I loved George Steck.

After coffee and a quick breakfast the next morning, we went old-school. I pulled out a printed map, Joe a compass. We confirmed our location as the head of Cranberry Canyon and hiked through the Supai to the top of the Redwall in no time. The night's rain had left the ground soggy. Soon we came upon fresh footprints. A few minutes later a group of hikers appeared.

Chatting revealed that the group—the National Outdoor Leadership School (NOLS), which included five teenage boys—came from Virginia. Two men told us they were guides. The only female identified herself as another guide and their trip leader.

"So, what hike are you guys doing?" was our next question.

"We're going down Cranberry, along the river to Kanab Creek, up Kanab, and out Scotty's Hollow to the rim," the TL reported. She sounded confident.

"Wow! That's a good one," I marveled, looking at the boys, then back at her. "Have you hiked down here much?"

"I've hiked the Canyon once before. This is the first time for the boys."

I felt my eyebrows raise. Considering the relative difficulty of their hike versus their Canyon hiking experience level, they were the equivalent of novice skiers attempting a black diamond run. Gary Ladd, in his foreword to *Loop Hikes II* (for reasons that should be obvious by now), specifically discourages just such a scenario, nicely summing up what you need in Canyon hiking experience before attempting one of George's loop hikes:

> The loops are for backpackers with Grand Canyon savvy—those with a bachelor's [degree] in maintained trails and a master's in the non-maintained. They are for those who understand that the terms "easy" and "difficult" are Teflon slippery, that resourcefulness is essential and that not all miles are created equal. Deception lurks on the loops. Take care.

Seeing my reaction as well as Joe and Vince's, she started digging in her pack. "I researched what we're doing for this hike by using this book." She pulled out George Steck's 272-page *Hiking Grand Canyon Loops*.[14]

"Whoa! That's a great book!" I blurted. While running into this group in a remote Canyon drainage was surprising, her lugging George's entire, now out-of-print book instead of a few photocopied pages triggered my unabashed astonishment.

"Yeah, the guy who wrote it, George Steck, was a good friend of mine."

"*Really?* That's cool."

---

14 In 2002, *Loop Hikes I* and *II* were combined into one volume.

"And believe it or not," I added, "we've got pages copied from the same book for our hike."

"Wow! No way!" She and the others in her group murmured in disbelief. After describing our intended hike, several seconds of awkward silence followed.

"Uhh ... did you see Ghost Rock?" one of us asked.

She hesitated. "Maybe ... but we're not sure." This almost assuredly meant no. While I found myself mentally applauding her ambition, leading the adolescent boys, and having done her homework using George's book, I still felt concerned. First, George's description for finding Ghost Rock was great, even for novices. Second, the figures are very distinct; in my view, their not finding Ghost Rock didn't bode well for their Canyon route-finding ability. Route-finding was an asset they needed for their intended hike and necessary for off-trail backpacking, as rockslides, wrong turns, and so forth can make printed route descriptions utterly obsolete.

"How are you boys doing?" Joe asked the mostly whupped-appearing Virginia boys, intentionally changing the subject. This elicited a few half-hearted "okays," shoulder shrugs, and head nods.

"We're all a little tired, but we'll be fine," their TL asserted.

"Well, good luck. Have a great trip," we told them as we headed out first.

"You, too."

While I still felt uneasy about the group's prospects, my mind lingered more on the woman having George's book with her. *How cool was that?!* He would've been so proud.

Moving along, we took in a "great view" of the Colorado River that George speaks of in his book, then worked our way eastward along the top of the Redwall, looking for the break we needed to descend to the river.

When three distinct but very steep and scary bays plunging into airy space appeared at the edge of the Redwall cliff, I pulled out my pages of George's "TAPEATS CREEK/KANAB CREEK LOOP."

In his description of how to descend below the Redwall, George wrote that the first bay offered the best descent. We explored it and found it dicey and exposed. Before committing to it, we decided to look at the other two. Kind of like guessing on the old television gameshow *Let's Make a Deal*. Which of the three mystery doors (in this case, bays) concealed the hidden prize? *Was it Bay #1? Or Bay #2? Perhaps it was Bay #3.* The second chute was a definite no-go, ending in a hundred-foot drop-off. In the third, the one farthest east, Vince and I made a short downclimb, then a traverse behind a large boulder. Vince, a good climber, led.

"Hey, Tom! There's a cairn here! It goes!" he hollered back up to me and Joe.

Looking down, a very steep and daunting several-hundred-foot ridge line of loose-looking boulders stood out just below Vince. It seemed like a doable route—if done with care—to the bottom. Vince and I were partway down, with Joe above us, when we saw the NOLS group approach. Like us, they had started down the first bay.

"Hey!" I hollered up to them. "That's not really the best route. We looked at it. You can get down over here. It's easier!"

"This is the one that George Steck says to use!" the leader yelled back.

Vince and I looked at each other.

"That first bay looks even worse from down here," Vince whispered to me. It did look bad, even for a good rock climber going up. Downclimbing it without protection while wearing a backpack? No thanks.

"We know!" I shouted back. "We have the same description, but that one looks really dangerous and involves some pretty risky climbing."

"I've climbed 5.9 before. I can do this!" she shouted.

Fine, but what about the boys?

"But it's easier and less risky over here! We're already past the worst spot, and there's a cairn!"

She went silent, probably a little annoyed. Probably a little embarrassed. From the mumbled tones, we guessed she was discussing the situation with her co-guide. Meanwhile, we hollered up to Joe, who'd been waiting on top for our report, to come on down. He yelled back that his knees hurt, and he'd decided it was time for him to abort the hike. I climbed back up to chat with him (and also to get his camera).

"My knees aren't too happy, Tom. I'm gonna head back," he confessed.

"Sorry to see you go, but I understand. We'll meet you at Indian Hollow in three days."

As he hiked back, I hustled over to the NOLS group.

"Hey, look," I said to the trip leader. "I'm not trying to tell you what to do, but it's a lot easier where we went, way less exposed and less dangerous." I kept my tone non-authoritarian. "We can also help you guys with your packs through the dangerous part. Once you're below that, it looks fairly straightforward following that ridgeline to the bottom." As I spoke, I pointed out our objective.

"Thanks, but we haven't decided yet," she responded.

"Okay. Well, good luck," I said before hiking back to Vince.

"What'd they say?" he asked, after I reached him.

"Not much. They haven't decided."

"Those boys are in so far over their heads. One of them could die here," Vince worried.

"Yep."

We studied the talus slope of loose Redwall scree below us, a very steep, eroding ridge line about 400 feet long. We both knew if we weren't careful, we could die here just as easily as the boys above. We inched down along the ridge, the gully to our right sheer and perhaps sixty feet deep. A fall into it would mean almost certain death.

After about thirty minutes of scrambling, we made it safely down. When we looked up again, the NOLS group was nowhere in sight. Deciding to wait no longer, we contoured east, crossing an ancient dry lakebed before dropping into Deer Creek. We found a commercial river trip's passengers lounging on the slickrock when we arrived in an area called the Patio. I recognized a couple of the guides from Arizona Raft Adventures. They didn't mind sharing some space and some food. After an hour, we all headed to the river, where the guides gave us a couple of beers and sodas from their stash. Vince and I then headed downstream.

By late afternoon, we arrived at Fishtail Canyon near River Mile 140 and set up a wind-blown camp. Despite the gusts, I had no complaints. It was a tee-shirt and shorts evening and not just because of the weather. Another one of my favorite features about desert canyons? *Little or no water = little or no bugs.* Mosquitos, gnats, and other annoying flying insects are mostly MIA down here, perfect for a guy like me with hypersensitivity to insect stings. Foregoing big, itchy, red welts in return for having to hunt for water is more than a fair tradeoff. I relish it, especially in camp and around mealtimes. *Not getting eaten while I am eating? How awesome is that?!*

Speaking of nourishment, after devouring gourmet rehydrated meals (a cushy comfort of the twenty-first century) under a spectacularly setting sun, Vince, ever the philosopher, dished up some food for thought.

"Tom, do you believe in heaven?"

His expression was sincere.

Vince Sutherland. *T McCullough*

"I like to think there is an afterlife, Vince. I really do. But my heaven isn't like most people's. Growing up, I remember trying to visualize God and heaven, but it was always hard. Now, heaven's easy, and it's always the same. I see Becky with me. We're both young, probably in our thirties. And I see my kids. They're innocent and energetic. We're down in a beautiful slickrock desert canyon, alongside a river. Like here. Around us are the spirits of close friends and family. That's my heaven. That's my bliss. I could live that for eternity."

I flipped the question on Vince.

"I'm not so sure, but yours sounds pretty good."

We spent the next day working our way up Kanab Creek. Evidence of the flash flood Weston had encountered two months earlier was all around us: snarls of tree branches, logs, leaves, mud-caking and other debris could be seen

Approaching Scotty's Castle in Kanab Creek. *Rich Rudow*

on the banks and boulders. About ten miles up, we approached a feature called Scotty's Castle, an obelisk-shaped butte of Redwall nearly as high as the 550-foot-tall Washington Monument. It towers over Kanab's little creek, fringed in this area by maidenhair ferns, agave cactus, and bear grass. Despite its tiny flow, the canyon walls echoed the clear-water creek's babble, the perfect background din for an embarrassingly light-sleeper like me, who likes white noise at night, wilderness or not.

We each laid our sleeping spots out on yoga-mat-sized sandy sections adjacent to the creek, then Vince pulled out the satellite phone and tried to phone Becky. It was something she insisted upon us doing, making it very clear she felt less than thrilled that we were going where Wes almost died.

"All right. Let's see if this baby works," Vince said as he dialed her number. Despite the perfectly clear sky, for nearly an hour, our attempt yielded nothing. Finally, for all of about two minutes, it connected. The call's brevity also drove home the gravity of Weston's earlier predicament and helped further explain his mindset after he escaped.

In the morning, we took a side hike up Scotty's Hollow to enjoy several stunning waterfalls and slickrock pools of clear, cold water. We could easily see why the NOLS group chose it for their exit point. (We didn't see them, nor did we expect to. While we never learned how their trip went, I didn't need to add their names to an updated edition of *Over the Edge*.)

Around midafternoon we reached the confluence of Kanab Creek with Jumpup Canyon. Seeing yet more evidence of flashflooding gave us pause. This spot marked the location of Weston's near-miss with the flood.

We walked over to the shadowy narrows of Jumpup Canyon and peered inside. Gray, fifty-foot-high, overhanging Muav walls created a sense of both dread and enchantment. Rather than going north and farther up Kanab as Wes had done, we needed to meander through Jumpup. With Wes and flashfloods still on my mind, traversing this limestone corridor triggered another thought, one I knew Wes would appreciate.

In the book, *Lord of the Rings: The Two Towers*, Helm's Deep is a gorge guarded by a fortress with dark and mysterious halls, and is the scene of a great battle. Jumpup is a gorge within a gorge. Similar to Helm's Deep, its stony innards reflect a battlefield. Deep excoriations on its limestone walls—war wounds—reflect eons of clashes with flashfloods. Slipping through Jumpup's scarred, overhanging, gray Muav walls also made me think of passing between the hardened, calloused, and cupped hands of giants. *One Hall to Rule Them All.*

After walking about three miles through Jumpup, we veered right

Jumpup Canyon narrows. *Rich Rudow*

again and into the narrows of Kwagunt Hollow; another two miles or so beyond that we set up camp in an open area beneath rustling cottonwood trees and near a clear slickrock pool. I pulled out my tarp, blew up my sleeping pad and lay down, taking in the sublime setting. *Do I believe in heaven? Yes. Of course I do. Right here. Right now.*

That evening we called Joe on the satellite phone and told him our plans had changed. Instead of Indian Hollow, we would come out at Sowats Point. This would save us a few miles of walking. He agreed to pick us up there.

The next morning while hiking out that final stretch, I frequently found myself staring across the Canyon to the south, daydreaming. Wes frequently came to mind, including conversations I'd had with both him and T McCullough shortly after Wes returned from his near-miss in Kanab Canyon.

"Something happened to Wes during that flood, Tom," T told me over the phone the day after Weston returned. He sounded both frustrated and concerned. I knew he meant this statement in reference to Weston's decision to break up with his girlfriend, T's sister Patricia, almost immediately after coming home. He'd told me what he intended to do. "She's wonderful. I know that, but I don't think we're right for each other, Dad. And I don't want to live a lie."

I told him that made me sad, but I respected his decision.

T expressed some understandable anger. "I think you really need to talk to him, Tom," he pressed. "He got tweaked in there." I told T I'd already spoken to Wes. Without giving him the details, I also told him he was right. Wes had gotten tweaked in there, but in a good way.

As we neared the rim, George's spirit—as it had at the beginning of the hike—came back into mind. So did Vince's question. And with the massive peninsula of Great Thumb Mesa coming into view, I couldn't help but think of Ioana Hociota, someone I had never met. Her vibrant spirit also felt close by.

She will always be here. Like George and Kenton and Harvey. Heaven for Grand Canyon hikers, for Grand Canyon lovers.

Within that reverie came thoughts of two others lured to Canyon fates. Both had walked the length, practically worshipping this landscape. Both had haunting, heart-rending endings.

Bill Ott.

CHAPTER FORTY-ONE

The Good Son

THE STORY OF BILL OTT

In silence and solitude, we find a spiritual oasis amidst the clamor of the world's voices and the tyranny of our unceasing conscious thoughts.

Frank Waters
Eternal Desert (1990)

April 1974

Tempe, Arizona, attorney Steve U'Ren laughed when he recalled watching his friend Bill Ott do an arm wind-up like a major league pitcher about to throw a fastball. But instead of a baseball, Ott was gripping the brand-new camping flashlight that another buddy, Keith Zieland, had handed him seconds earlier. Zieland considered Ott a serious outdoorsman and wanted his impression of the fancy flashlight he'd just bought; it had been advertised as unbreakable, he said. Ott hefted the object briefly for weight, sizing it up before hurling it at a block wall. The flashlight shattered. Ott turned to Zieland, whose mouth was agape.

"Keith," he hooted, "I hate to tell you this, but they lied to you again!" Ott—who later bought Zieland a new flashlight—burst out laughing. U'Ren never forgot that moment, one typical of Ott's quirky humor and somewhat eccentric, unpredictable personality.

U'Ren described another incident that reflected Ott's sometimes random behavior. While hiking together in the Canyon on February 13, 1981, within a mile of the Colorado River in Soap Creek Canyon, Ott suddenly stopped, then said to U'Ren, "Can you handle both of these packs to the river?"

"I think so," U'Ren replied. "Why?"

"I need to go back up and move my truck down to Lees Ferry. I want to start my walking from there so that I do all of it within the Canyon, below the rim." U'Ren, who knew about Ott's goal to become the first person to complete a lengthwise hike on the north side of Grand Canyon, agreed. As he wrestled with the extra pack, Ott reversed and headed back up Soap Creek.

Six feet tall and lean, Ott strode with a steady pace. But despite his long gait, it was well after dark when he arrived at River Mile 11 where U'Ren waited for him. More than a week later they walked into Nankoweap Canyon at River Mile 53. Here they took a layover day to hike up-canyon to the scenic Kolb Arch. That evening the two huddled around a bonfire and chatted as they sipped some of the bourbon Ott carried with him. In the morning, Ott made blueberry pancakes before they headed out along the Butte Fault route. Within three days, they arrived at Lava Canyon, River Mile 66, where they retrieved a cache Ott had hidden during a river trip several weeks earlier. Along with food, the cache contained an inexpensive inflatable raft with paddles. "Do you want me to leave it after I cross, just in case?" U'Ren asked.

"Nope. I'll see you later, Steve," Ott answered.

U'Ren hopped in and started to paddle from shore.

"Paddle fast!" Ott shouted as he waved, then turned and headed downstream along the riverbank...

"Bill definitely was not a Type A," recalled U'Ren. After being introduced in 1972 by a mutual friend in Tempe, the two men began hiking the nearby Superstition Wilderness Area together. By the time of their Grand Canyon hike, U'Ren had known Ott for nearly a decade and considered him a compatible hiking partner. He also knew that Ott, while incredibly bright, was also somewhat absent-minded and a procrastinator, waiting until the last minute to accomplish tasks, then fretting and fussing while doing them.

He particularly remembered Ott's short fuse when it came to the Canyon's backcountry use permit system. Because Ott dreaded engaging with the staff there, he intentionally avoided it. Too often, U'Ren would hear from Ott that he'd gone into the Backcountry Reservations Office (BRO) and come out fuming because he felt the staff had "no clue" about where he planned to hike or how he planned to do it. As a result, they were sometimes reluctant to give him the permits he wanted. Nonetheless, Ott credited at least part of the idea of walking the Canyon's length on the north side to the NPS ranger manning the BRO desk in 1979.

After completing an epic fifty-three-day trip below the rim, walking from Great Thumb to Lees Ferry, Ott went into the BRO and studied the topo maps on the wall behind the ranger on duty. The ranger, aware of Ott's monumental, mostly south-side hike, commented that no one had done the entire north side—Kenton Grua, the only person known to have walked the Canyon's length, had done it on the south. Sold on the concept, Ott told the ranger he'd return in two years to walk the entire north side of the Grand Canyon.

True to his word, in 1981 Ott felt ready and invited U'Ren to come with him; the invitation, he added, included the permit. Enticed, U'Ren agreed to go but told Ott he could only spare two weeks, not the nearly three months Ott believed the entire trip would take. He'd have to find someone else for the remainder, or go it alone. Ott chose the latter. This came as no surprise to U'Ren. Alone was something Ott usually preferred; it gave him flexibility. "I rarely keep any kind of schedule when I hike alone," he once wrote, adding, "I try to leave myself open to what the landscape has to offer and how I feel." So, for sixty-five days, he wandered the rugged terrain unaccompanied.

Around May 1, he arrived at Grand Wash Cliffs after a grueling seventy-eight days. Exhausted and needing to cross Lake Mead's large Pearce Ferry Bay, he tried to flag down a boat. Two buzzed close by, took one look at the disheveled backpacker, and sped off. Finally, a third boater gave him a ride.

After he returned to Phoenix he contacted two people, both of whom shared responsibility for his hike's success. Like so many others of the era seeking Canyon hiking advice, Ott had corresponded with Harvey Butchart. Before the hike they exchanged several letters, and Ott visited Harvey once in person. Harvey's counsel was, predictably, illuminating. After completing the hike, Ott wrote to Harvey, thanking him for helping make his quest a success. He also provided a concise report of the trip. Harvey responded with a gracious letter, congratulating Ott on his "epochal hike." In his reply Ott brushed the praise aside, then ended his letter by summing up his post-hike state of mind: "How fine is good society; how magnificent is solitude!"

The other person Ott checked in with—and first in order—was his mother. He owed his love for deserts, specifically America's biggest desert canyon, to her, both because of, and in *spite* of, her.

Born in Erie, Pennsylvania, in 1946, the oldest of four children, Ott had a brother and two sisters. He and his little brother suffered from asthma and psoriasis. In part to relieve those afflictions, when Ott was eight, his family moved to Florida. Yet, physical ailments were not the Ott children's biggest childhood challenge.

That infamous distinction belonged to their mother. Prone to rages, she usually targeted her husband. Otherwise, she zeroed in on her oldest boy, Bill. Younger sister Paula recalled her mom, who only had an eighth-grade education, as being "psychologically evil." She remembered once seeing her big brother down on his knees, crying, head bowed, hands clasped in prayer, begging his parents to quit fighting. It didn't work. Consequently, young Bill Ott often withdrew, first holing up in his room, later escaping to the outdoors.

Ott's parents divorced while he was in high school. After he graduated in 1964, his mother gained custody of the children and moved them all to Arizona. Ott got a job and turned over most of his salary to his mom. He also helped around the house and cared for his siblings.

Maternal gratitude proved hard to earn, however. His mother remained moody, quick-tempered, and verbally abusive. With Bill's father gone, Bill was the lightning rod for her fury. After one particular fight she kicked him out. To survive, Ott started working for an uncle making airplane machine parts. However, as a contrite son who believed *he* was the problem, he kept returning home, hoping to soothe his mother's mind and spirit.

The tragic death of his seventeen-year-old sister in a car accident shortly after moving to Phoenix made things worse. Ott's mother descended to an even darker place. Bill made it a point to come home, check on her, give her what money he could spare, help around the house, and take care of his younger siblings. He would then disappear into the desert, increasingly his place of refuge from a gloomy, dysfunctional home life.

He started taking classes at Arizona State University in Tempe, majoring in biology with a minor in mycology. But in 1967, despite needing only a few more credit hours for his degree, the twenty-one-year-old dropped out of college and enlisted in the US Air Force to avoid being drafted and sent to Vietnam.

Instead, he was deployed to Thailand, where he maintained and repaired Gatling-type guns.

After two years in the Air Force, Ott returned to Phoenix and took a series of odd jobs. His mother still raged, and the desert still beckoned. The two influences seemed directly proportional.

With increasing frequency, Ott sought out the desert during his days off. An avid reader, he also focused on learning about the landscape he loved, and became an amateur naturalist and geologist. His interests expanded beyond the central valley to the state, and eventually, lured him to the Grand Canyon. In the early 1970s he made his first Canyon hike. The newly discovered

Bill Ott's Air Force photo.

landscape offered him the most soothing solitude he had ever known, and it quickly became his favorite escape.

By the mid-1970s, he had backpacked a majority of the Canyon's designated trails, and like so many Grand Canyon hikers, he gravitated to trips on the Colorado River. Hired as a swamper by Moki Mac River Expeditions, he eventually worked his way up to full-time guide, gaining a reputation as someone who took his job and the Canyon seriously. While getting paid to hike and boat in his favorite setting seemed like a dream come true, what Ott really craved was the serenity that came with Canyon solitude.

In fall 1979, thirty-three-year-old Ott launched his first mammoth Grand Canyon backpacking trip, a nearly two-month-long trek on River Left. He began at Hermit's Rest, hiking thirty miles along the rim to an old stock trail near Great Thumb Point. There, he dropped below the rim and walked along the Esplanade to Mount Akaba, near River Mile 148, before working his way back upstream.

Six weeks later, at Lava Canyon, River Mile 66, he crossed the Colorado in a small inflatable raft before finishing his route to Lees Ferry on River Right. Friends accompanied him on three separate occasions during half of the hike; he hiked alone for the remainder. Echoing Robert Benson, he wrote: "Schedules and having to depend on others was not conducive to the type of interaction with the landscape that I intended for myself on such a walk."

Doing things on his own constituted a comfort zone. A lifelong bachelor, Ott came and went mostly as he pleased. He did have a few serious girlfriends, however. In 1982, for example, the year after he finished his full-length walk, he followed one of them to Vernal, Utah, and took a job as a river ranger at nearby Dinosaur National Monument. When the relationship ended in 1985, he returned to Arizona to be closer to his mother and to re-enroll in school. He now wanted a more financially stable career, one that not only paid better, but also was portable and offered potential for flexible hours. He chose nursing.

That fall, he signed up for the nursing program at Mesa Community College. After graduating, he worked in the Phoenix area for several years, and remained compelled to care for his mother—financially and medically—despite it proving to be a relatively thankless job. By the early 1990s, burned out and needing a change of scenery, he decided to make his exit again.

In 1995, he kissed his mother and Arizona goodbye and headed for the Pacific Northwest, where he intended to make a permanent home. He told his mother he would periodically return to care for her, and also knew he had to revisit what commanded an equal grip on his heart and soul: Grand Canyon. For nearly twenty years he faithfully made biannual pilgrimages to Arizona.

By 2010, as his mother became increasingly feeble, Ott was gripped by an all-consuming concept for a novel Canyon quest: locating and taking digital pictures of Archaic rock-art paintings left by ancient Canyon inhabitants—in particular, the art type known as Grand Canyon Polychrome Style. Then, through computer enhancement, he'd recreate the rock art images as they might have looked when freshly painted. Doing this had become an obsession.

During April 2012, buoyed by a confidence built by forty years of hiking the Canyon, Ott surrendered to the alluring beauty of these pictographs and embarked on what would be his last wilderness journey.

CHAPTER FORTY-TWO

Eternal Solitude

THE STORY OF BILL OTT (CONTINUED)

"I'll never stop wandering. And when the time comes to die, I'll find the wildest, loneliest, most desolate spot there is.".

Everett Ruess
Letter to Brother, 1932

1995

With everything he needed stuffed into a backpack, Bill Ott left Arizona for Oregon on a $250 motorcycle. The Oregon state motto fit his spirit: "She Flies With Her Own Wings." His trip ended at Cove, a town of about 500 in Oregon's northeast corner, where he told friend Scott Thybony he planned to pursue a "pseudo-Walden experiment."

Ott once described himself to Thybony as "a simple man." He also wrote, "I think I have always tried to 'get by' and not intrude on the world around me if possible ... keep my head down and a low profile as it were." He eventually bought a two-acre parcel and built his own cabin.

A self-taught carpenter, Ott processed all his lumber by hand. Eventually, he completed his tiny dream house. Part of his success came from his single-mindedness; he often obsessed about becoming proficient at something, such as learning to create beautiful stained glass, and persevered until he succeeded. Then, as he had done with the Arizona desert, he applied himself to learning about Oregon's natural world. This culminated in his unpublished book, "The Natural History of Kalmiopsis," a wilderness area located in southwestern Oregon's Siskiyou National Forest known for its extraordinary ecological diversity.

Beginning in the early 2000s, his interests turned to digital photography. After studying the craft in earnest, he found his personal niche in photographing rock art. Ott incorporated this skill into his biannual pilgrimages to the Southwest, in particular the Grand Canyon area. By August 2007, his skills had become so proficient, he received an invitation to display his work at the Southern Oregon Guild Gallery in Kerby. That invite, affirmation of his mastering the subtleties of early Photoshop techniques, fueled his enthusiasm to discover more rock art for re-creation. In early 2012, that eagerness came to a climactic peak, manifesting in an ambitious but risky Grand Canyon trip to find more that spring.

Before heading into the Canyon, good son that he was, Ott detoured to Phoenix to check on his now very frail mother. As usual, on arrival—and for the next several days before heading out—he directly handled her care, despite her being what many would classify as a "difficult patient," unappreciative and sometimes verbally and physically abusive. Notwithstanding, Ott told friends that after this rock-art reconnaissance trip, he hoped to move back to Arizona to be closer to her. She'd given him money she won years earlier gambling in Las Vegas and he'd use it to help pay for his move. At that point he'd become her permanent, full-time caretaker, an extremely demanding and depressing job but one he had resigned himself to take on after he finished his polychrome search.

At least 3,000 to 4,000 years old, multicolored Polychrome Style rock art (or "poly-chromatic" paintings) were created by some of the Grand Canyon's mysterious early inhabitants. The ancient graffiti, typically found under protected overhangs, appears to have been scrawled on the stone walls by someone using red, yellow, green, and white crayons. While some images obviously depict deer, bighorns, or humans, others are very abstract. For example, ancient artists frequently drew vertically elongated figures, from three to more than five feet tall. Many have bulbous heads but no faces (like Ghost Rock). Some of the elongated "bodies" are decorated with stripes or squares and have sticklike appendages. Others have none. Still others have dangling lines that squiggle like jellyfish tentacles. Regardless, the archaic rock art style is fascinating and generally considered to exist only in the Grand Canyon region on the north side of the Colorado River.

Hoping to find proof to the contrary, Ott chose the south side's Mohawk Canyon as his starting point. Mohawk, which intersects the Colorado at River Mile 171.5, is about seventeen miles long from rim to river. After hiking five miles down to the Esplanade level, he planned to take his sweet time (up to about four weeks) poking his nose into any nook, cranny, or overhang that hinted it might be hiding some polychrome rock within the twenty-five miles of sprawling Mars-scape between Mohawk and its sister canyon upstream, called National, which is comparable in size and shape.

Like Mohawk, National Canyon (which joins the Colorado four and a half miles upstream of Mohawk at River Mile 167) is big. It's about 19 miles long from rim to river. Also massive is the Supai platform between the two. On both sides of the river, the Esplanade Sandstone slickrock seems nearly endless. Again, they are about twenty-five miles apart. To appreciate Ott's goal within this convoluted terrain, imagine an ant looking for a food source on the crusty surface of a recently played-in but dried-out sandbox—one about the size of a basketball court. Moreover for Ott, any success in finding polychrome rock art required his locating something far more critical than food. *Water.* Indeed, his primary objective—and his life—hinged on it.

Well aware of this risk, a couple of years earlier, Ott had tried to explain to Thybony what inspired him, despite the danger. In addition to finding the polychrome rock art, he wanted to make even more enhanced photographic recreations, something he had been doing for sites off the North Rim for several years. They discussed several places each had seen along the expansive Esplanade between Kanab Creek and the Tuweep area. Ott told Thybony he wanted to find some new ones.

Aware that Thybony was at least as well acquainted with that area as he, Ott asked, "Okay, Scott, where *haven't* you searched?"

As Thybony well knew, Ott had excellent powers of observation. He also knew the north side had been visually picked over by archeologists and rock

The expanse of the Esplanade between Mohawk and National Canyons. *Rich Rudow*

art hunters, himself included, for decades. Where *hadn't* he searched? Thybony gave Ott his most honest answer. "Across the river on the south side. As far as I know, no one has looked over there."

The single biggest reason that no one "looked over there" is because the bulk of the territory is Hualapai Reservation, with very restricted access. Regardless, Thybony believed the likelihood of finding a new site on the south was minuscule, even for someone as skilled as Ott. Accepted wisdom on the topic held that Grand Canyon Polychrome Style was unique to the north side because the Colorado River provided a physical and cultural deterrent to any southward crossing by the ancient artists. Finding a southside site would be rare indeed.

Despite the slim chance of success, Thybony didn't try to dissuade Ott, and Ott seemed enthusiastic about the challenge. In a later note to Thybony, he wrote, "The fact that no one has done the wild undeveloped side is an added bonus I guess but not the 'reason' for the trip." Ott's likely main reason for the trip? The same as it had always been. Solitude.

In preparation, Steve U'Ren recalls that for this trip, Ott seemed extremely well organized, far more than usual. His planning had been meticulous, especially with food. U'Ren knew his friend had to be careful; Ott would be traveling alone for three weeks, maybe more, and hadn't cached any supplies in advance. Moreover, this would be the longest of his annual spring treks in the Grand Canyon. Again, Ott intended to explore on Hualapai tribal lands for almost a month, focusing on the area between Mohawk and National Canyons. Whether he found rock art or not, his plan called for him to exit by hiking up National Canyon from the Esplanade the seven miles back to the rim. From there he'd have to tromp ten more miles from the rim to Highway 16, which links Hualapai Hilltop and the Havasupai Trailhead with old Route 66. Once on this well-traveled highway, he'd hitchhike to Seligman, get a motel room, and find a way back to Flagstaff, where he'd left his truck at the house of a friend named Glenn Rink. Ott figured he could carry enough food to last about a month, if he rationed appropriately.

Rink, with whom Ott had stayed for a couple of nights before heading out, didn't agree. He told Ott he was not carrying enough food. In response, Ott patted his belly.

"Well then, I guess I'll have to live off of this."

Another concern was Ott's water supply—or rather, his lack of one. With his pack literally jam-packed, little room remained for water bottles; Ott could only stuff in a couple. He carried none in his hand, nor did he attach any to the outside of the pack. Meanwhile, the forecast called for warm and dry weather for most of his time inside the Canyon. Ott would need to find water, would *have* to find water. This did not seem improbable, but given the lack of rain that spring, finding a drink could prove difficult. In fact, one of the reasons U'Ren declined Ott's invitation was the questionable availability of water. But along with another fried, Keith Miller, he did agree to drive Ott to Mohawk.

During the drive north, U'Ren sensed Ott becoming more edgy as they neared the head of Mohawk Canyon. He admitted he didn't have a permit to hike on the Hualapai tribal lands, and knew he needed to get below the rim and out of sight as quickly as possible to avoid detection. The little-used, two-track dirt road that U'Ren was following came with an abundance of washboarding, ruts, and rocks; when they took a wrong fork and had to backtrack, Ott became even more flustered.

"Don't fuck up, Bill. Don't fuck up," U'Ren recalled Ott muttering to himself. Then, as they neared the edge of a feeder drainage that dropped into Mohawk proper, Ott suddenly blurted, "Stop!" Flinging open the door, he grabbed his pack and made some final adjustments. One last time, U'Ren offered Ott more water, but he declined. After shouldering his heavy pack, Ott shook hands with U'Ren, said goodbye, dropped into the drainage, and disappeared.

Three-and-a-half weeks later, U'Ren phoned Glenn Rink.

"Still haven't heard from Bill," he began, sounding concerned. "What do you think?"

"Let's give him five more days. He told me he might be in the Canyon up to thirty days."

On day thirty, with Ott still a no-show/no-call, U'Ren phoned Rink again. This time, they agreed that a search should be started. They made this decision despite Ott specifically telling Rink, "If I don't show up, don't send anybody to come looking for me."

Rink called friend and veteran Canyon backcountry ranger Bil Vandergraff, who in turn involved the NPS SAR team, despite the search area being outside NPS jurisdiction. Vandergraff also contacted Sergeant Aaron Dick, head of the Coconino County Sheriff Search and Rescue (CCSSAR) program. Dick quickly assembled a team and reached out to Rink and Thybony, who both knew the area, asking them to participate in the search.

Rink had work obligations to clear before getting involved, but Thybony was able to commit right away. After gathering gear and food for several days, he hopped aboard a Department of Public Safety (DPS) helicopter. During the flight, Thybony contemplated the nearly impossible odds of finding a human speck, far smaller than a cinder granule in a carpet, within the complicated terrain below.

The pilot dropped him and NPS EMT volunteer ranger Sueanne Kubicek on a Supai sandstone bench in Mohawk Canyon, where a boot print had reportedly been found. When word spread that a searcher had identified a single boot print on the east side of Mohawk, both Thybony and Rink remember feeling skeptical. Rink didn't think Ott had made it that far (over thirty miles from his starting point), while Thybony believed the "track" could easily have been an imprint caused by wild horses known to roam the area. Two horseshoe prints, partially overlapping, could easily morph into a boot-shape. The fact that while no one noted anything close to human tracks, Thybony's group found wild horse tracks between Mohawk and National, makes this a likely scenario.

About the same time, on day one of the search, CCSSAR volunteer searcher Michael Ghiglieri found a legitimate clue: a small Ziploc bag containing pills. Covered with dust, it had been stomped on by wild horses, and the plastic looked as if it had been nibbled by rodents. Had it slipped out of Ott's pack? Did losing his meds cause a medical problem? He was sixty-five. The pills in the Ziploc were later identified as ibuprofen. Yet other pills, found in his personal possessions (at home) turned out to be prescription medication for high blood pressure. Did Ott have a heart condition beyond high blood pressure? Did he have a heart attack? If he did, shouldn't they find his body sprawled somewhere?

Thybony and Kubicek considered this as they walked, searching where a hiker would most likely walk, then where one wouldn't. They also searched all the overhangs in their assigned sector, places Ott might have camped. They found nothing. No additional tracks. No evidence of camping. And, not surprising to Thybony, none of the elusive rock art Ott sought. More disconcerting, they also found no sign of water. This made Thybony uneasy. He couldn't help but think that lack of water, especially if Ott had been injured, likely played a role in his fate.

Canyoneer Rich Rudow, who may be the most experienced person alive when it comes to exploring in western Grand Canyon, couldn't agree more. He thinks water would have been an issue, injured or not. "That time of year, late April to early May, the surface pothole water can be good, then go to bleak within a week."

Unfortunately for Ott, who was likely aware of the forecast, inner-Canyon daytime highs went from warm to hot several days after his arrival, climbing to the mid-90s. Rudow believes that with those temperatures, any surface water would have evaporated within days.

Was Ott caught high and dry in a stony equivalent of the Sahara?

"That what I'd bet," adds Rudow. "I'm also guessing he would have needed at least six to eight liters of water per day, then more for his hike back out to the highway. Finding no surface water would've forced him to downclimb pour-offs and drainages just to get to shaded pothole water. He may have trapped himself between cliffs, going down one that he couldn't get back up but above one he couldn't downclimb. Yeah, he could've got to water going down National or Mohawk where perennial water can be found in both at the bottom of the

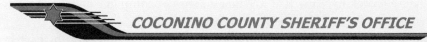

COCONINO COUNTY SHERIFF'S OFFICE

911 E Sawmill • Flagstaff, AZ 86001

MISSING PERSON

DATE: 05/07/2012   DR#: S12-01697

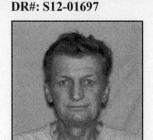

NAME: **William Anthony OTT**
DOB: **05/13/1946**
HEIGHT: **6'00"**
WEIGHT: **180 lbs**
EYES: **Blue**
HAIR: **Brown**
CLOTHING: **Unknown**

Redwall formation. Or he even could've made it to the river. But the Supai out there is really thick. We're talking like, 1,200 feet thick. The Redwall's even thicker at 1,400 feet. Just getting through these layers can be time-consuming and challenging, even if finding water wasn't critical. Plus, he had carrying capacity for only about three liters. He should've had twice that, especially for that long hike back out to the highway. If he stuck to his plan of continually exploring around, he'd need to somehow find water on the Esplanade for resupply at least twice a day. And it's one thing to try to find water when you're running low and you *want* to. It's totally another when you're completely out and you *have* to."

After three days and no luck, Glenn Rink was flown in with other fresh searchers, overlapping briefly with Thybony and Kubicek before the latter two flew out. Rink's equally futile efforts lasted three days before he returned to Flagstaff. The day Rink arrived home, Thybony showed up on his doorstep, eager to hear first-hand how the rest of the search had gone. When he pulled up, Thybony noticed the Ford Ranger pickup with Oregon plates parked at Rink's house. His heart sank. Seeing the truck, one of Ott's prized possessions, still at the house meant only one thing. There was no hope of finding Ott alive.

As Rink and Thybony chatted, Rink pulled out some large panoramic prints of rock art panels. Thybony recognized them as Ott's photos of Canyon polychrome pictographs. While Thybony had taken or seen plenty of photos of the sites, these images displayed shockingly higher levels of color and clarity, like seeing the fantastic, millennia-old art when it was new, the paint not quite dry.

Ott had painstakingly stitched together a series of computer-enhanced photos, bringing a thirty- to fifty-foot panel into a single image.

After Rink told Thybony that the search had been scaled back, he gave him some details. Rink reported that he and another searcher, Jesse Perry, had combed upper Mohawk Canyon. They found tracks believed to be Ott's going both directions. They continued to maneuver down-canyon to the Colorado, but no more tracks turned up. After camping at the river for the night, the next morning they went back up-canyon and encountered another searcher, NPS Tuweep ranger Todd Seliga. The NPS had flown Seliga, the most experienced remote-Canyon hiker they had, to Seligman. From there he caught a ride with other searchers out to the base camp on the rim. The Park's chopper then dropped him off at the head of National Canyon. Seliga hiked in, running into Rink and Perry in the Redwall. They discussed their best options, knowing that the search would probably have to be tapered off soon. They concluded that it would be best if Perry and Rink tried to contain the search on the west side of Mohawk and the east side of National, while Seliga would hike the Esplanade to National, then descend to the river.

The trio came away with nothing, not a single clue as to Ott's demise. Rink and Perry, however, did find an ominously coincidental inscription scratched under an overhang: out of food. If not for the date, 1947, Rink thought it sadly ironic that the etching could have been Ott's.

Finally, on May 25—after seven days of intense, multi-agency searching (twelve to fifteen people a day, employees from a variety of agencies, including CCSSAR, NPS, the Hualapai Nation, and Arizona DPS) and volunteers in temperatures that sometimes exceeded 90°F—workers called off the search. The CCSSAR effort, at 1,407 person-hours, was the largest ever for the agency to date; at more than $40,000, it blew most of the organization's annual budget. And the NPS, although not obligated to search areas within Hualapai Tribal jurisdiction, made three helicopter reconnaissance flights, costing thousands of dollars each and totaling more than fifty person-hours.

Ott was pronounced "deceased in absence" in the state of Oregon on May 2, 2012. Four days later, the state of Arizona did the same. This hit Ott's family—his mother and only surviving sister, Paula—hard. The official death announcements made a sad time even sadder. Only a year or so earlier Ott's younger brother had died from complications related to a longstanding lung disease. His death hadn't been a surprise, but the loss of Bill was; the unsolved mystery added to their anguish.

So, what happened?

Although considered least likely, even at the onset, foul play had to be excluded. Ott was in an extremely remote area. While he had few friends, he had fewer enemies, at least none that anybody knew of. He didn't do drugs, have unpaid debts, or engage in illegal activities. But he did have a $4,000 camera. Still, foul play seemed negligible, especially given the relative remoteness. How unlikely was it?

During the search, before dropping into Mohawk Canyon, Ghiglieri asked the Hualapais present, "Who goes in here [Mohawk Canyon], anyway?"

Two immediately gave the same response: "No one."

Yet a few miles down Mohawk, Ghiglieri and SAR partner Phil Aerts found a large cave directly on Ott's route containing, according to Ghiglieri's estimate, "at least fifty graffiti signatures by Hualapai."

Further, Scott Mascher, a former Yavapai County Sheriff, now retired, recalls having been on the plateau in 2010 near the vicinity of Ott's embarkation. Mascher, an avid Grand Canyon remote hiker as well as professional boatman, had taken permitted hikes on Hualapai tribal land in the western canyon for years. "This area gets more traffic than one might think, especially in comparison to the really remote stretches on the western end of the north rim."

After setting up camp near Mohawk, Mascher recalls how a truck suddenly roared up, off-roading across a sage flat. The driver slammed on the brakes and jumped out, shouting, "You're trespassing! You need to leave now!" The man wore a plaid shirt and a ballcap and had a holstered pistol.

"Wait! We have a permit to camp and hike! I'll show you!"

"I don't care! Leave, now!"

Mascher says the angry, armed man naturally made him nervous.

"So, I didn't argue. I started breaking down my tent, but he found it too slow. He yelled, 'Just throw it in your truck and get off our land now!' So, I did."

From his work in law enforcement, Mascher also has direct knowledge of an unsolved homicide in the area in 2011, the year before Ott disappeared.

"It was a Coconino County murder case that I became aware of from the sheriff's detective out of Flagstaff. A working cowboy for the Boquillas Ranch living at Camp 16 just off the Hualapai reservation boundary was shot and killed at the camp's house. To this day that murder remains an unsolved mystery."

Given his personal experience and law-enforcement knowledge, does Mascher think Ott met with foul play?

"While it certainly is possible, I think it's unlikely."

What about a heart attack? Again, Ott did have high blood pressure, a risk factor for heart disease. Besides being one of George Steck's close friends, John Azar was also close to Ott. He strongly doubts it. Plus, Azar says he knows "for a fact" that Ott didn't have heart disease. "Plus, he was a nurse," Azar points out. "He knew about meds and getting check-ups. He smoked a little weed on occasion but had never smoked cigarettes. He was in great shape."

Another disturbing possibility was debated. Was it suicide? Did Ott have a death wish and intentionally hid, then carried it out? His sister Paula, as well as close friends U'Ren, Rink, and Thybony, say no. He hadn't been depressed. He didn't leave a note. Plus, he had big plans for the future, including working on his rock art photographs and moving back to Arizona. An incident only a year before he went missing also argued against suicide or a premeditated disappearance. In April 2011, Ott had been hiking below the North Rim near Tuckup Canyon when he injured his leg. This slowed him so badly that he also ran out of water. His leg dragging, Ott made an intense effort to self-rescue, which he did, getting himself out a week overdue. He eventually hitchhiked to John Azar's place in Fredonia. For that hike, Azar says, Ott had a signal mirror with him, and he had it on his last hike as well. Rink corroborates this; he made sure Ott had a mirror before he left his house.

So, what about the comment Ott made to Rink, explicitly telling him not to send a search party if he failed to show up? While not directly suicidal, it does suggest a lack of motivation to live if something potentially fatal occurred. Rink believes it amounted to nothing more than a tongue-in-cheek remark.

Still, Paula Ott says she discovered some things at her brother's home that made her wonder. If he wasn't actively suicidal, did he have a premonition that something might happen? For example, they couldn't find any of his personal papers in his house, and his social security number had been written on a piece of paper and pinned to a board on the wall, readily accessible to anyone who might need it. Perhaps it meant nothing, but she found it odd.

It still leaves the question: How can a person disappear in canyon country, as he did, without a trace? While it seems unlikely, there is at least one precedent. In the middle of the Great Depression, twenty-one-year-old Everett Ruess went missing, never to be seen again, in the slickrock area of Davis Gulch, near the Escalante River above what is now Lake Powell.

A risk-taker, Ruess had been known to make dangerous climbs on exposed cliffs using ancient and eroding Moqui steps. Then, one day in 1934, he disappeared, his burro and camp found abandoned. Since then, no evidence of his possible demise has shown up, despite decades of extensive searching by countless people, including Scott Thybony, for his book, *The Disappearances*. Thybony concluded that the fearless young man with wanderlust likely fell into a slickrock canyon crevasse during a risky climb. Becoming wedged and unable to free himself, he would've eventually died, his remains perfectly and completely concealed by the fissure.

A similar fate is plausible for Ott. The convoluted slickrock where he wandered has hundreds of places for just such a lethal fall. Yet Ott had forty-four years on Reuss. Older and maybe wiser, he was also not a risk-taker. Ott's friends say he wouldn't have put himself in harm's way, at least not intentionally. Could he have been impaired by dehydration, or fallen in a desperate search to find water? Again, that's Rich Rudow's take.

Yet Rink reports that he and searcher Jesse Perry easily found water in a pothole where feral horses drink, above a drop in the Redwall going down into Mohawk. Rink believes Ott would have done the same. "I don't believe Bill had a water problem unless he lost his mobility for some reason," Rink

Reuss in Tsegi Canyon, July 1934. *Rainbow Bridge/Monument Valley Ansel Hall collection*

surmises. "Bill would have been able to find water as long as he was mobile. But once you lose mobility out there, you are in trouble. And that could happen as easily as having a badly sprained ankle."

Both Rink and Thybony speculate that Ott might have become seriously ill—a stroke or heart attack, perhaps. Rink also believes that whatever happened, did so within the first week. He suspects Ott was base-camped somewhere on the western side of Mohawk—not part of the primary search area—when that "something" happened. He doesn't think Ott spent much time (if any) on the east side of Mohawk, where—to Rink's disappointment—much of the search had focused because of the reported boot print found in the area. Unfortunately, the print, which Rink deemed "probably bogus," was never found again. Adding to Rink's frustration, the finder apparently failed to follow protocol by making a geo-reference point using GPS or taking photographs.

Unless Ott's remains are found, whatever may have contributed to his demise will remain unknown. What is unequivocal, however, is that Ott's main objective—aside from finding rock art—likely never changed: enjoying the Canyon's silence and solitude. Wherever he found it.

In this regard, despite being born more than a generation apart and the forty-four-year age difference at the times of their disappearances, Ruess and Ott shared similarities. The title of William "Bud" Rusho's book about Everett Ruess, *A Vagabond for Beauty,* could have doubled for a book about Ott. In his book, Rusho includes passages from Ruess's journal. Several months before he died, he wrote:

> I must pack my short life with interesting and creative activity....
> Then, and before physical deterioration obtrudes, I shall go on some last
> wilderness trip, to a place I have known and loved. I shall not return.

By all reports, Ruess, like Ott, harbored no suicidal inclinations. His comment, "I shall not return" from a potentially "last" wilderness trip is prefaced by "before physical deterioration obtrudes." While physical deterioration can occur at any age, it's less common in youth but inescapable with advanced age. Thus, one can infer that young Ruess's "goal" for his life's end referenced the distant future when he was an old man, rather than an intent to disappear as a young one.

John Azar believes Ott had a similar desire for his own last days and ultimately made a conscious decision to disappear and never be found: "He [Ott] was betting everything on finding the rock art and water. He already had extra weight for his camera and food. So he didn't carry enough water and ran out. When he found the first and second springs in Mohawk likely dry, I think he may have gotten desperate. He rolled the dice and he lost. He may have fallen, but even injured, it was not in Billy's nature to leave tracks. He almost stalked. I don't think he wanted to be found. That's why there's no trace of him. He crawled under an overhang where he'd be almost impossible to find. Then he let death take him."

Yet, Azar smiles when pondering that conclusion. "I think it was a pretty poignant ending for Billy."

Glenn Rink also smiles, then laughs, as he reminisces about his friend Ott. "He was pretty fuckin' weird. Quirky, but really knowledgeable, especially about the Canyon. And he was also really humble. He didn't like attention." Indeed, all those who knew him well believe Ott would probably have been annoyed by the search efforts, though they also think he might have been pleased by the outcome. Much earlier, in his 1981 journal written while walking the Canyon length, Ott pondered:

> Where is it I walk? Is this some magical paradise on another world
> or truly just a dry canyon in Arizona? I am awed again and again, and
> with more gentle rain it becomes the source of joy I have come to know
> here ... please let there not be an end to this.

CHAPTER FORTY-THREE

Leaving George in Better Hands

THE LIFE OF ROBERT BENSON

In life, it's not where you go. It's who you travel with.

Charles M. Schultz (1922–2000)

March 1983

At dawn, Robert Benson awoke to an unmistakably happy sound from the nearby tent. Benson lay silent and smiling in his own tent for half an hour, taking in the giggling. He felt closer to the two gigglers than to his own parents.

Eventually, Helen Steck unzipped their tent and stepped out, George on her heels. Helen, dressed for a polar expedition, then clambered into Elmo. George, only slightly less bundled, did the same. Then he fired up the engine and cranked the heater to full blast. Benson's thermometer read 40°F.

The threesome had camped a few miles from Pearce Ferry, in Mohave Desert country. After warming up Elmo, they quickly packed their gear and drove to Pearce Bay. There, they anticipated that Meadview River ranger Don Forester—who had picked up George and Benson at the end of their last hike, the eighty-day Ordeal by Rubble four months earlier—would likely arrive within the hour. Helen had eggs cooking and coffee brewing when Forester motored up in his cruiser boat. He joined them for breakfast.

Afterward, Benson, clad only in his trademark cut-off jeans and a long-sleeve shirt, made a final gear check before slinging his pack over his shoulder and hauling it down to Forester's boat. Once he, Helen, and George had hopped aboard, Forester steered the boat four miles upstream, anchoring at the Grand Wash Cliffs. While the cliffs marked the official end of the Grand Canyon, they also marked the unofficial beginning of Benson's colossal, 165-day hike following the Colorado River back upstream to Moab, Utah.

Benson appreciated having George and Helen there. Besides the moral support, he also knew Forester's shuttle likely wouldn't have happened without George's influence. For years, George had made it a point to get to know NPS rangers whom he respected, and that respect and effort were reciprocated. George and Helen had no problem coaxing Forester into participating in their tiny send-off for Benson. With the stunning Grand Wash Cliffs as a backdrop, the couple broke out some bubbly. Benson wrote: "George popped the champagne bottle while Helen pulled out four expensive Styrofoam cups. A toast to a new adventure!"

Not wanting to get caught "drinking on the job," Forester scanned for onlookers before imbibing. At 9:30 a.m., after a few snapshots, Benson headed up-canyon. He later jotted down this thought: "I made my first step into an adventure of the unknown. A piece of driftwood I found nearby served as my first walking stick."

His isolation lasted for about ten minutes. Hearing a motor behind him, he turned to see Forester's boat. George and Helen, still aboard, were giggling once more as they surprised him with one final good-bye. The

Helen and George Steck toasting Benson at the start of his upstream trek. *Don Forester*

whole gang toasted again, this time with cans of Coors. Benson stuffed one can into his pack for lunch, then gave farewell hugs. Like John and Paige Shunny, George and Helen also filled a role in Benson's life as beloved American foster parents.

That first night Benson made camp five miles upstream at Columbine Falls, a beautiful spot where a year-round stream pours over the edge of a Bright Angel Shale cliff. After settling in, Benson began journaling to fulfill his goal of "recording the day's important and trivial matters on paper."

True to his word, especially when it came to the trivial, Benson penned nearly 80,000 words (entirely in English) in his journal during his six-month upstream traverse.[15]

---

15 Combined with his writing rituals throughout the downstream portions the year before, the word count for his journals totaled an astounding 143,236, enough to create a book about the size of this one—all from a man for whom English was a second language.

Benson's first evening came straight from George's playbook: a happy hour of Mai Tais and hors d'oeuvres, followed by a delicious taco dinner with sour cream and tortilla chips. Afterward, he built a small fire and—consistent with his dichotomous nature—rather than rejoicing in his privacy, he lamented having no one to share it with.

The next day, he wrote that he made "lousy progress," going only a disappointing 3.5 river miles, 1.5 miles short of his goal. He grumbled, again, about the solitude—ironic, considering that in the past, hiking companions had often come in for some harsh criticism in his journal. George had earned especially scathing comments during the previous year's Ordeal by Rubble. However, in this day's entry, Benson's nostalgia is clear.

> A rotten day and I can't say I had fun. It was too early to lose my enthusiasm, but I can't just blame the weather for the depressed mood. I felt lonely. Until now I didn't realize that this was going to be a solo adventure. Every time I fall into this low state of mind, I question my urge to go on an adventure like this and the reasons I come up with. But there was hope that things will look brighter with a change of weather and scenery.

As the days grew longer and brighter, so did his attitude. On April 1st, he jovially described his permit-less (and undetected) crossing of Diamond Creek: "It's April Fool's day—I wonder how the Hualapais take a joke."

Another boost of excitement came less than a week later, on the afternoon of April 7, 1983. Near River Mile 202, two grizzled-looking men paddling canoes appeared. While an uncommon sighting, the real shock for Benson was that they had caught him from *behind,* paddling upstream against the Colorado River's hefty 17,000 cfs flow.

> I yelled until they noticed me and asked them to come on shore. Verlen Kruger and Steve Landick, two pioneers from Michigan, not just attempted to canoe up the Grand Canyon [sic], but included this section as part of a 3-year, 28,000 mile canoe challenge.

He added: "And I thought I was nuts."

The three men discussed their respective projects. Kruger and Landick seemed to be just as intrigued by Benson as he was by them. In Kruger's book about the journey (cowritten with Brand Frentz), *The Ultimate Canoe Challenge: 28,000 Miles Through North America,* Kruger recalls meeting Benson:

It was a long walk through tremendously difficult terrain, and we were impressed and delighted to hear his story. We talked about the kind of feelings that led people to take "impossible" trips, how you feel an urgency, that you have to do it, without really being able to give a sensible reason.

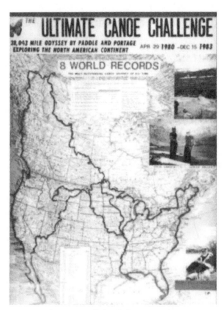

Book cover of the Ultimate Canoe Challenge.

Steve Landick and Verlen Kruger.
Robert Benson

Recharged and inspired by the two equally ambitious men, Benson pushed on. A few days later, he reached Havasu Canyon at River Mile 157.3, which he found swamped with people. Disgusted, he wrote, "Havasu Falls looked like Miami Beach, a fleshpot worse than Phantom."

Two weeks later, he arrived at Elves Chasm, a travertine grotto with spectacular waterfalls formed by Royal Arch Creek at River Mile 117. For a while, he had it all to himself and did some exploring. When he returned to the river, he saw that a Wilderness River Adventures boat had pulled in with only a couple of guides on board. Curious, he approached and asked why. "We're dead-heading," they told him, describing a quick, passenger-less trip to pick up clients at the Whitmore Wash helipad. The head boatman, Ron "Shadow" Ellis, told Benson he'd heard of him, even referencing Benson's disastrous fall. Pleased, Benson wrote about the moment: "Once again, I got reminded that my identity was becoming popular when Ron asked me if I was the guy that hiked the Canyon with broken bones."

Shadow invited him to join their group for dinner at a camp downstream. Not wanting to retrace his route, Benson declined. Undeterred, Shadow offered him an alternative: over six pounds of raw steak. That, Benson gladly accepted, writing, "It felt like Christmas."

The next day, as Benson neared Bass Rapid at River Mile 108.4, he encountered another commercial motor rig. This one, however, was loaded with passengers. Still, the boatmen did not hesitate to invite him to join them for the evening; this time, he accepted. Hopping aboard, he joined them as they motored their Western River Expeditions boat to the right shore for camp. Within minutes a platoon of kayaks appeared. Baffled by the trip's large size, Benson learned that the expedition was a "boatman training trip" led by the NPS's Kim Crumbo. Benson was in for another pleasant surprise: George Steck's son, Stanley, a newly hired NPS boatman, was part of the crew.

Benson deemed the evening's dinner "excellent—steaks and potato salad." He also noted that as part of the evening's celebration, Terry Brian, one of the river rangers, had hefted in sixty pounds of booze. Earlier that day, Brian hiked out from Phantom on a mission to "save the spirit of the cruise." The "save" hinged on Brian buying more alcohol for the trip and then successfully delivering it before the boaters got too far downstream. Arriving on the rim, Brian literally ran to Babbitt's General Store in Grand Canyon Village, bought the liquor, finagled a ride to the South Bass Trailhead, then hustled seven miles back to the river down the South Bass Trail. Amazingly, Brian and his load—six six-packs of beer and various bottles of hard stuff—arrived intact before sunset.

The next morning, the group invited Benson to hang out with them during their layover day, but he declined, motivated by an urge to move on. After they shuttled him back to River Left, he scrambled up to the Tonto Trail. Four days later, on May 17, he reached Havasupai Gardens (HG). After a brief visit with Ranger Rod Losson, he covered the six miles down Bright Angel Trail to Phantom Ranch to do laundry and enjoy a few beers in the canteen. Despite being a little tipsy, he hiked back to HG that evening, arriving just before dark.

In the morning, he jogged back to Phantom once again to take advantage of the staff's invitation to join them for breakfast. In addition to pancakes, bacon, eggs, toast, and coffee, they dished Benson plenty of attention, asking him about his hiking exploits, which he had no problem sharing.

After breakfast, Benson hiked back up to the Tonto Platform with Ranger Jennifer Burns, following the old "miner's route" in a ravine just west of the Silver Bridge. Along the way, they chatted about the new backcountry management plan. Besides wanting to make his name and exploits known, Benson had learned from George the importance of greasing the wheels of potentially beneficial Canyon relationships, especially with the NPS. This meant schmoozing with rangers like Burns at every opportunity. After reaching the Tonto Trail, Burns headed out the South Kaibab Trail while Benson hiked the four miles westward to HG.

That afternoon, while sipping beers from a stash he'd placed in Losson's fridge, Benson began reorganizing his food and gear. Losson agreed to have Benson's sleeping bag packed out by mule; Benson assured him he wouldn't need it, as the weather would only get hotter. Around 8:30 that night Benson used the ranger's phone to call George Steck and they finalized plans to meet at the Little Colorado River in five days.

Benson arrived at the Little Colorado on May 21, two days early; this allowed him at least three layover days, depending on when George arrived. Complying with NPS regulations that prohibit camping close to the confluence, he set up his camp on the river ledges about a mile upstream from the mouth. Then he took his pack frame and headed another mile-and-a-half up the Little Colorado to retrieve his cache of three five-gallon metal cans. He strapped the awkward load of nearly eighty pounds of food and beer to the frame, then lugged it back to his camp.

With time to kill and temperatures now in the mid- to upper nineties, he lounged and journaled while chugging river-cold beers. He also blew up his previously stashed "super-raft" to paddle around in a small lagoon near the mouth, then swam and took a soapless bath.[16] For a while he also hung out and drank beer with local river legend and guide Curtis "Whale" Hansen.[17] Whale, a gregarious, heavy-set Vietnam vet who drove motor rigs for Hatch River Expeditions, helped Benson retrieve a stockpile of beer he'd earlier bribed guide Tony "TA" Anderson to hide for him near the confluence. TA had left the stash along with a "treasure map" to another resupply upstream at River Mile 21.7.

Now well supplied with beer, Benson promised himself not to bum any off boaters. Instead, he continued lounging, waiting for George to hike in from the Tanner Trail then across the Beamer. On his third layover day, the man he admired as much as any finally arrived.

> Not too long, around 5:00 p.m., a character with a blue pack appeared in the distance. I ran towards him to greet the weather-beaten hiker. At the brink of dying from dehydration he made it to camp with me. The beers were cold and George began to chug them down like water. While exchanging stories and the latest news, a considerable amount of beer cans began to pile up.

---

16 Endangered humpback chub fish congregate in the Little Colorado near the confluence. NPS regulations prohibit soap use here.
17 Whale's 1995 suicide inspired the formation of a nonprofit for suicide prevention, Grand Canyon's Whale Foundation.

Benson and George enjoying beers near the LCR. *Steck family archives*

The next morning, relieved of excess beer weight from the previous day's celebration and unburdened by a cumbersome load of water, the two made good time traversing upstream along the riverbank on the level Tapeats ledges. But the days became hotter and longer, and within a couple of miles, the Tapeats petered out. Heat and sidehilling took its toll on the then fifty-eight-year-old Steck, and his pace dwindled to about half of Benson's. Besides walking slower, the distance between his stops shortened and his rest times lengthened. Benson became increasingly concerned when this pattern continued for several days. George mostly blamed it on his ailing back. Several minor stumbles and one bad fall didn't help.

On May 31, near Eminence Break at River Mile 44, George plopped down. "I'm done," he confessed to Benson. "I'm going to hitchhike a boat ride out." Benson didn't try to talk George out of it.

By coincidence, their stopping point coincided to where Kenton Grua had also quit hiking during his first lengthwise attempt in 1973. Luckily, boats appeared within forty-five minutes. More fortuitously, NPS boatman and friend Kim Crumbo was part of the trip, as was Don Forester's wife. Crumbo didn't hesitate, agreeing to take George to Phantom, where he could hike to the South Rim. While relieved, George knew he would miss his young backpacking buddy. Likewise, Benson would miss his oldest and closest hiking friend. What neither knew was that this would be their last hike together.

Of George's departure, a saddened but relieved Benson wrote:

> It probably was a wise decision although I didn't feel too happy about losing my companion. I sent 4 rolls of film out with him and traded them some trash for some fresh cheese. Then goodbye to George, he was in better hands now.

Self-portrait at a polychrome rock art panel.
Robert Benson collection

CHAPTER FORTY-FOUR

Receipts in a Shoebox

THE LIFE OF ROBERT BENSON (CONTINUED)

And you run, and you run to catch up with the sun but it's sinking
Racing around to come up behind you again
The sun is the same in a relative way but you're older
Shorter of breath and one day closer to death…

Pink Floyd
"Time"/*Dark Side of the Moon* (1973)

June 1983

After George rode downriver from Eminence Break Camp, Benson plodded alone in the opposite direction. On June 8, 1983, three days later, he set up camp at Saltwater Wash, River Mile 12. A Western Rivers motor rig appeared and veered over. Boatman Bill Skinner, whom Benson knew, introduced Benson to his passengers, then described the hiker's ambitious goal, now well within reach. Benson basked in the attention.

> The big surprise came when he presented a bottle of champagne as a congratulation gift to the Grand Canyon finale. I thought it was a really neat idea. The passengers must have been instructed to be prepared to meet a rare character, since I got flooded by questions and snap shots.

June 9, a Thursday, marked Benson's final camp in Grand Canyon. The upbeat buzz from the previous day's attention with Skinner's group evaporated and his emotions seemed to flatten. He wrote that he didn't feel "depressed in any way nor look[ing] forward to any change." But he did add, "Tonight was just another camp amidst the glamour and beauty of Canyon Country."

The following morning, Benson hiked to River Mile 8, the mouth of Jackass Creek. Believing the Colorado's high-water flows would likely make it impractical to walk farther upstream below the rim and along the river, he chose to hike the three miles out Jackass Canyon, then another two to the highway. At 10:15, he reached Highway 89, which came as a bit of a shock.

> The first reaction of my senses told me of a difference in air quality. Even before the first car passed by, I smelled the strong fumes of gasoline and exhaust fumes. The air simply stunk. The absence of those pollutants over the past months had sharpened my senses.

Turned off by the sight and smell of vehicles, he didn't bother to hitchhike. Instead, he walked five miles to Marble Canyon Lodge. Using the payphone, he called the Shunny house. No one picked up. Next, he tried Stan Jones, who lived in nearby Page. That call also went unanswered. So he began hiking east, just as his original plans called for, through Echo Pass, up onto Highway 89, roughly ten miles from Page. Lonely and uninspired, he eventually changed his mind about hitchhiking and stuck out his thumb.

Within minutes, a truck driver for Wilderness River Adventurers picked him up. The driver not only took him to Page, but also dropped him off right at Stan Jones's house. Benson knocked on Jones's door. He had knocked on that same door for the first time in 1980, intrigued to meet the man many called "Mr. Lake Powell." At that time Benson had little interest in Jones's obsession, the massive, 186-mile-long reservoir. Instead, he was in search of information about the mysterious slickrock country that surrounded it, the other 87 percent of the Glen Canyon National Recreation Area (GCNRA). Jones reportedly knew as much about this backcountry as he did the reservoir.

Jones hadn't always been Mr. Lake Powell. An Illinois native, in his previous life Jones worked for the Walt Disney Company in the 1950s as a publicist for the popular *Davy Crockett* movie and the even more popular *Mickey Mouse Club* television show.

Then in 1967, wanting out of the southern California rat race, he moved to Page. Taken by the high desert with its heart-stirring red rock and the rising lake's cobalt-blue water, he devoted the rest of his life to boating, hiking, and researching the region, becoming its foremost expert. By 1980, the sixty-two-year-old had written several books and articles about the place, which he published through his business, Sun Country Publications.

Flattered by Benson's inquiry, Jones had freely shared his expertise. The two corresponded by mail for the next couple of years before Benson started his mega-hike. Like Benson, Jones kept journals of his explorations, which he called "ramblings." While Jones believed he did a fairly good job documenting his backcountry encounters in field notes and maps, Benson's journals both stunned and humbled him. He described them as "monumental by comparison."

So impressed was Jones that he offered to financially sponsor Benson's trips as well as publish his "monumental" writings. He later devoted an entire chapter to Benson in his 1998 book, *Stan Jones' Ramblings: By Boat and Boot in Lake Powell Country.* He titled the chapter "Robert Benson—Master

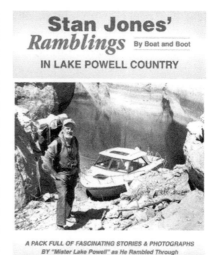

Stan Jones's book cover.

Hiker" and said this of the hiking prodigy: "His pocket notebooks were models of meticulous memorabilia, his many penciled pages so lucid and inclusive that they read like nearly-finished manuscripts…. Benson's collection of USGS maps contained the most and neatest entries I have ever seen penciled in by an amateur cartographer. His dozens of references to springs, streams, cascades, fords, oases, aboriginal and Indian trails, pictographs, petroglyphs, unusual rock formations, and campsites bear witness to the fact that Robert was not 'just a hiker' but was, rather, a very aware student of the natural world in which he felt most at home."

Now, three years later, Benson found Jones's house unoccupied. So, he sat down and waited. Jones's daughter-in-law, Betty Slater, who eventually stopped by to drop off some mail, told Benson that Jones and his wife, Alice, were boating on the lake and would probably return in two to three days. She offered him a place to stay, but he politely declined. Instead, he camped at the local campground and waited for the couple to return. Benson wound up spending several days with them, resting, sipping margaritas, and enjoying Alice's cooking. He paid "rent" by helping the Joneses with landscaping. Alice recalled that Benson's speech had a subtle underlying accent, which she correctly guessed was German. One day she asked him about it. He looked down at his feet then up at the horizon. Softly, after a long moment of silence, he replied with the story John Shunny helped him fabricate and rehearse. "I'm American but I was raised in Minnesota by my German grandmother. She was an immigrant who knew very little English. I spoke German before I went to school to be taught the language of America."

Clearly, being of German descent did not evoke pride in the young man. Jones, who would later encourage Benson to write a book about his exploits, recalled that each time he suggested it to Benson, Benson seemed ambivalent—a little excited, but fearful as well at the thought of publicity. Jones came to believe that his reluctance stemmed from being in America illegally.

At any rate, during Benson's stay Jones repeatedly urged him to consider writing a book after completing the hike. He even went as far as offering to ghostwrite, then publish it through his company. Benson admitted being flattered but continued to decline and frequently changed the subject, the deflection typically blamed on his stomach. That and "bad water."

Benson retrieving a cache.
Robert Benson

Jones called his Page physician friend, Dr. Gus Scott, to discuss Benson's complaints, believing that Benson had contracted giardia despite his having religiously treated all the water he drank with iodine. Upon hearing the story and at Jones's urging, Dr. Scott called in a prescription to a local pharmacy for Flagyl. Even so, he doubted that diagnosis and wondered, because of the reported chronicity of Benson's stomach ailments, whether the young man might have hepatitis. (He didn't.)

While Robert wouldn't commit to writing a book, he did agree to an interview Stan set up with a reporter for the *Lake Powell Chronicle*. Meanwhile, he hoped the Flagyl would kick in. Placebo or not, within two days it seemed to do the trick and Benson was ready to pull on his boots once again. That night he wrote: "missing the sounds of a stream or river, like in the Grand Canyon."

On June 19, in broiling heat, Jones dropped off Benson near Navajo Creek on Lake Powell's southern shore and helped him don his backpack, a new one Jones had purchased for him as a parting gift. They exchanged handshakes that, Jones mused, "can only be felt by outdoorsmen that have mutual respect for each other."

For several minutes Jones observed "the most accomplished hiker I have ever known" moving machine-like upstream despite the elevated temperature. At the top of a distant knoll, Benson briefly stopped, turned, and waved one last time before disappearing into the slickrock.

Methodically, he worked his way north, past arm after arm after arm of sprawling Lake Powell. After six weeks of circumnavigating or bisecting nearly fifty slickrock side canyons—some fifteen to twenty miles in length and all under incessant sun—Benson arrived at the San Juan River. There, he veered into a tributary called Grand Gulch and then up to Collins Canyon, where he ascended to a spectacular overlook.

Writing in his journal that night, he reported feeling down, and that his "physical problem" had returned.

> I feel like I'm being robbed of my whole existence. It's worse than the situation last year when I kept hiking after the accident. Physical pain doesn't seem to bother me as much as the battle between mind and body that I am going through now.

He also observed that the fun aspect of his trip had ended some time ago. However, he would keep going "for the commitment and also the flicker of hope that things will change for the better again."

Yet, as Moab, Utah, and the end of his more than five-month-long über-hike drew near, even that "flicker of hope" seemed to snuff out. At Dripping Springs Wash, less than ten miles from his final destination, Benson stopped again. With mosquitoes biting, dark clouds rolling in, and his stomach churning, he decided to call it quits.

> I almost felt like a coward, suddenly aiming for a quick end. But 163 days was a long time—maybe too long.
>
> It seemed like an eternity since I passed places like Lava Falls and Havasu, yet the memories are as fresh as if they happened yesterday. I successfully realized a dream, an idea which I didn't let go since the day it was born, many years ago. I was tired and worn out now, looking forward to some rest of mind and body.
>
> This August 29th at 12:30 p.m., I turned away from the past 5½ months, trying to aim my thoughts for the events ahead and preparing myself for the switch to civilization.... My mind kept returning to the past ...
>
> I was walking on a paved road now. It didn't feel right, as if a pavement was not meant for walking. At 5:00 p.m. I reached the portal, the threshold of a different world—Moab. In town I tried to contact some boatmen I had met along the way but they were on the River right now. That scratched the celebration. Somehow, I didn't feel that glorious anymore.

On March 14, 1984, a little over six months later, Robert Eschka Benson drove his 1974 Jeep into the Carson National Forest two hours north of Albuquerque. Rolling into a clearing, he parked and got out. Receipts for the roll of duct tape and a long hose he'd just purchased were stuffed into his coat pocket. Normally, he put receipts in a shoebox, part of an obsessive recordkeeping routine. By now, a decade after he'd arrived in the US, the box contained piles of receipts, an ongoing catalog of his frugal lifestyle. However, that day's receipts wouldn't make it into the shoebox.

Benson spent several minutes configuring the hose and taping it into position, securing one end to the tail pipe and pulling the other end through the driver's-side window. After climbing back into the Jeep and rolling up the window until it gently pinched the hose, he opened a quart of premixed Jose Cuervo margarita and began sipping. He also inserted a cassette tape into the tape player and pressed play. Starting the Jeep's engine, he settled back to listen to Pink Floyd's *Dark Side of the Moon*...

The next day hikers discovered Benson's lifeless body. His death shocked the Shunny family as well as the Stecks and other friends whom John Shunny, executor of Benson's modest estate, informed.

He'd searched Benson's address book and found 170 names. Listed first was Benson's mother, Alma Eschka, in Weidenberg, Germany. She had only seen her son twice since he had left for America eight years earlier. Both visits had required her to travel to New Mexico. After receiving the heartbreaking news, she and other family members asked Shunny to refrain from revealing that Benson had taken his own life.

Shunny honored this request in the notes he sent. He also made copies of Benson's journals and sent Alma the originals. Shunny gave George Steck a copy of the journals as well as Benson's original maps, slides, and slide projector. For himself and his family, Shunny kept some of the exotic wood Benson had collected, intending someday to build a drafting table.

Shunny arranged for Benson's body to be cremated. He sent half of the ashes to Alma and—at her request—gave the other half to George to spread in the Grand Canyon.

Receipt for hiking boots.
Robert Benson collection

```
Dear Friend of Robert,
       Robert Benson died unexpectedly on March 15. He had lived with
us off and on since 1976, and Paige and I had come to regard him
as another son. At his death, he was 28 and had been planning an-
other Grand Canyon trip.
       This summer, we plan to visit his mother, Alma Eschka, in
Germany.
       In going through his effects, including his address book, we
came across your name. We'd be happy to meet and talk with you,
should you ever pass through Albuquerque.
                                           Sincerely yours,

       John Shunny
       2517 Cutler NE
       Albuquerque, N.M.
       87106
```

John Shunny's note about Robert Benson's death. *Robert Benson collection*

When those who knew him learned that Benson's death was a suicide, it didn't come as a tremendous surprise. George Steck, for one, believed several incidents had been prophetic. For example, during Thanksgiving dinner in the El Tovar's dining room in 1982, after completing their *Ordeal by Rubble* hike George had noted:

> Helen always gets people to say what they're thankful for. So, we're all hanging there doing that. And we met a friend of Stanley's, Larry, so Larry tells what he's thankful for. Robert, he's not thankful for anything. And Larry says "C'mon Robert! You're gonna have to give in eventually. You might as well make it easier." But he said "No, I'm not thankful for anything."
> Finally, I broke the impasse by saying "Well, Robert, can't you at least be thankful for the fact that you don't have anything to be thankful for?" Yes, he could subscribe to that. That was what he was thankful for.

A month later, Benson took the Stecks out for a pre-Christmas meal. George described the disturbing conversation Benson had with Helen:

> After dinner he wanted to speak to Helen alone—he didn't want me there—and what he was telling Helen was, he wanted Helen to treat him the same way she would treat the bag boy at the supermarket. He didn't

want to be incorporated into our family, the extended family, anymore. He didn't want to be invited to the house for dinners and things. And she didn't pick up on that. Later she realized that was his way of saying goodbye to us.

Furthermore, George recalled, "He'd told me right at the beginning that he intended to kill himself before he was thirty. I guess he wanted to give me the option of not investing time in him if he was not going to be around for very long. I don't know why he told me, or felt he had to tell me at the time, but it just must have been on his mind a lot."

Benson was twenty-eight when he took his life. He had made no known previous suicide attempts. Yet he seems to have harbored some more thinly veiled suicidal ideations. For example, when Elias Butler interviewed George for *Grand Obsession*, George commented that Benson flirted with death in the form of risky behavior:

> He could take chances like he was defying death to come get him. He could do things that I couldn't do. Or, he would do things that I would not be willing to do. One place, down near Toroweap [Overlook] would be a good example. Someplace in the Redwall where the Redwall [makes a whistling noise], it goes down. Well, he has a photograph of his feet standing on the edge of that cliff with just his heels on solid rock and the toes and the rest of his boots out over space, hanging in the air. And he's taking a picture down thru those feet to the river below. It would seem to me that when you were looking that way, you'd get vertigo. Maybe he was hoping that would happen.

With his toes hanging in space, not only could minor vertigo have sent him to his death, so could have a gust of wind. Or a simple nudge. What ultimately pushed him over his own emotional edge into suicide will never be known. He left no note, nor had he openly discussed his thoughts during those last few days.

One incident, however, may have been what thrust Benson past his tipping point. In June 1983, near the end of his mega-hike, Benson's father died. John Shunny learned this in a letter from an Eschka family member and shared it with George. Both chose to wait to tell Benson until he finished his trek.

According to Pete Shunny, Benson—whom Pete considered to be a serious, rather humorless person who frequently seemed indifferent to or mostly unaffected by joy, grief, pleasure, or pain—shrugged off his father's passing. "It's not a big deal to me. We were never close," he told Peter.

Still, Benson's German family began urging, then insisting, that he return to Germany not only to see his immediate family but to help fill his father's absence. His mother and his paternal uncle even traveled to the US to try to persuade him. But Benson made it very clear to his German family—and to his American one—that he would not be leaving.

Benson with his mother. *Robert Benson collection*

Doing so might reveal his false identity to US Immigration, for which he would be jailed and deported. So again, he said no.

After his suicide, the Stecks, the Shunnys, Stan Jones, and others who knew Benson came to believe the pressure to return to Germany on top of the risk of losing all he had come to love drove him to the brink.

Did it?

While a chance existed that his identity might have been discovered, how likely was it? Benson died in 1984. The world, especially airline travel, was vastly different than it is today.

There was no Transportation Security Administration (TSA). You booked flights by phone or in person and paid by credit card, check, or cash. On flight departure day, you turned up at the gate, showed a driver's license for in-country flights to prove your identity, and got your boarding pass. No X-ray machines. No pat-downs. No internet identity searches. Flying was simple, not to mention, fun.

Although he would've needed a passport to fly internationally, Benson had an excellent fake driver's license as well as a perfectly forged Social Security card and birth certificate. He had no criminal record, had never been arrested, and had paid taxes for nearly a decade. The likelihood of discovery at the airport check-in or when getting a passport? Pretty much nonexistent.

Did he find his family's pressure to return overwhelming? Did he feel overrun with guilt? The fact that he hadn't gone back or seen his family in nearly a decade speaks against that. If his father's negativity had repulsed him all those years before, that, too, had disappeared.

Which still leaves the big question: What *really* drove Benson to suicide?

"Many men are love-starved for their fathers (and fathers for their sons) and deny it. To let this 'out of the bag' is to face a great deal of anger, rejection, and sadness," writes Deryl Goldenberg, PhD, in *The Psychology Behind Strained Father Son Relationships.*

Benson would never let such a "cat" out of his bag. Clearly such a demonstration would constitute a sign of weakness. His dad had taught him that. So, he kept his cat, stuffed deep inside, where it repeatedly clawed at both his mind and body, producing symptoms that alcohol would only mask and no antibiotic could ever cure.

In his 1998 essay, "Absent Fathers: Effects on Abandoned Sons," Dennis Balcom writes:

> Many adult sons abandoned by their fathers have difficulty developing and sustaining self-esteem, forming lasting emotional attachments, recognizing their feelings, or being expressive with their adult partners and children. These men must turn their attention toward their absent fathers and resolve the mystery of their absence to ensure that their current intimate relationships can succeed.

It doesn't seem out of the realm of possibility that Benson's suicide was spurred by poor self-esteem and feelings of worthlessness, the result of unrequited love, emotional abandonment, and rejection from a parent. Further, most research concludes that the best hope for long-term success and favorable outcomes is via re-establishing some greater level of communication between parent and adult child. Even if not part of Benson's conscious daily thoughts, he may have harbored such hope. While his father lived, a chance at acceptance did, too. With his father's death, that possibility—as well as "proving" his worth by his unprecedented hike—was gone. A lifelong emotional wound could never heal properly.

⌒〰⌒

During a river trip on the day after Christmas 1983, NPS archeologist Helen Fairley went exploring with friend Michael Collier in Kanab Canyon. They encountered a lone hiker. As they talked, Fairley recognized a slight German accent. She remembered that the man, who introduced himself as Robert Benson and said he was on a two-week solo sojourn, seemed cheerful, with no hint of depression.

On January 8, 1984, after his two weeks alone, Benson rimmed out. Getting another Canyon fix seemed to help his disposition, as later that month, with his doldrums apparently passed, Benson invited David Kiel and his wife Rebecca on a thirteen-day trek around Great Thumb during spring. He hoped it would aid the Kiels in their "Walk the River Grand, from Source to Sea" hike. To David Kiel, Benson's tone sounded upbeat and optimistic. Three weeks later he wrote this to a friend: "There is this idea going around my head of another extended hike in the Summer – Fall '85. This time only from Lee's Ferry to Pierce's on the northside again, but it will top the two previous hikes in difficulty in physical requirements ("Super trip")."

About the same time, Benson wrote Stan Jones that he was reconsidering the book deal (something he also mentioned in his letter to the Kiels), partially to recoup the "$10,000" the trip cost him. "Should I decide on any publication, I would be very interested in doing business with you." Surprised by Benson's sudden turnabout and willingness to "go public," Jones surmised that Benson may have felt a new sense of security, that "Congress would sweep the [undocumented] monkey from his shoulders." Either that, or he "took smug pride in his eight years of evading detection as an alien and wished to taunt the system."

Benson began showing his slides and giving lectures on his hiking exploits for groups in Albuquerque. Then for whatever reason, all that new-found enthusiasm began to fade.

During the last six weeks of his life, something caused a drastic change in

Robert Benson letter to David Kiel, 1984. *Courtesy David Kiel*

Benson's mindset. Increasingly sullen, he cut back interactions with others, preferring even more solitude than usual. Perhaps most telling, for the first time in nearly a decade, he stopped hiking. Why the self-imposed exile from what he loved most: exploring Canyon Country on foot? Was this a personal punishment for letting the chance to reconcile with his father slip away? No one will ever know, but in this "exile," his zest for life seems to have slipped into the void.

Hiking was Benson's lifeline. Like an antibiotic salve, it may have soothed an open wound in his heart. Without the Canyon, Benson's psychological wound might have started to fester, then became an overwhelming infection—like sepsis.

Left untreated, sepsis is fatal.

Once, engulfed in the sweltering heat and dead silence of Glen Canyon slickrock, Benson described the depth of his bond to Canyon Country, possibly the truest and most self-revelatory words he'd ever put on paper: "Being and hiking in the canyons means my whole life."

Robert Benson looking at the Supai Narrows.
Robert Benson

CHAPTER FORTY-FIVE

Within Canyon Shadows

KANAB POINT TO TUWEEP (THE FINAL LEG)

It's part of what we call the Shadow, all the dark parts of us we can't face. It's the thing that, if we don't deal with it, eventually poisons our lives.

Michael Gruber
The Good Son (2010)

December 1997

"Do you think you've got it?" Norma asked.

"I don't know. If I push any harder, I'm going to harpoon his little leg to the table."

My comment to my nurse emerged during a medical procedure involving a large, hollow needle and a very small shin bone, a combination used only in life-or-death situations. My patient, an unresponsive and barely breathing three-week-old, had weighed 7.5 pounds at birth. Today, he topped out at only four-and-a-half. The drastic weight loss, instead of an expected one-to-two-pound weight gain, underscored the direness of his situation and clearly suggested that his critically ill condition was far more than hypothermia. The cause(s) for the extreme weight loss or "failure to thrive," would have to be addressed tomorrow—*if he survived today.* Pinching his pencil-thick tibia between the fingers of my left hand, I was trying to push the needle tip into it using my right.

"Okay. Go ahead and try it," I told Norma, indicating that she should open the IV line and see if the fluid would flow through into the bone marrow.

"Nope. No flow," she said, both voice and face grim.

Beads of sweat broke out on my forehead.

Just minutes earlier, I had been enjoying the Grand Canyon Clinic's annual staff Christmas party, hosted by my colleague Dr. Jim Wurgler at his home. Less than an hour into it, Jim's wife, Jodie, told me the clinic had called and I was needed immediately. I sprinted through the cold night air our emergency entrance and bolted in.

Norma McDowell was the RN on duty. I had worked with Norma multiple times before at our sister clinic, the Williams Healthcare Center in Williams, Arizona. She offered to cover during the Christmas party. The newborn, a baby boy, was lying under a bright light on an exam table in front of her. He was tiny. Having never worked in an neonatal intensive care unit (ICU), he was the smallest patient I had ever seen. Worse yet, he was clearly the sickest.

His skin appeared gray and mottled; his breathing, rapid and shallow. Every several seconds, his head and neck spasmed in occasional seizure-like contortions. And with every labored breath, his ribs sucked in. I touched his skin. It felt cold. Very cold.

"Mom says she put her baby boy down for a nap in a back bedroom," Norma reported. "When she came back to feed him, he wouldn't wake up."

Per mom, who was panicking, both her pregnancy and the delivery had been normal. After his birth, mother and son returned to their home at Grand Canyon's South Rim, a place called "Supai Camp" about three miles from the clinic and my family's own house in Grand Canyon Village. Earlier that evening, mom had put the baby down for a nap, then went to take a shower in the camp's separate shower house. The baby was left under grandma's watch. Unfortunately, the fire in their house's woodstove—the house's only source of heat—had died down. When mom returned, she checked on her infant son. After finding him cold and unresponsive, she loaded him in the car and raced over here.

A body temperature below 95°F indicates significant, potentially life-threatening hypothermia; this baby's rectal temperature topped out at 89.1°F, by far the lowest temperature I had seen in a person still alive. Yet it wasn't the worst case of hypothermia (at least not yet) that I directly knew of at Grand Canyon. The other one, coincidentally but not surprisingly, also occurred at Supai Camp.

✎

In 1922—thirty-nine years after the US government sequestered the Grand Canyon's Havasupai people on a 518-acre reservation within the Canyon and three years after Grand Canyon became a National Park—the NPS set aside 160 acres for Havasupai families at what became known as "Supai Camp." The naming reflected NPS reliance on Havasupai workers to build much of the

Camp and park's infrastructure. For many of the Havasupai people now unable to hunt and gather, their survival options were reduced to low-paying jobs as maids, janitors, and dishwashers for the Fred Harvey Company. Supai Camp, just three miles from Grand Canyon Village down Rowe Well Road, allowed this work force to live close by, in housing the company neither paid for nor maintained.

The homes were two- to three-bedroom cottages with electricity and water but no gas, indoor plumbing, or central heating (the houses were heated with woodstoves in the main room). The "camp" name was apt; simple dwellings and lack of amenities made living there much like camping. One building served as a community bathroom and shower area. The NPS encouraged Havasupai families to relocate there and pay a nominal $5/month cabin rent.

By the early 1990s when I started working at the Grand Canyon Clinic, most of the Supai Camp houses had deteriorated into dilapidated shacks. On the first of several house calls I made there (on my off time) during a very cold night, I checked on Harriet, a sweet, elderly Havasupai woman who had leukemia. Though she had become quite weak, she never failed to be kind and pleasant. That night she told me, "I'm not long for this world, doctor." Several weeks later neighbors found her frozen to death in her cabin. She had apparently become so weak that she had been unable to maintain a fire in her woodstove.

Now, five years after Harriet's death, I focused intently on this hypothermic infant. Norma had positioned the baby on his back on an exam table so the bright, warm light could bathe his scrawny little body. He received supplemental oxygen through an infant mask, and Norma gently massaged his tiny form to rouse and rewarm him. Although conceptually simple, she had to exercise caution. A too-vigorous jostling could send the baby into cardiac arrest; cold heart muscle is prone to potentially lethal, abnormal rhythms.

I worked with Norma, doing more of the same. Despite our efforts, the baby's breathing became increasingly shallow and his color worsened. Every few seconds he made a faint, high-pitched sound like that of an injured rabbit. We checked his blood sugar; it was critically low. Further, his shriveled skin, rapid heart rate, and a dry diaper also signaled advanced dehydration. To make any progress here, we needed to insert an IV line through which we could administer warm IV fluids and glucose, and we needed to do it now.

Norma, calm under pressure and with over thirty years of experience, was the perfect nurse for this situation. She desperately scanned for a vein that might be a potential IV site, including on the scalp, where veins are typically prominent on newborns. But because of the dehydration, this baby's peripheral veins had shrunk to virtual nonexistence. Knowing minutes mattered in this life-or-death situation, we discussed trying another, more invasive option.

I held my breath as I tried to push the needle into his tiny tibia, the shin about the size and shape of the middle bone

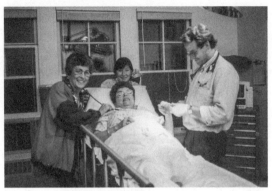

Playing doctor for real, 1993.

of my index finger. I hadn't been taught this procedure during my medical training. Back then, I instead had learned the emergency "cutdown" procedure to be used on infants when veins could not be accessed on the surface: slice open the skin over a large vein with a scalpel, aiming for the inside of the lower leg above the ankle. Next, dissect down through the tissue until you find the vein, then insert a catheter. Often a bloody and messy procedure, it could leave a large scar. Worst of all, it was time-consuming.

I had learned a newer shin-bone procedure—intraosseous vascular access— only a couple years earlier in a class called "Pediatric Advanced Life Support," or PALS for short. Intraosseous needles had become the go-to time-saver in situations such as these. If we could pull this off, it would allow us to administer the warm saline and glucose directly into the bone marrow, where it could be absorbed into the bloodstream. I pushed harder, feeling the needle tip going into bone. Ominously, the baby didn't even flinch.

It may sound ironic, but even during emergencies like these and after seven years on the job as a park doctor, my life and career still felt mostly like a dreamscape, living and working in my favorite place. Despite the long hours and the high-stress moments, I loved the job.

Yet I had no idea that Grand Canyon National Park even had a clinic before being hired in July 1990. Accepting the job required that I live in the park. The typical "commute" from my house to the clinic was an idyllic three-minute saunter through the woods, often shooing deer and elk out of the way. In emergencies, that commute became a thirty-second sprint.

Grand Canyon Clinic, open 24/7 year-round, employed two physicians: Dr. Jim Wurgler, my colleague and mentor, and me. We saw appointments, walk-ins, and emergencies. On alternate nights, we were on call for the spectrum of after-hours emergencies, including heart attacks, strokes, infections, trauma, and drunks. When a life or limb teetered in the balance, we had to intervene quickly, flawlessly. In moments like those, with the stress nearly overwhelming, I remember thinking, *How'd I get myself into this?* The answer revolved mainly around one person.

⌒〰⌒

"All right. I have seven boys," my devout Irish Catholic mother pointed out. "At least one of you should be a priest, and one of you a doctor." Of the several occupations she had chosen for me and my brothers, she seemed to hold these two in highest regard.

For many reasons, I've always been a momma's boy, a mom-pleaser. But I remember thinking: *A priest? That ain't happening. At least not with me. Girls are way too fascinating. I'd like one someday. I'll be a doctor. Let one of my other brothers, Dave or Terry or Jim or John or Joe or Jerry, take that priest job.*

Fortunately, I had an aptitude for academics, so my mother steered me to medicine—a noble career she called it—and a path out of the poverty in which our family lived.

After my parents divorced, when I was ten years old, she moved us to Flagstaff. The Grand Canyon, close, cheap, and iconic, became our big vacation destination every summer. I fell in love with the place and everything about it, especially the nightly talks by interpretive rangers. Partly, as a result of those chats, I grew to love history; I even pursued it as an undergraduate degree in college, with an emphasis on the American Southwest. Along the way to my diploma, I fulfilled the requirements to apply to medical school. When I was accepted by the University of Arizona's College of Medicine in Tucson, my backup plan to join the National Park Service and work at Grand Canyon as an interpretive ranger became moot.

As a medical student, I found the journey to becoming a doctor far more arduous than I anticipated, and much more stressful. In fact, I liken it to undertaking a remote, off-trail backpacking trip into the Grand Canyon, especially that first one.

You start out relatively naïve but fresh and energized. Then almost

Back row: Jim, my mom, Marsha, John. Front row: me, Joe, Lucky the dog, Jerry. Flagstaff Arizona circa 1974.
(Missing: siblings Pam, Dave, Terry)

instantly the going gets rough. You quickly become physically and emotionally exhausted, sometimes feeling abused by your surroundings. Far too often you also sense that, despite your intense efforts, you aren't covering any ground, that the destination is no closer. Periodically, you're cliffed out and confronted by terrifying exposure. Worst of all, sometimes you feel completely lost, convinced you took the wrong path. But just as in hiking Grand Canyon, the farther you go, the harder it is to turn around. So, you keep going. And going. *And going.* All the while, you hope and pray that the destination will have been worth the journey…

⌁

"Try it now," I urged Norma.

Once again, she twisted the IV line's valve to the open position. We both held our breath.

"Nope! It's still not going! There's no flow!"

The heart monitor revealed the infant's heart rate beginning to plummet, along with his oxygen levels.

"Start bagging him," I instructed a second nurse, one we had called in for further assistance. "Norma, hold off on chest compressions for a minute," I added.

The other nurse started pushing oxygenated air through a tiny facemask into the baby's lungs. As she did I drove the needle ever so slightly harder into the infant's shin, twisting as I pushed, trying to get it to just puncture the bony cortex and enter the marrow without poking it out the other side. I held my breath. More beads of sweat appeared on my forehead. Norma noticed.

"How many of these have you done?"

"One," I grimaced as I pushed the needle. "On a chicken bone."

January 2016

Why would a cowboy leave his saddle? We asked ourselves as we stared at the cowboy-camp relic. Wes, Connor, T, Vince, and I found it and other abandoned cowboy gear under an overhang near a spectacular collection of polychrome rock art. It seemed to us that a saddle would be the most prized and expensive item a cowboy owned, aside from the animal who wore it. His horse must've died, gotten lost, or become incapacitated. Nearby, we found an inscription: "Stu Stubbs, 1939, age 22." We contemplated what might have befallen Mr. Stubbs as we ate lunch.

The previous day we had enjoyed John Azar's cooking and hospitality in Fredonia. Following an early breakfast, John and his friend Virgil shuttled the four boys and me out to the rim of Kanab Canyon through four inches of snow.

The abandoned saddle we found. *Tom Myers*

After dropping us off, John promised to pick us up at Tuweep at the end of our hike in five days.

Snow and slush concealed our barely visible route as we dropped off the rim. It also made footing precarious, especially while toting heavy packs, and spurred anxiety on top of the other mixed emotions I'd been coping with.

For Wes and me, this was our last leg.

Pelted by waves of rain and sleet, we trekked westward along the Esplanade. As the sun set, the shower became a full downpour. Blizzard conditions prevailed on the rim above us. We'd beaten the snow by only a few hours; if we'd arrived any later, our trek would have been impossible.

Freezing and sopping wet despite rain gear, we opted to call it an early evening, and ducked into our tents. The constant pattering of rain was a bonus for me; the white noise helped me sleep long and soundly. Waking, I felt refreshed and more clearheaded than I had been in God only knew how long.

After packing up our soggy gear, we headed into a wall of fog and mist that had slunk into every side canyon, gulch, and cleft like a fantastic gaseous intelligence in a science fiction movie. Icy fingers from the rims draped the cliffs

On the snowy wet Esplanade. *T McCullough*

in an ethereal white, lending the Canyon a mystical appearance that reminded me of the White Cliffs of Dover.

In my imagination, these Canyon cliffs, towering over the burnt scarlet and rusty burgundies of the widening Esplanade Sandstone, also became a Jurassic coast and a briny red sea parted by the Canyon's inner gorge. Puddles glinted in the minor undulations on what is otherwise nearly ocean-flat table rock. Beyond the coolness, the relative smoothness for walking, and the visual delight, we were also relieved of the burden of carrying water. We could quench our thirst by dipping a water bottle into a pothole or simply lying down and lapping directly from it. The fresh, ice-cold "sea water" tasted marvelous.

When the mist lifted, the view expanded to what western Grand Canyon is famous for: seemingly endless slickrock beneath an equally expansive sky. The Canyon's "big sky" country, where one feels extra small. Despite the weather, we took time to walk an extra half mile, then climb 400 feet to the summit of a humble little butte sporting one of my all-time favorite Grand Canyon names: the Cork. As the rain pummeled us, we hooted and hollered from atop it.

Finally, on our penultimate day, the rain stopped. Snow draped the rim and talus above us and, again, wispy clouds filled much of the Canyon. Flashes of sunlight, like flames in a fire, breached the scene. That juxtaposition—wispy white clouds among a dancing kaleidoscope of Canyon color highlighted by flickers of sunshine—was beyond breathtaking.

It always is.

Kenton Grua would likely be the first to agree. On a wintery March 26, 1976, while encountering similar views, he journaled: "The day is magical, it's snowing lightly, the clouds fill the Canyon but at times open to brilliantly light up shimmering walls and buttes. We feel as though it's all a dream, that we are walking through a vision of heaven."

After passing Tuckup Canyon, I told the boys we were close to two tiny, man-made treasures I really wanted to see. I had hoped their location would be revealed by sunlight glinting off the material they were made of, but, given the overcast and the shadows, I knew this would be unlikely. Plus, they had been intentionally placed where they wouldn't be easily discovered, lest they be damaged, stolen, or otherwise removed.

Yes, they would likely be cloaked in shadow, like so many things.

1984

For a while, George Steck carried Benson's ashes in a soap dish. To honor his mother's request, George periodically sprinkled some of the ashes in the

Canyon, including off the rim at Cape Solitude. One day, while standing at Grandview Point, he dumped all that remained, abruptly ending the ritual. He thought Benson would have been good with that. Yet he still wanted to do something more permanent to honor him and his Canyon legacy.

Shortly thereafter, George drilled four small holes in the granite underneath an overhang in a side canyon about a mile upstream of Havasu Canyon. River runners call it "Paradise" with good reason: a small waterfall flows over a Muav Limestone cliff festooned with travertine and ferns, then splashes into the river. It's a stunning spot.

With loving care, George placed a plaque he had made for Benson, inscribed with Psalm 23 in Benson's native tongue: *Er weidet mich auf einer grünen Aue, und führet mich zum frischen Wasser.* "He makes me lie down in green pastures and leads me to fresh water."

The plaque George Steck had made for Robert Benson. *Steck family archives*

Although George had bolted the plaque in place, it disappeared several years later. He never knew who took it, but he suspected the culprit was the NPS. He came to this conclusion after he learned the drill holes had been filled in with rock-colored epoxy to conceal them. Angry and disappointed, George grumbled to friends that he hoped the plaque had been destroyed. "Better that than have it take up space in some bureaucrat's file cabinet."

A rumor also began to circulate that the plaque hadn't been destroyed but removed from Paradise to "save it." As river runners began discovering it, word got out that the NPS would soon be on a mission to remove it. So, someone "rescued" the plaque by removing it before the park did. That same someone placed it in a more remote location less likely to be found. George preferred that rumor to the file cabinet fate.

So did I.

Eventually, through the Canyon grapevine, I learned that the plaque relocation was no rumor. I also got a tip as to where it might now be found, along with another memorial plaque for the man who had made the first. I told the boys I wanted us to take a detour to find them. They agreed, which inspired me, for the first time on the trip (and the first time in a long time), to become the bellwether for our fivesome.

As we walked, the Mohawk Canyon area to the south filled our view; I could not help but think of Bill Ott. He had probably hiked on the same level, looking for polychrome sites like the ones we'd seen on this trip. In my mind's eye I pictured him there. Shortly before he disappeared, Ott and I had exchanged several emails. I mentioned my goal to walk the length with Wes. He had responded kindly: "Sounds like a nice project to do with your son. Have fun."

Closing in on where the plaques were reported to be, I quickened my pace. As I scanned the cliff faces in front of me, my thoughts were still on Ott. I pondered his childhood, especially his relationship with his dysfunctional mother. Did that relationship drive him to continually seek refuge and solitude in the world's most famous canyon? Beyond its inspirational beauty, the nonjudgmental "nature" of Nature can be healing. While it does not welcome us—nor does it care a whit whether we live or die—neither does it deter us. Instead, it allows everyone equal, nondiscriminatory, unlimited—but not always easy—access.

My thoughts lingered on Ott's death. Had he intentionally disappeared? Did he want to fade off into the sunset in the Grand Canyon? Did he want to take his last breath in the spectacular place he loved?

Many people have chosen to do so.

As these unanswerable questions circled, my thoughts switched back to George Steck. My source told me his plaque was conveniently (and appropriately) next to Robert Benson's. I had respected and loved that pot-bellied old fart for so many reasons. In addition to hiking the Grand Canyon, he defined his life by his dedication to his profession and to fatherhood, and by his love and faithfulness to his wife. He reigned as my Canyon hiking hero, and I'd let him know that. Even so, thinking about one of my last interactions with George made me sad.

George Steck and me at the Cremation Canyon party, 1998.
Gary Ladd

We'd been chatting when he told me about his plans for his last loop hike, the "Old Geezer hike." He rattled off the names of those invited. From the numbers, I knew he had room for a couple more. Usually not one to invite myself along, I gushed, "I'd really love to go, George, that is if you could fit me in."

"Yeah, okay, we'll see," he hedged.

I never heard back from him. The hike went on without me. He filled the spots with other people, several he didn't even know, guests of others on the permit. Disappointingly for me,

I *never* did a loop hike with George. And I never let him know how hurt I was to be excluded in this way by a man I looked up to as a surrogate father. Now, searching for his plaque, I found myself getting misty-eyed.

I looked back toward the boys. For some reason they had stopped far behind me. *Why aren't they following?* Anxious, my sense of urgency soared. I needed to find the plaques quickly, on my own now, I guessed, while they waited, patient but clearly not captivated as I was, and ready to move along.

Fading jet contrails etched the sky. *Are any of those pilots gazing down into the Canyon right now?* Scott Thybony's brother John came to mind. He died in a helicopter, not as a result of enemy fire, but rather as a consequence of flying miscalculations between his and another sight-seeing aircraft. John experienced struggles at home growing up, moved far away from his parents (primarily his father), and risked his life by volunteering to fight in a war he ultimately didn't agree with. Did he, too, seek out the Grand Canyon as a way to heal wounds inflicted by a dysfunctional relationship with his father as well as the scars of Vietnam? He had given up on flying after the war, but years later relented to fly routinely over Grand Canyon, the place in which his fate was sealed.

Finally, my thoughts zeroed in on Robert Benson. What was it that had really brought him to that final brink, to killing himself? And what was his father actually like? The image was disturbingly easy to imagine. I saw a brainwashed man, deeply rooted in the Nazi philosophy of racial superiority, viciously lashing out at young Robert Eschka. Was he disgusted by his son? Did he reject and torment Robert for perceived imperfections?

Suddenly, all these emotions resonated, especially Benson's death. My heart began to race as my thoughts lurched back to my own childhood, then early adulthood, and to what lurked in dark shadows of my own life—things I'd long blocked out but never forgotten completely.

The gusts of cold wind that buffeted me carried with them a terrible rush of anguish, embarrassment, and fear that felt all too familiar as my mind transported me back to a gray, wet day in 1984, much like this one; 1984—the same year Robert Benson had committed suicide. Although we had never met and, on the surface, would seem to have nothing in common except a love for hiking the Grand Canyon, we were once very much kindred in spirit.

Sunlight bathing the Esplanade in Western Grand Canyon after a storm. *Rich Rudow*

CHAPTER FORTY-SIX

Endings, Rewritten

KANAB POINT TO TUWEEP (CONTINUED)

Do you care what's happening around you?
Do your senses know the changes when they come?
Can you see yourself reflected in the seasons?
Can you understand the need to carry on?

—John Denver
"Season Suite: Spring"/Rocky Mountain High

"It is in your moments of decision that your destiny is shaped."

Tony Robbins
Awaken the Giant Within (1992)

October 2000

"Hey, you guys, I have something I want to show you." Artist Bruce Aiken proceeded to display his new painting to George Steck and me. "I call it a 'macro,'" he added. The portraiture represented a close-up of fossilized roots he had found in a piece of sandstone from the Supai. The twisted and intertwined reddish-brown root casts projected three-dimensionally off the stone. It reminded me of a pile of French fries covered in dried-up ketchup.

"It's my new style. What do you think?" he asked.

I moved in for a closer look. His "new style" definitely diverged from his old. It was more abstract, which I found less appealing.

"Well, it certainly is intricate," I began diplomatically, trying for tact. "If you like it, I like it, too, Bruce."

We both looked at George. He stared at the painting, his expression as flat as the canvas.

"I think it stinks," Steck declared bluntly. "You need to go back to your old style, Bruce." George loved Aiken's work and had commissioned him to do two paintings, which now hung in his house. This gave him some leeway to be candid. We all chuckled.

Since 1972, Bruce and Mary Aiken had lived at Roaring Springs, four miles down the North Kaibab Trail and 2,500 feet below the rim. They raised their family there while Bruce worked as the pumphouse operator for the NPS. Large pumps less than a mile up-canyon from the Aikens' home pushed water from Roaring Springs almost a half-mile straight up to the North Rim for the use of visitors and residents alike. Bruce's job was to make sure the pumps continued to do theirs.

Between shifts, he painted. His true passions were art and raising his children. Doing both down in Grand Canyon had made him regionally famous. Once their three kids were grown and gone, Bruce and Mary found their empty inner-Canyon nest invaded by people like me and George, fans of Bruce Aiken and lovers of the Grand Canyon. Admittedly, it also served as a perfect respite during a cross-canyon hike.

The Aikens invited us to an overnight stay during our October 2000 three-day, rim-to-rim crossing. In addition to George and me, the Aikens also invited Becky, our three kids, friends Ken and Annie Phillips and their kids Connor and Chloe, and yet another friend, fifty-nine-year-old Sandy Nevills-Reiff, the mother of my Canyoneers buddy, Greg Reiff.

Bruce and Mary made room for George and Sandy to sleep in their house. The rest of us bedded down on the large helipad adjacent to the house. The howling wind rattling the trees made for a restless night. Part of my insomnia also came from mentally replaying an incident that had occurred during the hike down.

Our daughters Brittany and Alex hiked with Becky, along with Annie Phillips and Connor's sister, Chloe. Five-year-old Wes and seven-year-old Connor were walking with me and I told them stories to distract them from the tedium of hiking. I could hear Connor's footsteps behind me, until I didn't.

I glanced back. Connor had vanished.

"Connor! Connor! Where are you?" I shouted as I spun around looking for him. He neither appeared nor answered.

The timing couldn't have been worse. Despite Wes weighing about forty pounds, I had brought his old "baby" backpack just in case he bonked. Minutes earlier, I'd stuffed him into it when he started dragging. Now as I spun and twisted while scanning for Connor, the additional load made my movements awkward and unbalanced. The same for any running, which I tried. Weston's little body bounced and jerked back and forth the entire time.

"Where's Connor, Daddy?" Wes asked as I searched, his voice trembling.

"I don't know. I need to find him!" I knelt, wrangled off the pack, then yanked Wes out of it. "You have to wait here! Don't move!" I ordered, holding a finger toward his face. I ran a short way back up the trail and looked around. Still no Connor. I looked behind me and saw Wes following.

"WES! YOU NEED TO WAIT! STOP!"

He started to cry.

"Sorry, Wes! Please wait here! I'm going to check by the creek!" I scrambled down to find Connor sitting quietly on a rock and staring at the rushing water. He seemed mesmerized.

"Connor! What are you doing?!" I scolded, my tone harsh.

"Nothing," he blurted, obviously startled.

"Don't ever do that again! You can't walk off like that!"

His lower lip stuck out and started to tremble. Then his head and shoulders shrank down. "Sorry, Tom," he softly said between tears, clearly embarrassed by my scolding, and probably a little afraid.

"It's okay, Connor." I gave him a hug. "You just scared me! I can't let anything happen to you. I love you! Never walk off like that again, okay?"

"Okay," he whispered, head still down.

Connor and Weston on South Kaibab Trail, 2000. *Tom Myers*

"Are we good?" I asked, smiling and rubbing his back.

"Yes." He looked up and smiled back. Fortunately, when I explained the incident to Annie, she took it in stride. "He does things like that sometimes," she said.

The next day, I instructed both Connor and Wes to walk in front of me. I vowed to keep Connor constantly in my sight. The two made it easy by holding hands.

Sixteen years had passed between that cross-canyon traverse in 2000 and our current Kanab-to-Tuweep hike. Now the boys walked in front of me in a nostalgic throwback and a shocking reminder of the passage of time. Their chatter—a mix of politics, climbing jargon, and crude jokes—had little in common with their deep conversations as little boys about pizza, Space Rangers, and the Pokémon cards they collected. Between eye-blinks, it seemed, they had grown into men—thankfully, humble, kind, and considerate men.

Annie and Ken once told me that they believed hiking the Canyon's length had saved Connor's life. Like Wes, during adolescence he had gone to a dark place, they said; the entire Phillips family was worried. Connor mentioned the experience to me as well. "I was miserable in high school. I felt that was all there was. I didn't know there was anything else. If you weren't one of the cool or really popular people, you were nobody. I just got into gaming, hanging out with all the other losers and nerds."

As we passed Tuckup Canyon, more memories from that 2000 October rim-to-rim hike resurged, particularly carrying Weston's forty pounds in a baby backpack. Now, at six feet, three inches and 200 pounds, he could carry me. His strength, stamina, speed, and climbing skills far exceeded mine, even during my prime. Most astounding was his ability to spot hiking and climbing routes through the cliffs. Like a bighorn, Wes had a sense for choosing the right path.

He'd also chosen the right path in life. That one, however, did not come so naturally.

When he began to struggle with depression during his middle and late teens, Becky and I did what most parents do under those circumstances: We blamed ourselves. We also entered that torturous feedback loop of analyzing and re-analyzing where and when and how we had gone wrong. I found this process especially hard, as any parent does when feeling somehow responsible for their struggling child. In Weston's case, it didn't help that I believed he had inherited a tendency for brutal self-judgment and depression from me.

Yet my mother always insisted that I wasn't a moody or brooding child. On the contrary, she claimed, I was happy-go-lucky. Still, collectively, my childhood left me with some hefty baggage in terms of self-worth. Much of it, I later came to understand, resulted from my relationship—or lack thereof—with my father. My dad, perhaps like Benson's, was frequently not a nice man.

Born during the depths of the Great Depression and raised on a Missouri farm, after a brief military stint he attended college, the first in his family to do so. My father then went on to become a general practice (GP) doctor and work in a rural midwestern town with less than 2,000 people. Ironically for a physician, sarcasm and doling out humiliation came all too naturally to him, at least while at home. At other times, so did physical violence, especially when under the influence of alcohol, which was a problem for him. My mom told us stressors of his job drove him to drink. In the end, if not the cause, the booze at least abetted in the destruction of his marriage, his practice, and much of his life.

As a child, insecure and unable to sleep, I sucked my thumb until around age seven. Worse yet, when I did sleep, I wet the bed. Try as I might, I had no control over this and it continued until after I turned twelve. As if those two nightly rituals weren't bad enough, to help myself fall asleep, I also rolled my head back and forth. It was both distracting and soothing, like sucking my thumb; unlike the thumb-sucking, however, the head rolling continued well into my teens. Maybe because it scrambled any racing thoughts or worry (sometimes I fretted that it was also scrambling my brain). Maybe because it worked like white noise. It also relieved my increasingly frequent tension headaches. I'd do it for minutes, even hours, off and on, all night. My dad, who nicknamed me "Thumb," found these behaviors annoying and me disappointing because I couldn't control them.

After my parents divorced, my mother moved us west. My dad, who had accepted custody of four of his nine kids (including me) in the settlement agreement, ultimately opted for none. Instead, he just disappeared. While I felt incredible relief in the moment, this betrayal would become the foundation of my insecurity. There was no goodbye from him. No letters. No phone calls. No hugs. No child support. Nothing. While our living in relative poverty was tough, I could cope with going hungry at times or the "trailer trash" looks flashed our way when we used food stamps. I came to tolerate the teasing I got for my mom's bowl haircuts, for wearing patched, high-water pants; cheap tee-shirts (sometimes smelling like dried urine from having been slept in the night before); and worn-out tennis shoes. I could stomach the embarrassment of driving around in our beat-up station wagon. I also learned to deal with my own self-loathing for being a thumb-sucking, bed-wetting, head-roller. What I couldn't seem to accept, however, was my father's disregard and disgust of me. It plagued me, gnawed at me, haunted me.

One of my brothers, Dave, tracked our father down nearly a decade later in the boondocks of Canada. I remember my feeling of sadness … sadness that my dad hadn't died. Dying would have explained things. That he was still alive and out of touch signaled an intentional indifference. I felt of no consequence in my father's eyes. None of us were. How could we be so inadequate, so insignificant, so unworthy of love, that someone who helped bring us into this world could kick us to the curb forever?

With that mindset and at my mom's behest, I made a vow to become a doctor. As much as I credit my mother for this inspiration, I would be remiss to not also include the negative influence of my dad. I wanted to prove that I wasn't worthless. That I had value. I could be someone, maybe even a doctor—*like you, Dad*—if I worked hard enough. To that end, by age twenty-one I had done well enough to have a shot at getting into medical school. I also had friends and a steady job. Still, my insecurities stayed with me.

It all came to a head one day.

On a rainy afternoon in August 1984, I sought out my closest friend, Mark Crane. I hadn't slept in days; again, while I'd never been a great sleeper, this period had been an exceptionally rough stretch. I needed to talk to someone. *Badly*. I had just tried to break up with the one-and-only girlfriend (before Becky) I'd ever had. I knew we weren't right for each other, but I felt like a miserable failure because I couldn't make it work.

She scolded that I was cruel, that I'd broken her heart; she'd wanted to marry me, she sobbed uncontrollably. All of which exacerbated my long-standing self-esteem issues. I felt utterly and completely worthless.

Tears in my eyes, I tried to hide my embarrassment when I arrived at Mark's dorm room. Reluctant to spill my guts, I only spoke of the break-up, one of my own doing. All the while, dark thoughts circulated through my head, ones he had no way of knowing. If he had, I'm sure he would have intervened, and I would've probably melted down. I have never blamed Mark for not reading my mind that day. He, too, had been taught to be tough, to "pick himself up by his bootstraps" when he felt down.

"Ah, you'll get over it," he assured me. "I never really liked her anyway."

"Yeah, well … okay. I'll see you later."

I left quickly. Despite what I had just told him, I decided he wouldn't see me later. Nor would anyone else, at least not that way. My way to ensure that was eighty miles away.

Hopping into my Ford Pinto, I drove north. Once I arrived at the South Rim, I would take the shuttle bus to the Abyss area off Hermit Road and its 1,200-foot drop. I wouldn't jump. No need to. I would just close my eyes and step off.

As I drove, the rain became a downpour and the rivulets streaming down the windshield rivaled the ones on my face. What happened next is still a blur. What I do recall is losing sight of the road and suddenly swerving and skidding on the slick highway. Panicked and hyperventilating when I managed to stop, it occurred to me that I had almost achieved my goal early. Then I thought of my mom, my brothers and sisters, and the painful aftermath my suicide would leave for them.

I turned my car around.

2016

Now, more than thirty years later, I looked back at the boys far behind me. They hadn't moved. Roiling with mixed emotions, including anger that they didn't seem willing to help me look for the plaques I felt were so important, I gave up my search and headed back to join them. I tried to hide how rattled I felt. Unsuccessfully.

"Why didn't you guys come?" I grumbled. "I told you I wanted to see those plaques. I've wanted to see them for years. It meant a lot to me. I didn't think it was asking that much." Abruptly, tears flooded my eyes. This embarrassed me and made things worse. I closed my eyes and turned my head away.

More memories of that 1984 monsoon day flooded back.

After I got back to Flagstaff, I decided to reach out to a close friend who was finishing up her master's degree in psychology. She lived and worked as the head resident at a women's-only dorm. I also worked there, primarily on weekends, as a desk clerk on the graveyard shift—my second job in addition to working as a night clerk at Travelodge. Between the two jobs, I was "on-call" five nights a week.

Despite my exhaustion, I felt thrilled to find Colleen at home. For several hours, I did the talking and the crying, she did the listening, then offered honest, sincere feedback. We were both drained by the time I went home and—finally— slept. Her friendship and insights helped save my life that day.

Four months later, with the holidays fast approaching, I relapsed. I found myself retreating from life and spending my time alone and in my own head. Despite reaching out to Colleen, family, and friends, I still wasn't fully convinced that I was honorable or worthy of happiness. Vulnerable, I knew I needed yet more help but from a different source. I sought out my neutral, nonjudgmental "friend," the natural landscape to the north that I loved more than any other.

I also sought out my "little brother," David. At nine years old, he too, struggled. Three years earlier, I had joined Big Brothers and Big Sisters of Flagstaff, a program where adult men and women take on roles of older siblings or surrogate parents for the one who is absent in single-parent homes. My own mom had enrolled us in the program when we had arrived in town a decade earlier, and I wanted to give back to a boy who seemed to be in the same difficult place I had been.

Not once during the two years I'd known him had David heard from his father. For David, I hoped to be the father figure I never had. That year, I wanted to celebrate New Year's with him at the Grand Canyon. It would be my third such celebration in a row but a first for David, who'd never before camped or backpacked. Although David's mom seemed nervous, which made me a little jittery, too, she allowed him to go…

January 1, 1985. New Year's Day. I climbed out of our tent at Havasupai Garden shortly after the sun came up. Not long after, David poked his head out.

"I'm ready to go fishing!" he announced.

So we hiked to the river, did some fishing, and spent time in the canteen at Phantom Ranch. That night, we camped again at Havasupai Garden. On January 2, we hiked out. I coaxed and encouraged David the entire way, bribing him with candy and the promise of a burger and fries once we reached the rim. When we finally did, he seemed overjoyed.

"Wow! I did it, Tom! That was the coolest thing I've ever done in my life!" he exulted.

I smiled at him, then looked back to the Canyon. The color—the brilliant blue above and the rainbows in rock below—were more striking than ever. I closed my eyes and took a long, deep breath. The crisp, cold air, spiced with pine and juniper, inflated my lungs. It was the most gratifying breath of my life.

Tears welled in my eyes. Nothing had actually changed, yet everything had changed. Completing that hike with David was a defining moment for me. A renaissance moment. I felt reborn. *I am a good person. I am a decent man. I am a worthy man.* The Grand Canyon had been part savior; the Bright Angel Trail, my Road to Damascus.

"Are you okay?" he worried, noticing my tears.

"I'm great. Just great. Thank you." I hugged him.

2016 (continued)

Suddenly I felt an arm around me. Opening my eyes, I saw the arm belonged to Wes. "I'm really sorry, Dad," he apologized. "I didn't know seeing those plaques meant that much to you." He gave me a wonderful father-son hug. "I'll go out there with you if you want. We can still do it."

I peered intently into his eyes. As I had, he'd somehow gotten through his own dark time by hiking in the Canyon. I tried to wipe my tears away. Instead, more came.

"Dad, I'm sorry. Really. We can go out there." He wore an expression of heartfelt concern.

"Oh, Wes, it's all right. This really isn't about the plaques. It's about life and finding your way. Being here with you means everything to me. There was a time when I almost guaranteed it would not have happened. It was pretty close. And for a while, there was a time when Mom and I were worried we might lose you," I faltered, noticing the tears in his eyes, as well.

"I hope you know these trips were mostly about just hanging out with you, being part of your life, something I never had with my own dad. That's what I really wanted, to spend time with you and experience this place together. It was so hard at times, even scary, but I wouldn't have missed it for the world. We're going to be done tomorrow, but I don't want *this*," I motioned with my hand from him to myself, "me and you, to ever end. I love you, Wes."

"I love you too, Dad," he said, hugging me yet again.

✧

We reached the Tuweep that afternoon. During the last couple of days, we'd fantasized repeatedly about food—junk food mainly: something fatty, something sweet, something salty, all with lots of calories. Although I told Becky it would be okay if she didn't plan a celebration for Wes and me after finishing our dream mega-hike, I secretly hoped she might surprise us. Maybe she'd clandestinely arrang for a delivery of pizza, or burgers and fries, maybe with John Azar's help?

When we arrived, Tuweep backcountry ranger Todd Seliga welcomed us with open arms. The warmth of the ranger station, like Todd's reception, felt

Tuweep Ranger Station. *Amy Martin*

great. Bless his heart, he made a spectacular vegetarian meal that included a great spinach, tomato, and feta cheese salad, as well as a side of sweet potatoes with butter. We gorged ourselves.

The next morning, we munched a breakfast of granola bars and oatmeal while we waited for Azar to pick us up. He rolled up in the Yukon at midmorning, stepping out in his standard sweatpants, sweatshirt, moccasins, and little wool beanie.

"I brought you boys some food," he said, glancing at Wes and his buddies. "There's some fried chicken here, and donuts, chips, and soda."

The boys looked at John as though he were a god, then pounced on the food, thanking him between mouthfuls.

Less than an hour later we were pummeling Todd with our goodbyes, then we piled into my truck.

"So, John, what's on your agenda for today?" I leaned back against the headrest as we pulled out.

"Well," he hesitated, "I think I'm gonna boil up some eggs and potatoes and make a potato salad." I looked over my shoulder at Wes. He wore a huge, ear-to-ear grin. So did the other boys.

The dented Yukon rattled familiarly over the frozen washboards. The bumpy road made all of its idiot lights—brakes, service engine, seatbelts—flash. Nuisances I couldn't fix, still, they filled me with a mix of pride and sentimentality. The many shuttle trips had taken a toll on the old beast. But, ahhh! What memories it helped us make!

As sunlight flooded the valley ahead, I glanced back at Wes again. Despite the banging, he had fallen asleep leaning against the window. I couldn't help but think of how he had done the same thing after we squeezed our first lengthwise hike into our busy lives, going down Cathedral Wash and out Rider: seven-and-a-half years, sixteen section hikes, nearly sixty hiking days, and more than 600 miles earlier.

Now 20, he had a short-cropped beard that was better than anything I could grow. He was a man now—a good, decent, resilient one. In so many ways the Grand Canyon had made him a better person. Inspiration and lessons gleaned from navigating these cliffs had helped him—as they had me, a generation earlier—learn to navigate life.

Both he and Connor had confided in me that the Canyon changed their attitudes from despondency and disdain to eager engagement and hope for the future. Insecurity was replaced with self-confidence. Self-doubt with self-worth. Fear with courage. And indifference with love.

In that moment my mind went—as it frequently does—to the movie *It's a Wonderful Life*. In this classic 1946 film starring James Stewart, Stewart's

character, George Bailey, strongly considers suicide on Christmas Eve, contemplating jumping off a bridge into an icy, raging river. Rescued by his guardian angel, Clarence, the despondent Bailey tells Clarence, "I wish I had never been born." Clarence proceeds to show George the heart-rending flip side of his life, had he not been around to live it. More specifically, Clarence highlights the impact George has had on others.

Looking at Wes and reflecting on my own life—as a son, brother, husband, and father, as well as a physician—I knew too well how a single, snap decision could have altered all of those roles, forever. I decided not to go there. Instead, like George Bailey at the end of the movie, I chose to focus on my good fortune: the opportunity to touch so many lives. *And to be touched by so many.* I didn't dwell on what might have been, but marveled at what has been. In that time of introspection, I knew the Grand Canyon's role could not be overestimated. And to this day, I continue to marvel at the Canyon's capacity to edit a future. To make wonderful moments and wonderful lives. To rewrite endings. It is a landscape truly worthy of the "life-changing" cliché.

And lifesaving, in more ways than one.

September 2008

"There's someone here I'd like you to meet, Wes. He's a little younger than you."

During a drive back from a hike in the South Bass area, I made a detour and pulled into Supai Camp. The changes here astounded me; it looked vastly different than the first time I had ventured here on a house call to see Harriet, the Supai woman with leukemia. The old bungalows had been refurbished, upgraded. Several new houses sported wrap-around decks.

With thirteen-year-old Wes beside me, I walked over to a resident I saw standing outside, someone I knew and was hoping to find at home.

"Hello," I said, calling out her name. She turned to me.

"Oh! Dr. Myers! Hi!"

I hugged her, introduced Wes, and we chatted.

"Is your grandson around?"

"He's over there," she pointed, then led us a short distance to a clearing.

Shirtless and riding a bike, the now nearly 11-year-old Havasupai boy looked happy and healthy. Like Supai Camp, the difference in his appearance from when I'd first seen him shocked me. He had been so sickly and tiny and hovering at death's door that night. Back then, I could easily hold his failing wisp of a body in one hand. He braked his bike and approached, looking a little bewildered.

"Do you remember me?" I asked, smiling. I had seen him a few other times, but several years had passed.

He smiled back, but shook his head no.

"That's okay. I'll never forget you though." I introduced Wes.

"Can I see your leg?" I asked.

"Which one?" he replied, perplexed by my question.

"Gosh, I can't remember. Can you show me both?"

"Sure," he shrugged.

I squatted down and peered at his shins.

"Whatcha lookin' for?"

I told them both the story of that fateful night when I had struggled with the needle and against catastrophic failure.

His legs appeared symmetrical, normal. I squinted at the area just below his knees. Then I saw it. A tiny scar about the size of a pencil tip. Vivid memories of that December night nearly a dozen years ago swirled in my mind. As warm fluid and sugar had run into his bloodstream via his bone marrow and oxygenated air had filled his lungs, he began to perk up, his critical condition improving. Finally, he was stable enough to be life-flighted by helicopter to Phoenix Children's Hospital, where he remained for nearly a month, including a week in the neonatal ICU.

"You were a pretty sick little guy that night," I sighed.

I looked back up at him.

"Are you having a good summer, getting some good rides in?"

"Yep!" he grinned.

"That's awesome! It's great to see you!" I gave him a high-five.

"Thanks!" He pedaled off, legs cranking hard, his back tire kicking up a little dust devil.

"Wow! That's pretty cool, Dad," Wes remarked after we got back into the Yukon.

"You know what's really cool?" I asked.

"What?"

"*You*. Thanks for coming," I added. "It was a lot of fun."

"Yeah, that was a really great hike. We should do another one," he mused.

Hmmm … He was older now, strong and fit for his age. He'd already accumulated an unusual amount of Canyon hiking experience. I felt something familiar twitch on my back. Something that had taken up residence there in 1985.

"Well, Wes, now that you mention it. I was wondering …"

Wes grinned, interrupting me. "Sure, Dad."

Wes and me, 2016. *Connor Phillips*

All proceeds from the sale of this book will be donated
to the Grand Canyon Conservancy in memory of Robert
Eschka Benson. The Conservancy was founded in 1932 and
is Grand Canyon National Park's official philanthropic and
collaborative partner. I do this in the hope that the healing
powers of the Grand Canyon, which the Conservancy has
done so much to support over the years, will touch the life
of someone in need. To learn more about the Conservancy's
work, visit grandcanyon.org.

Sources

In writing this book, I relied on letters, journals, interviews, emails, and personal conversations I had with many of the people (some now deceased) who appear in these pages. Conversations were recreated to the best of my memory and ability. Although the wording is not verbatim, they accurately represent the sense of those exchanges.

Articles and Archives
Barrett, Robert. "First Through Marble Canyon on Foot: Hard Not to Panic, Ain't It?" *The Arizona Republic,* 30 May, 1976.
Benson, Robert Eschuka [sic]. Transcribed hiking logs. Special Collections, Cline Library, Northern Arizona University, Flagstaff.
Butler, Elias. Interview with George Steck. Special Collections, Cline Library, Northern Arizona University, Flagstaff.
Grua, Kenton. Hiking journals. Private collection.
Kiel, David, and Rebecca Kiel. "Walk the River Grand" and hiking journals. Private collection
Moore, Kenny. "Grandeur and Torment." *Sports Illustrated,* 30 March, 1985.
Steck, George. Hiking journals. Private collection.
Steiger, Lew. Interview with Kenton Grua. Special Collections, Cline Library, Northern Arizona University, Flagstaff.

Books and Suggested Reading
Butler, Elias, and Tom Myers. *Grand Obsession: Harvey Butchart and the Exploration of Grand Canyon.* Puma Press, 2007.
Fedarko, Kevin. *The Emerald Mile: The Epic Story of the Fastest Ride in History Through the Heart of the Grand Canyon.* Scribner, 2013.
Canyon. Scribner, 2024.
Fletcher, Colin. *The Man Who Walked Through Time.* Vintage reissue, 2014.
Ghiglieri, Michael, and Thomas Myers. *Over the Edge: Death in Grand Canyon.* 3rd ed. Puma Press, 2024.
Jones, Stan. *Stan Jones' Ramblings by Boat and Boot in Lake Powell Country.* Sun Country, 1998.
Steck, George. *Hiking Grand Canyon Loops.* Falcon Guides, 2002.
Thybony, Scott. *A Guide to Hiking the Inner Canyon.* Grand Canyon Natural History Association, 1989.
Wehrman, Robert. *Walking Man: The Secret Life of Colin Fletcher.* BookBaby, 2016.

Acknowledgments

When it comes to creative endeavors like writing, I have come to believe that—as in athletics—the very best are born, not made. That said, I'm also convinced that a good story makes up for a lack of natural talent. So does great editing.

Mainly because of one person, I think I appear to be a far better writer than I actually am. Susan Tasaki, my editor, is brilliant and the consummate professional in her craft. She came out of retirement to help me. Her patience with my amateur efforts was humbling. More importantly, she never tried to change my narrative voice; she just made it very clear when she thought I was off key.

Next, I wanted my book to look timeless. I think it does, thanks to Mary Williams, an unsung hero of the Grand Canyon and Flagstaff literary communities for more than three decades. When it comes to book layout and design, Mary is the best. Spending many hours working with her to put "icing on the cake" was a pure joy.

My son-in-law David's parents, Karen and John Robertson, went way beyond the call of family to help out with line editing and painstaking proofreading. I found myself embarrassed, relieved, and incredibly grateful that they caught and corrected a multitude of errors.

I also leaned on friends for draft reading and additional editorial help (and who are still friends, despite that). These include my business partner and co-author of *Over the Edge*, Michael Ghiglieri. Michael's sincere and often brutal critiques resulted in me killing more of my "darlings" than I can count. Elias Butler, my co-author for *Grand Obsession* (and the best listener I know), used a softer, gentler, but equally effective approach to achieve the same result. Also helpful was physician and novelist Dr. Sandra Miller. Sandra convinced me that finding my voice through the use of medical metaphors could be fun and original . . . and it was.

Hazel Clark and Bronze Black stepped up for initial book design and layout, and Bronze also contributed to the gorgeous book cover—his fourth for me.

I also can't say enough about Gary Ladd. He donated amazing photos (the fantastic cover shot is one of his), and gave thoughtful, encouraging feedback. Best of all? Sharing Steck stories.

Helen and Wayne Ranney were such an inspiration. They both read early drafts, and convinced me that the moral of the story was worth the grueling effort and time.

Scott Thybony, a longstanding hiking hero with an impressive spectrum of Canyon knowledge, provided invaluable insights on Harvey Butchart; George Steck; Bill Ott; and, of course, his brother John. He also fact-checked much of the book.

Kevin Fedarko, whom I consider the most gifted writer to ever pen words about the Grand Canyon, knows this book would not have happened without him, and he knows why. He also provided an incredibly kind blurb.

Annette McGivney, another amazing writer, read it, got it, and did the same.

Richard ("Q") Quartaroli, an outstanding Canyon historian and fact-checker, assisted me without hesitation, as he has for more than thirty years.

Tom Martin, as usual, went out of his way to help. This included river-trip support for our Diamond Down hiking legs as well as draft fact-checking, proofreading, and photo donation. He also surprised me with one of the best hugs of my life after he finished reading the book.

Michelle Grua, Ellen Tibbetts, and Bart Henderson shared great memories of Kenton Grua, as well as photos; Michelle also graciously shared Kenton's journal.

Paula Ott, Glenn Rink, and Steve U'Ren were invaluable in articulating Bill Ott's story, as were Mindy Karlsberger (formerly Thybony) with John Thybony's and Andy Holycross with Ioana Hociota's.

Dave Kiel and Rebecca Just (formerly Kiel) were incredibly gracious and patient in sharing their story and photos.

Pete Shunny and Sara Steck provided priceless insight into Robert Benson. Pete also gave me Robert's "shoebox" of memorabilia; I am so grateful that he saw its value and hung onto it.

John Azar and Todd Seliga served up hospitality as well as their homes to the boys and me. John also provided captivating stories and photos about Steck, Benson, and Ott.

Andy Holycross is a man of character and true blue. Getting to know him better through emotionally intense discussions of Ioana Hociota touched me more deeply than I would've ever imagined.

Rich Rudow, second only to Harvey Butchart as the Grand Canyon's greatest explorer, made selfless contributions to nearly every facet of the book. Plus, he donated world-class photos.

Ron Mitchell is a true gem of a man. Meeting and getting to know him was like interacting with living history. He and his thoughtful wife Patti are wonderful people.

Others who also helped significantly with draft reading, proofreading, photos, or general feedback: George Bain, Mike Buchheit, John Crowley, Dr. David Graham, Karen Greg, Eric Gueissaz, Julie Hammonds, Bryan and Dustin Lord, Suzi Martin, Scott Masher, Pete McBride, Theresa McMullen, Ken and Annie Phillips, and Pete Runge.

The following individuals helped in too many ways to list, not the least by providing much-needed encouragement: Chris Atwood, Bruce Babbitt, Jan Balsom, Scott Baxter, Jay and Janet Bawcom, Scott Baxter, Kim Besom, John Blaustein, Phillip Bremer, Don Lee Brown, Bill Burger, Billy and Karen Cordasco, Gene Couch, Dr. Mark Crane, Helen Fairley, Don Forester, Dr. Erinn Gallagher, Dan Hall, Steve Hirst, Colleen Hyde, Richard Jackson, Kamran Javadi, Matthias Kawski, Peggy Kolar, Amy Martin, Steve Martin, Don Mattox, Troy McReynolds, Dove Menkes, Anne Miller, Dave Mortenson, Alan and Roberta Motter, Jim Ohlman, Carla Olson, Rudi Petschek, Robby Pitagora, Pam and Clair Quist, Sandy and Greg Reiff, Arnie Richards, John Southrey, the Steck clan (Allen, Mike, Stan, Ricia, Lee, and Sara), Lew Steiger, Larry Stevens, Russell Sullivan, Monte Tillinghast, Sally Underwood, Bryan Wisher, and David Zickl.

My penultimate thanks go to those with whom I've shared the Grand Canyon at the deepest level (literally and/or figuratively) and for whom I care deeply:

"The boys" (Connor, Vince, and T), my other sons.

Nephew Peter Bremer, as selfless and thoughtful as they come.

Sons-in-law Ethan Dyer and David Robertson, great guys who love my daughters and make them happy.

My mom, Sharon Myers, who never abandoned me and introduced me to the Grand Canyon.

Finally, my most heartfelt appreciation and gratitude go to the greatest loves of my life:

Daughters Brittany and Alexandra, so strong and determined, yet so gentle, selfless, and kind.

Son Wes, the best adventuring buddy of my life and someone I greatly respect and admire.

And most of all, Becky, my wife of nearly forty years. A wonderful and loving person, she gave our kids their best attributes. She also put up with this book, the "third person in our marriage," for way too long.

Wes looking back from a lava dome near River Mile 183, 2015.

Tom Myers has worked at Grand Canyon as a physician since 1990 and serves as local medical advisor for the NPS. A dedicated explorer of the Canyon backcountry since his late teens, he also has a special interest in Grand Canyon human history and wilderness medicine. An amateur writer, historian, and researcher in his free time, he has co-authored/authored multiple Grand Canyon-related publications, including four other books and numerous medical journal articles. He and his wife Becky live in Flagstaff, Arizona, and have three grown children and two grandchildren.

Also by Tom Myers:

Fateful Journey: Injury and Death on Colorado River Trips in Grand Canyon
(with Lawrence E. Stevens and Christopher Becker) 1999

Over the Edge: Death in Grand Canyon (with Michael P. Ghiglieri) 2001; 3rd
Edition 2024; 2016 National Outdoor Book Award, Classic

Grand Obsession: Harvey Butchart and the Exploration of Grand Canyon (with
Elias Butler) 2007; 2008 National Outdoor Book Award, History/Biography

Flipped Out for Grand Canyon (with Bronze Black) 2015
All proceeds donated to Grand Canyon Youth

How Not To Die At Grand Canyon (Pocket Guide) 2020
All proceeds donated to Grand Canyon National Park Preventive Search and
Rescue